C000007067

DISKI

Dissertationen zur Künstlichen Intelligenz

Mit Unterstützung des Fachbereichs 1 „Künstliche Intelligenz“ der Gesellschaft für Informatik e.V. herausgegeben von

The Problem of Tuning Metaheuristics

as seen from a machine learning perspective

Mauro Birattari

Mauro Birattari
IRIDIA, Université Libre de Bruxelles
Avenue Franklin Roosevelt 50
CP 194/6
B-1050, Brussels
Belgium
Email: mbiro@ulb.ac.be

A dissertation submitted to the
Université Libre de Bruxelles
Faculté de Sciences Appliquées
IRIDIA – Institut de Recherches Interdisciplinaires
et de Développements en Intelligence Artificielle

Accepted on the recommendation of:
Prof. M. Dorigo

Die Deutsche Bibliothek lists this publication in the *Deutsche Nationalbibliografie*;
detailed bibliographic data is available on the Internet at
http://dnb.ddb.de.

"infix" is a joint imprint of Akademische Verlagsgesellschaft Aka GmbH and IOS Press BV (Amsterdam)

Reproduced from PDF supplied by the author
Printing and Binding: Hundt Druck GmbH, Köln
Printed in Germany

ISSN 0941-5769
ISBN 3-89838-292-3
ISBN 1-58603-551-7

To my father

who provided me with a proper unit system for measuring the world

The thesis

The problem of tuning a metaheuristic can be profitably formalized and solved as a machine learning problem

This dissertation was discussed in a public defense held at the Université Libre de Bruxelles, Brussels, Belgium, on December 20, 2004. In this occasion, Mauro Birattari was awarded a *European Doctorate* title in applied sciences.

Composition of the jury:

Hugues Bersini
Professor, Université Libre de Bruxelles, Brussels, Belgium
Secretary of the jury

Andrea Bonarini
Associate Professor, Politecnico di Milano, Milan, Italy
Foreign expert

Gianluca Bontempi
Associate Professor, Université Libre de Bruxelles, Brussels, Belgium
Member of the jury

Christine Decaestecker
Senior Research Associate of the Belgian National Fund for Scientific Research
Member of the jury

Marco Dorigo
Research Director of the Belgian National Fund for Scientific Research
Thesis supervisor

Philippe Van Ham
Professor, Université Libre de Bruxelles, Brussels, Belgium
Chairman of the jury

External referees:

Wolfgang Bibel
Professor, Technische Universität Darmstadt, Darmstadt, Germany

Ben Paechter
Professor, Napier University, Edinburgh, United Kingdom

Foreword

Combinatorial optimization problems are of high academical and practical importance. They arise in a great number of fields including science, economics, and engineering. Unfortunately, many combinatorial problems belong to the class of *NP*-hard problems. From a practical point of view, this implies that the computational resources needed for solving these problems are formidable in typical realistic settings. More technically, the computational resources needed grow exponentially with the dimension of the problem.

These hard optimization problems are typically dealt with using the heuristics methods studied in Artificial Intelligence. Although heuristics are not formally guaranteed to find the optimal solution of a given problem, they have empirically shown the ability of finding high quality solutions using a limited amount of computational resources. The main drawback of heuristics is that they are problem-specific and that developing a new heuristic for a given problem is particularly demanding.

Metaheuristics are a promising alternative. Like heuristics, metaheuristics are able to find good solutions to hard combinatorial optimization problems using a reasonable amount of computational resources. They present the further advantage of being problem-independent and much more flexible in practice. Example of metaheuristics are simulated annealing, tabu search, evolutionary computation, iterated local search, and ant colony optimization. In order to be flexible, metaheuristics have a number of parameters that need to be tuned before they can be used. Although an out-of-the-box implementation of a metaheuristic often obtains fairly good results, a careful tuning is needed when state-of-the-art results are sought. It is widely recognized in the technical literature that tuning is crucial to the success of a metaheuristic. Nevertheless, relatively little attention has been given to the issue. It should be noted, for example, that a precise definition of the tuning problem is still missing and that tuning is still considered as an art. Typically, scientists and practitioners still tune their algorithms by hand, guided solely by their experience and by some rules-of-thumb.

With this thesis, Mauro Birattari has succeeded in laying the foundations for a scientific approach to tuning metaheuristics. His most remarkable intuition has been to understand that the tuning problem has much in common with the typical problems faced in machine learning, a very active area of Artificial

Intelligence. Thanks to this intuition, Mauro Birattari was able to import in the field of metaheuristics the right ideas and methods from the more mature area of machine learning. He succeeded thus in providing an elegant formal definition of the metaheuristics tuning problem and, then, in proposing F-Race, an effective algorithm for its solution. Always from a machine learning perspective, Mauro Birattari critically discusses the research methodology currently adopted in the metaheuristics area. He highlights some flaws, and proposes some guidelines for future empirical investigations.

The thesis contains also an experimental analysis of F-Race and some examples of practical applications. Among others, it presents a feasibility study carried out by the German-based software company SAP that concerns the possible use of F-Race for tuning a commercial computer program for vehicle routing and scheduling problems. Moreover, it discusses the successful use of F-Race for tuning the best performing algorithm submitted to the *International Timetabling Competition* organized in 2003 by the *Metaheuristics Network* and sponsored by PATAT, the international series of conferences on the *Practice and Theory of Automated Timetabling*.

The thesis is well-structured and beautifully written. Mauro has the uncommon ability to formally frame a problem, find solutions, and communicate the results of his research. This thesis is particularly clear and easily understandable, notwithstanding its complexity and the amount of details. Moreover, it is really a pleasure to read. Due to the originality of Mauro's contribution and to the high relevance of the problem he addresses, I expect that his work will have an important impact on the whole metaheuristics research community.

PROF. MARCO DORIGO

Brussels, Belgium
June 2005

Original contributions

The following is a summary of the main contributions proposed in the thesis:

The framework: The thesis defines the framework in which the problem of tuning metaheuristics emerges, and describes this problem as a *generalization* problem presenting a number of features that are akin to those that characterize machine learning problems.

Formal position of the tuning problem: The thesis gives a formal definition of the tuning problem in which the key role is played by the notion of a probability measure P_I defined over the space of the instances.

Formal analysis of the evaluation problem: The thesis proposes a formal analysis of the Monte Carlo estimation of the performance of a metaheuristic on the basis of a number of observations.

Definition of tuning algorithms: The thesis introduces a number of tuning algorithms. Beside the trivial *brute-force* approach, the class of *racing* algorithms for tuning and, in particular, *F-Race* are introduced.

Empirical analysis: The thesis proposes an accurately designed and statistically sound experimental evaluation of the tuning algorithms introduced. An innovative re-sampling methodology is adopted for the first time in the context of the empirical analysis of metaheuristics.

Applications: The thesis discusses a number of successful applications of *F-Race* and of related algorithms. Among them, the use of a *racing* algorithm for designing a hybrid metaheuristic that outperformed all competitors in the *International Timetabling Competition*, and a feasibility study carried out by the German-based software company SAP, that concerned the possible use of *F-Race* for tuning a commercial computer program for vehicle routing and scheduling problems.

Experimental methodology: The thesis discusses a number of methodological issues and, in particular, some catches related to the practice of tuning. The notion of *over-tuning* is introduced that parallels the already well understood machine learning concept of *over-fitting*.

Moreover, the following contributions are contained in the Annexes:

Analysis of *ant colony optimization*: An original description of *ant colony optimization* is proposed in the terms of optimal control and dynamic programming. Moreover, the model-based search framework is introduced which accommodates a number of combinatorial optimization methods including *ant colony optimization*.

***Lazy learning* for local regression:** An original *lazy learning* algorithm is described and some evidence is provided that it can be an effective alternative to state-of-the-art supervised learning methods for tackling the regression problem.

Finally, two software packages, lazy and race, have been developed to be used with R, the free software suite for statistical computing and graphics. These packages, which are distributed, free of charge, under the GNU General Public License, are available for download from the official site of *The Comprehensive* R *Archive Network*.

Statement

This thesis describes an original research carried out by the author. This work has not been previously submitted to the Université Libre de Bruxelles or to any other university for the award of any degree. Nevertheless, some chapters of this thesis are partially based on articles that, during his doctoral studies, the author, together with a number of co-workers, has published or submitted for publication in the scientific literature.

Preliminary versions of the formal statement of the tuning problem given in Chapter 3 and of the description of the *F-Race* algorithm given in Chapter 4 are contained in:

Birattari, M., Stützle, T., Paquete, L., & Varrentrapp, K. (2002). A racing algorithm for configuring metaheuristics. In Langdon, W. B., Cantú-Paz, E., Mathias, K., Roy, R., Davis, D., Poli, R., Balakrishnan, K., Honavar, V., Rudolph, G., Wegener, J., Bull, L., Potter, M. A., Schultz, A. C., Miller, J. F., Burke, E., & Jonoska, N. (Eds.), *Proceedings of the Genetic and Evolutionary Computation Conference*, pp. 11–18, Morgan Kaufmann. San Francisco, CA, USA.

Footnote 5, page 70, is inspired by the following work:

Piscopo, C. & Birattari, M. (2002). Invention vs. discovery. A critical discussion. In Lange, S., Satoh, K., & Smith, C. H. (Eds.), *Discovery Science. 5th International Conference, DS2002*, volume 2534 of *LNCS*, pp. 457–462, Springer-Verlag. Berlin, Germany.

The formal analysis of the problem of the empirical estimation of the performance of a metaheuristic given in Section 4.1 has been already made public in:

Birattari, M. (2004). On the estimation of the expected performance of a metaheuristic on a class of instances. How many instances, how many runs? Technical Report TR/IRIDIA/2004-01, IRIDIA, Université Libre de Bruxelles, Brussels, Belgium.

The description given in Chapter 5 of the computing environment in which the experimental analysis proposed in the thesis was performed, is based on:

Labella, T. H. & Birattari, M. (2004). Polyphemus: De abacorum racemo. Technical Report TR/IRIDIA/2004-15, IRIDIA, Université Libre de Bruxelles, Brussels, Belgium.

The analysis given in Section 5.2.1 of the metaheuristics for the UNIVERSITY-COURSE TIMETABLING problem developed by the *Metaheuristics Network* is based on:

Rossi-Doria, O., Sampels, M., Birattari, M., Chiarandini, M., Dorigo, M., Gambardella, L. M., Knowles, J., Manfrin, M., Mastrolilli, M., Paechter, B., Paquete, L., & Stützle., T. (2003). A comparison of the performance of different metaheuristics on the timetabling problem. In Burke, E. & De Causmaecker, P. (Eds.), *Practice and Theory of Automated Timetabling, 4th International Conference, PATAT 2002*, volume 2740 of *LNCS*, pp. 329–351, Springer-Verlag, Berlin, Germany.

In particular, the graphs given in Figure 5.18, page 153, were obtained by Michael Samples and are reproduced in the thesis by courtesy of their author:

Sampels, M. (2002). Metaheuristics for the timetabling problem. Results of a comparison within the Metaheuristics Network.
`http://iridia.ulb.ac.be/~msampels/ttmn.data/`.

The discussion proposed in Section 5.2.2 on the use of the *F-Race* algorithm for designing hybrid metaheuristics for the UNIVERSITY-COURSE TIMETABLING problem is based on the following two works:

Chiarandini, M., Socha, K., Birattari, M., & Rossi-Doria, O. (2003). International timetabling competition. a hybrid approach. Technical Report AIDA-03-04, FG Intellektik, FB Informatik, Technische Universität Darmstadt, Darmstadt, Germany.

Chiarandini, M., Birattari, M., Socha, K., & Rossi-Doria, O. (2004). An effective hybrid approach for the university course timetabling problem. *Journal of Scheduling*. Accepted for publication.

The description of the racing algorithm for feature selection given in Section 5.2.3 is based on:

Bontempi, G., Birattari, M., & Meyer, P. E. (2004). Combining lazy learning, racing and subsampling for effective feature selection. Technical Report 527, Département d'Informatique, Université Libre de Bruxelles, Brussels, Belgium. Submitted for publication.

The analysis of the experimental methodology proposed in Chapter 6 is partially based on:

Zlochin, M., Birattari, M., & Dorigo, M. (2004). Towards a theory of practice in metaheuristics design. A machine learning perspective. Technical Report MCS04-01, Computer Science and Applied Mathematics, The Weizmann Institute of Science, Rehovot, Israel. Submitted for journal publication.

The proof given in Appendix 6.A, page 192, of the biasedness of the best of the realizations of a set of random variables as an estimator of the corresponding random variable itself, has been refined through a number of interesting and useful discussion with Gianluca Bontempi, Mark Zlochin, T. Halva Labella, Bruno

Marchal, Daniele Catanzaro, and Philippe Smets.

The concept of *mental image* plays an important role in the analysis given in Annex A of ant colony optimization from the point of view of optimal control theory and reinforcement learning. The use of this concept in Aristotle and Thomas Aquinas, and more in general in Ancient and Medieval epistemology has been deeply discussed with Carlotta Piscopo. The precise meaning of the Ancient Greek term *phantasma*, and a research of occurrences of this term in the original Greek and Latin texts were provided by Scilla Goria.

The description of ant colony optimization given in Annex A is based on the following works:

Birattari, M., Di Caro, G., & Dorigo, M. (2000). For a formal foundation of the Ant Programming approach to combinatorial optimization. Part 1: The problem, the representation, and the genearl solution strategy. Technical Report TR-H-301, ATR-Human Information Processing Labs, Kyoto, Japan.

Birattari, M. (2001). On the formal foundation of ant programming. Mémoire de DEA, Université Libre de Bruxelles, Brussels, Belgium.

Birattari, M., Di Caro, G., & Dorigo, M. (2002). Toward the formal foundation of ant programming. In Dorigo, M., Di Caro, G., & Sampels, M. (Eds.), *Ant Algorithms, 3rd International Workshop, ANTS 2002*, volume 2463 of *LNCS*, pp. 188–201, Springer-Verlag. Berlin, Germany.

Dorigo, M., Zlochin, M., Meuleau, N., & M.Birattari (2002). Updating ACO pheromones using stochastic gradient ascent and cross-entropy methods. In Cagnoni, S., Gottlieb, J., Hart, E., Middendorf, M., & Raidl, R. (Eds.), *Applications of Evolutionary Computing, EvoWorkshop 2002: EvoCOP, EvoIASP, EvoSTIM/EvoPLAN*, volume 2279 of *LNCS*, pp. 21–30, Springer-Verlag. Berlin, Germany.

Zlochin, M., Birattari, M., Meuleau, N., & Dorigo, M. (2004). Model-based search for combinatorial optimization: A critical survey. *Annals of Operations Research, 131*(1–4):373–395.

The description of the *lazy learning* algorithm given in Annex B is based on:

Birattari, M., Bontempi, G., & Bersini, H. (1999). Lazy learning meets the recursive least-squares algorithm. In Kearns, M. S., Solla, S. A., & Cohn, D. A. (Eds.), *Advances in Neural Information Processing Systems 11*, pp. 375–381, MIT Press. Cambridge, MA, USA.

Birattari, M. & Bontempi, G. (1999). Lazy learning vs. Speedy Gonzales: A fast algorithm for recursive identification and recursive validation of local constant models. Technical Report TR/IRIDIA/1999-6, IRIDIA, Université Libre de Bruxelles, Brussels, Belgium.

Bontempi, G., Birattari, M., & Bersini, H. (1999). Lazy learners at work: The lazy learning toolbox. In *EUFIT'99: The 7th European Congress on Intelligent Techniques and Soft Computing, Abstract Booklet with CD Rom*, ELITE Foundation. Aachen, Germany.

Two software packages have been developed by the author and made available in the public domain under the GNU General Public License[1] of the Free Software Foundation:

Birattari, M. (2003). The race package for R. Racing methods for the selection of the best. Technical Report TR/IRIDIA/2003-37, IRIDIA, Université Libre de Bruxelles, Brussels, Belgium. Package available at:
`http://cran.r-project.org/src/contrib/Descriptions/race.html`.

Birattari, M. & Bontempi G. (2003). The lazy package for R. Lazy learning for local regression. Technical Report TR/IRIDIA/2003-38, IRIDIA, Université Libre de Bruxelles, Brussels, Belgium. Package available at:
`http://cran.r-project.org/src/contrib/Descriptions/lazy.html`.

The latter had been previously released as a package for Matlab™:

Birattari, M. & Bontempi, G. (1999). The lazy learning toolbox. For use with Matlab. Technical Report TR/IRIDIA/1999-7, IRIDIA, Université Libre de Bruxelles, Brussels, Belgium.

This thesis was typeset by the author using LaTeX. The research work described in the body of the thesis was carried out using exclusively free software: GNU Emacs, R, CVS, gcc, among others. In particular, all computers used for developing code, running experiments, writing reports, articles, and the thesis itself were running a GNU/Linux operating system, mostly the Debian distribution, but also Red Hat and Suse. The author warmly endorse all the software adopted.

No animals were harmed during the making of this thesis.

M. B.

Brussels, Belgium
October 2004

[1] `http://www.gnu.org/copyleft/gpl.html`

Acknowledgments

I acknowledge financial support from a number of institutions: The very initial phase of my Ph.D. studies was funded by the *Région wallonne* through a FIRST Project carried out at IRIDIA, Université Libre de Bruxelles, Brussels, Belgium, under the supervision of Prof. Hugues Bersini, and in collaboration with the FaFer Usinor steel company in Charleroi, Belgium. For six months my research was funded by the AASS lab, Örebro Universitet, Örebro, Sweden, where I have been working under the supervision of Prof. Alessandro Saffiotti and Dr. Tom Duckett. From April 2001 to June 2004, my Ph.D. studies have been supported by the *Metaheuristics Network*, a Training and Research Network funded by the Improving Human Potential Programme of the Commission of the European Communities, under contract number HPRN-CT-1999-00106. In the framework of the *Metaheuristics Network*, I had the unique opportunity of working with two different research groups: I have been for one year with INTELLEKTIK, Technische Universität Darmstadt, Darmstadt, Germany, where my work has been supervised by Prof. Wolfgang Bibel and Dr. Thomas Stützle. Since April 2002, I have been with IRIDIA, Université Libre de Bruxelles, Brussels, Belgium, where I have been supervised by Prof. Marco Dorigo. Starting from July 2004, my Ph.D. studies have been funded by the *actions de recherche concertées* of the *Communauté française de Belgique* through the research project *ANTS* directed by Prof. Marco Dorigo.

I started my research career back in 1996 with my Master's thesis at the Politecnico di Milano, Milan, Italy, under the supervision of Prof. Andrea Bonarini and Prof. Gianluca Bontempi. I really owe much to Gianluca: I have learned from him many of the tricks that compose my repertoire and that have been so useful in the research that led to this thesis.

While I was working at my Master's thesis, Gianluca introduced me to IDSIA, Istituto Dalle Molle di Studi sull'Intelligenza Artificiale, Lugano, Switzerland, where I met Prof. Luca Maria Gambardella and Prof. Marco Dorigo. Later on, I had the great pleasure to work with Luca within the *Metaheuristics Network*, and Marco became my Ph.D. supervisor at IRIDIA.

Always thanks to Gianluca, I joined IRIDIA as an exchange undergraduate student. There I had the chance to be supervised by Prof. Hugues Bersini. Hugues has an extraordinary talent in charming students and in making them involved in his fascinating researches in the domain of artificial intelligence.

I am much indebted to the great friend of mine Gianni Di Caro, for introducing me to ant colony optimization back in 1998. The never-ending discussions we had on the issue played a major role in shaping my point of view on metaheuristics.

With Dr. Mark Zlochin I shared my interest for the analysis of metaheuristics from the machine learning point of view. Mark is extremely knowledgeable in statistics and machine learning theory: Working with him has been very useful for the development of my thesis ... and very fun, indeed!

This work would have been simply impossible without the support of Dr. Thomas Stützle. It was Thomas who attracted my attention to the problem of tuning metaheuristics and who suggested that my machine learning background could be profitably employed on this problem. Thomas has been very helpful in these years: In all phases of my research I could rely on his advice and on his great experience.

Prof. Marco Dorigo has supervised this work of mine, and more in general my research activities since 2000. Marco has been the perfect supervisor: He has been extremely supportive and his advice on all aspects of my research and my scientific activity has been really invaluable. Most of all I want to acknowledge here the value that Marco kept adding to my research through comments, discussions, and brainstorming sessions: Extremely knowledgeable in ant colony optimization *(bien sûr!)*, metaheuristics, machine learning and, in general, in all topics I touch in my work, Marco really seemed taking pleasure in diving into the gory details of my work. During these years, I had much to learn from Marco, and not only on scientific issues directly related to my thesis. Indeed, Marco gave me the chance to assist him in various tasks such as writing reports and project proposals, managing research projects, supervising students, organizing events, *etc.* I had therefore the opportunity to observe his activities from a privileged position and to acquire skills that will be very useful in my future career.

Beside Marco and Thomas, I wish to thank the senior scientists in charge of the other nodes of the *Metaheuristics Network*, in particular, Prof. Luca M. Gambardella and Prof. Ben Paechter. A special thanks goes to the young researchers of the *Metaheuristics Network* and to all other researchers that have been somehow involved in the research activities of the network: Leonora Bianchi, Dr. Christian Blum, Dr. Thomas Bousonville, Marco Chiarandini, Dr. Matthijs den Besten, Dr. Irina Dumitrescu, Dr. Stefka Fidanova, Dr. Joshua Knowles, Philip Kostuch, Max Manfrin, Dr. Monaldo Mastrolilli, Dr. Nicolas Meuleau, Fabrizio Oliverio, Luís Paquete, Dr. Marco Pranzo, Dr. Andrea Roli, Dr. Olivia Rossi-Doria, Dr. Erol Sahin, Dr. Michael Sampels, Tommaso Schiavinotto, Krzysztof Socha, and Klaus Varrentrapp. These years of research together have been blood, toil, sweat, and tears (and admittedly also a couple of beers) but they have been a great pleasure and a great satisfaction to me: Thank you all!

Moreover, I wish to thank all (previously unmentioned) people I have been working with at IRIDIA: Prof. Philippe Smets, Dr. Bruno Marchal, Vittorio Gorrini, Dr. Edy Bertolissi, Dr. Nick Bradshaw, Antoine Duchâteau, Dr. Jorge Gasós, Francesco Allevi, Emanuele Persico, Prof. Philip Miller, Thomas Halva Labella, Vito Trianni, Roderich Groß, Shervin Nouyan, Christos Ampatzis, Daniele Catanzaro, Julia Handl, Dr. Patrice Latinne, Prof. Masaaki Minagawa, Roberto Pirotta, Dr. Mohamed Ben Haddou, Dr. Tom Lenaerts, Colin Molter, Pierre Sener, Christophe Philemotte, Pierre Philippe, Utku Salihoglu, Dr. Frank Vanden Berghen, Nathanäel Ackerman, François-Xavier Willems, Maria J. Blesa, Fabiola Boldrini, Michela Lunghi, Roberto Ghizzioli, and Muriel Decreton; and all (previously unmentioned) people I have been working with at INTELLEKTIK: Dr. Gunter Grieser, Dr. Peter Grigoriev, Dr. Ulrich Scholz, Dr. Sergey Yevtushenko, Dr. Hesham Khalil, and Maria Tiedemann.

On a more personal basis, I wish to thank Grzegorz Cielniak, Danae Riveros, Candice Roufosse, Elena Lanzoni, Scilla Goria, Luca Di Mauro, Johann Sebastian Bach, Jacques Brel, Jean-Pierre Van Roy of *Cantillon*, Jean-Luis Dits of *La Brasserie à Vapeur*, Armand Debelder of *Drie Fonteinen*, *Le Musée du Cinéma* of Brussels, Aldo Piatti, all my old friends at *Bu-Sen Bresso* judo club, Bouzian El Amri, Lionel Hebrant, and the ULB judo club.

I thank all my family for their love and support: Giulia, Francesco, Adriano, Lorena, Filippo, Rita, Giuseppe, my grandparents Franco, Valeria, Meri, and Lino, my brother Luca and Stefania, my mother Anna, my father Claudio, Vladimiro and Carlotta.

Carlotta, in particular, has shared with me each single good or bad moment in the last ten years: For this reason, and for many others, I really love her very much ... and I deeply appreciate her perseverance :-)

* * *

This work of mine is dedicated to my father for all what he gave me and for all what he taught me. Especially for explaining me, many years ago, what happens to the steps of an escalator when they get to the top ... and most of all, for managing to teach me to ask this kind of questions! My father taught me to pay attention to things, to take pleasure in wondering first, and to look for rational explanations immediately afterwards. My approach to the issues discussed in this thesis, proudly reflects his teachings: *Wonder en is gheen wonder.*[†]

M. B.

Brussels, Belgium
October 2004

[†] *What appears a miracle is not a miracle*, the motto of the scientist and civil engineer Simon Stevin (1548–1620).

Contents

Car sans généralisation, la prévision est impossible. Les circonstances où l'on a opéré ne se reproduiront jamais toutes à la fois. Le fait observé ne recommencera donc jamais; la seule chose que l'on puisse affirmer, c'est que dans des circonstances analogues, un fait analogue se produira. Pour prévoir il faut donc au moins invoquer l'analogie, c'est-à-dire déjà généraliser.†

Henri Poincaré

Chapter 1

Introduction

Aiming at the best is one of the most fundamental traits of intelligence. In all activities, human beings tend to maximize benefit or, equivalently, to minimize inconvenience in some context-dependent sense. The pursuit of the best appears so connatural with the human mind that when we do not recognize it in somebody's behavior we readily qualify him/her as *irrational.*

Quite naturally, along the centuries man has devoted much effort to the development of formal tools that help in spotting optimality. Mathematical optimization, as we know it nowadays, is the result of this effort: A collection of powerful methods and algorithms for tackling a large variety of different problems. In the contemporary world, optimization plays an extremely important role in all branches of engineering and has therefore a huge economical relevance. During the last two decades in particular, the ever increasing availability of computing power has further enlarged the set of optimization problems that can be effectively handled.

The history of optimization methods has been dominated by two different and possibly competing concerns: On the one hand, an optimization method should be *efficient*, that is, it should be able to find some highly satisfactory solution and it should be able to do it quickly. On the other hand, it should be *manageable*,

†*Because without generalization, prediction is impossible. Circumstances in which we have operated will never reproduce all together at the same time. Therefore, an observed event will never reappear; the only thing we could state is that in analogous circumstances, an analogous event will happen. In order to make a prediction, it is therefore necessary to resort at least to analogy, that is, indeed, to generalize.*

that is, it should be easy to use and, in case, easy to adapt with possibly some minor modifications, to other optimization problems different from, but somehow similar to the one for which it was originally developed.

Of these two concerns, *efficiency* appears as the most basic one while *manageability* is a concern of a higher order related to the problem of engineering and optimizing the process of developing optimization algorithms themselves. Nevertheless, the *manageability* concern had a major role in shaping the whole optimization field. It should be indeed recognized that the very existence of optimization subfields—such as, for example, continuous vs. discrete optimization—or the concept of *optimization problem* as a collection of instances, are the most noticeable implications of the *manageability* concern. As a matter of fact, the ultimate goal of optimization is to solve specific problems emerging in the real-world. Nevertheless, rather than solving each single specific problem by itself and re-starting from scratch with the research when a new problem is given, it seems advisable to recognize that different specific problems have some common structure and can be profitably considered as different *instances* of a same problem. This abstraction step, although seemingly obvious, is fundamental for the formal development of optimization. It opens indeed the way to the development of optimization algorithms and to the formal analysis of their properties.

In the development of combinatorial optimization—the optimization subfield that is the focus of this thesis—the role played by the *manageability* concern emerges clearly and is tightly connected with the deepest motivations underlying the research presented in the thesis itself. Many combinatorial optimization problems of great economical relevance are believed to be particularly difficult to solve. This belief is formally expressed in the computational complexity theory by saying that they are *NP-hard*.[1] As a practical consequence, an exact solution to instances of such problems can possibly require a huge amount of computation time in order to be produced. For such problems it is customary to have recourse to *heuristics*, that is, problem-specific algorithms that implement some *reasonable* strategy for obtaining a *sufficiently good* solution in a *suitably short* amount of time: Heuristics do not provide any theoretical guarantee on the quality of the solution they might produce and, at most, they come with some positive record of successful applications to instances of the problem for which they had been devised. Notwithstanding this lack of theoretical support, heuristics have met some notable success on many different problems of practical relevance and have therefore proven, in practice, to be able to provide a positive answer to the *efficiency* concerns.

The major drawbacks of heuristics derive from their problem-dependent nature: Although ideas that were proven successful in tackling other problems might be useful when a new problem is given, each problem presents its own peculiar-

[1]See for example Garey & Johnson (1979). An introduction to these concepts is given in Section 2.1.4.

ities and pitfalls. As a consequence, in order to design an effective heuristic for a given problem, a wealth of problem-specific information is needed. Moreover, often the development of a heuristic is a labor-intensive activity and a great intellectual challenge that requires the attention of a highly skilled practitioner and therefore entails major economical costs. Clearly these drawbacks substantially limit the *manageability* of heuristics.

In the last two decades, a new class of algorithms emerged, the so called *metaheuristics* (Glover, 1986). Metaheuristics are general algorithmic templates that can be easily adapted to solve the most different optimization problems. In other words, a metaheuristic defines some high-level and abstract principles for organizing a search in the space of the solutions of a generic optimization problem. When a given new optimization problem has to be tackled, some steps need to be taken before the metaheuristic is operational. From the point of view of the practitioner that adapts a metaheuristic to a problem, the metaheuristic is best seen as a modular structure coming with a set of components, each typically provided with a set of free parameters. The task of the practitioner consists in properly selecting the components to be included in the actual implementation, assembling them, and finally providing values for their free parameters. In any case, these steps require much less effort than the development from scratch of an *ad hoc* heuristic and, in this sense, metaheuristics are apparently more *manageable* than their forerunner heuristics.

Most often, even a quick-and-dirty implementation of a metaheuristic is able to obtain fairly good results. Nevertheless, an out-of-the-box implementation of a metaheuristic for a given problem does not typically equal the performance of an *ad hoc* heuristic, when the latter is available. The high flexibility of metaheuristics allows fairly good results on a large class of potential problems but, at the same time, it prevents from obtaining excellent results on each of them: Clearly, a sort of *efficiency/manageability* trade-off must exist.

If state-of-the-art results are needed, some extra effort is often necessary. In such a case, the practitioner should inject some problem-specific knowledge in the implementation of the metaheuristic and, most of all, should take extra care in properly designing the structure and in tuning the free parameters of the metaheuristic in order to match the specific features of the problem at hand and of the specific class of instances that one wishes to solve. Typically, practitioners *craft* a good structure supported only by their own experience and tune the parameters by hand in a *trial-and-error* procedure guided by some *rules-of-thumb*. No formal tool or statistical methodology is usually adopted in this phase and much rests upon personal feelings and sensations. This approach, beside being extremely tedious, is error prone, scarcely reproducible, and expensive.

The research presented in this thesis aims precisely at defining an automatic procedure for configuring and fine-tuning metaheuristics. Our involvement in the issue stems from the conviction that the development of an automatic tuning procedure is a *conditio sine qua non* for fully accomplishing the "revolution" of the combinatorial optimization field that began with the introduction of metaheuristics: Since the ultimate goal of metaheuristics is to drastically reduce and eventually get rid of the effort needed for designing effective optimization algorithms when new problems arise, automatic configuration and tuning should be considered as an integral part of the research on metaheuristics. We are confident that a proper automatic tuning procedure would indeed allow the definition of a general-purpose optimization approach that conjugate high *manageability* with state-of-the-art *efficiency*.

Although the crucial role of tuning is acknowledged in the literature, see for example Barr *et al.* (1995), relatively little attention has been given to the issue. Admittedly, some works have been published describing tuning methods and even if some of them are manifestly brilliant (Coy *et al.*, 2001; Adenso-Díaz & Laguna, 2002) and possibly very promising, our personal analysis of the literature led us to the conclusion that the very nature of the tuning problem remained so far misunderstood. The main contribution of the thesis consists in a formal definition of the tuning problem: As it is made clear in the body of the thesis, the tuning problem has the characteristics of a machine learning problem. Indeed tuning consists in finding the *best* possible configuration of the algorithm at hand, where with *best* configuration we mean the one which is deemed to yield the best results on the instances that the algorithm will be eventually faced with, once operational. Clearly, these instances are not known beforehand, and in particular during the tuning phase itself. Tuning has therefore to rely on other instances, *tuning instances* in the following, that should be reasonably considered as *representative* of the whole class of instances that the algorithm will eventually encounter. This process of substitution entails the assumption that the results obtained on the tuning instances by the metaheuristic, indeed by each of its configurations, can be *extended* to the whole class of interest. To be more explicit, when tuning a metaheuristic we are ready to accept the hypothesis that since tuning instances are somehow *similar* to the instances that could be possibly encountered once in operation, the results obtained on the former should be, in turn, *similar* to those that would be obtained on the latter. In this precise sense, the tuning problem is a genuine *generalization* problem that can be profitably framed, formalized, and solved in a machine learning setting.

Accordingly, machine learning concepts and methods play a key role in the thesis: The definition of the tuning problem, the tuning algorithms proposed, and the experimental methodology adopted, liberally take inspiration from the machine learning literature and bring therefore some fresh ideas to the optimization community. In particular, the definition of the tuning problem rests on the concept of *class of instances*, which is formally captured by considering a probability measure over the space of the instances of the optimization problem at hand. An exhaustive discussion of the issue is given in the thesis, it suffices here to notice that the adoption of a probabilistic model in this context is rather atypical and, according to our personal experience, almost *disturbing* for optimization practitioners. When we adopted this *probabilistic approach* for the first time in Birattari *et al.* (2002), we were convinced it was absolutely novel in the optimization literature. Only afterwards, we became aware that, although with different aims and in a different context, it had been already used by Wolpert & Macready in their seminal works on the *no free lunch* theorem (1996; 1997). Apparently, this element was so unusual for the optimization community that it went unnoticed—and not only to us. Indeed, subsequent works on the *no free lunch* theorem presented by other author have developed many elements of the original results by Wolpert & Macready (1996, 1997) but have dropped all reference to a probability measure over the space of instances—see for example Radcliffe & Surry (1995), Schumacher *et al.* (2001), Igel & Toussaint (2003), and Corne & Knowles (2003). It is interesting to notice that the adoption of a probabilistic model of the space of the instances must be really some characteristic trait of an analysis of optimization issues from a machine learning point of view: It is indeed a key element in this thesis as it is, even if with very different aims, in the work of Wolpert & Macready (1996, 1997), authors that have a strong machine learning background and are mostly active, David Wolpert in particular, within the machine learning community.

Another original element in the thesis, that also stems from a well established practice in machine learning, is the experimental methodology adopted. In the machine learning literature, great attention is payed to a clear separation between data used for training a learning machine and data used for its assessment. Machine learning practitioners are well aware of the risks associated with a violation of this separation, that is, the risk of seriously overestimating the performance of a learning approach. *Over-fitting* is the concept that is typically invoked for describing this phenomenon and different theoretical works have been devoted to its analysis—see for example Geman *et al.* (1992) and Vapnik (1995, 1998). Unfortunately, no similar awareness exists within the optimization community of the risks deriving from assessing the performance of a metaheuristic on the same instances that where used for tuning its parameters. In the thesis we call *over-tuning* the over specialization of a metaheuristic for a specific instance, or group of instances: In particular, we stress the need to assess the performance of a metaheuristic on fresh instances that where not previously used for configuring or fine-tuning the parameters of the metaheuristic itself. This ensures an *unbiased* evaluation of the metaheuristic under analysis.

Always concerning the experimental methodology adopted in the thesis, a further original element borrowed from the machine learning practice is the re-sampling strategy that was used in the comparison of the tuning algorithms discussed in the thesis and in the analysis of the risks associated with the aforementioned *over-tuning* concept. Re-sampling methods (Good, 2001) such as, for example, the *bootstrap* (Efron & Tibshirani, 1997), are statistical methods that are effectively used for enhancing the significance of the conclusions that can be drawn from a given data sample. Rather than using the given sample directly, re-sampling methods prescribe that a number of *pseudo-samples* be generated by sampling, possibly with replacement, the original data. All subsequent analysis is then performed on the so obtained *pseudo-samples*. These methods are commonly employed by machine learning practitioners but, to the best of our knowledge, they have never been adopted before in the empirical analysis of metaheuristics. Nevertheless, re-sampling methods are particularly suitable for research in metaheuristics and in the thesis they allow to *simulate* an extremely large number of runs of the metaheuristics under analysis and to draw therefore conclusions that would have been impractical to reach by actual computation.[2]

The structure of the thesis

Beside this Chapter 1, also Chapter 2 is of a marked introductory nature. It is composed of two parts: On the one hand, Section 2.1 introduces some background knowledge about combinatorial optimization and metaheuristics. In particular, this section provides a critical review of the literature concerning the empirical evaluation of metaheuristics and the fine-tuning of their parameters. On the other hand, Section 2.2 introduces the supervised learning problem and in particular the *racing* class of algorithms that were originally proposed within the machine learning community for solving the model selection problem. These algorithms serve in this thesis as a source of inspiration for tackling the problem of tuning metaheuristics.

Chapter 3 gives a precise definition of the tuning problem that is considered in the rest of the thesis. First, an informal definition is given through an example of a typical situation in which the tuning problem emerges. Then, a formal position of the problem is proposed, which gives a precise mathematical meaning to each of the elements highlighted in the informal example. The role played by Chapter 3 is of key importance for the development of the thesis: To the best of our knowledge, our definition of the tuning problem is the first formal definition of this problem given in the literature. It has the merit of revealing the true nature of the problem of tuning metaheuristics and to show its tight relationship with the supervised learning problem and in particular with model selection.

Chapter 4 presents the *racing* class of algorithms for solving the tuning problem defined in Chapter 3. These *racing* algorithms are inspired by some algorithms introduced within the machine learning community for solving the model selection problem. In particular, the *F-Race* algorithm is introduced. *F-Race* belongs to the family of *racing* algorithms but it is characterized by the adoption of a novel statistical test, the *Friedman two-way analysis of variance by*

[2]As an example, the analysis summarized in Figure 6.2, page 182 of Chapter 6, is based on 80600 *simulated* runs of *iterated local search*, each taking 10 s of computations on the kind of machine adopted, an AMD Athlon™ XP 1400-based personal computer. If actually executed, these runs would have taken more than $8{\times}10^{13}$ s, that is, more than 2.5 million years: Quite a considerable time ... especially when you wish to include the result in your Ph.D. thesis!

ranks (Conover, 1999), that had never been considered before in the design of *racing* algorithms. As it is explained in the body of the chapter, the Friedman test appears particularly suitable in the context of metaheuristics tuning. The chapter defines also some simpler *brute-force* algorithms that for their characteristics, as it will be made clear in the chapter itself, serve in our research as an appropriate yardstick for measuring the performance of the tuning algorithms developed in the thesis. As a by-product of the development of *F-Race* and of the other tuning algorithms presented in the chapter, Section 4.1 proposes a formal analysis of the problem of evaluating the expected performance of a generic stochastic algorithm, such as a metaheuristic or one of its configuration. This analysis has a major impact on the empirical study described in Chapter 5 and informs the discussion on the experimental methodology proposed in Chapter 6.

Chapter 5 proposes an empirical evaluation of the tuning algorithms introduced in the thesis. The chapter is composed of two parts aiming both, each on the basis of different pieces of evidence, at showing the effectiveness of the algorithms under analysis: On the one hand, Section 5.1 proposes a formal empirical analysis in which the *racing* algorithms discussed in the thesis are compared, under controlled conditions, with some *brute-force* methods that serve as a yardstick. In this section, two tuning problems are considered. In the first, the metaheuristic to be tuned is *iterated local search* and the optimization problem considered is the QUADRATIC ASSIGNMENT problem. In the second, the algorithm is *ant colony optimization* and the problem is the TRAVELING SALESMAN problem. For both tuning problems, the differences in the performance of the algorithms under analysis are assessed through appropriate statistical tests of significance, and a number of graphs are proposed that help visualize and understand the characteristics of the algorithms themselves. On the other hand, Section 5.2 reports some examples of practical applications of the *racing* algorithms presented in the thesis. These examples do not provide any formal comparison with other methods and are more of a *qualitative* rather than *quantitative* nature. Their goal is to show that the proposed algorithms have the flexibility and usability that are necessary to make them appealing for practical applications.

Chapter 6 is of a rather philosophical nature and proposes a critical discussion of the experimental methodology currently adopted in many works that present empirical analysis of metaheuristics. On the basis of the definition of the tuning problem given in Chapter 3, and in particular of the formal analysis of the problem of evaluating the expected performance of a metaheuristic given in Section 4.1, we are in the position of highlighting some pitfalls in the current methodology and proposing an alternative approach.

Each chapter of the thesis is concluded by a section devoted to a discussion and a critical evaluation of the material presented in the chapter itself. Final conclusions are drawn in Chapter 7, which proposes an overview of the results presented in the thesis, puts them in perspective, and highlights possible extensions and future research directions.

The *Metaheuristics Network*
IRIDIA, Université Libre de Bruxelles, Brussels, Belgium
INTELLEKTIK, Technische Universität Darmstadt, Darmstadt, Germany
CSG, Technische Universiteit Eindhoven, Eindhoven, The Netherlands
Istituto Dalle Molle di Studi sull'Intelligenza Artificiale, Manno, Switzerland
ECRG, Napier University, Edinburgh, United Kingdom
EuroBios, Paris, France
AntOptima, Lugano, Switzerland

Table 1.1: Five academic research groups and two companies have been involved in the activities of the *Metaheuristics Network* that covered the time period between September 2000 and August 2004.

Further material is given in the annexes: They cover topics that, although directly related to the issues discussed in the thesis, have been judged not strictly necessary for following the logical flow of the arguments. In particular, Annex A proposes an original analysis from a machine learning perspective of *ant colony optimization*, one of the metaheuristics discussed in the thesis. On the other hand, Annex B is an overview of *lazy learning*, a supervised learning method that is mentioned on several occasions in the thesis.

The Metaheuristics Network

The research presented in this thesis was carried out in the framework of the ***Metaheuristics Network*** which provided the original motivations, the research environment, and the necessary funding. The *Metaheuristics Network* is a Training and Research Network funded by the Improving Human Potential Programme of the Commission of the European Communities, under contract number HPRN-CT-1999-00106. According to the official contract of the *Metaheuristics Network* (2000):

> *The goal of the* Metaheuristics Network *is to deepen the understanding of metaheuristics so that they can be applied more effectively to the solution of important practical combinatorial optimisation problems.*

The activities of the *Metaheuristics Network* started in September 2000 and were accomplished in August 2004. A total of seven nodes have been involved: five academic research groups and two companies—see Table 1.1 for a list of the participants.

The research method of the *Metaheuristics Network* has been mostly experimental. Along the four year life period of the project, different combinatorial optimization problems were studied. The network tackled first some well understood academic problems such as MAXIMUM SATISFIABILITY and QUADRATIC

ASSIGNMENT. Once the network was properly set up, the focus moved to more challenging problems: one year was devoted to scheduling problems, in particular GROUP SHOP SCHEDULING (Sampels *et al.*, 2002), one year to timetabling problems, in particular UNIVERSITY-COURSE TIMETABLING (Rossi-Doria *et al.*, 2003), and finally one year to vehicle routing problems, in particular VEHICLE ROUTING WITH STOCHASTIC DEMAND (Bianchi *et al.*, 2004). For each of the aforementioned problems, a number of metaheuristics were implemented including *simulated annealing*, *tabu search*, *evolutionary computation*, *iterated local search*, and *ant colony optimization*.[3] The study of each problem has been organized in three phases. During the **first phase**, one single node would conduct a preliminary analysis of the problem. This node would be the one with the most significant background experience on the problem at hand. The goal of the first phase would be to highlight the most interesting features of the problem itself, point out possible pitfalls, define a class of instances of interest, and implement a common software library including data structures, an input/output interface and other software components such as an appropriate local search.[4] In the **second phase**, each of the academic research groups would implement a different metaheuristic on the basis of the common software library developed in the first phase. These versions of the algorithms were supposed to be bare-bone implementations of the basic principles of each metaheuristic aiming at providing an understanding of their potential, without a direct concern to performance. The second phase would conclude with an empirical analysis of the metaheuristic implemented. In the **third phase**, a stronger interaction among the network nodes would take place with the aim of designing some high-performing, possibly hybrid, metaheuristics based on the experience gathered during the first two phases.

Parallel to the activity of the academic nodes, the industrial nodes would study the possibility of adopting the metaheuristics under analysis for the solution of real-world problems similar to those studied by the academic partners. A continuous exchange of information and experience between academic and industrial partners resulted to be highly beneficial for both since it gave the academic researchers the chance to measure the practical relevance of their work, and gave the industrial researcher a wealth of new and promising ideas.

The author of this thesis joined the *Metaheuristics Network* in April 2001 and spent 12 months with INTELLEKTIK in Darmstadt, Germany, and 28 months with IRIDIA in Brussels, Belgium. The original analysis of the tuning problem and its formal definition were produced while the author was with INTELLEKTIK. The tuning algorithms presented in the thesis were first employed for tuning the parameters of the two metaheuristics, namely *simulated annealing* and *iterated*

[3]These algorithms are introduced in Section 2.1.7.

[4]See Section 2.1, in particular Sections 2.1.6 and 2.1.7, for an introductory discussion on the role of local search in the implementation of metaheuristics.

local search, developed by INTELLEKTIK for the second phase of the research on UNIVERSITY-COURSE TIMETABLING. When the author moved to Brussels, the same tuning approach was adopted for re-shaping the *ant colony optimization* algorithm implemented at IRIDIA. During the third phase of the research on the timetabling problem, a joint research involving IRIDIA, INTELLEKTIK, and ECRG was set up with the aim of producing a high-performing algorithm for timetabling by combining features of different metaheuristics that were proven successful during the second phase. In this effort for producing an hybrid metaheuristic, a fundamental role was played by a semi-automatic tuning procedure derived from the methods presented in this thesis. The resulting algorithm outperformed all algorithms submitted to the *International Timetabling Competition* organized in 2003 by the *Metaheuristics Network* and sponsored by PATAT, the international series of conferences on the *Practice and Theory of Automated Timetabling*. Moreover, the ideas presented in this thesis had a major impact in refining the experimental methodology adopted by the *Metaheuristics Network* for the empirical assessment of the algorithms developed within the network. In particular, the analysis of the problem of evaluating the expected performance of a metaheuristic, as presented in Section 4.1, led to the definition of a novel experimental protocol that was first adopted for the assessment of the metaheuristics developed for the vehicle routing problem.

Denn wer, ohne ein bestimmtes Problem vor Auge zu haben, nach Methoden sucht, dessen Suchen ist meist vergeblich.[†]

David Hilbert

Chapter 2

Background and state-of-the-art

Although the problem of tuning metaheuristics is highly relevant in practical applications and notwithstanding the general acknowledgment of this fact, no well defined and established methodology exists for tackling it. Indeed, the most striking element emerging from the literature is that the problem even lacks of a clear and explicit definition which, in our opinion, indicates that a full understanding of its very nature is still missing.[1] As a consequence, the analysis of the state-of-the-art that we propose in this chapter will be unavoidably "in the negative:" It will be characterized more vividly by what is missing in the literature rather than by what is present.

This chapter is composed of two parts: On the one hand Section 2.1 introduces some background knowledge about combinatorial optimization and metaheuristics. More in the specific, Section 2.1.8 describes the current practice in tuning metaheuristics, and some related issues discussed in the literature, such as, for example, the definition of an experimental methodology. On the other hand, Section 2.2 introduces the supervised learning problem while Section 2.2.7 describes a class of model selection methods adopted by the machine learning community.

These two parts, which might admittedly seem quite unrelated, are connected precisely by the definition of the tuning problem that, despite (and indeed due to) its absence from the literature, is the pivot of this chapter and of the whole thesis. The connection is made clear in the main body of the thesis: The definition of the tuning problem proposed in Chapter 3 shows that tuning metaheuristics can be indeed described as a learning problem. Furthermore, Chapter 4 introduces an algorithm that belongs precisely to the class described in Section 2.2.7, and that can be effectively used for tackling the tuning problem, as it is shown by some experimental results and examples of applications proposed in Chapter 5.

[†] *He who seeks for methods without having a definite problem in mind seeks for the most part in vain.*

[1] To the best of our knowledge, the first formal formulation of the tuning problem and its description as a generalization problem akin to those faced in machine learning was given in Birattari *et al.* (2002).

2.1 Metaheuristics for combinatorial optimization

The goal of this section is to provide some background knowledge on the use of metaheuristics for combinatorial optimization and to report on the current state-of the-art for what concerns the problem of tuning metaheuristics.

In this Section 2.1.1 we briefly propose some historical and philosophical facts about optimization. In Section 2.1.2 we give a formal description of the optimization problem and in Section 2.1.3 we introduce the problem of combinatorial optimization. In Sections 2.1.4 and 2.1.5 we provide an overview of some important theoretical results on the complexity of combinatorial optimization problems and on the *a priori* equivalence of optimization algorithms. In Section 2.1.6 we introduce the concept of metaheuristic and in Section 2.1.7 we provide a bird's-eye view of the most popular metaheuristics. Finally, in Section 2.1.7 we discuss the problem of tuning metaheuristics as it appears in the literature.

2.1.1 A philosophical and historical perspective

Optimization problems are extremely relevant and arise in any human activity as they represent the rationalization of the natural impulse of all intelligent beings to aim at *the best.*

In a broad sense, *to optimize* means to select among a set of possibilities the best one. In such a sense, man has always implicitly optimized since the night of the times: Which fruit to pick from that tree? Which animal to hunt in that herd? Which cave to spend the night in?

In a more formal sense, by optimization we mean a rational process that involves the explicit definition, typically in the formal language of mathematics, of a search domain and of a criterion. The first historical evidence of a rationally posed optimization problem arrived to us through Simplicius (VIth century) who quotes now lost works in which it appears that before Aristotle, that is before the IVth century before Christ, it was known that among all plane figures of same perimeter the circle is the one of largest surface and that among all solid of same surface the sphere is the one of largest volume.

In the 19 b.C, the Latin poet Vergil reports the legend of the foundation of the city of Carthage, about 800 b.C.:

> *Devenere locos, ubi nunc ingentia cernis*
> *moenia surgentemque novae Karthaginis arcem,*
> *mercatique solum, facti de nomine Byrsam,*
> *taurino quantum possent circumdare tergo.*[‡]
> *Publius Vergilius Maro,* Æneid, Book I.

The Phoenician Queen Dido reached North African after fleeing her country to escape from her brother, the tyrant Pygmalion. Once on the coasts of the Tunisian

[‡] *Then came they to these lands where now thine eyes behold yon walls and yonder citadel of newly rising Carthage. For a price they measured round so much of Afric soil as one bull's hide encircles, and the spot received its name, the Byrsa.*

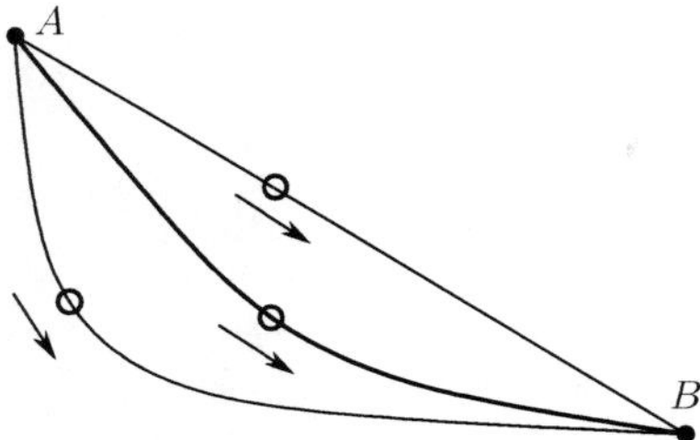

Figure 2.1: The *brachistochrone* problem proposed by Bernoulli in 1696: Among all possible paths joining two points A and B in the vertical plane, find the one which minimizes the time of descent of an object moving under gravity along the path itself.

gulf, she managed to persuade the local chief to give her as much land as she could enclose within the hide of a bull. She is reported to have cut the hide into thin strips, joined them into a rope, and laid the latter out along a *semicircle*, using the Mediterranean coast as a supplementary boundary: By shaping the rope into a semicircle, Dido solved the problem of *maximizing* the enclosed surface while satisfying an isoperimetric constraint.[2]

The great scientists of the XVII and XVIII centuries posed and solved other optimization problems. Isaac Newton (1642–1729), Christian Huygens (1629–1695), and Leonhard Euler (1707–1789) study the problem—sadly enough, a military application—of maximizing the range of a projectile as a function of the initial elevation. In 1687 Newton studies a problem of hydrodynamic: minimize water resistance by varying the shape of an object propelled through the water. In 1696, Johann Bernoulli (1667–1748) challenges the mathematicians of his time to solve the *brachistochrone*[3] problem (Bernoulli, 1696): Given two points in the vertical plane, find the shape of a wire joining the two points which minimizes the time of descent on a small bead that slides along the wire under gravity—see Figure 2.1 for a graphical representation of the problem. Five mathematicians found a solution using different techniques: Johann Bernoulli himself, Newton, Jacob Bernoulli (1654–1705), Leibniz (1646–1716), and de L'Hôpital (1661–1704).[4]

Nowadays, optimization problems emerge in all branches of engineering: the very act of *designing*, which characterizes the activity of an engineer, is in its wholeness, at least ideally, an optimization problem: Among all possible designs

[2] An interesting account of the history of optimization is given in the introduction of the optimal control book by Alexéev *et al.* (1982).

[3] From the Greek βράχιστος, shortest and χρόνος, time.

[4] Galileo (1564–1642) had already analyzed a similar problem but without obtaining a general solution (Galilei, 1638).

find the one that satisfies a set of given constraints and minimizes the costs.[5]

Nevertheless, the importance of optimization problems is not restricted to technology and to human artefacts but extended curiously also to natural sciences: It appears so *natural* to pursue the best, that philosophers and scientists became convinced that Nature itself, *in some sense*, optimizes. The least-time principle of Pierre de Fermat (1601–1665) is a first major example in the history of science: It asserts that the actual path between two points taken by a beam of light is the one which is traversed in the least time. About half a century later, in his philosophical work *Théodicée* (1710), Leibniz claims that the universe is *the best possible*.[6] Such a philosophical claim had a great influence on the development of the *principle of least-action* which is an assertion about the nature of motion that provides an alternative approach to mechanics completely independent of Newton's laws.[7] First formulated in 1750 by Maupertuis (1698–1759) in a somehow naive form, the principle of least-action was then refined and further developed by great mathematicians such as Euler, Lagrange,[8] and William R. Hamilton (1805–1865). This principle is indeed one of the greatest generalizations in all physical science, although not fully appreciated until the advent of quantum mechanics in the XXth century.[9] Variations on the least-action principle have proved useful in general relativity theory, quantum field theory, and particle physics. As a result, this principle lies at the core of much of contemporary theoretical physics.

2.1.2 The optimization problem

Formally, an **instance of an optimization problem** is a pair (S, f) where S is a generic set of *solutions* and $f : S \rightarrow \mathbb{R}$ is a function that associates a *cost* to each solution. The problem is to find a $\bar{s} \in S$ for which:

$$f(\bar{s}) \leq f(s) \qquad \text{for all } s \in S. \tag{2.1}$$

Such an element $\bar{s}$ is called an *optimal solution* to the given instance.[10] As a shorthand notation, in the thesis we will write:

$$\bar{s} = \arg\min_{s \in S} f(s), \tag{2.2}$$

[5]Alternatively, a constraint is given on the costs in the form of a *budget*, and one wishes to maximize some measure of performance.

[6]Without being perfect, otherwise it would be indistinguishable from God.

[7]A remarkable introduction to classical mechanics seen from this perspective is given in Lanczos (1985).

[8]Giuseppe Lodovico Lagrangia (1736–1813).

[9]Ernst Mach in his influential history of mechanics (Mach, 1893) does not even mention the principle of least-action nor Hamilton's formalization of mechanics.

[10]It is customary to formulate optimization problems as *minimization problems*. Clearly, any minimization problem (S, f) can be transformed into a maximization problem (S, g) by simply considering $g = -f$ and reversing the inequality in Equation 2.1. In this case, it is said that the function g assigns a *value* to each solution in S.

where with "arg min" we denote the element of the set S for which the minimum is attained.[11]

For convenience, along the centuries different classes of optimization problems, each characterized by specific properties of the set of solutions and of the cost function, where identified and studied separately. Nonlinear programming, convex programming, linear programming, calculus of variation, and optimal control are just examples of subfields of applied mathematics that focused on a specific class of optimization problems.[12]

2.1.3 Combinatorial optimization

In this thesis, we focus on *combinatorial optimization problems*, which are optimization problems characterized by a *finite* set of solutions S, that is typically defined as a subset of all possible *combinations* or *permutations* of given *components*. The following example will serve as an introduction to this class of problems:

> **Brel's Problem**[13]
>
> Your partner wants to visit the cities of Vierzon, Vesoul, Honfleur, Hamburg, and Paris. You are not really happy about this trip: you would rather visit Antwerp!
>
> In order to make the trip slightly less unpleasant, you wish at least to go along the shortest tour that passes through all the given cities.

In this example, which our reader will have certainly recognized as an instance of the well known TRAVELING SALESMAN problem, the set of solutions is the set composed of all possible permutations of the given cities.

More formally, we define an **instance of a combinatorial optimization problem** to be a pair (S, f) where S is a *finite* set of solutions, and $f : S \to \mathbb{R}$ is a function that associates a *cost* to each solution. The problem is to find an optimal solution $\bar{s} = \arg\min_{s \in S} f(s)$.

As already mentioned above, an instance is typically given in terms of some set C of *components*: The set of solutions S is some appropriate subset of the power set $\mathcal{P}(\mathrm{C})$ of the components C, and the cost function f is computed on the basis of the components themselves.[14]

---

[11] We suppose here that S is closed. Under this assumption, the minimum of f on S indeed exists. If this minimum is attained for more than one element of S, it is a matter of indifference which one is considered. Some authors prefer thinking that "arg min" defines the set $\bar{S} \subset S$ of all optimal solutions for which Equation 2.1 holds. Accordingly, they write $\bar{S} = \arg\min_{s \in S} f(s)$. The two conventions are equivalent and both acceptable: In the thesis, we adopt consistently the one defined in Equation 2.2.

[12] See Pierre (1986) for a comprehensive introduction to optimization theory.

[13] This problem was first illustrated, albeit not in its optimization form, in Brel (1968).

We call a **combinatorial optimization problem** a set of instances that share the same *structure* for what concerns the set S and the cost function f, that is, the same way of constraining the set $\mathcal{P}(\mathrm{C})$ for obtaining S, and the same general procedure for assigning a cost to a solution on the basis of its components.

The process of defining a combinatorial optimization problem as an abstraction from single instances is clearly somehow arbitrary and it is justified solely by convenience: Thanks to this abstraction we can developed algorithms that apply to the whole set of instances we gather into a problem, rather than develop *ad hoc* algorithms for each instance. The same holds true for the formal proofs of properties common to all instances of a same problem.

Some combinatorial optimization problems

In addition to the already mentioned TRAVELING SALESMAN, other relevant combinatorial problems that are considered in this thesis are MAXIMUM SATISFIABILITY, QUADRATIC ASSIGNMENT, and TIMETABLING. We give in the following a brief description of these problems.

MAXIMUM SATISFIABILITY

A set $U = \{u_1, u_2, \ldots, u_m\}$ of boolean variables and a set $C = \{c_1, c_2, \ldots, c_n\}$ of *clauses* are given. A *truth assignment* for U is a function $\phi : U \to \{0, 1\}$. We say that $u \in U$ is *true* under ϕ, if $\phi(u) = 1$. Otherwise, if $\phi(u) = 0$, we say that u is false. If $u \in U$ is a variable, u and $\overline{u}$ are *literals* over U: The literal $\overline{u}$ is true if and only if u is false. A clause $c \in C$ is a set of literals over U. It represents the disjunction of its literal and it is therefore satisfied by a truth assignment ϕ if and only if at least one of its members if true under ϕ. The problem consists in finding the truth assignment that minimizes the number of clauses that remain unsatisfied. It is easy to verify that the number of possible truth assignments is $2^{|U|}$ and that the set of possible solutions is the power set of U.

[14]For definiteness, we provide here a formal definition of an instance of the TRAVELING SALESMAN problem in its asymmetric and integer version.

The set $\mathrm{C} = V \cup E \cup D$ of components is the union of:

- a set V of vertices, each representing a city to visit;
- a set $E = \{e : e = \langle v_j, v_k \rangle \text{ where } v_j, v_k \in V, \text{ and } j \neq k\}$ of edges each representing a connection between an ordered pair of cities;
- a function $D : E \to \mathbb{Z}^+$ encoding the distance between two cities in V, and represented here as a set of ordered pairs: $W = \{w : w = \langle e, d \rangle \text{ where } e \in E \text{ and } d \in \mathbb{Z}^+\}$.

On the basis of the components C we can define the pair (S, f): The set of solutions is given as
$$S = \{s \in \mathcal{P}(E) \subset \mathcal{P}(\mathrm{C}) : |s| = |V| - 1,\ \forall v \in V\ \exists e_1, e_2 \in s\colon e_1 = \langle v, v_j \rangle, e_2 = \langle v_k, v \rangle \text{ for some } v_j, v_k \in V\}$$
and the cost function is defined as $f(s) = \sum_{e \in s} D(e)$, where $D(e) = d$ if $\exists w \in W\colon w = \langle e, d \rangle$.

QUADRATIC ASSIGNMENT
This problem consists in assigning n facilities to n locations: Two matrices A and B are given, where a_{vw} is the *distance* between locations v and w, and $b_{v'w'}$ is the *flow* between facilities v' and w'. The goal is to find an optimal assignment, that is, a permutation $s = \{s_1, s_2, \ldots, s_n\}$ of index set $\{1, 2, \ldots, n\}$ that minimizes the function:

$$f(s) = \sum_{v=1}^{n} \sum_{w=1}^{n} b_{vw} a_{s_v s_w},$$

where s_v denotes the location which facility v is assigned to, and the term $b_{vw} a_{s_v s_w}$ represents the cost contribution of simultaneously assigning facility v to location s_v, and facility w to location s_w.

TIMETABLING
The TIMETABLING problem (Schaerf, 1995; Cooper & Kingston, 1995; de Werra, 1995, 1997) exists in a number of variants. We consider here the UNIVERSITY-COURSE TIMETABLING problem (Burke *et al.*, 1994, 1995; Schaerf, 1995; Di Gaspero & Shaerf, 2001), as defined by the *Metaheuristics Network* for its research activity and for the *International Timetabling Competition*.[15] A set of classrooms is given together with a set of lessons and a set of time-slots. A list of attending students and a list of classroom requirements (for example, a video-projector or a minimum size) are associated with each lesson. Similarly, each classroom is associated with a list of requirements that it is able to satisfy. The set S of feasible solutions contains all the assignments lesson/classroom/timeslot that satisfy the following two constraints: (i) no student should have overlapping courses, and (ii) no lesson should be held in a classroom that is too small for containing the number of student that are supposed to attend. The problem consists in finding a feasible solution that minimizes the number of the following events: (i) a student has only one hour of class on a day; (ii) a student has more than two hours of class in a row; (iii) a student has class in the last time-slot of a day. A formal description of the problem defined by the *Metaheuristics Network* was given by Manfrin (2003) and by Socha (2003b).

Combinatorial optimization problems, and in particular some of them including MAXIMUM SATISFIABILITY, QUADRATIC ASSIGNMENT and TIMETABLING, are particularly *hard* to solve in a precise sense that is made clear in Section 2.1.4.

[15] `http://www.idsia.ch/ttcomp2002`

2.1.4 On the computational complexity of algorithms

When one designs an algorithm, he is in general interested in making it as *efficient* as possible, where the efficiency of an algorithm is typically measured in terms of its computation *time*.[16]

Efficiency is such a critical factor in the design of algorithms that it dictated a criterion for classifying combinatorial optimization problems: A problem is considered *well-solved* when an algorithm is available that solves *efficiently* **all** its instances. It is an accepted and meaningful convention (Edmonds, 1965) to call "*efficient*" an algorithm that computes in a time that grows not more than polynomially in the *size* of the instance, where the latter is the amount of data needed to encode the instance itself in a reasonably *compact* form, that is, for example, without extra padding characters or without unnecessary information.[17] For definiteness, let us consider the TRAVELING SALESMAN problem. In order to encode a generic instance we need to list the cities and to encode, say in binary form, the distance between each *pair* of them: The amount of information needed grows *quadratically*—and therefore polynomially—in the number of cities. The number of cities can therefore be informally taken as a measure of the size of an instance.[18]

So far, no efficient algorithm has been devised for solving the TRAVELING SALESMAN problem. The same holds for a large number of other relevant problems: Notwithstanding the efforts of the research community, there is still a *class of hard* problems for which no efficient algorithm is available.

---

[16]Clearly, the computation time of an algorithm depends on the speed and on the specific architecture of the computer on which it runs. A machine independent measure can be obtained in terms of the number of elementary operation needed by some abstract computation model such as, for example, a Turing machine (Mandrioli & Ghezzi, 1987). Nevertheless, in the framework of this thesis an informal understanding of this concept will suffice. Another remark is worth mentioning here: when studying the complexity of an algorithm, another factor to be considered beside the computation time is the amount of memory needed by the computation. Also this issue is beyond the scope of this thesis. We refer the reader to a text book of theoretical computer science, such as Mandrioli & Ghezzi (1987), for a formal presentation of these concepts.

[17]In the following, we will often use the wording "polynomial-time algorithm" as a short hand for denoting an algorithm that solves each instance of a given problem in a time that is bounded by a polynomial function of the size of the instance itself. Similarly, the explicit reference to the size of the instance at hand will be understood in the expression "the algorithm computes in polynomial time."

[18]The actual amount of information needed to encode the instance depends on the specific encoding we adopt. In any case, for any ***reasonable*** encoding, the amount of information will not grow more than polynomially with the number of cities. The mismatch between what we informally call the ***size***—number of cities—and the actual amount of information needed to encode the instance does not cause any harm here since we are interested in making a distinction between the "good" algorithms that compute polynomially, and the "bad" ones that do not: an algorithm computes polynomially in the actual amount of information needed under a specific encoding, **if and only if** it computes polynomially with respect to the number of cities.

It has been theoretically proved[19] that if an algorithm were available to solve in polynomial time one of the members of this class of hard problems, also all the others could be solved in polynomial time. In fact, the problems belonging to this class enjoy the property that each of them can be reduced to each of the others in polynomial time; that is, each instance of each of the problems belonging to the class can be transformed, in polynomial time, into a corresponding instance of each of the other problems in the class. It follows that if we had an efficient algorithm for one of the problems of the class, we could solve in polynomial time each instance of any other problem by simply transforming it into an instance of the problem we are able to solve, and then solve the latter: Both operations can be completed in polynomial time and therefore the whole computation would be polynomial. As a consequence, either all the problems in such a class are solvable in polynomial time, or none of them is. So far, there is no formal proof of neither of the two alternatives.

Decision problems and the *NP*-complete class

The concept outlined above are formalized by the theory of computational complexity and in particular by the so called ***NP*-completeness** theory (Garey & Johnson, 1979). This theory deals with the class of *decision problems*, that is, those problems whose answer is either *yes* or *no*. It does not refer directly to combinatorial optimization, which is the focus of this thesis. Nevertheless, its results can be extended also to optimization problems as we show in the next subsection. The TRAVELING SALESMAN problem serves also here as a valuable example, in this case, of a decision problem:

> TRAVELING SALESMAN
> In the decision version of the TRAVELING SALESMAN problem, a set of cities is given, together with the distance between each pair of them. The question is: *Does a tour exists that visits all of them once and only once and whose length is less than a given value L?*

The focus of the *NP*-completeness theory is more precisely on the class of decision problems that can be solved in polynomial time by a *nondeterministic* machine. By a polynomial nondeterministic machine we mean a fictious device that for any instance admitting a positive answer is able to show in polynomial time that the answer is indeed positive. With reference to the TRAVELING SALESMAN problem, for example, if the instance at hand admits a tour of length less than L and therefore the answer to the question is positive, a polynomial nondeterministic machine needs simply to *guess and hit* an appropriate solution and then show, in polynomial time, that indeed its length is less than L. This definition of a polynomial nondeterministic machine involves some sort of *magic* in the ability

[19] See Garey & Johnson (1979) for an organic account of the subject.

of the machine to guess the appropriate solution. Clearly, no such machine exists and the definition we gave serves solely as a formalization of the concept of polynomial-time verifiability of solutions.

The class of all problems that can be solved in polynomial time by a nondeterministic machine is called *NP*. As a subset of *NP* we define the class *P* of all those problems that can be solved in polynomial time by a *deterministic* machine, which indeed embodies the concept of an algorithm.[20] Clearly, all problems in *P* are also in *NP*: If the instance at hand admits a positive answer, the deterministic machine needs first to find an appropriate solution and then to verify that the solution indeed satisfies the question. A corresponding nondeterministic machine can rely on a sort of oracle for finding the appropriate solution instantaneously and then jumps immediately to the verification phase. The verification phase for the two machines is the same: they differ in the fact that the deterministic one needs first to find the solution. The computation time of the nondeterministic machine will be no longer than the one of the deterministic one. If the computation time of the deterministic machine is polynomially bounded, that is, if the problem is in *P*, also the computation time of the nondeterministic one will be polynomially bounded, and therefore the problem will be also in *NP*. Thus, $P \subset NP$

Now the question is whether $NP \setminus P$ is empty or not. In other words, if there exists any *inherently intractable* decision problem in *NP*, that is a decision problem whose solutions can be verified in polynomial time but for which no known or unknown algorithm exists that can tell in polynomial time if any given instance admits a positive answer. This is nowadays one of the most interesting open questions in mathematics and theoretical computer science, both from a speculative point of view and for the economical relevance of its practical implications.

What we know for sure is that there are some decision problems for which nobody so far has been able to find a polynomial-time algorithm. Moreover, it has been shown that a specific problem known as SATISFIABILITY is, in a precise sense we will make clear presently, *the hardest* problem in *NP* (Cook, 1971).

SATISFIABILITY
A set $U = \{u_1, u_2, \dots, u_m\}$ of boolean variables and a set $C = \{c_1, c_2, \dots, c_n\}$ of *clauses* are given. A *truth assignment* for U is a function $\phi : U \to \{0, 1\}$. We say that $u \in U$ is *true* under the truth assignment ϕ, if $\phi(u) = 1$. Otherwise, if $\phi(u) = 0$, we say that u is false. If $u \in U$ is a variable, u and $\overline{u}$ are *literals* over U: the literal $\overline{u}$ is true if and only if u is false. A clause $c \in C$ is a set of literals over U. It represents the disjunction of its literals and it is therefore satisfied by a truth assignment ϕ if and only if at least one of its members if

[20] Theoreticians formalize this concepts in terms of the Turing machine. We can informally think of a normal computer program that runs on our desktop.

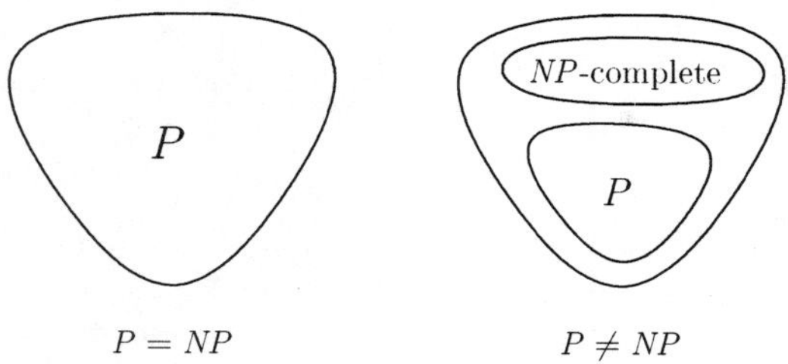

Figure 2.2: The *NP* class under the two possible hypothesis. On the left hand side: if $P = NP$, all decision problems in *NP* can be solved in polynomial time. On the right hand side: if $P \neq NP$, the set $NP \setminus P$ is at least populated by the *NP*-complete class which includes, among others, the SATISFIABILITY problem.

> true under ϕ. The question is whether there exists a truth assignment that satisfies all clauses.

It has been shown that all problems in *NP* can be *reduced* to SATISFIABILITY in polynomial time (Cook, 1971; Karp, 1972). This means that any instance of any problem in *NP* can be transformed, within a time bounded by a polynomial function of the size of the instance itself, into a corresponding instance of SATISFIABILITY. If we were able to solve in polynomial time all instances of SATISFIABILITY, we would be able to solve in polynomial time any instance of any *NP* problem. In this precise sense, no problem in *NP* can be harder than SATISFIABILITY: If we were able to show that SATISFIABILITY can be solved in polynomial time, *NP* would be a subset of *P*, and since the opposite holds as it was shown above, the two sets would be equal.

On the other hand, since the proof that SATISFIABILITY is the hardest problems in *NP*, many other problems were proved *as hard as* SATISFIABILITY. In general, a problem Π_1 is proved *at least as hard as* problem Π_2 if each instance of Π_2 can be transformed in polynomial time into a corresponding instance of Π_1. The class of problems that enjoy the property of being the *hardest* in *NP* is called the class of *NP*-complete problems: If $NP \setminus P$ is not empty, it is populated, at least, by the class of *NP*-complete problems, as graphically illustrated in Figure 2.2.

Optimization problems and the *NP*-hard class

The concepts outlined in the previous subsection concerning the computational complexity of decision problems can be extended to any kind of problem and in particular to combinatorial optimization problems. For definiteness, we restrict to the latter in the rest of our discussion. A combinatorial optimization problem Π_o

is said to be *at least as hard as* a decision problem Π_d if for each instance i_d of Π_d, we can define in polynomial time an instance i_o of Π_o such that the knowledge of an optimal solution to i_o would enable us to answer either in the positive or in the negative to the question associated to i_d. Some examples will help clarifying this definition.

The similarity is apparent between the optimization problem MAXIMUM SATISFIABILITY defined at page 16 and the decision problem SATISFIABILITY defined at page 20. Given an instance of SATISFIABILITY we can immediately obtain a corresponding instance of MAXIMUM SATISFIABILITY: the sets U of variables and C of clauses of the latter are taken to be exactly those of the former. If an optimal solution $\bar{s}$ of the MAXIMUM SATISFIABILITY instance is available, we can compute in polynomial time its cost $f(\bar{s})$, that is, the number of clauses that are left unsatisfied. If $f(\bar{s}) = 0$ the answer to the original SATISFIABILITY instance is *yes*. Otherwise, since no other solution s might leave unsatisfied less clauses than $\bar{s}$, we can safely conclude that the original set of clauses cannot be satisfied and that the answer to the original SATISFIABILITY instance is *no*.

Even more apparent is the similarity between the decision version and the optimization version of the TRAVELING SALESMAN problem. Also in this case, given an instance of the decision problem where the question is whether a tour exists whose length is less than a given L, we can immediately obtain the corresponding optimization version: same cities and same distances between each pair of them. If the optimal solution of the optimization instance is available, we can compute in polynomial time its length and we can compare it with L. If it is shorter we answer in the positive to the original decision problem. Otherwise, we answer in the negative.

From these examples it emerges clearly that if a polynomial-time algorithm existed for solving the optimization problem, also the corresponding decision problem would be solvable in polynomial time via the former. In this sense MAXIMUM SATISFIABILITY and the optimization version of TRAVELING SALESMAN are *at least as hard as* SATISFIABILITY and the decision version of TRAVELING SALESMAN, respectively. The class of all problems that are *as hard as* a *NP*-complete problem is called the class of ***NP*-hard** problems.

2.1.5 On the *a priori* equivalence of search algorithms

Another corpus of important theoretical results on optimization algorithms goes under the suggestive name of *no free lunch* theorems (Wolpert & Macready, 1996). These results concern the problem of optimization from a rather abstract point of view. They do not refer, at least in their original form, to any specific algorithm or to any of the above mentioned combinatorial optimization problems. Indeed, the *no free lunch* theorem holds for an abstract model of the optimization process, and only recently some theoretical result has been proposed (Schumacher *et al.*, 2001; Igel & Toussaint, 2003) that aims at bridging the gap between the abstract framework of the *no free lunch* theorem and the actual practice in combinatorial optimization.

Let us consider all possible mappings $f : S \to \mathcal{Y}$ between two *finite* sets S and $\mathcal{Y}$, where S is the space of solutions and $\mathcal{Y}$ is the range of their values. The space of all such possible mapping is $\mathcal{F} = \mathcal{Y}^S$. We define a *trace* of length m to be a sequence of pairs:

$$T_m = \{(s_1, y_1), \ldots, (s_m, y_m)\}, \tag{2.3}$$

where $y_j = f(s_j)$. Moreover, let T_m^s and T_m^y be the sequences of the visited solutions and of their values, respectively. Further, let $T_m^s[j] = s_j$ denote the j-th component of T_m^s, and $T_m^y[j] = y_j$ the j-th component of T_m^y. With the notation

$$T_m||(s_{m+1}, y_{m+1}) = \{(s_1, y_1), \ldots, (s_m, y_m), (s_{m+1}, y_{m+1})\}, \tag{2.4}$$

we indicate the operation of *appending* the pair (s_{m+1}, y_{m+1}) to the sequence T_m, in order to obtain the sequence T_{m+1}.

The set of all possible sequences of length m is given by $\mathcal{T}_m = (S \times \mathcal{Y})^m$, and the set of all sequences of any length by $\mathcal{T} = \bigcup_{m \geq 0} \mathcal{T}_m$.

Let us define a *deterministic non-retracing search algorithm*, for short simply *algorithm* in the rest of the section, the mapping $a : \mathcal{T} \to S$ that maps a sequence T into a solution. In particular, we require a not to revisit solutions, that is, $a : T \mapsto \{s \in S : s \notin T^s\}$.

With the notation $T_m(a, f)$ we denote the sequence of length m of pairs (s_j, y_j) visited by the algorithm a when dealing with the problem f. To be more explicit:

$$\begin{array}{lll}
s_1 = a(\emptyset), & y_1 = f(s_1), & T_1(a,f) = \{(s_1, y_1)\}; \\
s_2 = a(T_1(a,f)), & y_2 = f(s_2), & T_2(a,f) = T_1(a,f)||(s_2, y_2); \\
\ldots & \ldots & \ldots \\
s_j = a(T_{j-1}(a,f)), & y_j = f(s_j), & T_j(a,f) = T_{j-1}(a,f)||(s_j, y_j); \\
\ldots & \ldots & \ldots \\
s_m = a(T_{m-1}(a,f)), & y_m = f(s_m), & T_m(a,f) = T_{m-1}(a,f)||(s_m, y_m).
\end{array}$$

The performance of the algorithm a on the function f for what concerns a search of m steps is a function $\Phi(T_m^y(a,f))$ of the values $y_j = f(s_j)$ associated to the solutions s_j visited by a. Typically, we are interested in the best solution found by a during the search:

$$\Phi(T_m^y(a,f)) = \min_j y_j, \qquad \text{with } y_j \in T_m^y(a,f). \tag{2.5}$$

Let us define the quantity $P(T_m^y|f, m, a)$ that is the probability of obtaining a certain sequence of values $y_1, \ldots, y_m$, given that we are searching the function f with algorithm a. Indeed, since we focus here on *deterministic* algorithms,

$$P(T_m^y|f, m, a) = \delta\left(T_m^y, T_m^y(a,f)\right),$$

where δ is Kronecker's function: $P(T^y_m|f,m,a) = 1$ if $T^y_m = T^y_m(a,f)$ and it is null otherwise.[21]

Having defined the abstract model of optimization, we are now able to enunciate the main theorem:

No Free Lunch Theorem. *For any pair of algorithms a and b:*

$$\sum_{f\in\mathcal{F}} P(T^y_m|f,m,a) = \sum_{f\in\mathcal{F}} P(T^y_m|f,m,b). \tag{2.6}$$

A proof of the theorem is given in Wolpert & Macready (1996).

From the *no free lunch* theorem, it follows that, for any measure of performance $\Phi(T^y_m)$, $P(\Phi(T^y_m)|f,m,a)$ averaged over all functions $f \in \mathcal{F}$, is independent from the algorithm a.[22] This means that if on a subset $\mathcal{F}' \subset \mathcal{F}$, the algorithm a obtains on average better results than b, on the complement $\overline{\mathcal{F}'} = \mathcal{F} \setminus \mathcal{F}'$, b would perform better than a.

In this sense, the *no free lunch* theorem has been intended as an argument in favor of the *specialization* of algorithms: for a given algorithm a find a subset of optimization problems $\mathcal{F}_a$ on which a obtains good results. Alternatively, for a restricted set $\mathcal{F}' \subset \mathcal{F}$ of optimization problems find the best algorithm.

Since the publication of the *no free lunch* theorem (Wolpert & Macready, 1997), research has therefore focused on the problem of finding classes of problems over which the *no free lunch* theorem does not hold. In particular, an important question is whether the *no free lunch* theorem holds over the instances of a given combinatorial optimization problem such as TRAVELING SALESMAN, MAXIMUM SATISFIABILITY, QUADRATIC ASSIGNMENT, and TIMETABLING.

A final answer to this question is not available, yet. Nonetheless, some interesting results that go in this direction have been recently published. In particular, Schumacher *et al.* (2001) proposed a *sharpened* version of the *no free lunch* theorem based on the concept of *closeness* of a set $\mathcal{F}'$ of functions under permutation.

[21] An important element that should be noted is that the probabilistic framework proposed by Wolpert & Macready (1996) implicitly contains much of the elements of the tuning problem as it is formalized in Chapter 3. In particular, it contains the idea of a distribution of probability over the space of the instances, which is fundamental for a correct definition of the problem of tuning metaheuristics and which is thus the key element of this thesis. Unfortunately for the scientific community—but fortunately for us, since this gave us the chance to investigate in this thesis some previously unexplored domain—the full implications of the adoption of a probabilistic framework went overlooked so far.

[22] Other statements descend or are equivalent to the *no free lunch* theorem. For example, it holds (Radcliffe & Surry, 1995) that for any two algorithms a and b, and any function f, there exists another function g such that: $T^y_m(a,f) = T^y_m(b,g)$, that is, a function g on which b obtains the same sequence of values that a obtains on f. Moreover, the *no free lunch* theorem has been extended to multiobjective optimization in the Pareto sense (Corne & Knowles, 2003). Such equivalent statements or extensions are extremely interesting but they are not relevant in our discussion.

Let us first define a permutation of the set S to be a one-to-one function $\sigma : S \to S$ of S onto itself. A permutation of a function $f : S \to \mathcal{Y}$ is a function $\sigma f : S \to \mathcal{Y}$ such that $\sigma f(s) = f\big(\sigma^{-1}(s)\big)$. The set of functions $\mathcal{F}'$ is closed under permutation if for all $f \in \mathcal{F}'$, also $\sigma f \in \mathcal{F}'$. Schumacher *et al.* (2001) proved the following:

No Free Lunch Theorem (sharpened). *The* no free lunch *theorem holds for a set $\mathcal{F}'$ if and only if $\mathcal{F}'$ is closed under permutation. That is, for any pair of algorithms a and b:*

$$\sum_{f \in \mathcal{F}'} P(T_m^y | f, m, a) = \sum_{f \in \mathcal{F}'} P(T_m^y | f, m, b),$$

if and only if for all $f \in \mathcal{F}'$, also $\sigma f \in \mathcal{F}'$.

Elaborating further on the result obtained by Schumacher *et al.* (2001), Igel & Toussaint (2003) formulate the conjecture that for the combinatorial optimization problems considered in practice, the *no free lunch* theorem does not hold. This conjecture is based on two orders of considerations. The first, which in our personal view is not fully convincing, is that the fraction of subset of $\mathcal{F} = \mathcal{Y}^S$ that are closed under permutation tends to zero when $|S|$ grows. The second, which we consider much more interesting, is based on topological considerations on the space S of combinatorial optimization problems. Igel & Toussaint (2003) start their argumentation by showing that a non-trivial neighborhood[23] is not invariant under permutation. They describe then two constraints defined in terms of the concept of neighborhood.

1. For a given neighborhood relation ν and a given function f, let the *maximum steepness* $z_\nu^{\max}(f)$ be:

   $$z_\nu^{\max}(f) = \max_{s_j, s_k \in S \wedge \nu(s_j, s_k) = 1} D_\mathcal{Y}\big(f(s_j), f(s_k)\big),$$

   where $D_\mathcal{Y} : \mathcal{Y} \times \mathcal{Y} \to \mathbb{R}$ is some metric defined on $\mathcal{Y}$. It holds that: If the maximum steepness $z^{\max}(f) = \mathcal{Y}$ of every function $f \in \mathcal{F}'$ is constrained to be smaller than the range of f, than the set $\mathcal{F}'$ is not closed under permutation.

2. Let a *local minimum* of a function f be a solution $\tilde{s}$ for which $f(\tilde{s}) \leq f(s)$ for all s such that $\nu(\tilde{s}, s) = 1$. Moreover, let the $\mathcal{Y}$-histogram of a function f be a mapping $h_f : \mathcal{Y} \to \mathrm{N}$ such that $h_f(y)$ counts the number of solutions

[23]Let a ***neighborhood*** relation on S be a symmetric function $\nu : S \times S \to \{0, 1\}$. Two solutions $s_j, s_k \in S$ are called ***neighbors*** if $\nu(s_j, s_k) = 1$. In the following we will use also the notation $s_j \in \mathcal{N}(s_k)$ or $s_k \in \mathcal{N}(s_j)$ if $\nu(s_j, s_k) = 1$. A neighborhood structure is called ***non-trivial*** if and only if there exist four solutions $s_j, s_k, s_v, s_w \in S$ such that $s_j \neq s_k \wedge \nu(s_j, s_k) = 1$ and $s_v \neq s_w \wedge \nu(s_v, s_w) = 1$.

$s \in S$ that are mapped into y by f. Let us define now $l_\nu^{\max}(f)$ to be the maximum number of local minima that any function $f' \in \mathcal{F}'$, which shares the same $\mathcal{Y}$-histogram with f, can have. If the number $l_\nu^{\max}(f)$ for every function $f \in \mathcal{F}'$ is constrained to be smaller than the maximum number of local minima that a function belonging to $\mathcal{F}$ can have, then $\mathcal{F}'$ is not closed under permutation.

According to Igel & Toussaint, these elements indicate that the *no free lunch* theorem should not hold on the classes of combinatorial optimization problems that are of practical relevance. Although these results appears very interesting, the authörs fail to indicate practical examples of classes of problem for which the *no free lunch* theorem does not hold. The specific question whether the *no free lunch* theorem holds true on the instances of TRAVELING SALESMAN, MAXIMUM SATISFIABILITY, QUADRATIC ASSIGNMENT, and TIMETABLING is still open.

2.1.6 Exact algorithms, heuristics, and metaheuristics

Due to the economical relevance of combinatorial optimization problems and to their diversity, a large number of algorithms were devised for their solution. These algorithms can be classified as either *exact* or *approximate*.[24]

Exact algorithms are guaranteed to find an optimal solution to any instance within an instance-dependent run-time. Unfortunately, since many problems of interest happen to be *NP*-hard, no polynomial-time algorithm is so far known that solves them efficiently: The instance-dependent run-time cannot be bound, for what concerns known algorithm, by any polynomial function of the size of the instance. As a consequence, for many problems the applicability of exact methods remains constrained to relatively small instances and a large share of instances remains computationally intractable.

On the other hand, approximate methods are not guaranteed to find an optimal solution but, in practice, they are often able to find good solutions, albeit possibly suboptimal, in a relative short time.

We need to elaborate more on this concept since it will be one of the key issues in the development of the thesis. In practical applications we are often faced with *extremely large* instances and *too short* time. Clearly, both qualifications *large* and *short* for the size of the instance and for the time, respectively, are nothing but relative: Given the available computing resources and the speed of the best exact algorithm we can adopt for the problem at hand, we call *large* an instance that cannot be solved by our algorithm within the available amount of time. Vice

[24]The classification of algorithms into *exact*, *heuristics*, and *metaheuristics* that we adopt in this thesis is admittedly rather simplistic. Further sub-categories could be possibly defined and a sharper taxonomy could be given—see Papadimitriou & Steiglitz (1998). Notwithstanding its roughness, the classification we adopt in this section will properly serve the purpose of the thesis.

versa, we say we have *short* time when within that amount of time we are not able to solve the given instance with our algorithm.

In any case, when facing a practical problem we typically have to find the best possible solution in the given amount of time, however overwhelming its size might be. If the given time is larger than the time needed by the available exact algorithms, practitioners have to resort to approximate ones.[25]

A term adopted in the operations research literature to denote an approximate algorithm is *heuristic*.[26] In its typical usage within the research community, this term indicates an algorithm that comes with no guarantee of optimality but that appears nonetheless sound and dictated by common sense, and that, first of all, happens to work in practice.

Typically, a heuristic is tailored to a specific problem and heavily relies on the peculiarities of the search space and of the cost function of the problem itself. This means that designing a heuristic for a new problem is a particularly labor-intensive activity. It requires to acquire a first-hand understanding of the characteristics of the problem under analysis in order to exploit its intimate characteristics and to delve into its depths. In the general case, the knowledge of heuristics previously devised for other problems cannot be directly extended to the new one and might be therefore of little help.

With the primary goal of reducing the development effort of approximate algorithms, the so called *metaheuristics* were introduced.[27] A metaheuristic is a high-level and problem-independent definition of a search strategy that can then be specialized to the specific optimization problem at hand. They are typically based on one or both of the following two non exclusive general principles: (i) the incremental *construction* of a solution component by component; (ii) the *modification* of a given complete solution.

For definiteness, let us give a description of the most basic metaheuristics based on the second of the above mentioned principles: *local search*.[28] *Local search*

[25] Waiting for faster computers to appear on the market is not an option here: Given the nonpolynomial rate at which the time needed to solve an instance of a *NP*-hard problem grows with its size, an increment of a factor 2 or even 10 in the speed of computers will have a very little impact on the size of the largest instance we can solve. For what concerns the computational issues relate to *NP*-hard problems, it appears we cannot rely on the development of the hardware technology. Admittedly, there are a lot of rumors on quantum computing and on its possible impact on the solution of *NP*-hard problems. Yet, given the current state of development of quantum computing, it seems quite unlikely that our generation will be able to witness its practical impact on the combinatorial optimization field.

[26] From the Ancient Greek εὑρίσκω, I find or I discover.

[27] The term *metaheuristics* [Gr. μετά, after or beyond + εὑρίσκω, I find or discover] was first used in Glover (1986) but became widely adopted only more recently. Another term that has been often used as an alternative is *modern heuristics* (Reeves, 1995).

[28] *Local search* is so *basic* as a metaheuristics that it could be considered as a degenerate case. Some readers might hardly accept to call *local search* a metaheuristic on its own and would rather consider it as *component* often included in other metaheuristics. They would in any case agree with us that many metaheuristics, if (im)properly tuned, degenerate to a

is based on the concept of *neighborhood* of a solution: For using *local search*, we need to define a rule to associate to each solution $s \in S$, a set $\mathcal{N}(s) \subset S$ called a neighborhood of s. A solution $\tilde{s}$ is called a *local optimum* if none of the solutions in its neighborhood has a lower cost: $f(\tilde{s}) \leq f(s), \forall s \in \mathcal{N}(\tilde{s})$. Having defined the concepts of neighborhood and of local optimum we are now in the position of describing the algorithm. *Local search* is an iterative procedure that, starting from an initial solution s_1, at the generic iteration j searches the neighborhood $\mathcal{N}(s_j)$ of the current solution s_j according to some strategy. If a solution $s' \in \mathcal{N}(s_j)$ is found for which $f(s') < f(s_j)$ the procedure is iterated on $s_{j+1} = s'$, otherwise the procedure stops and s_j is returned as best solution found.

It is apparent from this description that the returned solution might at most be guaranteed to be a *local optimum* and that no prove of *global* optimality can be produced by the method.

Different flavors of *local search* might be implemented according to the way the neighborhood of the current solution is searched: for example, we mention here the *best improvement* strategy according to which we enumerate all the solutions in the neighborhood and then we move to the one of minor cost, if the latter is less than the one of the current solution. As an alternative, we might adopt a *first improvement* strategy according to which we move the current solution as soon as we find another solution in the neighborhood whose cost is lower. When adopting the first improvement strategy we can either enumerate deterministically the whole neighborhood or sample it stochastically. This second option is appealing if the neighborhood is particularly large, however in this case we loose the possibility of proving that the returned solution is at least a local optimum.[29]

Another element of the algorithm that was left undefined in the description given above is the criterion adopted for generating the initial solution. In general, when *local search* is intended as a stand-alone algorithm, as in the description we give here, the initial solution is randomly selected in S.[30] In this case, *local search* is a *stochastic* algorithm in the sense that different runs of *local search* return different solutions with typically different costs.[31]

In order to *specialize* the generic *local search* procedure that we have described

simple *local search*. The reason we present here such a degenerate case is indeed the fact that it offers the opportunity of highlighting some general traits of metaheuristics without the burden of unessential details. Methods that are more widely-accepted as being metaheuristics are introduced in Section 2.1.7.

[29] In general, this is not a real concern, at least in applications.

[30] This remark will result clearer after Section 2.1.7: Some metaheuristics adopt *local search* as a component for *refining* solutions. In this case, the initial solution is not randomly selected but it is indeed the solution that needs to be *refined*.

[31] Clearly, if a stochastic first improvement strategy is adopted for searching the neighborhood, the overall algorithm is stochastic even if the initial solution is selected deterministically: different run of the *local search* starting all from the same initial solution would typically end in different local optima.

to a specific problem we need to define, in a meaningful way for the problem itself, what should be considered a neighborhood and what should be the strategy for searching it. Once these element are specified, the *local search* for the given problem is defined.

Having in mind *local search* as an example, we summarize here the key characteristics of metaheuristics: Metaheuristics are stochastic, problem-independent, approximate algorithms for tackling combinatorial optimization problems. They are a valid alternative to more traditional methods when the available computation time is too short for adopting exact techniques and when the available understanding of the problem is too limited for developing an *ad hoc* heuristic.

2.1.7 A bird's-eye view of most popular metaheuristics

In this section we provide the reader with a brief description of the most widely adopted metaheuristics. We do not mean our excursus to be neither complete nor detailed: We refer the interested reader to more specific publications that survey the metaheuristics field such as Blum & Roli (2003).[32] In particular, in the following we limit ourself to a brief description of the concepts characterizing each metaheuristic without entering the details of the various variants in which each of them has been implemented. For what concerns *iterated local search* and *ant colony optimization*, the two metaheuristics we consider in our experimental analysis, more details on the specific implementations we adopt are provided in Chapter 5. Moreover, in Annex A we propose two contributions to the formal analysis of *ant colony optimization*. In the first, we formalize *ant colony optimization* in the language of dynamic programming and optimal control; in the second, we introduce the framework of *model-based search* into which *ant colony optimization* can be cast together with other optimization procedures such as *stochastic gradient descent* and the *cross-entropy* method.

Random restart

The main drawback of *local search* is that it often returns unsatisfactory solutions when the search remains trapped in a high-cost local minimum. The most immediate (and trivial) way of tackling this drawback is *random restart*, which consists in repeating a *local search* more than once, starting each time from a new randomly-selected initial solution. The rationale here is that if (i) the fraction of *low-cost* local minima[33] is sufficiently large and if (ii) local minima are uniformly distributed in the search space, by repeating the *local search* procedure a suffi-

[32] French-speaking readers may consider also Dréo *et al.* (2003).

[33] We adopt here and in the following the informal expression *low-cost* local minima to indicate those local minima that, although suboptimal, have a cost that is *sufficiently* close to that of the global optimum. They are therefore solutions that can be defined as satisfactory.

ciently large number of times the probability will be quite high of hitting at least once a satisfactory local minimum.

Unfortunately, in many practical applications neither of the two hypotheses is justified. Nevertheless, given the simplicity of *random restart*, practitioners often implement this approach when confronted with a new problem, for having some benchmark result to serve as a baseline against which more sophisticated metaheuristics can be compared.

Iterated local search

Another simple approach that, contrary to random restart, is extremely effective in practice, is *iterated local search* (Lourenço *et al.*, 2002). Again contrary to random restart, the underlying hypothesis is here that low-cost local-minima are clustered. *Iterated local search* consists in a sequence of runs of *local search* where the initial solution of a *local search* is obtained by a *perturbation* of the local minimum found by the previous one. In order for this mechanism to be effective, the perturbation should not move the position of the new starting point too far from the previous local optimum, otherwise the search will loose the focus from the currently explored area. At the same time, the perturbation should not be too feeble, otherwise the *local search* risks to converge back to the same local optimum already reached by the previous descent.

Simulated annealing

Simulated annealing (Kirkpatrick *et al.*, 1983; Cerny, 1985) is inspired by the annealing process of crystals. The aim of the physical annealing process is to obtain a perfect crystal, which is characterized by a state of minimum energy. The process consists in heating a crystal and then in cooling it slowly: if cooling is too fast, the final crystal will present irregularities and defects. On the other hand, if temperature is decreased slowly, the crystal has the possibility of reaching a minimum-energy state.

Simulated annealing for combinatorial optimization consists in a random walk through the space S of solutions properly endowed with a structure of neighborhood as the one defined for *local search*. A parameter called *temperature* regulates the walk: given the current solution s, a candidate solution s' is randomly selected in $\mathcal{N}(s)$. With a probability

$$p_{s,s'}(\mathsf{T}) = \begin{cases} 1 & \text{if } f(s') < f(s), \\ \exp\left(\frac{f(s)-f(s')}{\mathsf{T}}\right) & \text{otherwise,} \end{cases}$$

the solution s' is *accepted*: the process moves to s' and the procedure is iterated. If s' is not accepted, an alternative solution $s'' \in \mathcal{N}(s)$ is sampled, and so on.

The *temperature* is slowly decreased during the search with the consequence that at the beginning of the search the probability of accepting non-improving solution is higher and then it decreases over time. This device helps in quitting the basin of attraction of high-cost local minima that might be encountered in the early stages of the search.

Tabu search

First introduced in Glover (1986) on the basis of early ideas formulated a decade before (Glover, 1977), *tabu search* is nowadays among the most cited metaheuristics. In its basic implementation, *tabu search* adopts a device called *tabu list* for trying to escape from local minima and avoid cycles. The tabu list is a *first-in first-out* queue of previously visited solutions. It is used within a search approach that is somehow similar to the *best improvement* strategy of *local search*: A neighborhood structure is defined on the set S of solutions; the search starts from an initial solution s_1 and proceeds iteratively; at the generic step j, when the current solution is s_j, the tabu list TL_j contains $s_j, s_{j-1}, \ldots, s_{j-L+1}$, that is, the last k solutions visited, where the length of the tabu list L is a parameter of the algorithm. The new current solution is set to $s_{j+1} = s' \notin TL_j$, where $f(s') \leq f(s)$, $\forall s \in \mathcal{N}(s_j) \setminus TL_j$. The process is then iterated.

In words, *tabu search* keeps memory of the previously visited solutions and moves from solution to solution selecting at each step the best option out of those in the neighborhood, yet avoiding some *tabu* moves.

Evolutionary computation

Evolutionary computation is inspired by the ability shown by populations of living beings to evolve and adapt to changing conditions, under the pressure of natural selection (Darwin, 1859). A variety of slightly different approaches have been developed: *evolutionary programming* (Fogel, 1962; Fogel *et al.*, 1966), *evolutionary strategies* (Rechenberg, 1973) and *genetic algorithms* (Holland, 1975; Goldberg, 1989). The latter are mainly applied in combinatorial optimization.

The terminology adopted by the adepts of *evolutionary computation* is peculiar and deeply rooted in the biological metaphor: *Evolutionary computation* deals with a *population* of *individuals*, which represent solutions. Each individual is described by a *chromosome*, which is a collection of *genes*, that is, a string of symbols—*alleles* in the parlance—as, for example, $\{0, 1\}$ if a binary encoding is adopted. The *fitness* $\mathcal{F}_{it}(s)$ of an individual s is an appropriate decreasing function of the cost $f(s)$. In other words, $\mathcal{F}_{it}(s') > \mathcal{F}_{it}(s'')$ if and only if $f(s') < f(s'')$.

Evolutionary computation is an iterative procedure. At each step, a *generation* of individual is considered. A group of individuals with a high fitness is selected for *reproduction* and therefore will pass its genetic material to future generations. Reproduction consists in *mating* two of the selected individuals, the *parents*, for obtaining two new individuals whose chromosomes are made of segments of their parents' chromosomes. This operation is called *cross-over*. Another mechanism, called *mutation*, is adopted for injecting diversity in the population. It consists in randomly flipping, with some properly defined low probability, the value of some genes.

A version of evolutionary computation called *memetic algorithms* (Moscato, 1989) prescribes that parents be refined through *local search* before mating. In this way, they do not pass to future generations their original genetic material but rather an improved version. Despite the little biological plausibility of this *Lamarckian* inheritance,[34] the use of *local search* was shown to be particularly effective (Brady, 1985; Nissen, 1994; Vaessens *et al.*, 1996).

Ant colony optimization

Ant colony optimization (Dorigo, 1992; Dorigo *et al.*, 1999; Dorigo & Stützle, 2004) is a metaheuristic inspired by the foraging behavior of ant colonies: It can be observed (Goss *et al.*, 1989) that, in order to find the shortest path from a nest to a food source, ant colonies exploit a positive feedback mechanism by using a form of indirect communication called stigmergy (Grassé, 1959), based on the laying and detection of pheromone trails.

The goal of *ant colony optimization* is to find a path of minimum cost on a weighted graph.[35] To this end, a number of paths are generated in a Monte Carlo fashion, and the cost of these paths is used to bias the generation of further paths. This process is iterated with the aim of gathering more and more information on the graph and eventually produce a path of minimum cost.

Each path is generated sequentially. In the pictorial description of *ant colony optimization*, the generation of a path is described as the walk of an *ant* on the graph. At each node the ant randomly selects which edge to traverse on the basis of a set of parameters, called *pheromone*, which are associated to each edge: A high value of the pheromone for an edge increases its probability of being traversed. Once a walk is concluded and a solution is obtained, the ant traces back its path and deposits further pheromone on the traversed edges. The amount of pheromone released is some appropriate decreasing function of the cost of the solution so that edges composing low-cost solutions get reinforced the most and increase their probability of being selected by future ants.

The performance of *ant colony optimization* can be significantly improved by using *local search* for refining the solution found by an ant before updating the pheromone trail (Dorigo & Gambardella, 1997; Stützle & Hoos, 1998, 1999).

---

[34] Jean-Baptiste Lamarck (1744–1829) has been a great zoologist of its times and a forerunner of the theory of evolution. Unfortunately, his name is nowadays associated merely with a discredited theory of heredity: The "inheritance of acquired traits" (Lamarck, 1809).

[35] In order to tackle, a generic combinatorial optimization problem with *ant colony optimization*, the problem must be properly encoded into a shortest path problem. Such an encoding is always possible: An overview of the many different problems that have been so far effectively handled with this approach can be found in Dorigo & Di Caro (1999) and in Dorigo & Stützle (2004).

2.1.8 Current practice in tuning metaheuristics

As it appears from the brief descriptions given in Section 2.1.7, a metaheuristic is not properly an *algorithm* but rather a set of concepts that serve as guidelines for tackling an optimization problem. It is convenient to look at a metaheuristic as at an *algorithmic template* that needs to be instantiated to yield a fully functioning algorithm. In most of the cases, namely for *local search*-related metaheuristics, a neighborhood structure has to be defined over the set of solutions. In all cases, a number of parameters, either numerical or categorical or both, has to be tuned.

The importance of tuning is generally recognized by the research community: It is apparent to anybody who has some direct experience with metaheuristics that these methods are quite sensitive to the value of their parameters and that a careful tuning typically improves the performance in a significant way.

In this section, we first discuss the literature on the general problem of experimentally measuring the performance of a metaheuristic. Indeed, since tuning consists in selecting the best configuration of an algorithm, the basic ability of comparing two (or more) alternatives plays a fundamental role. We then describe the state-of-the-art in tuning metaheuristics and finally we present some optimization algorithms that perform a sort of *on-line* tuning of their parameters. The latter are not further discussed in the thesis and are mentioned here only for the sake of completeness.

Experimental analysis of algorithms

This section briefly reviews a number of papers that have been published about the empirical analysis of stochastic optimization algorithms and metaheuristics in particular. Most of these papers give some general suggestions on how to conduct an experimental campaign, highlight some common mistakes, and propose some guidelines. In particular, they all advocate the adoption of sound statistical procedures and of a rigorous experimental design.

The content of these papers is not particularly original and any good book of design and analysis of experiments such as Dean & Voss (1999) or Montgomery (2000) covers most of the technical issues discussed therein. Nevertheless, these papers were neither useless nor redundant: They had a fundamental didactic role and greatly contributed to the development of metaheuristics and more in general of operations research. Indeed, up to the publications of these papers, the operation research community was not particularly familiar with statistics and these papers had the merit of explaining the importance of a correct empirical analysis and of providing useful guidelines. It is our personal opinion that the message of these papers greatly improved the quality of published papers even if much has still to be done in this direction: Unfortunately, still nowadays too many of the papers published on metaheuristics feature some extremely poor, incorrect, and inconsistent experimental analysis.

The first works on the empirical evaluation of optimization algorithms started appearing in the eighties: Golden & Stewart (1985) and Golden *et al.* (1986). McGeoch (1986) presents some case studies of empirical analysis of algorithms. McGeoch (1992) discusses the adoption of variance reduction techniques in the empirical analysis of algorithm. Barr *et al.* (1995), McGeoch (1996), and Johnson (2002), which are considered milestones on the issue, discuss various aspects of the design and analysis of experiments with stochastic optimization algorithms. Gent & Walsh (1994) and Gent *et al.* (1997) discuss a list of typical pitfalls encountered when performing an experimental analysis. Hooker (1994) argues that an empirical analysis of algorithms is more informative and practically useful than a theoretical one. Strangely enough from our point of view, at the very beginning of the paper the author disposes of the idea of considering a probability distributions over the instances and judges it as *unreflective of reality*. This idea is central in the formal position of the tuning problem we give in Chapter 3. This definition captures a typical problem faced in practical applications where thinking of a probability distribution over the space of the instances is, in our view, extremely natural. Further, as it is shown in Chapter 5, the method we develop for tuning metaheuristics, which is based on a probabilistic model of the space of the instances, proved to be particularly effective in practical applications. Hooker (1995) advocates an experimental practice that should *describe* algorithms rather than *compare* them. In particular, the author insists on the need of obtaining a *model* of algorithms that should highlight the effect of one or more factors on the performance of the algorithm itself. To this aim, a specific factor, say for instance the use of *local search* to refine solutions in *ant colony optimization*, should be singled out and two otherwise identical implementation of the metaheuristic at hand should be compared: one including this factor and the other not. Out of such a comparison, much can be learned about the role played by the factor under analysis. McGeoch & Moret (1999) give general advice on how to present experimental results in written papers and in oral presentations.

Since the above excursus on algorithm experimentation is necessarily incomplete, we refer the interested reader to McGeoch (2002) for a thorough bibliography of the field.

Approaches to tuning algorithms

In the vast majority of the cases, metaheuristics are tuned by hand in a *trial-and-error* procedure guided by some rules of thumb. This approach is typically adopted in most of the research papers dealing with metaheuristics. Few researchers declare it explicitly and show to be aware of the limitation of the approach—see for instance Van Breedam (1995) and Gendreau *et al.* (1994)—while the vast majority do not even spend a word on the issue.

The trial-and-error approach presents many drawbacks of different nature. It will be sufficient to highlight here two of them concerning primarily industrial applications and academic research, respectively. A major issue with this approach for what concerns the large-scale industrial application of metaheuristics is that it is extremely time-consuming, labor-intensive, and it requires the attention of a particularly skilled practitioner, typically the person that implemented the algorithm or in any case somebody who is well acquainted with it. On the other hand, for what concerns academic works on metaheuristics, the adoption of this approach risks to invalidate any conclusion drawn from the experimental comparison of different algorithms: Typically, researchers are not equally acquainted with all algorithms under analysis and moreover, though acting in the best faith, they are more keen to devote their attention to their algorithm of choice rather than to the others.

Possibly influenced by the above mentioned paper by Hooker (1995), some authors adopted a methodology based on factorial design, which is characteristic of a *descriptive* analysis. Therefore, rather than solving directly the tuning problem they pass through the possibly more complex intermediate problem of understanding the relative importance of each parameter of the algorithm. For example, Xu & Kelly (1996) try to identify the relative contribution of five different components of a tabu-search.[36] They disable each component one at a time, execute the resulting algorithm on seven instances and compare the results and draw conclusions on the effectiveness of each component. Furthermore, the authors consider different values of the parameters of the most effective components and select the best value. Parson & Johnson (1997) and Van Breedam (1996) use a similar approach. Xu *et al.* (1998) describe a more general approach which is nonetheless based on the same basic idea of a factorial analysis. It is worth mentioning here that in order to compare different alternatives, the authors adopt, even if in a rather different context, the same statistical tests that we consider in Chapter 4 for defining our tuning algorithm *F-Race*, namely, the Friedman test and the Wilcoxon test (Conover, 1999).

Another approach to tuning that has been adopted for example in Coy *et al.* (2001) and in Adenso-Díaz & Laguna (2002), is based on the method that in the statistical literature is known as *response surface methodology* (Dean & Voss, 1999; Montgomery, 2000; Myers & Montgomery, 2002).[37] This method, which is akin to a *gradient descent* or a *local search*, consists in an iterative search in the space of the parameters that can be roughly described as follows: A metric is defined on the space of the parameters which assigns a *distance* between each pair of configurations of the metaheuristic to be tuned. The search starts in some point of the parameter space, that is, for some given values of the parameters, and moves iteratively in the parameter space considering a sequences of points.

---

[36] Namely: network flow moves, swap moves, tabu short-term memory, restart/recovery strategy, and a procedure based on the solution of a TRAVELING SALESMAN problem for finding the best sequence of customers on a route.

[37] A related method developed in the machine learning community for tackling stochastic optimization problems is described in Moore & Schneider (1996).

At the generic iteration of the search process, the metaheuristic is tested for the value of the parameters corresponding to the current point and for those corresponding to neighboring points. If the results observed in the current point are better than those observed in the considered neighborhood, the search is stopped and the values of the parameters corresponding to the current point are returned. Otherwise the current point is moved to the best point in the considered neighborhood and the process is iterated.[38] Clearly, the described search scheme is not guaranteed to find the globally optimal value of the parameters. Nonetheless, it typically finds good configurations.[39] The main drawback of this approach is the fact that it requires that a metric be defined in the parameter space. While this assumption does not pose any problem if the parameters are *ordinal* variables, either discrete or continuous, it does not hold in the case of *categorical* variables, that is, for variables whose possible values cannot be meaningfully ordered. Unfortunately, when tuning metaheuristics, it often happens to deal with variables of this kind. Let us think for example to the case of the definition of a neighborhood structure for a local search. Typically, a variety of options can be considered and no meaningful *distance* can be defined among them.

More in general, the major limitation of all above mentioned works is that they lack of a clear definition of the tuning problem itself. In particular, almost all of them—a notable exception is Coy *et al.* (2001)—fail to notice that tuning has always to be conceived *with respect to* a specific class of instances. Moreover, they lack of a precise statement of which specific figure of merit—such as, for example, the average performance over the class—that the tuning process is expected to optimize. We show in Chapter 3 that these limitations can be overcome thanks to the definition of a probabilistic measure over the space of the instances.

On-line tuning

For the sake of completeness, we mention here a class of optimization algorithms that perform a sort of automatic *on-line* tuning. They do not play any role in the following of the thesis since they are meant to solve a problem that is quite different from the tuning problem we define in Chapter 3, yet we briefly introduce these methods since they bear some logical connection with the subject of the

[38] An interesting feature of the method described in Adenso-Díaz & Laguna (2002) that deserves mentioning here is the adoption of the so called *Taguchi design* (Taguchi, 1987; Roy, 1990): The neighborhood of the current point is defined as the collection of points that rest on the vertices of an hypercube centered in the current point itself. This neighborhood is not explored exhaustively but only a fraction of the vertices is considered Byrne & Taguchi (1987).

[39] The reader might be tempted to suggest to restart the search from other randomly selected points in the parameters space giving rise to a search procedure akin to ***random restart***. More in general, all the schemes implemented by the metaheuristics described in Section 2.1.7 could be adopted for organizing the search. In other words, this would amount to using a metaheuristic for tuning metaheuristics but, unfortunately, this would simply beg the question generating a *regressio ad infinitum*.

thesis. In particular, *on-line* tuning is typically based on some machine learning technique, belonging often to the reinforcement learning literature.[40]

The key idea behind on-line tuning is to modify some parameters of the search algorithm while performing the search itself. This approach is particularly appealing when one is supposed to solve one single instance, typically large and complex. This contrasts with the methods we discuss in the thesis, that are thought for handling the situation in which one is called to solve a possibly large number of instances.

One of the first influential descriptions of on-line adjustment of the parameters of an algorithm is given in Battiti & Tecchiolli (1994) where the authors introduce a ***tabu search*** where the length of the tabu list is optimized on-line. In Battiti (1996) the same idea is extended and the *reactive search* framework is defined as a metaheuristic in which a feedback on the search is obtained and used to modify some parameters, while the search itself is still in progress.

Zhang & Dietterich (1996) use a reinforcement learning method where the value function is approximated with a neural network, in order to tackle a scheduling problem.[41] A more detailed description of the method is given in Zhang & Dietterich (1998).

In Boyan & Moore (1997, 2000) the ***stage*** method is developed which is based on the idea of predicting the outcome of a local search on the basis of information on its starting point. The prediction is performed using a *lazy learning* approach—see Section 2.2.6 for a brief introduction to this class of machine learning methods. Moll *et al.* (1999) extend the ***stage*** method adding the possibility of refining *off-line* the informations gathered along the search. A related approach that aims at predicting the performance of different heuristics on a given instance is described in Allen & Minton (1996). The reinforcement learning formalism is adopted also in Miagkikh & Punch III (1999) for tackling the QUADRATIC ASSIGNMENT problem. Birkendorf & Simon (1998) describe ***boost***, a method that learns along a search to improve given solutions. Prais & Ribeiro (2000) describe a *reactive GRASP* in which the parameters of the algorithm are self-adjusted along the search according to the quality of the solutions previously found. The method considers a list of different acceptable values for the parameters to be varied on-line. The actual value to be used is stochastically selected with probabilities that are updated along the search on the basis of the observed results. In Su *et al.* (2001), linear regression is used to predict, over multiple ***simulated annealing*** runs, the long term outcome achieved by starting from a given initial solution. In ***evolutionary computation*** literature, the idea of on-line tuning is much older and can be found in Rechenberg (1973) and Schwefel (1981). More recently, it has been proposed in the works of Toussaint (2001) and Liang *et al.* (2001).

[40] See Section 2.2.2 for a brief introduction to reinforcement learning. A thorough presentation of reinforcement learning is given in Sutton & Barto (1998).

[41] More precisely, the problem at hand was a job-shop scheduling problem originating from a practical problem faced by NASA: the space shuttle payload processing.

2.2 The problem of supervised learning

Supervised learning plays a major role in this thesis as a source of inspirations at many different levels. Among them: the definition of the problem of tuning metaheuristics given in Chapter 3, the algorithm proposed in Chapter 4 for the solution of this problem, the critical analysis given in Chapter 6 of the experimental methodology currently adopted in evaluating metaheuristics, and finally some elements of the experimental protocol adopted in Chapter 5.

In order to give some precise reference to the reader, this chapter introduces and discuss the supervised learning problem. In Section 2.2.1 we propose an historical and philosophical introduction to machine learning in general. Section 2.2.2 introduces the three main subfield composing contemporary machine learning: *supervised learning*, *unsupervised learning*, and *reinforcement learning*. In Section 2.2.3 we restrict our attention to supervised learning and we give a formal definition of its typical problem. Sections 2.2.4 and 2.2.5 give a formal meaning, within the framework of supervised learning, to the concepts of *induction* and *generalization*, respectively Section 2.2.6 discusses the current practice in supervised learning. In particular, it proposes an overviews some popular supervised learning methods and a discussion of some problems that have to be faced such as, for instance, the problem of model selection. Finally, Section 2.2.7 presents the so called *racing* approach for solving the model selection problem.

2.2.1 A philosophical and historical perspective

Machine learning played a central role in artificial intelligence since its very beginning. With artificial intelligence, machine learning has shared a form of *split personality disorder* being attracted by two competing attitudes that we call here the *mystical* and the *pragmatic* one. The former is related to the old dream of *being as God* and therefore giving life to a creature. The latter, is related to the probably equally ancient dream of humanity of being freed from labor.

On the one hand, in the naive view of machine learning that descend from the mystical attitude, the *intelligent* machine is man's *alter ego*: created by man but enjoying then an independent life, almost in *competition* with its creator. In particular, the machine is expected to *surprise* its creator by showing it is able to *learn*, that is, to do things it was not designed for. This view is deeply rooted in the myth and in the literature: The themes of the creature is found in the Greek myth of *Pygmalion and Galatea* (Rose, 1928), and reappears, often with moralistic connotations, in the Jewish legend of the *Golem* (Idel, 1983), in *Frankenstein* (Shelley, 1818), *Pinocchio* (Collodi, 1883) and then in a large number of the science-fiction literary works and movies of the last century. Among them *R.U.R* (Capek, 1920), *Metropolis* (Lang, 1927), the many novels by Asimov—see Clarke (1993, 1994) and references therein—*2001: A Space Odyssey* (Kubrick, 1968), *Blade Runner* (Scott, 1982), *Terminator* (Cameron,

1984), and *Matrix* (Wachowski & Wachowski, 1999).

On the other hand, in the critical view of machine learning leaning toward the pragmatic attitude, the *intelligent* machine is rather an extension of man. A useful tool, much more sophisticated than a telephone or a bulldozer, but still of the same nature of a wedge or a lever: A device the engineer explicitly designs to solve a specific class of problems in a given context, or possibly set of contexts.

The two attitudes have been tightly interwoven and *in some sense* both gave a contribution to the field. As the reader might have already understood, we definitely lean towards the pragmatic attitude and we are rather skeptical about the mystical one: the very names we chose to denote the two attitudes betray our feelings on the issue. Nevertheless, we have to recognize the *pragmatic* value of assuming a *mystical* attitude when the point is raising funds for financing the research: The field has always enjoyed some considerable funding, not always justified by actual achievements. This could happen also thanks to a conspicuous coverage by the media that have always been especially attracted by the *oddity* of the project of creating an *intelligent machine.*

The research in machine learning has not followed a linear path and, in time, researchers focused their attention on quite different paradigms, including connectionism, symbolic learning, and inductive learning. An introduction to these different approaches is given in Carbonell (1990) and in Shavlik & Dietterich (1990). Among them, the one that is relevant in this thesis is the connectionist which is closely related to the supervised learning problem discussed in Section 2.2.3 and in the following ones.[42] The connectionist approach to machine learning started being explored in the early works of the 1950s and 1960s with the two-fold goal of deepening the understanding of human brain and developing a learning machine taking inspiration from neurophysiology. Several works concentrated on the development and the analysis of models of neurons. In particular, Rosenblatt (1958) proposed the model that is known under the name of *perceptron*, forerunner of modern neural networks. More precisely, the perceptron is a *single-layered* neural network, that is, a network whose neurons are directly connected either with the input or with the output. For such a model Rosenblatt (1958) was able to find a training rule; on the other hand, a general training rule for the generic multi-layered networks seemed out of reach, at least at those times. The perceptron attracted much of the research interests in machine learning for a decade: An account of the machine learning of those times is given in Nilsson (1965). An abrupt stop to the research on the perceptron followed the publication of the work by Minsky & Papert (1969) in which some severe limitations of this model were highlighted. In particular, Minsky & Papert (1969)

[42]Indeed, the connectionist paradigm is broader than its application to supervised learning. It includes, among others, applications to clustering (Kohonen, 1982) and dynamic systems (Hopfield, 1982; Elman, 1990). In the framework of the thesis it is sufficient to restrict our attention to the "classical" feed-forward neural network of which we give a description in Section 2.2.6 and, more in particular, in Figure 2.7.

showed that the perceptron is essentially a linear device and is therefore ruled out in the large majority of practical applications. This result discouraged further research on the perceptron and had the effect of diverting the attention of the machine learning community away from all neural inspired methods. Only 20 years later, Rumelhart *et al.* (1986) were able to find a training rule for multi-layered neural networks which, contrary to the perceptron, are known to be capable of approximating any continuous function. Following this result, the interest of the community switched back to the connectionist approach. During the last 15 years, the field of neural network has flourished favoring the development of the research on supervised learning. The neural network *renaissance*, probably under the pressure of the increasing amount of practical applications, has *pragmatically* focused on the engineering aspects of neural networks to the detriment of the neurological plausibility of the proposed models. Currently, most of the approaches discussed within the neural network community, think for instance to the *support vector machines* (Vapnik, 1998; Cristianini & Shawe-Taylor, 2000), have little in common with the human brain and rest on the contrary on solid statistical and theoretical basis (Devroye *et al.*, 1996; Kearns & Vazirani, 1997; Vapnik, 1998).

2.2.2 The three main problems of machine learning

Humans, and animals in general, react to their environment and perform different actions in response to the inputs they receive. It is generally considered a sign of the intelligence of a subject if its responses change over time and become more and more effective. When this happens, we say that the subject is able to *learn*. The field of machine learning studies learning algorithms, which specify how the changes in the learner's behavior depend on the inputs received and on feedback from the environment. Depending on the feedback we can distinguish between the following forms of machine learning: *supervised learning*, *unsupervised learning*, and *reinforcement learning*. In this thesis we deal with the problem of tuning metaheuristics that, as we make clear in Chapter 3, has much in common with supervised learning. It is mostly for the sake completeness that we introduce in this section also unsupervised and reinforcement learning.

Supervised learning. On one extreme, *supervised learning* involves some sort of interaction between the learner and a *supervisor*. The learner is provided with a set of examples of the behavior of the supervisor that it is supposed to reproduce. Each example consists in an *input/output* pair, where the output is the response of the supervisor to the given input. The learner has then the chance to directly compare, for what concerns the given examples, its response to the one provided by the supervisor. On the basis of this comparison, the learner can properly adjust its behavior in a way that is more likely to produce the appropriate response the following time it receives the same input. As an example, we can consider a simple *classification* problem: The learner is called to recognize fruits. In order to train the learner, the supervisor provides some apples, oranges, peaches and bananas, and show them to the learner associating to each fruit the correct name. The learner has access to some features of each fruit, say color, smoothness of the surface, shape, size, *etc.* Its tasks consists in associating a fruit name to a set of values of the observed features. Beside the classification problem, another important supervised learning problem is *regression estimation* where rather than with categorical variables as in classification, we deal with continuous quantities. In general, the supervised learning practice is much entangled with other well established research fields such as statistics (Barnett, 1999), econometrics (Campbell *et al.*, 1997), and system identification (Ljung, 1987): The issue in supervised learning, as in the aforementioned field, is to *model* some phenomenon and to acquire the ability to perform *predictions*.

Unsupervised learning. On the other extreme, *unsupervised learning* does not provide for passing any feedback to the learner. Instead, the learner receives only input data and it is expected to cluster them in a *meaningful* way. In unsupervised learning, the learner's task consists in detecting similarities and differences among the input patterns. As an example of unsupervised learning, we can consider a perceptual system. In artificial vision a typical problem consists in detecting and locating the objects that populate an image. This problem can be possibly solved by a learning agent that is able to *cluster* the pixels of the image in such a way that each cluster represents a different object.

Reinforcement learning. A third alternative between the two extremes is represented by *Reinforcement learning* (Sutton & Barto, 1998), even if it is admittedly much closer to supervised learning. In reinforcement learning the learning agent performs a *sequence* of actions which change the state of the environment, and receives a sequences of *rewards* and/or *punishments* as a feedback. What complicates the framework is the fact that the feedback received by the agent is typically *temporally delayed* and a direct action-feedback mapping cannot be easily established. Examples of reinforcement learning problems appear in many field such as robotics and game playing (Samuel, 1959; Tesauro, 1992). Early research in reinforcement learning was strongly connected with psychology and cognitive sciences. Nowadays, the strong link has been recognized between reinforcement learning and other fields of applied mathematics such as dynamic programming (Bellman, 1957) and optimal control (Bertsekas, 1995a).

2.2.3 Supervised learning

The general problem of supervised learning can be defined in terms of the following three elements (Vapnik, 1995, 1998):

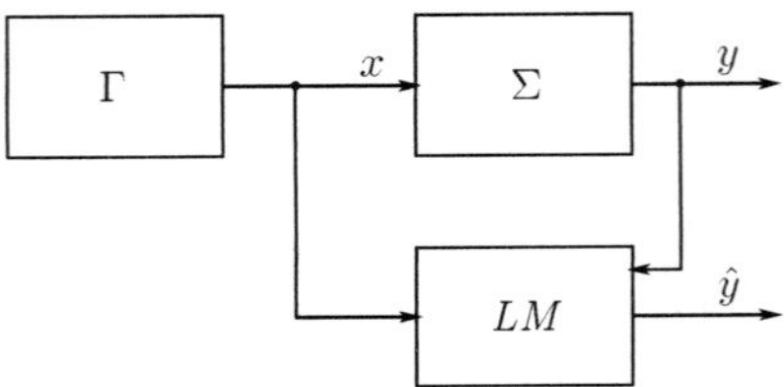

Figure 2.3: A graphical representation of the supervised learning problem. During the training phase, the learning machine *LM* observes a *training set* composed of input-output pairs (x, y), where y is the response of the supervisor Σ to the input x. On the basis of this training set, *LM* is supposed to *learn* the behavior of the supervisor: to a new input x, *LM* is supposed to respond with an output $\hat{y}$ that should be as close as possible to the output y returned by the supervisor.

- A generator Γ of random data $x \in \mathbb{R}^d$, independently and identically distributed according to a *fixed but unknown* distribution $P(x)$;
- A supervisor Σ that, for a given input x, returns an output $y \in \mathbb{R}$ according to a *fixed but unknown* conditional distribution $P(y|x)$;[43]
- A learning machine *LM* which is able to implement a set of functions $g(x, \alpha)$ with $\alpha \in \Lambda$.[44]

In this context, graphically represented in Figure 2.3, we will say that the machine *LM learns* the behavior of the supervisor Σ if it is able to select among the possible functions $g(x, \alpha)$ the one that better approximates the behavior of the supervisor. The selection is made on the basis of a *training set*:

$$\mathcal{Z} = \{(x_1, y_1), (x_2, y_2), \ldots, (x_N, y_N)\}.$$

composed of N input-output pairs, independently and identically distributed according to the *fixed but unknown* distribution $P(x, y) = P(x)P(y|x)$.

For a given input x, we can measure the so called *loss function*

$$\mathcal{L}\big(y, g(x, \alpha)\big),$$

[43]This is the most general case which includes the possibility that the supervisor selects the output as a function $y = f(x)$ of the input. In this case $P(y|x) = \delta\big(y, f(x)\big)$, where δ is Kronecker's function.

[44]The fact that we consider a parametric set of functions $\{g(x, \alpha) : \alpha \in \Lambda\}$ is not a restriction since the nature of α is left unspecified and Λ is therefore an arbitrary set: it could contain numbers, vectors, or any other arbitrary abstract element.

which quantifies the discrepancy between the prediction $\hat{y} = g(x, \alpha)$ obtained by the learning machine and the actual response of the supervisor. As we will see presently, the function $\mathcal{L}$ must be properly defined in a meaningful way according to the specific nature of the learning problem at hand.

Having defined the *loss* for a specific input x we can now state that the goal of the learning machine is to minimize the *expected value* of $\mathcal{L}$ with respect to the joint input-output distribution $P(x, y)$. This quantity is called the *risk functional*:

$$R(\alpha) = \int \mathcal{L}(y, g(x, \alpha))\, \mathrm{d}P(x, y). \tag{2.7}$$

More precisely, the goal of a learning process is to find among all possible functions $g(x, \alpha)$, with $\alpha \in \Lambda$, the function $f(x, \bar{\alpha})$ that minimizes the functional $R(\alpha)$ when the joint distribution $P(x, y)$ is unknown but a training set $\mathcal{Z}$ is given. We could write:

$$\bar{\alpha} = \arg\min_{\alpha \in \Lambda} R(\alpha).$$

From this definition, the similarities and the differences are apparent between the supervised learning problem and the optimization problem introduced in Section 2.1.2: In both cases a set of object is given together with a criterion that measures the desirability of each of the objects. Nevertheless, in the definition of the supervised learning problem the criterion cannot be analytically computed since the joint distribution $P(x, y)$ appearing in Equation 2.7 is unknown. Because of this difference, the supervised learning problem cannot be trivially reduced to an optimization problem and a considerably different conceptual framework has to be developed.

The definition of the supervised learning problem we gave above is rather general and comprises different specific subproblems. Among them, the most studied in the literature are the problem of *pattern recognition* and the problem of *regression estimation*.

Pattern recognition

In the pattern recognition problem (Duda *et al.*, 2001) the supervisor observes a pattern x and determines to which of k classes it belongs. The learning machine is required to learn to perform the classifications of new patterns on the basis of a set of examples of patterns classified by the supervisor.

Using the formal apparatus defined above, we can express the pattern recognition problem as follows: The patterns appear randomly and independently according to a *fixed but unknown* distribution $P(x)$. The supervisor classifies each pattern into one of k classes. We assume that the supervisor performs the classification according to a *fixed but unknown* conditional distribution $P(y|x)$, where $y \in \{1, 2, \dots, k\}$.[45] Neither $P(x)$ nor $P(y|x)$ are known; however, we know

[45] The case in which the supervisor assigns a class to a pattern in a deterministic way is a

they exist and are fixed. Therefore, the joint distribution $P(x, y) = P(y|x)P(x)$ exists, even if it is unknown. The only source of available information is a set $\mathcal{Z} = \{x_j, y_j\}_{j=1}^N$ of N patterns classified by the supervisor.

The learning machine implements a set of functions $g(x, \alpha)$, with $\alpha \in \Lambda$, which might take only k values $\{1, 2, \ldots, k\}$.

In this context, it is natural to consider the following simple *loss* function:

$$\mathcal{L}\left(y, g(x, \alpha)\right) = \begin{cases} 0 & \text{if } y = g(x, \alpha), \\ 1 & \text{if } y \neq g(x, \alpha); \end{cases} \tag{2.8}$$

that is, an *indicator function* for the subset of misclassified patterns.[46] When the loss function is defined as in Equation 2.8, the *risk* functional,

$$R(\alpha) = \int \mathcal{L}\big(y, g(x, \alpha)\big)\, \mathrm{d}P(x, y).$$

represents the overall probability that the learning machine incurs in a classification error.

Regression estimation

Let us consider the stochastic relation between two variables $x \in \mathbb{R}^d$ and $y \in \mathbb{R}$ such that, given x, the value of y is obtained as a result of a random experiment dominated by the conditional distribution $P(y|x)$. Further, let the value of the variable x be randomly extracted according to a distribution $P(x)$. Neither $P(y|x)$ nor $P(x)$ are known but they exists and are fixed. Thus the joint distribution $P(x, y) = P(y|x)P(x)$ exists and is fixed, even if unknown.

Estimating the stochastic dependency between the variables x and y on the basis of a set of independent and identically distributed examples $\mathcal{Z} = \{x_j, y_j\}_{j=1}^N$ means to estimate the conditional distribution $P(y|x)$ which is typically a particularly hard task. In many applications we do not need a complete description of the stochastic dependency and the conditional expectation is sufficient:

$$E[y|x] = r(x) = \int y\, \mathrm{d}P(y|x).$$

The (deterministic) function r that associates to each value of x the expected value of y conditioned to x is called the *regression* function. Accordingly, the

particular case. The advantage of the general formulation is that it accounts for misclassified patterns and/or errors in the database of examples, situations which are typical in real-world applications.

[46]More complex loss functions can be considered, as well. Let us think, for instance, of the case in which some sort of errors are to be penalized more than others. Medical diagnosis is an example: false-negatives are usually much more dramatic errors than false-positives. The latter typically lead to further examinations that can spot the error; on the other hand, the former leave a disease undetected and untreated which could be possibly fatal to the patient.

problem of estimating the regression function on the basis of a set of examples is known as *regression estimation.*

In can be shown that the problem of regression estimation can be solved by a learning machines that is able to implement the functions in $\{g(x, \alpha) : \alpha \in \Lambda\}$ and that minimizes a risk functional where the loss function is defined as

$$\mathcal{L}(y, g(x, \alpha)) = (y - g(x, \alpha))^2, \tag{2.9}$$

that is as the quadratic error. Indeed the minimum of the risk functional

$$R(\alpha) = \int (y - g(x, \alpha))^2 \, \mathrm{d}P(x, y) \tag{2.10}$$

is attained at the regression function, that is, for the $\bar{\alpha}$ for which $g(x, \bar{\alpha}) = r(x)$, if the regression function belongs to the set $\{g(x, \alpha) : \alpha \in \Lambda\}$. On the other hand, if the regression function does not belong to the aforementioned set, the $\bar{\alpha}$ for which the risk is minimized is such that among all functions in the set, $g(x, \bar{\alpha})$ is the closest to $r(x)$ in the L_2 metric:[47]

$$\sqrt{\int (r(x) - g(x, \bar{\alpha}))^2 \, \mathrm{d}P(x, y)} \leq \sqrt{\int (r(x) - g(x, \alpha))^2 \, \mathrm{d}P(x, y)} \qquad \forall \alpha \in \Lambda.$$

2.2.4 The minimization of the empirical risk

As we have shown in Section 2.2.3, the problems of both pattern recognition and regression estimation can be reduced to the problem of minimizing the risk functional

$$R(\alpha) = \int \mathcal{L}(y, g(x, \alpha)) \, \mathrm{d}P(x, y), \tag{2.13}$$

[47]In order to prove the statement, let us consider the following decomposition of the loss function defined in Equation 2.9:

$$\begin{aligned} (y - g(x, \alpha))^2 &= (y - r(x) + r(x) - g(x, \alpha))^2 \\ &= (y - r(x))^2 + (r(x) - g(x, \alpha))^2 + 2(y - r(x))(r(x) - g(x, \alpha)). \end{aligned} \tag{2.11}$$

The risk functional is therefore

$$R(\alpha) = \int (y - r(x))^2 \, \mathrm{d}P(x, y) + \int (r(x) - g(x, \alpha))^2 \, \mathrm{d}P(x), \tag{2.12}$$

since the integral with respect to y of the third term in Equation 2.11 is null.

The first term in Equation 2.12 does not depend on α, therefore the minimum of $R(\alpha)$ is attained at the same $\bar{\alpha}$ at which the minimum of the second term in Equation 2.12 is attained. It follows that the minimum of the risk is attained at the regression function if there exists an $\bar{\alpha} \in \Lambda$ such that $g(x, \bar{\alpha}) = r(x)$—in words, if the regression function belongs to the set of functions implemented by the learning machine. On the other hand, if the regression function does not belong to the set of function spawned by Λ, the minimum of the risk is attained at $\bar{\alpha} \in \Lambda$ for which $g(x, \bar{\alpha})$ is the closest possible to the regression in the L_2 metric.

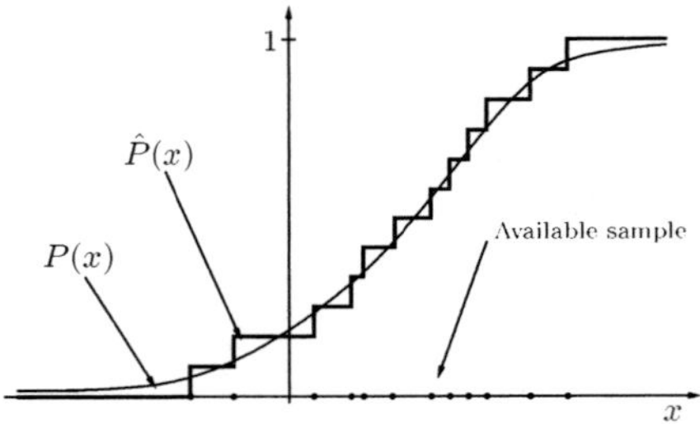

Figure 2.4: In this univariate example, the actual distribution $P(x)$ is approximated by the empirical distribution $\hat{P}(x)$ based on the sample $\{x_1, x_2, \ldots, x_N\}$, represented by the black dots on the horizontal axis.

in the case where the joint distribution $P(x, y)$ is fixed but unknown and a training set

$$\mathcal{Z} = \{(x_1, y_1), (x_2, y_2), \ldots, (x_N, y_N)\},$$

composed of N observations is available. Since $P(x, y)$ is unknown, an analytical solution to this problem is not possible: we are not able to find directly the function $g(x, \bar{\alpha})$ for which $R(\alpha)$ is minimized. It is therefore necessary to empirically approximate the optimal solution on the basis of the available training set. A viable solution, possibly the most intuitive, is based on the so called *principle of maximum entropy* (Papoulis, 1991) which, in this context, prescribes to approximate the unknown distribution $P(x, y)$ with its empirical counterpart obtained from $\mathcal{Z}$, that is, the stair-wise $\hat{P}(x, y)$—see Figure 2.4 for a visual example.[48] As a consequence, we can approximate the risk defined in Equation 2.13 with the so called *empirical risk*

$$R_{\text{emp}}(\alpha) = \int \mathcal{L}\big(y, g(x, \alpha)\big)\, \mathrm{d}\hat{P}(x, y) = \frac{1}{N}\sum_{j=1}^{N} \mathcal{L}\big(y_j, g(x_j, \alpha)\big), \tag{2.14}$$

obtained on the basis of the training set $\mathcal{Z}$.

The above described procedure defines the *induction principle* that in the literature is known as the *empirical risk minimization*:[49] The original problem

[48] According to the Glivenko-Cantelli theorem, when the number of observations tends to infinity, the empirical distribution converges in probability, in the uniform metric, to the actual distribution. See Vapnik (1998) for a proof of the theorem, its generalization, and a thorough discussion of all implications for what concerns the formal development of the machine learning theory.

[49] Together with the *empirical risk minimization*, a more advanced principle, the *structural risk minimization*, is discussed in Vapnik (1998). This new principle stems from the analysis

of minimizing the risk $R(\alpha)$ is reduced to the minimization of $R_{\text{emp}}(\alpha)$. Thus, in order to reproduce the behavior of the supervisor, the learning machine rather than using the function $g(x, \bar{\alpha})$ that minimizes $R(\alpha)$, uses the function $g(x, \alpha_N)$ that minimizes the empirical risk $R_{\text{emp}}(\alpha)$ constructed on the basis of the N examples contained in $\mathcal{Z}$. Formally:

$$\alpha_N = \arg\min_{\alpha \in \Lambda} R_{\text{emp}}(\alpha).$$

It is worth noticing here that in the case of a regression estimation problem where the loss function is defined as in Equation 2.9, the empirical risk is:

$$R_{\text{emp}}(\alpha) = \frac{1}{N} \sum_{j=1}^{N} \left(y_j - f(x_j, \alpha)\right)^2,$$

and therefore the *empirical risk minimization* amounts to the classical least-squares method. On the other hand, in the case of pattern recognition when the loss function is defined as in Equation 2.8, it is easy to observe that the *empirical risk minimization* is equivalent to the minimization of the number of classification error on the training set, which is the most intuitive way of training a model in pattern recognition (Duda *et al.*, 2001).

2.2.5 The theory of generalization

We say that a machine LM is able to *generalize* if, on the basis of a training set $\mathcal{Z} = \{x_j, y_j\}_{j=1}^N$ containing examples of the responses $y_1, \dots, y_N$ given by a supervisor Σ to the input values $x_1, \dots, x_N$, it is able to predict the responses of Σ also for what concerns new values of the input variable that are not contained in $\mathcal{Z}$.

If the learning machine were able to minimize the risk functional $R(\alpha)$ and could use the minimizing function $g(x, \bar{\alpha})$, generalization would be guaranteed by definition. Yet, being $P(x, y)$ unknown, the machine LM has to be content with some approximation. As we have seen in Section 2.2.4, the *empirical risk minimization* principle prescribes that LM should adopt $g(x, \alpha_N)$, to approximate $g(x, \bar{\alpha})$, that is, the function that minimizes the empirical risk defined on the basis of $\mathcal{Z}$.

The function $g(x, \alpha_N)$ enjoys by definition the property of being the best one in the set $\{g(x, \alpha) : \alpha \in \Lambda\}$ at reproducing the responses of the supervisor when we restrict to the training set $\mathcal{Z}$. Nonetheless, no guarantee is available for what concerns input values that are not included in $\mathcal{Z}$.

---

of the limitations of the former.

In the next subsection, we sketch an analysis of the limitations of the *empirical risk minimization* because it serves as an introduction to concepts that will be useful in the course of the thesis, namely in Chapter 6. On the contrary, we do not enter in the details of the ***structural risk minimization*** principle because this would go beyond the scope of our work. We refer the reader to Vapnik (1998).

VC-dimension

In this paragraph we propose some introductory elements of the so called *generalization theory* (Vapnik, 1998) whose goal is precisely to define a set of conditions under which it is guaranteed that $g(x, \alpha_N)$ is a good approximation of $g(x, \bar{\alpha})$ and therefore that a learning machine which follows the *empirical risk minimization* principle is able to generalize properly to new data.

Formally, the *empirical risk minimization* principle is said to be *consistent* for a set of functions $Q(z, \alpha) = \mathcal{L}(y, g(x, \alpha))$ with $\alpha \in \Lambda$, and for the joint density $P(z) = P(x, y)$, if the following two sequences converge in probability to the same limit:

$$R(\alpha_N) \xrightarrow[N \to \infty]{prob} \inf_{\alpha \in \Lambda} R(\alpha),$$

$$R_{\text{emp}}(\alpha_N) \xrightarrow[N \to \infty]{prob} \inf_{\alpha \in \Lambda} R(\alpha),$$

where α_N denotes the optimal value of α obtained by minimizing the empirical risk on the basis of a training set $\mathcal{Z}$ composed of N examples, and where $\inf_{\alpha \in \Lambda} R(\alpha)$ is the *infimum* of the risk for $\alpha \in \Lambda$. In words, the principle is consistent if for training sets of increasing size, the sequence of functions $Q(z, \alpha_N)$, with $N = 1, 2, \ldots$, are such that both the risk and the empirical risk converge in probability to the minimal possible value of the risk.

The **key theorem** of learning theory, due to Vapnik & Chervonenkis (1991), can be stated as follows: Let $\{Q(z, \alpha) : \alpha \in \Lambda\}$ be a set of functions such that $A \leq R(\alpha) \leq B$ for all $\alpha \in \Lambda$. In order for the *empirical risk minimization* to be consistent, it is necessary and sufficient that $R_{\text{emp}}(\alpha)$ uniformly converge to the actual value $R(\alpha)$ on the whole set $\{Q(z, \alpha) : \alpha \in \Lambda\}$, in the following sense:

$$\lim_{N \to \infty} Prob \left\{ \sup_{\alpha \in \Lambda} \left(R(\alpha) - R_{\text{emp}}(\alpha) \right) > \epsilon \right\} = 0, \quad \forall \epsilon > 0. \tag{2.15}$$

According to this theorem, the *empirical risk minimization* is consistent if and only if $R_{\text{emp}}(\alpha)$ *uniformly* converges to $R(\alpha)$.

It is worth noticing that the key theorem is a *worst-case analysis*: it states that the consistency the *empirical risk minimization* depends on the *worst* function, in the sense defined in Equation 2.15, among those in the set $\{Q(z, \alpha) : \alpha \in \Lambda\}$.

Given the results stated by the key theorem and, in particular, given the structure of Equation 2.15, the importance of defining bounds on the difference $R(\alpha) - R_{\text{emp}}(\alpha)$ becomes apparent. In these bounds, a fundamental role is played by the concept of *VC-dimension* of a learning machine (Vapnik & Chervonenkis, 1971) which is a scalar h, measuring the complexity of the machine itself. The important theoretical results concerning the VC-dimension is that if h is finite, the uniform convergence—in the sense given in Equation 2.15—of $R_{\text{emp}}(\alpha)$ to $R(\alpha)$ is guaranteed and therefore the *empirical risk minimization* is consistent.

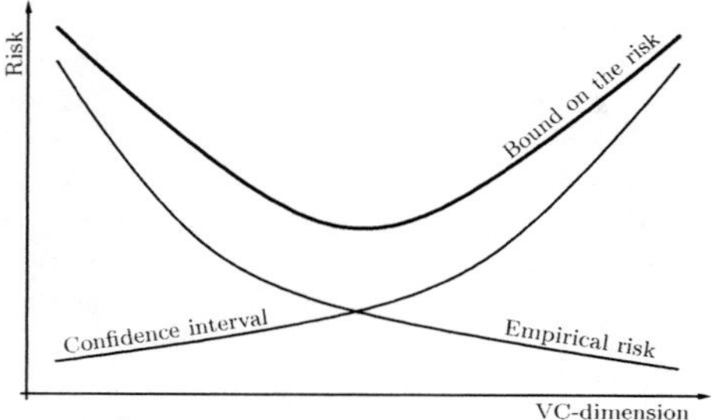

Figure 2.5: When the VC-dimension grows, the empirical risk decreases but the confidence interval increases. The overall result is that the bound on the actual risk, which is the composition of the two contributions decreases initially and then increases again.

Moreover in the non-asymptotic case, that is, when the size N of the training set $\mathcal{Z}$ is finite, it can be shown that for a set $\mathcal{Q} = \{Q(z, \alpha) : \alpha \in \Lambda\}$ of functions for which $0 \leq Q(z, \alpha) \leq B$, the following inequality holds with probability $1 - \eta$:

$$R(\alpha_N) \leq R_{\text{emp}}(\alpha_N) + \frac{B\mathcal{E}}{2}\left(1 + \sqrt{1 + \frac{4R_{\text{emp}}(\alpha_N)}{B\mathcal{E}}}\right), \tag{2.16}$$

where, if the cardinality of the set of functions is finite, that is, if $|\mathcal{Q}| < \infty$,

$$\mathcal{E} = 2\,\frac{\ln|\mathcal{Q}| - \ln\eta}{N}, \tag{2.17}$$

and therefore $\mathcal{E}$ is not a function of the VC-dimension h. On the other hand, if the cardinality of $\mathcal{Q}$ is infinite, and the VC-dimension of the learning machine is h, it results:

$$\mathcal{E} = 4\,\frac{h(\ln 2N/h + 1) - \ln\eta/4}{N}. \tag{2.18}$$

On the basis of these results we can state that the *empirical risk minimization* is a valid *induction* principle when the size N of the training set is large, say $N > 20h$. In this case, $\mathcal{E}$ is small, the second summand on the right hand side of Equation 2.16 is thus small as well, and the actual value of the risk is to be expected to be close to the empirical risk. On the other hand, if the ratio N/h is small, a low value of $R_{\text{emp}}(\alpha_N)$ does not guarantee that also the actual risk functional $R(\alpha_N)$ is small. In this case the second summand on the right hand side of Equation 2.16 cannot be neglected and can be considered as a *confidence interval* of the estimate of the actual risk provided by its empirical counterpart. Figure 2.5 offers a graphical representation of the relation among the terms of Equation 2.16 for a fixed value of N and varying h.

The bias/variance dilemma

Another analysis that somehow parallels the one based on the concept of VC-dimension and that allows a useful insight into many aspects of supervised learning is known in the literature under the name of *bias/variance decomposition* (Geman *et al.*, 1992). The core of this analysis consists in showing that the prediction error yielded by a function $g(x, \alpha)$ can be decomposed into two components: the *bias* and the *variance*. We sketch in the following the analysis as proposed in Geman *et al.* (1992).

In order to make explicit the dependency on the training set $\mathcal{Z}$ of the selected function, we adopt here the notation $g(x, \alpha_{\mathcal{Z}})$ in place of the previously adopted $g(x, \alpha_N)$. Let us consider first a specific training set $\mathcal{Z}'$. A measure of the quality of the prediction for a given input x' yielded by $g(x', \alpha_{\mathcal{Z}'})$, where $\alpha_{\mathcal{Z}'}$ has been selected on the basis of the given training set $\mathcal{Z}'$, is given by the expected value of the square of the error:

$$E\left[\left(y - g(x, \alpha_{\mathcal{Z}})\right)^2 \middle| x = x', \mathcal{Z} = \mathcal{Z}'\right],$$

where the expectation is taken with respect to the marginal distribution $P(y|x)$, for a given input $x = x'$. This quantity can be decomposed[50] as:

$$\begin{aligned} E\left[\left(y - g(x, \alpha_{\mathcal{Z}})\right)^2 \middle| x = x', \mathcal{Z} = \mathcal{Z}'\right] &= \\ = E\left[\left(y - E[y|x]\right)^2 \middle| x = x', \mathcal{Z} = \mathcal{Z}'\right] &+ \left(g(x', \alpha_{\mathcal{Z}'}) - E[y|x']\right)^2. \end{aligned}$$

It can be noticed that the first summand on the right hand side does not depend neither on the training set $\mathcal{Z}$, nor on any choice that could be possibly operated by the learning machine: Indeed, it is simply the variance of the output y given the input x. As far as an evaluation of the prediction produced by the learning machine is concerned, we can therefore restrict our attention to the second summand, that is, to the square of the difference between the prediction $g(x', \alpha_{\mathcal{Z}'})$ and the regression function $r(x') = E[y|x']$:

$$\left(g(x', \alpha_{\mathcal{Z}'}) - E[y|x']\right)^2. \tag{2.19}$$

Let us consider now all possible training sets. A measure of the quality of the prediction yielded by the learning machine is given by the expected value, with respect to all possible training sets, of the quantity given in Equation 2.19:

$$E_{\mathcal{Z}}\left[\left(g(x', \alpha_{\mathcal{Z}}) - E[y|x']\right)^2\right], \tag{2.20}$$

where the subscript $\mathcal{Z}$ in $E_{\mathcal{Z}}$ is there to stress that the expectation is taken with respect to all possible training sets.

[50] See Note 47 and, in particular, Equation 2.11.

It might happen that for a specific training set $\mathcal{Z}'$, the selected function $g(x, \alpha_{\mathcal{Z}'})$ produces good predictions of $E[y|x]$, while for another training set $\mathcal{Z}''$, the prediction obtained by $g(x, \alpha_{\mathcal{Z}''})$ is particularly poor. Formally, this concern can be expressed by decomposing the expectation given in Equation 2.20 as:

$$E_{\mathcal{Z}}\Big[\big(g(x', \alpha_{\mathcal{Z}}) - E[y|x']\big)^2\Big] =$$
$$= \big(E_{\mathcal{Z}}[g(x', \alpha_{\mathcal{Z}})] - E[y|x']\big)^2 + E_{\mathcal{Z}}\Big[\big(g(x', \alpha_{\mathcal{Z}}) - E_{\mathcal{Z}}[g(x', \alpha_{\mathcal{Z}})]\big)^2\Big], \quad (2.21)$$

where the two terms on the right hand side are the square of the *bias* and the *variance*, respectively.[51] The *bias* measures the difference between the *expected* prediction and the regression function.

Even if the bias component is small, that is, if *on average* the predictions are good, the learning machine could be affected by a large *variance*: The learning machine could be, in other words, extremely sensitive to the characteristics of the specific set of examples used for training.

Going back to the general problem of machine learning, the conclusion that can be drawn from the *bias/variance* analysis is that the choice of the structure of the set $\mathcal{G} = \{g(x, \alpha) : \alpha \in \Lambda\}$ to be adopted by the learning machine, always involves a trade-off.

On the one hand, the higher is the *complexity* of the set $\mathcal{G}$, the higher is its flexibility and generality, and the higher is the chance that at least one of the function in $\mathcal{G}$ is able to closely reproduce the behavior of the supervisor. In this case, the *bias* component is small. Nonetheless, since the training set if finite and typically relatively small, it might be difficult to identify the correct element of $\mathcal{G}$: The learning machine could be extremely sensitive to the particular realization of the training set and the prediction could therefore be affected by a large *variance*.

On the other hand, if the learning machine implements a simple and more restricted set of functions $\mathcal{G} = \{g(x, \alpha) : \alpha \in \Lambda\}$, say belonging to a simple

[51]It results:

$$\begin{aligned}
&E_{\mathcal{Z}}\Big[\big(g(x', \alpha_{\mathcal{Z}}) - E[y|x']\big)^2\Big] = \\
&\quad = E_{\mathcal{Z}}\Big[\Big(\big(g(x', \alpha_{\mathcal{Z}}) - E_{\mathcal{Z}}[g(x', \alpha_{\mathcal{Z}})]\big) + \big(E_{\mathcal{Z}}[g(x', \alpha_{\mathcal{Z}})] - E[y|x']\big)\Big)^2\Big] \\
&\quad = E_{\mathcal{Z}}\Big[\big(g(x', \alpha_{\mathcal{Z}}) - E_{\mathcal{Z}}[g(x', \alpha_{\mathcal{Z}})]\big)^2\Big] + E_{\mathcal{Z}}\Big[\big(E_{\mathcal{Z}}[g(x', \alpha_{\mathcal{Z}})] - E[y|x']\big)^2\Big] + \\
&\qquad + 2\,E_{\mathcal{Z}}\Big[\big(g(x', \alpha_{\mathcal{Z}}) - E_{\mathcal{Z}}[g(x', \alpha_{\mathcal{Z}})]\big)\big(E_{\mathcal{Z}}[g(x', \alpha_{\mathcal{Z}})] - E[y|x']\big)\Big] \\
&\quad = E_{\mathcal{Z}}\Big[\big(g(x', \alpha_{\mathcal{Z}}) - E_{\mathcal{Z}}[g(x', \alpha_{\mathcal{Z}})]\big)^2\Big] + \big(E_{\mathcal{Z}}[g(x', \alpha_{\mathcal{Z}})] - E[y|x']\big)^2 + \\
&\qquad + 2\,E_{\mathcal{Z}}\Big[g(x', \alpha_{\mathcal{Z}}) - E_{\mathcal{Z}}[g(x', \alpha_{\mathcal{Z}})]\Big]\big(E_{\mathcal{Z}}[g(x', \alpha_{\mathcal{Z}})] - E[y|x']\big) \\
&\quad = \big(E_{\mathcal{Z}}[g(x', \alpha_{\mathcal{Z}})] - E[y|x']\big)^2 + E_{\mathcal{Z}}\Big[\big(g(x', \alpha_{\mathcal{Z}}) - E_{\mathcal{Z}}[g(x', \alpha_{\mathcal{Z}})]\big)^2\Big].
\end{aligned}$$

The two summands in the last line are the square of the *bias* and the *variance*, respectively.

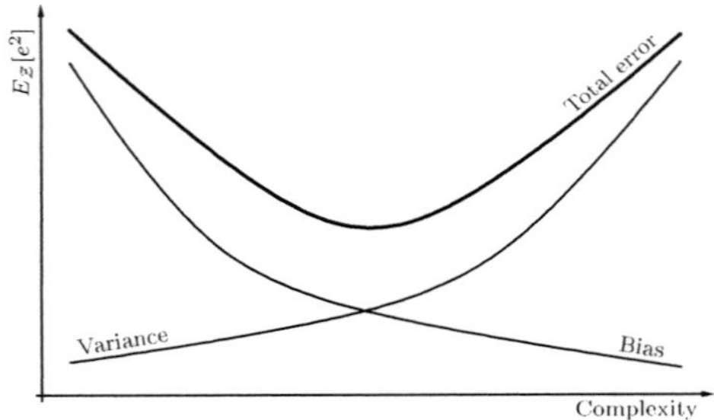

Figure 2.6: When the complexity of the learning machine grows, the *bias* decreases but the *variance* increases. The overall result is that the expectation on the square of the prediction error, which is the composition of the two contributions, decreases initially and then increases again.

parametric family described by a small number of parameters, the risk is high that none of the functions in $\mathcal{G}$ properly reproduces the behavior of the supervisor. In this case, the *bias* will be high. Yet, the *variance* will be small since the value of the few parameters spawning the family of functions can be identified with low uncertainty on the basis of any possible training sets.

For a limited number of available training examples, when the complexity of the set $\mathcal{G}$ increases, the *bias* component typically decreases while the *variance* component increases. The overall result, graphically shown in Figure 2.6, is that the expected value of the squared error initially decreases with the complexity of the learning machine, and then increases again. On the basis of the *bias/variance analysis*, we observe therefore a result that is qualitatively similar to the one reached through the analysis based on the concept of VC-dimension.

2.2.6 Supervised learning in practice

We cannot expect to convey here much of the complexity of the supervised learning practice. In particular we do not enter into the details of the various learning approaches but we limit our discussion to the general elements that appear in the supervised learning practice irrespectively of the specific approach adopted.[52] We

[52] For the sake of precision, the subsection **From observations to data** is of truly general character while the following subsection **Parametric and structural identification**, refers more properly to the approaches based on what Vapnik calls the principle of ***empirical risk minimization***—see Section 2.2.4 and Note 49.

Despite the central place they occupy in contemporary supervised learning, the more recently proposed approaches that according to the classification introduced by Vapnik (1998) follow the principle of ***structural risk minimization***, are less relevant in the context of this thesis. For

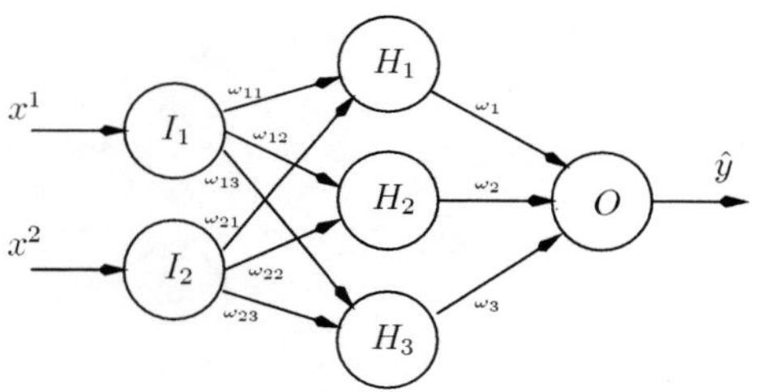

(a) A *feed-forward neural network* with bidimensional input, monodimensional output, and 3 neurons in the hidden layer.

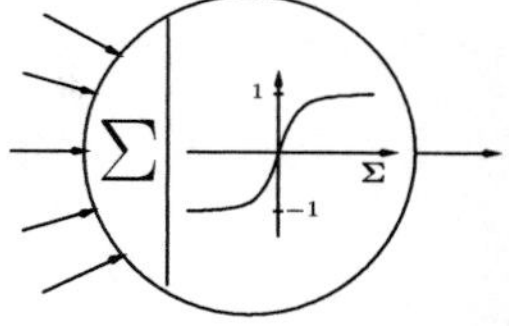

(b) Graphical representation of a neuron: The input signals are summed and the result is nonlinearly scaled through a sigmoidal function.

Figure 2.7: Feed-forward neural networks are *universal approximators* (Cybenko, 1989; Hornik *et al.*, 1989; Hecht-Nielsen, 1989), that is, provided they are endowed with a sufficient number of neuron in the hidden layer and the parameters ω_{ij} and ω_j are properly tuned, they are able to approximate arbitrarily well any continuous function.

need only to introduce here a quite high-level taxonomy of learning approaches, and to mention some algorithms that are discussed in the following of the thesis.

Learning approaches can be classified according to a variety of criteria. Beside the classification based on the dichotomy *empirical/structural risk minimization*, already presented in Section 2.2.4, other orthogonal criteria exist in the literature. One of them is based on the *global/local* dichotomy:

On the one hand, global approaches try to reproduce the behavior of the supervisor using a single functional approximator that covers the whole input space. As an example, the learning machine could try to reproduce the behavior of the supervisor using a polynomial, say a first degree polynomial. In this case, given an input $x \in \mathbb{R}^d$, the learning machine would try to predict the response y of the supervisor with an $\hat{y}$ which is a linear combination of the component of x—usually a constant term is included in order to account for an offset. In other words, the learning machine describes the supervisor as a hyperplane in the combined $d+1$-dimensional input/output space. A classical example of a global approach which is widely adopted in practical applications, is represented by *feed-forward neural networks* (Bishop, 1995)—see Figure 2.7.

On the other hand, local approaches reduce the original problem into a set of subproblems: The learning machine consists of a set of local models, each specialized on a different area of the input domain. When an input x is given, the output

a presentation and a discussion of such approaches, we refer the interested reader to Vapnik (1998) and in particular to Cristianini & Shawe-Taylor (2000).

$\hat{y}$ is obtained by appropriately combining the outputs of the local models whose domain comprise the input x. A variety of local methods have been proposed in the literature. Among them the *hierarchical* approaches such as *classification and regression trees* (Breiman *et al.*, 1984), *multivariate regression splines* (Friedman, 1991), *ID3* (Quinlan, 1993b), *hierarchical mixture of experts* (Jordan & Jacobs, 1994), *radial basis functions* (Powell, 1987), *piecewise linear models* (Billings & Voon, 1987; Skeppstedt *et al.*, 1992), and the *neuro-fuzzy approach* (Takagi & Sugeno, 1985; Jang, 1993). Other local approaches belong to the statistics and time-series prediction literature such as the *state-dependent models* (Priestley, 1988) and *threshold AR* (Tong, 1990), and others based on *splines* (Kavli, 1993). Moreover, it is worth noticing here that some forms of *gain scheduling* (Shamma & Athanas, 1990) adopted in the field of automatic control share much of the rationale which is behind the local approach in supervised learning. Johansen & Foss (1993) defined the general class of models called *local model networks* which comprises, under certain conditions, most of the aforementioned local approaches.

A further classification which is of interest in this thesis is the one based on the *eager/lazy* dichotomy:

On the one hand, *eager* approaches use the training set $\mathcal{Z}$, as soon as it becomes available, in order to extract a *compact* representation of the phenomenon at hand. The data are than discarded and only the compact representation is retained. The latter is then used to perform subsequent predictions. All approaches mentioned so far, both global and local, are *eager*.

On the other hand, *lazy* approaches (Aha, 1997), which are typically local, do not provide for any training phase: When the data $\mathcal{Z}$ becomes available, no computation is performed apart from properly storing the data, which are never discarded in favor of a model. For this reason, within certain communities such as the artificial intelligence community, *lazy* approaches are also known as *memory-based* methods. Only when a prediction is explicitly required for a precise value x' of the input, the *lazy* method retrieves from the database a typically tiny subset $\mathcal{Z}' \subset \mathcal{Z}$ of examples which are considered relevant according to some criteria, and use them to perform a prediction. In some cases, the extraction of the prediction from $\mathcal{Z}'$ is trivial: In *nearest-neighbor*, which is the prototypical *lazy* approach, when an input x' is given, the subset $\mathcal{Z}'$ retrieved from the database consists of only one example, the pair (x'', y''), where, in some metric, x'' is the closest to x' among all other x appearing in the database. The value y'' is then immediately returned as a prediction of the output of x'. In other cases, the operations that are performed are much more complex: In the case of the *adaptive lazy learning* (Birattari *et al.*, 1999), a complete modeling procedure including model selection and validation is performed for each prediction. This justifies the name *just-in-time modeling* (Cybenko, 1996; Stenman *et al.*, 1996) which is used within the system identification and control community to address *lazy* methods. *Lazy learning* is further discussed in Annex B.

From observations to data

In this section we briefly discuss the different logical steps that are needed to cast a real-world problem into the formal framework of supervised learning described in Section 2.2.3 and graphically represented in Figure 2.3. Although some elements of these phases can be, at least partially automatized, they typically require the intervention of the human designer of the learning machine.

Observation and analysis: The first step consists in an observation and analysis of the phenomenon at hand with the goal of spotting a set of measurable quantities apt to give a complete description of the phenomenon itself. In general, during this phase the available knowledge is limited and does not allow a correct selection of the set of variables that are *necessary and sufficient* to represent univocally the phenomenon. This phase is typically rather gross: We try to measure the largest possible number of variables—a limit being imposed by the economical cost of measurements—postponing the selection of the most informative to following stages of the learning process. The partial result produced by the observation and analysis phase is a set of *raw data* which represent the first possible form of representation of the phenomenon at hand. Notwithstanding its seeming triviality, this phase is particularly delicate since in the observation of the phenomenon we introduce some *a priori* knowledge that can be possibly groundless. The critical aspect of the phase is connected to the fact that a non accurate selection of the variables to be measured and therefore the exclusion of some possibly relevant ones, makes the most sophisticated learning algorithm powerless. The lack of a variable might be rather expensive since it requires, when already in subsequent phases of the learning process, to go back to the observation and analysis of the phenomenon and to redesign the criteria for data acquisition.

Preprocessing: During this phase the raw data are treated and prepared for the training of the learning machine. The preprocessing of data is not always necessary even if it is typically recommendable. Preprocessing operations might depend on the characteristics of the data, of the problem at hand, and of the specific learning approach that one wishes to adopt. The operations that are more often performed consist in removing seasonal trends if the data come from the observation of time-series, scaling, filtering out noise, and possibly suppressing outliers (Fayyad *et al.*, 1996). Experience indicates that a good data preprocessing allows for a more rapid and robust training of learning machines—see for instance Masters (1995).

Feature extraction: The goal of this phase is to extract from the pre-processed data a limited set of *predictors* of the phenomenon at hand. We wish to find the most *economical* representation of the information contained in the data that is necessary for training the learning machine. This phase is necessary for avoiding *collinearity* of data (Montgomery & Peck, 1992) in the input space, and to reduce the effects of the phenomenon that is known in the literature as the *curse of dimensionality* (Bellman, 1961), that is, the exponential explosion of the size of the problem with the growth of the number of variables considered. The typical ways that are followed in order to reduce the number of variables include *feature selection*, which consists in selecting the most predictive input variables, and *principal component analysis* (Myers, 1994) which consists in an appropriate linear combination of the original variables.

The result of the phases we just described is a set $\mathcal{Z} = \{(x_j, y_j)\}_{j=1}^N$ of input/output pairs, as described in Section 2.2.3, that can be fed to the learning machine for its training.

Parametric and structural identification

Let us consider now the practical problem of finding the function in $\mathcal{G} = \{g(x, \alpha) : \alpha \in \Lambda\}$ that minimizes the *empirical risk* $R_{\text{emp}}(\alpha) = \sum_{j=1}^N (y_j - g(x_j, \alpha))^2$. If the class $\mathcal{G}$ is particularly simple, it is typically possible to search it directly. The following two examples will serve to clarify this issue.

Linear models

Let us consider the case in which

$$g(x, \alpha) = \alpha_0 + \sum_{l=1}^{d} \alpha_l x^l, \qquad (2.22)$$

where x^l, with $l = 1 \dots d$, are the component of the input $x \in \mathbb{R}^d$; and α_l, with $l = 0 \dots d$, are the component of the parameters vector $\alpha \in \Lambda = \mathbb{R}^{d+1}$. In this case, an analytical solution is immediately available in closed form.[53] The same holds true for all classes of functions that are linear in their parameter α such as, for instance, the class

[53]The derivation is particularly simple in matrix notation. Let Y be a vector whose j-th component is y_j and X a $N \times d+1$ matrix whose j-th row is $1, x_j^1, x_j^2 \dots, x_j^d$, that is, the vector x_j with a prefixed 1 that accounts for the constant term in Equation 2.22. It results:

$$R_{\text{emp}}(\alpha) = \sum_{j=1}^{N} \Big(y_j - \alpha_0 - \sum_{l=1}^{d} \alpha_l x_j^l\Big)^2 = (Y - X\alpha)^T (Y - X\alpha).$$

In order to minimize $R_{\text{emp}}(\alpha)$, it is necessary and sufficient for $\bar{\alpha}$ to be a zero of the gradient $\nabla R_{\text{emp}}(\alpha) = -2X^T + 2X^T X\alpha$ of the empirical risk. Since the gradient of $R_{\text{emp}}(\alpha)$ is linear in α, it follows immediately that: $\bar{\alpha} = \left[X^T X\right]^{-1} X^T Y$. In words, in order to find the function that minimizes the empirical risk it is sufficient in this case to solve a linear system of equations of order $d + 1$, where d is the dimensionality of the input space.

of the polynomials $g(x,\alpha) = \sum_{l_1 l_2 \dots l_k} \alpha_{l_1 l_2 \dots l_k} x^{l_1} x^{l_2} \dots x^{l_k}$ of generic degree k,[54] or more in general all classes of functions that can be represented as a linear combination of terms: $g(x,\alpha) = \sum_{l=0}^{L} \alpha_l \Psi_l(x)$, where Ψ_l, with $l = 0 \dots L$ are a set of *basis functions*.

Neural networks with a fixed number of neurons

Let us consider a neural network whose hidden layer contains *exactly* k neurons. For a given training set $\mathcal{Z}$, training the network amounts to a search in the space of the parameters

$$\alpha = (\omega_{11} \dots \omega_{1k}, \omega_{21} \dots \omega_{2k} \dots \omega_{d1} \dots \omega_{dk}, \omega_1 \dots \omega_k) \in \mathbb{R}^{k(d+1)},$$

where the meaning of ω_{lm} and ω_l is the one given in Figure 2.7. In this case, a closed-form solution to the problem of minimizing the empirical risk is not available since, given the nonlinearity of the response of the neurons—see Figure 2.7(b)—the gradient of the empirical risk is not linear in the parameters. Nevertheless, an iterative search based on gradient descent can be performed through the so called *back-propagation* algorithm (Rumelhart *et al.*, 1986, 1995). Even if such a search is not guaranteed to find the global minimum of $R_{\text{emp}}(\alpha)$, it is typically able to find good local minima.

At first sight, these two examples appear conclusive: Given a training set and a parametric family of models—polynomials in the first example, neural networks in the second—we are able to find a set of parameters that minimizes the empirical risk. In the first of the examples, the optimal parameters are even given in closed form. Moreover, both polynomials (Weierstraß, 1885a,b) and neural networks (Cybenko, 1989; Hornik *et al.*, 1989) enjoy the property of being *universal approximators*: Provided the degree for polynomials, or the number of hidden neuron for neural networks, is sufficiently high, these models are able to approximate arbitrarily well any continuous function.

Unfortunately, at a closer analysis the situation is not so reassuring and the supervised learning practice is much more complex than that. The property of being a *universal approximators* enjoyed by a class of models, is in practice much more a *curse* rather than a *blessing*. It results indeed in a high *variance* of the fitted model that, as previously showed in Figure 2.6, washes out the advantages of being a universal approximator, that is, of having an arbitrarily low *bias*.

Practitioners call this phenomenon *over-fitting*: If the class $\mathcal{G}$ is too *rich and expressive* the fitted model will whimsically follow the *noise*, that is, the accidental peculiarities of the given training set, rather than extracting the essential traits of the underlying regression function.

[54] Here the indexes $l_1 l_2 \dots l_k$ range between 0 and d, $\alpha_{l_1 l_2 \dots l_k} = \alpha_{m_1 m_2 \dots m_k}$ if $m_1 m_2 \dots m_k$ is a permutation of $l_1 l_2 \dots l_k$, and we adopt the convention that $x^0 = 1$, so that the resulting $g(x,\alpha)$ is a non homogeneous polynomial of degree k.

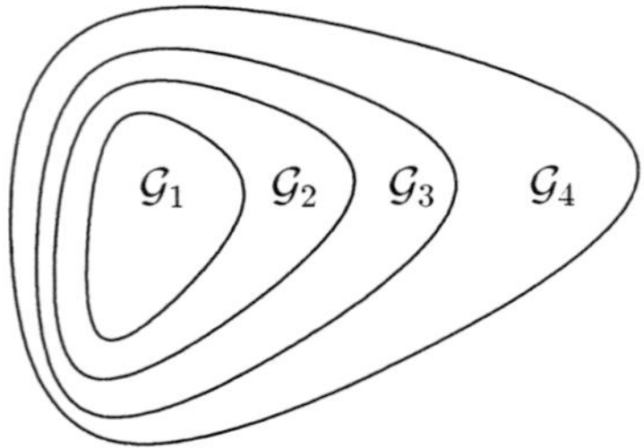

Figure 2.8: The class of functions is organized as a structure of nested subclasses.

In order to handle this problem, the supervised learning practice prescribes a *two-level* procedure composed of a **parametric identification** and of a **structural identification**: The overall class of function $\mathcal{G} = \{g(x, \alpha) : \alpha \in \Lambda\}$ is structured into a nested sequence of subclasses $\mathcal{G}_1 \subset \mathcal{G}_2 \subset \cdots \subset \mathcal{G}_K$, where $\mathcal{G}_k = \{g(x, \alpha) : \alpha \in \Lambda_k\}$—see Figure 2.8 for a graphical representation of the concept. The subclasses are such that each of them is *easily* searchable: Going back to the two examples discussed above, $\mathcal{G}_k$ could be the class of all polynomials of degree k or the class of all neural networks whose hidden layer is composed of k neurons. The **parametric identification** consists in finding, within each of the subclasses $\mathcal{G}_k$, the value α_N^k of the parameters that minimizes the empirical risk. On the other hand, the **structural identification** consists in selecting the best among the functions $g(x, \alpha_N^1), g(x, \alpha_N^2), \ldots, g(x, \alpha_N^K)$, which indirectly amounts to selecting the best of the subclasses $\mathcal{G}_1, \mathcal{G}_2, \ldots, \mathcal{G}_K$. While the parametric identification relies on the empirical risk minimization principle, the structural identification has to be based on some other criterion of selection. Indeed, since the functions $g(x, \alpha_N^1), g(x, \alpha_N^2), \ldots, g(x, \alpha_N^K)$ belong to subclasses of increasing complexity, the associate values of the empirical risk is an approximation more and more by defect of the actual risk. On the basis of Inequality 2.16, it is to be expected that the difference $R(\alpha_N^k) - R_{\text{emp}}(\alpha_N^k)$ increases with k. For this reason, the selection of the best among $g(x, \alpha_N^1), g(x, \alpha_N^2), \ldots, g(x, \alpha_N^K)$ is performed on the basis of the mean squared error these models present over a set of examples, called *validation set* or *test set*, that were not used during the parametric identification phase. The mean squared error on a *fresh* dataset is indeed an unbiased estimate of the actual risk.

To summarize, the two-level learning procedure consists in the following steps:

1. Split the original set $\mathcal{Z}$ of examples into two subsets: a training set $\mathcal{Z}_{\text{tr}}$ and a validation set $\mathcal{Z}_{\text{ts}}$;

2. Define a structure of nested subclasses of models: $\mathcal{G}_1 \subset \mathcal{G}_2 \subset \cdots \subset \mathcal{G}_K$,

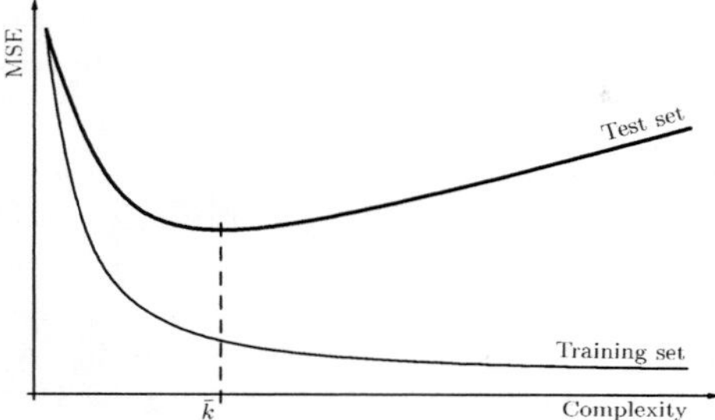

Figure 2.9: Mean squared error on the training set and on the test set. The error on the training set decreases monotonically with the complexity while the error on the training set, which is an unbiased estimate of the actual risk, decreases initially and then increases again.

with $\mathcal{G}_k = \{g(x, \alpha) : \alpha \in \Lambda_k\}$;

3. Within each subclass $\mathcal{G}_k$ find the function $g(x, \alpha^k_{\mathcal{Z}_{\text{tr}}})$ which minimizes the empirical risk calculated on the basis of the training set $\mathcal{Z}_{\text{tr}}$;

4. Validate on the test set $\mathcal{Z}_{\text{ts}}$ each of the functions $g(x, \alpha^k_{\mathcal{Z}_{\text{tr}}})$, with $k = 1 \dots K$.

5. Select among the K functions $g(x, \alpha^k_{\mathcal{Z}_{\text{tr}}})$, with $k = 1 \dots K$, the function $g(x, \alpha^{\bar{k}}_{\mathcal{Z}_{\text{tr}}})$ that obtains the best measure of performance on the validation set.[55]

The separation between a parametric identification and a structural identification phase results particularly effective in practice. In particular, the validation of the fitted models plays a fundamental role in avoiding over-fitting. The typical trend of the error on the training set and on the test set with increasing complexity is shown in Figure 2.9. The error on the training set decreases monotonically with the complexity of the subclass: the larger is the class, the lower is the bias component of the error and the lower gets the value of the empirical risk. On the other hand, the error on the test set, which is an unbiased estimate of the actual risk, decreases initially and then increases again: In a first phase, the increasing

[55] More complex schemes exists. One which is frequently applied in practice is called *cross-validation* (Stone, 1974; Kohavi, 1995) and consists in splitting the original set of example $\mathcal{Z}$ into L subsets $\mathcal{Z}_1, \mathcal{Z}_2, \dots, \mathcal{Z}_L$ of approximately the same size. In turn, one of these subsets, say $\mathcal{Z}_l$ is held-out and the others $\mathcal{Z} \setminus \mathcal{Z}_l$ are used for performing a parametric identification. Let $g(x, \alpha^{-l})$ be the model fitted on $\mathcal{Z} \setminus \mathcal{Z}_l$ and $\text{MSE}_l = 1/|\mathcal{Z}_l| \sum_{j \in \mathcal{Z}_l} (y_j - g(x_j, \alpha^{-l}))^2$ the *mean squared error* on $\mathcal{Z}_l$ used as validation set. The same procedure is iterated over all the subsets. The overall performance index is given by $\text{MSE} = 1/L \sum_{l=1}^{L} \text{MSE}_l$.

complexity of the considered class of functions improves the performance. Passed a certain optimal value for the complexity, the model starts over-fitting and the overall performance deteriorates.

2.2.7 Racing methods for model selection

In this section, we present and discuss a class of algorithms, known as *racing* algorithms, proposed within the machine learning community for solving the model selection problem (Maron & Moore, 1994). These algorithms are particularly relevant in this thesis because they serve as source of inspiration for tackling the problem of tuning metaheuristics. In particular, Chapter 4 introduces *F-Race*, an algorithm we developed which proved to be able to handle effectively the tuning problem and which, as its name suggests, belongs to the class of *racing* algorithms.

In Maron & Moore (1994) *Hoeffding race* is proposed as a method for accelerating model selection in supervised learning.[56] In particular, Maron & Moore are interested in selecting the set of best structural parameters for a memory based method. The measure of performance is here the *mean squared error* computed through the *leave-one-out* validation method which is an extreme form of cross-validation[57] where the held-out sets consist of just one example. In other words, leave-one-out consists in predicting each example in the available set on the basis of all other examples; a measure of the accuracy of the model structure at hand is then given by the average of the N observed squared errors, if N is the number of examples in the data set. Formally, the leave-one-out mean squared error of a given model is:

$$\hat{\mu}^{loo} = \frac{1}{N}\sum_{l=1}^{N}\left(y_l - \hat{y}_l^{-l}\right)^2, \tag{2.23}$$

where $\hat{y}_l^{-l}$ is the prediction of the output y_l obtained by the model at hand on the basis of all available examples but (x_l, y_l).

In the general case, leave-one-out is a very expensive procedure: it requires *training* N times the model structure, once on each of the N subsets of size $N-1$ that can be extracted from a database of N examples. Memory-based approaches are an exception in this respect: In memory-based methods no real training phase is involved and the computation time needed for performing k predictions, each on the basis of a different set of examples, amounts exactly to the time needed for performing k predictions, all of them on the basis of the same set of examples.[58]

[56] The main idea behind the method had been previously exposed in Maron's Master's thesis (1994).

[57] See note 55.

[58] This is clearly not true in the general case. For instance, in case of neural networks the training phase is rather time consuming: When given a new set of examples, a neural network is not able to directly perform predictions on the basis of this set. A training phase, typically

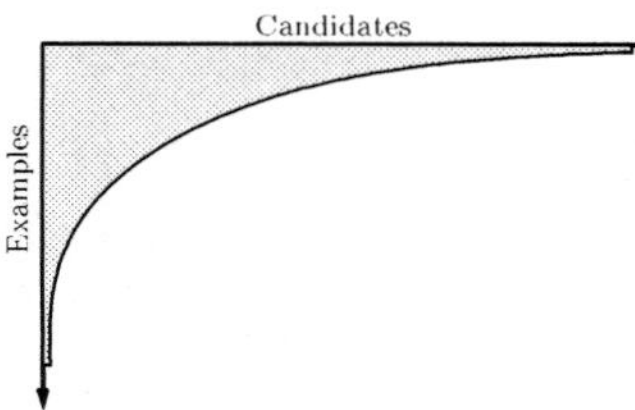

Figure 2.10: Graphical representation of the amount of computation involved in *Hoeffding race*. The leave-one-out evaluation of the candidate model structures is performed incrementally: One often the other, the examples of the dataset are put aside, each of the candidates performs a prediction of the output of the held-out example and the estimate of the leave-one-out measure for each candidate is updated. As soon as sufficient evidence is gathered that a candidate is suboptimal, it is discarded from further evaluation. As the evaluation proceeds, it focuses thus more and more on the most promising candidates.

The main idea introduced in Maron & Moore (1994) with *Hoeffding race*—idea that then characterized the whole class of *racing* algorithms—is that the search for the best model structure can be speeded up by discarding inferior candidates as soon as sufficient evidence is gathered against them. Indeed, the evaluation of the leave-one-out measure $\hat{\mu}^{loo}(\theta)$ concerning the generic candidate θ, can be performed incrementally: Being the average of N squared errors, each regarding one of the N examples in the dataset, this quantity can be approximated by the average $\hat{\mu}_k^{loo}(\theta)$ which is calculated on any subset of size k of these errors. It should be noted that, irrespectively of the size k of the sample considered, the average calculated on this sample is an *unbiased* estimate of the mean squared error $\mu(\theta)$ and that, moreover, the variance of such an estimate decreases with k. As the computation proceeds and the estimate of the leave-one-out measure for the candidates gets sharper and sharper, a statistical test of hypothesis can be adopted for deciding if the observed difference in the leave-one-out estimates of the given candidates is significant. In this case, the inferior candidates are discarded from the race and will not be further evaluated—see Figure 2.10 for a graphical representation of a race.

The original *racing* algorithm, *Hoeffding race*, adopted as statistical test one based on a Hoeffding's formula (Hoeffding, 1963) concerning the confidence on the empirical mean of k positive numbers $c_1, \dots, c_k$, sampled independently from the same distribution, when an upper bound on the random variable c is known. The probability that the true mean μ of the random variable c is more than ϵ

based on some variant of the back-propagation algorithm, is needed before the neural network is operational.

from the empirical mean $\hat{\mu}_k = 1/k \sum_{l=1}^{k} c_l$ is:

$$Prob\{|\mu - \hat{\mu}_k| > \epsilon\} < 2e^{-2k\epsilon^2/B^2} \tag{2.24}$$

where B is an upper bound on c. On the basis of Inequality 2.24 it is possible to define an interval $[\hat{\mu}_k - \epsilon, \hat{\mu}_k + \epsilon]$ around the empirical mean $\hat{\mu}_k$ in which the true mean μ should be with a confidence $1 - \delta$, formally:

$$Prob\{|\mu - \hat{\mu}(k)| > \epsilon\} < \delta.$$

It follows that after having observed k numbers $c_1, \dots, c_k$, we are able to establish that, with confidence $1 - \delta$, the true mean μ is within a distance ϵ from the empirical estimate $\hat{\mu}_k$ where:

$$\epsilon = \sqrt{\frac{B^2 \log(2/\delta)}{2k}}. \tag{2.25}$$

The *Hoeffding race* algorithm exploits Hoeffding's bound and defines, for each candidate θ, an interval

$$I_k(\theta) = [L_k(\theta), U_k(\theta)] = [\hat{\mu}_k^{loo}(\theta) - \epsilon, \hat{\mu}_k^{loo}(\theta) + \epsilon], \tag{2.26}$$

where $\hat{\mu}_k^{loo}(\theta)$ is a leave-one-out estimate based on k predictions of the true mean squared error $\mu(\theta)$ associated with candidate θ. On the basis of 2.25, the interval $I_k(\theta)$ is such that it contains the true value of $\mu(\theta)$ with confidence $1 - \delta$.

Hoeffding race starts with a collection of candidates and proceeds considering iteratively the examples in a given dataset of size N. At step k the k-th example in the dataset, (x_k, y_k), is held-out and all candidates in the race are called to predict the output y_k on the basis of all other examples in the dataset. For the generic candidate θ, the error $e_k(\theta) = y_k - \hat{y}_k^{-k}(\theta)$ is used to update the estimated leave-one-out mean squared error $\hat{\mu}_k^{loo}(\theta) = 1/k \sum_{l=1}^{k} e_l^2(\theta)$. Moreover, thanks to Equation 2.26, an upper bound $U_k(\theta)$ and a lower bound $L_k(\theta)$ are given for the true mean square error $\mu(\theta)$ of candidate θ. After completing step k and before iterating the procedure, all candidates whose lower bound rests above the upper bound of the best candidate so far are eliminated from the race and will not be considered for further evaluation. See Figure 2.11 for a graphical representation. On the basis of Equation 2.25, the elimination of *each* candidate configuration is performed with confidence at least equal to $1 - \delta$, that is, the probability of eliminating a candidate whose true mean square error is indeed better than the one of the best candidate so far, is less than $1 - \delta$. As the evaluation of the surviving candidates proceeds and more and more examples are considered in the leave-one-out procedure, the intervals $I_k(\theta)$ around the empirical estimates get tighter and the selection procedure gets sharper and sharper.

The main advantage of the adoption of a selection procedure based on Inequality 2.24, is the nonparametric nature of this inequality which implies that

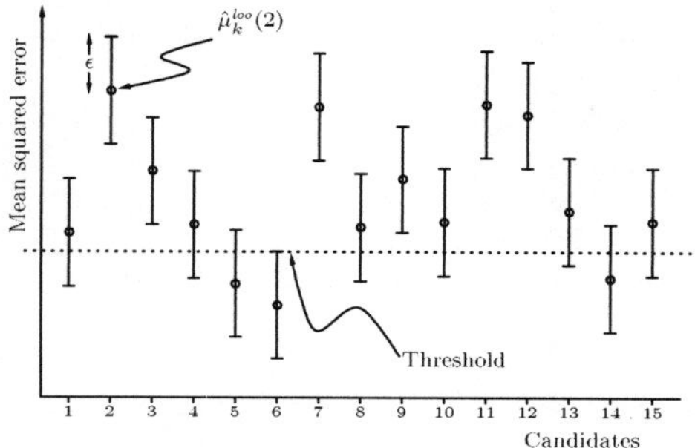

Figure 2.11: An example: After say k steps, candidate 6 is the best in the group and the upper bound on its estimate defines the value of the *threshold*. All candidates whose lower bound rest above the threshold are discarded. In this specific example, candidates 2, 3, 7, 9, 11, and 12 are eliminated. For each candidate θ, upper and lower bound are both ϵ-far from the estimated mean squared error $\hat{\mu}_k^{loo}(\theta)$.

its validity is guaranteed irrespectively of the distribution of the stochastic variables involved. The down side is represented by the fact that in most applications either no bound B is given on the observations, or the available bound is so loose to make Inequality 2.24 unusable. In their original works, Maron & Moore adopt an *estimate* of the unknown bound. This detail of the algorithm is indeed left unexplained in the first paper on *Hoeffding race* and is described only in a subsequent paper (Maron & Moore, 1997). The estimate is obtained empirically as the maximum squared error observed on an initial number of test examples. In Maron & Moore (1997), the authors describe a *Hoeffding race* procedure that starts discarding inferior candidates only after having observed their behavior on 30 test cases. During this preliminary phase, the bound is estimated. This solution is rather questionable from different points of view. First, the empirical estimation of the maximum of a distribution is particularly problematic.[59] Second, the Hoeffding bound given in Inequality 2.24 is is not valid in this context since the upper bound B is unknown and it is replaced here by an approximation by defect. Third, the 30 initial evaluations of all candidates can be a large

[59]It is indeed always biased, since all possible observations are by definition less or equal the quantity to be estimated. Even worse, the uncertainty on the estimate does not decrease with the size of the sample—as it does, for instance, in the case of the estimation of the expected value. Indeed, irrespectively of the size of the sample, it is always possible that the observed variable might assume an arbitrary large value which might emerge with very low probability: In virtue of its low probability, such a large value might fail to reveal itself in samples of any arbitrary size.

amount of computation time if the number of candidates is large and this reduces the practical applicability of the method.

Notwithstanding these issues with the use of the Hoeffding bound, the idea behind the *racing* approach is very appealing. In order to overcome the above mentioned problems while still exploiting the core racing idea, some new *racing* algorithms based on a different statistical tests were proposed in Moore & Lee (1994). Among them, *BRACE* is based on Bayesian statistics and implements a statistical technique known as *blocking* (Box *et al.*, 1978; Dean & Voss, 1999; Montgomery, 2000). A *block design* is an experimental setting that is possibly adopted when two or more candidates have to be compared and that improves the precision with which the comparison is made. A *block* is a set of relatively homogeneous experimental conditions under which all candidates are tested.[60] In the context of the selection of the best candidate on the basis of a leave-one-out validation, adopting a *block design* is particularly natural and simple: Indeed each of the surviving candidates is tested on *the same* examples. Each example is therefore a *block* in the considered design.

In *BRACE*, for each example (x_k, y_k) in the dataset and for each pair of candidates still in the race, say candidates θ and θ', we are interested in the quantity $h_k(\theta, \theta')$ defined by:

$$h_k(\theta, \theta') = e_k^2(\theta) - e_k^2(\theta').$$

where $e_k(\theta) = y_k - \hat{y}_k^{-k}(\theta)$ and $e_k(\theta') = y_k - \hat{y}_k^{-k}(\theta')$ are the errors yielded on the k-th example by candidate θ and θ' respectively. The sign of $h_k(\theta, \theta')$ indicates which of the two candidates obtained a better performance on example k: if it is negative, candidate θ was better than θ'; if it is positive, the other way around. During the race, the algorithm incrementally estimates the mean value $\hat{\mu}_k(\theta, \theta')$ and the variance $\hat{\sigma}_k^2(\theta, \theta')$ of $h_k(\theta, \theta')$, for each pair θ and θ' in the race. On the basis of these estimates a set of statistical tests is performed at each step of the algorithm to check if some candidate is significantly worse than any other. In this case, the inferior candidate is discarded from the race. Under some general conditions, the statistical test adopted in *BRACE* is equivalent to a *paired t-test* (Sheskin, 2000) performed between each pair of surviving candidates. Contrary to the test adopted in *Hoeffding race*, the *t-test* is a parametric procedure and therefore it relies on some assumptions concerning the stochastic variables involved, namely,

[60] An example might help here. Let us suppose we wish to compare the braking distance of three different cars under a variety of conditions. A *block* is here the definition of each of these conditions: initial speed, temperature and humidity of the road surface, wear and tear of tires, *etc.* A *block design* prescribes that the three cars should be tested in the same conditions. For instance, the experiments concerning a block could be performed in the following way: A road segment is selected and one after the other, possibly in a randomly selected order, the three cars, which have previously covered the same number of kilometers, are driven at a predefined speed along the road segment and when a predefined position is reached the brakes are applied. On a given *block* the cars should be tested within a reasonably short period of time to minimize the variations of the atmospheric and road surface conditions.

it assumes that the quantities $h_k(\theta, \theta')$ are normally distributed. Notwithstanding these limitation, *BRACE* proved to be very effective and is reported to yield better results than *Hoeffding race* (Moore & Lee, 1994; Maron & Moore, 1997). We definitely agree with the proponents of the method when they ascribe the observed superiority to the effectiveness of the *block design*.

It is worth noticing here that the strength of *Hoeffding race* is the adoption of a nonparametric test, even if the adopted test requires the knowledge of a bound on the observed error and this reduces dramatically the range of applicability of the method. On the other hand, *BRACE* proves that the adoption of a *block design* is particularly effective in a racing setting. Nonetheless, in order to include this feature, the authors had to adopt a parametric statistical test whose applicability is restricted by the hypothesis that the quantities involved should be normally distributed. *F-Race* (Birattari *et al.*, 2002), the racing method we propose in Chapter 4 for tuning metaheuristics, joins in one single algorithm the best features of *Hoeffding race* and of *BRACE*. Indeed, *F-Race* is based on the *Friedman two-way analysis of variance by ranks*, also known simply as *Friedman test*, which implements a *block design* in an extremely natural way and, at the same time, is nonparametric and therefore does not rely on any assumption on the distribution of the stochastic quantities under analysis.

2.3 Discussion

This chapter has introduced two research fields: **combinatorial optimization**, and **supervised learning**. These two fields are somehow related: as we pointed out in Section 2.2.3 while solving a learning problem, an optimization problem has to be solved as a subproblem. Nonetheless, supervised learning cannot be trivially reduced to optimization and requires the development of a considerably different conceptual framework. The presence of an introduction to these two different fields is justified by the interdisciplinary character of the thesis: The focus of the thesis in on the problem of tuning metaheuristics but most of the contributions, both in the formal definition of the tuning problem and in the development of a tuning algorithm, come from machine learning ideas.

The problem of tuning metaheuristics emerged in the optimization field only quite recently. Metaheuristics are a relative young class of algorithms which present features that are quite different from those of other optimization algorithms. In particular, most optimization algorithms are designed for solving a specific optimization problem. On the other hand, metaheuristics are problem-independent approaches to optimization: Rather than as *algorithms*, they should be more properly seen as general *algorithmic templates* that need to be instantiated on the specific problem at hand in order to yield a fully functioning algorithm. It is precisely in this process of *instantiation* that the need of some tuning procedure emerges: In order to be a true multi-purpose approach and to lend itself to the solution of a wide range of different optimization problems, a metaheuristic comes with a set of different modules that may be possibly included or not, and with a variety of parameters to be tuned. So far, metaheuristics have been tuned by hand on the basis of some *rules-of-thumb*: Such a manual approach is without doubts time-consuming and tedious and relies completely on human experience and intuition. Although viable in academic studies, this approach to tuning does not fit the needs of a large scale adoption of metaheuristics in real-world applications.

To overcome these limitations, some energy has been devoted by the research community to the definition of some automatic tuning procedures. In our view, much of the effort in this direction has been frustrated by the fact that a precise definition of the tuning problem is still missing and that its true nature has not been completely understood.

The main contribution of this thesis consists precisely in giving a formal definition of the tuning problem which, as we will see in Chapter 3, happens to highlight the similarities between the tuning problem itself and the supervised learning problem. Moreover, the tuning algorithm *F-Race*, presented in Chapter 4, belongs to the class of *racing* algorithms introduced in the machine learning community for solving the model selection problem—see Section 2.2.7. Further contributions discussed in the thesis that derive from machine learning ideas are the experimental methodology adopted in Chapter 5, and much of the analysis proposed in Chapter 6.

Galileo formulated the problem of determining the velocity of light, but did not solve it. The formulation of a problem is often more essential than its solution, which may be merely a matter of mathematical or experimental skill. To raise new problems, new possibilities, to regard old problems from a new angle, requires creative imagination and marks real advance in science.

Albert Einstein and Leopold Infeld

Chapter 3

Statement of the tuning problem

Metaheuristics are general algorithmic templates whose components need to be instantiated and properly tuned in order to yield a fully functioning algorithm. We call a *configuration* of a metaheuristic any possible instantiation of this template while with the expression *tuning problem* we denote the problem of properly instantiating the template, that is, the problem of choosing among the set of possible components and assigning specific values to all free parameters.

As practitioners know, metaheuristics are in general quite sensitive to the value of their parameters and a careful fine-tuning typically improves the performance in a significant way. This chapter is devoted to the definition of a formal framework in which the tuning problem can be cast and solved. Before entering in the technical details, an informal description of a typical situation in which the tuning problem arises is given in Section 3.1. In Section 3.2 we give the formal position of the problem and in Section 3.3 we discuss some possible extensions and variants. Section 3.4 summarizes and discusses the results presented in the chapter.

3.1 An informal example

The tuning problem is best introduced by an informal example: MARIO'S PIZZA DELIVERY problem. This simple example has the merit of including all the elements that characterize tuning problems as they occur in the real-world. These elements are cast into a formal framework in Section 3.2.

Mario's pizza delivery

Mario has a very successful wood-oven pizza restaurant that delivers pizzas all over the city to his many customers. Mario's is open around the clock and collects orders on the phone. Every 30 minutes, a delivery boy packs on the back of his motorbike the pizzas to be delivered to the customers that called during the last 30 minutes, he has a quick look of 1 minute at the city map for scheduling the delivery tour, and then he hits the road to deliver a still smoking pizza to Mario's aficionados.

Despite the exceptional amount of work at the restaurant, Mario reads a lot: He learned about metaheuristics and he wants to give them a try. What metaheuristic should he use for scheduling the delivery tours? What should be the values of the free parameters? In order to have an answer to these questions, he makes a deal with your lab: If within one month you produce a high-performing metaheuristic for scheduling his delivery tours, you will have 1000 coupons, each valid for one of Mario's famous pizzas.

We are already in the position of highlighting the following elements of Mario's problem that start shedding light on the problem of tuning metaheuristics in general:

1. Scheduling each of the delivery tours is a combinatorial optimization problem, namely a traveling salesman problem, that can be solved with a metaheuristic.[1]

2. Every 30 minutes a new instance has to be solved: Mario's problem is indeed characterized by a **stream of instances**.

3. A limited amount of time of 1 minute is available for solving each instance: The boy has to leave fairly quickly in order to be able to deliver a still smoking pizza.

4. Another time constraint is given: we are supposed to produce a fine-tuned metaheuristic within one month.

Before proceeding further in our analysis of the tuning problem, an important point has to be made clear. In the example, we are supposed to produce a "high-performing" metaheuristic for scheduling Mario's delivery tours but no precise meaning has been given, so far, to this sentence. In order to explicitly define

[1]Our choice to refer to traveling salesman in our informal presentation of the tuning problem was mostly guided by the sake of clarity: Since we expect our readers to be fairly familiar with it, they will not be distracted by its details and will rather focus on the tuning problem which is the real issue in the example.

a criterion for measuring the quality of a metaheuristic, two different orders of considerations are needed, the first pertains to the evaluation of the performance on **a single instance**, while the second extends the measure of the performance to **a whole class of instances**. While the former is rather simple to handle, the second is of a more subtle nature and is intimately related to the actual original contribution of the whole chapter.

Measuring the performance on a single instance

For what concerns the evaluation of the performance of a metaheuristic on **a single instance**, two issues have to be considered.

First, an appropriate cost function has to be defined. In Mario's example, the length of the tour found by the metaheuristic in the given amount of time appears as a natural and reasonable choice. Other functions could be equally reasonable. For example, the expected time needed for completing the tour is a measure that is somehow related to the tour length but that could be more appropriate if some streets are known to be particularly congested and therefore require, in order to be covered, a longer time than other of equal length, but typically less congested. Yet another cost function for which similar considerations hold is the amount of fuel needed by the boy's motorbike for completing the tour. The selection among these and other possible cost functions is very problem-specific and does not have any direct impact on the definition of the tuning problem. In this thesis, we always take for granted that an appropriate cost function has been defined for the underlying optimization problem.

Second, a metaheuristic is a stochastic algorithm and therefore different runs on a same instance will typically produce different solutions, each characterized by a different cost. When observing a stochastic quantity, as in this case the cost, we are typically interested in its *expected value*.[2] A single run of the algorithm on the instance at hand produces by itself an unbiased estimate of the expected value.[3] If we were interested in a better estimate for what concerns a specific instance, we would consider the average of more runs in order to have a reduced variance.

Measuring the performance on a whole class of instances

For what concerns the evaluation of the performance over **a whole class of instances**, a deeper insight has to be gained. Before proceeding further, we need to elaborate on the very notion of *class of instances*. To this aim, we need to define

[2]The possibility of adopting other statistics different from the expected value is discussed in Section 3.3.4.

[3]An estimator $\hat{q}$ of a quantity q a is said to be *unbiased* if $E[\hat{q}] = q$. Otherwise, it is called *biased* with bias $b = E[\hat{q}] - q$. The variance $\sigma^2_{\hat{q}}$ of $\hat{q}$ is $\sigma^2_{\hat{q}} = E\left[(\hat{q} - E[\hat{q}])^2\right]$. See Mendenhall *et al.* (1986) for an organic introduction to estimation theory.

some sort of model of how the stream of instances observed by Mario is generated. It should be noticed that among all possible TRAVELING SALESMAN instances, some will be more likely to occur than others. For example, the morphological features of the city itself rules out a large share of possible instances: An instance presenting nodes that fall outside the urban area will never occur. The same applies if a node of the instance is placed in a non residential area, such as the middle of a park, an industrial area, the bed of a river, and so on: no customer will ever request a delivery in such areas. On the contrary, an instance is more likely to occur if one of the nodes is placed, for example, at the university dorms: students are known to consume large amounts of pizza. Similarly, if Mario has heavily (and successfully) advertised in some neighborhoods, it is to be expected that instances that present nodes in these neighborhoods will occur more likely than those that do not.

The above discussion makes quite natural the introduction of a probabilistic model of the stream of instances. We consider here a simple probabilistic model, namely one in which the instances in the stream are independently and identically distributed. This simple model will serve the purpose of this section and of most of the thesis. A discussion of more general models is given in Sections 3.3.1 and 3.3.2. In the terms of a probabilistic model it is now possible to give a meaning to the notion of performance over a whole class of instances: we define the performance over a class of instances to be the *expected value*[4] of the performance over the instances of the class or, more roughly speaking, the average of the performance obtained on each instance, weighted by the probability that each instance occurs.

Having defined an appropriate way for measuring the performance of a metaheuristic both on a single instance and on a whole class of instances, we are now in the position of stating the tuning problem.

The ultimate goal of tuning

With respect to the concept of *stream of instances* we can state that the ultimate goal of tuning is to select a proper configuration that maximizes the performance on the instances that we will face in the future.

It goes without saying that future instances are not known in advance and, in particular, they are not available during the tuning phase. Nevertheless, some statistical properties of future instances can be extracted from past observations. Such a statement rests on the very basic assumption underlying any scientific investigation or any technological development: the hypothesis of *regularity of nature.*[5] On the basis of this typically implicit hypothesis, we expect that in

[4]Also for what concerns the performance over a class of instances, different statistics can be considered. A discussion is given in Section 3.3.4.

[5]This is not to endorse a vision of science based on induction (Piscopo & Birattari, 2002). Indeed, even if we question the idea that inductive inference, justified on the basis of the

Figure 3.1: When tuning a metaheuristic, we aim at optimizing its performance on future instances, but only past instances are available. On the basis of an hypothesis of *regularity of nature*, we assume that future instance will be generated by the same mechanism that generated the ones observed in the past. Namely, we assume that both past and future instances are extracted according to the same probabilistic model.

some sense **the past informs on the future** and that it is therefore possible to *generalize* past experience to future events. In this precise sense, tuning a metaheuristic is a genuine learning problem. This observation justifies the formal position of the tuning problem we give in Section 3.2 and the tuning algorithm we present in Chapter 4, which are both heavily influenced by concepts and methods pertaining to the machine learning field. On the other hand, the successful position of the problem and the applications of the algorithm will clarify the full implications of the statement and all its practical relevance.

In practice, the tuning process is a selection of the best configuration, performed on the basis of instances observed in the past. With reference again to MARIO'S problem, we may observe that the actual reason for developing a metaheuristic for scheduling delivery tours is that it will be then (hopefully) employed in practice at the restaurant. The **life-cycle**[6] of our metaheuristics is composed of two phases:

hypothesis of *regularity of nature*, is a solid ground for a final validation of scientific theories, we have to recognize to this hypothesis a fundamental regulative role. This position is already clear in Hume's writings: David Hume addressed the issue in the 18th century in a particularly influential way, and no analysis has managed to evade Hume's critique ever since. Hume became skeptical on the possibility of giving a logical justification to the practice of inferring knowledge about future events from past experience. He pointed out that all justifications of induction present some major logical flaw, in particular, justifying induction on the grounds that it has worked in the past relies on a circular argument.

According to Hume (1748), any inference from the past to the future is based solely on what he calls *custom* or *habit* and to which, in any case, he confers great practical relevance:

> *Custom, then, is the great guide of human life. It is that principle alone which renders our experience useful to us, and makes us expect, for the future, a similar train of events with those which have appeared in the past. Without the influence of custom, we should be entirely ignorant of every matter of fact beyond what is immediately present to the memory and senses. We should never know how to adjust means to ends, or to employ our natural powers in the production of any effect. There would be an end at once of all action, as well as of the chief part of speculation.*
> David Hume.

[6]A discussion of the notion of *life-cycle model* for metaheuristics is given in Chapter 6.

A development phase which takes place at our workshop and during which we develop the code and we tune the algorithm.

A production phase during which the algorithm is *located in its production environment*, that is, Mario's pizza restaurant.

These phases are disjoint in time and separated by the moment in which the metaheuristic leaves the workshop to enter the location of exploitation. Of these two phases, the former relies on past instances while the latter will have to deal with future ones. The link between the two is ensured by the hypothesis that the future will be *in some sense* similar to the past. Namely, both past and future instances belong to the same **class of instances** and are therefore generated according to the same mechanism: They are independently sampled from the same *unknown* distribution.

3.2 The formal position of the problem

In order to give a formal definition of the general problem of tuning a metaheuristic, we consider the following objects:

- Θ is the set of candidate configurations.
- I is the typically infinite set of instances.
- P_I is a probability measure over the set I of instances: With some abuse of notation, we indicate with $P_I(i)$ the probability that the instance i is selected for being solved.[7]
- $t : I \to \mathbb{R}$ is a function associating to every instance the computation time that is allocated to it.
- c is a random variable representing the cost of the best solution found by running configuration θ on instance i for $t(i)$ seconds.[8]
- $C \subset \mathbb{R}$ is the range of c, that is, the possible values for the cost of the best solution found in a run of a configuration $\theta \in \Theta$ on an instance $i \in I$.
- P_C is a probability measure over the set C: With the notation[9] $P_C(c|\theta, i)$, we indicate the probability that c is the cost of the best solution found by running for $t(i)$ seconds configuration θ on instance i.

[7]Since a probability measure is associated to (sub)sets and not to single elements, the correct notation should be $P_I(\{i\})$. Our notational abuse consists therefore in using the same symbol i both for the element $i \in I$, and for the singleton $\{i\} \subset I$.

[8]In the following, the dependency of c on t will be often implicit.

[9]The same remark as in Note 7 applies here.

- $\mathcal{C}(\theta) = \mathcal{C}(\theta|\Theta, I, P_I, P_C, t)$ is the criterion that needs to be optimized with respect to θ. In the most general case it measures in some sense the desirability of θ.

- T is the total amount of time available for experimenting with the given candidate configurations on the available instances before delivering the selected configuration.

On the basis of these concepts, the problem of configuring a metaheuristic can be formally described by the 7-tuple $\langle\Theta, I, P_I, P_C, t, \mathcal{C}, T\rangle$. The solution of this problem is the configuration $\bar{\theta}$ such that:

$$\bar{\theta} = \arg\min_{\theta} \mathcal{C}(\theta). \tag{3.1}$$

As far as the criterion $\mathcal{C}$ is concerned, different alternatives are possible—see Section 3.3.4 for a discussion of the issue. In the following, we consider the optimization of the expected value of the cost c. This criterion is adopted in many different applications and, besides being quite natural, it is often very convenient from both the theoretical and the practical point of view. Formally:

$$\mathcal{C}(\theta) = E_{I,C}[c] = \int c \, \mathrm{d}P_C(c|\theta, i) \, \mathrm{d}P_I(i), \tag{3.2}$$

where the expectation is considered with respect to both P_I and P_C, and the integration is taken in the Lebesgue sense (Billingsley, 1986).

The measures P_I and P_C are usually not explicitly available and the analytical solution of the integrals in Equation 3.2, one for each configuration θ, is not possible. In order to overcome this limitation, the integrals defined in Equation 3.2 can be estimated in a Monte Carlo fashion on the basis of a training set of instances, as it is shown in Chapter 4.

It is worth noticing here that a possible difficulty might arise with Equation 3.2 if for a given configuration θ, an instance i with $P_I(i) > 0$ exists, such that the probability is non null that θ fails to find any feasible solution of i within the given amount of time $t(i)$. Since it results natural to assign an infinite value to c in case of failure in retrieving a feasible solution, the integral given in Equation 3.2 does not converge under this circumstances, and we should assign an infinite value to the criterion $\mathcal{C}(\theta)$. In any case, notwithstanding the unaesthetic nature of dealing with infinite quantities, this does not cause any major theoretical nor practical problem.[10]

[10]Often an upper bound $B(i)$ on the cost of the solutions of instance i is available. In such a case, one might wish to assign the value $B(i)$ to c if configuration θ fails to find any feasible solution of i within time $t(i)$. In this case the problem of dealing with infinite quantities does not even arise.

3.3 Possible variants and extensions

The formal definition of the tuning problem that is provided in Section 3.2 is general enough to cover a wide range of practical problems. Nevertheless, it does not directly include all possible specific tuning problems that practitioners are called to face in the real-world when tackling optimization problems with metaheuristics.

This section describes some possible cases and discusses how to describe them in the terms of the formal definition given in Section 3.2.

3.3.1 Problem subclasses and *a priori* information

In the definition of the tuning problem given in this chapter, a tacit assumption is made that instances are *a priori* indistinguishable. In such a case, the tuning problem is stated as the problem of finding the configuration θ that provides the lowest expected cost over the whole class of instances. On the other hand, if an *indicator* is available which provides a way to distinguish among instances and to cluster them into subclasses in a meaningful way, such information can be used to reformulate the original tuning problem into a collection of subproblems, each referring to one of the subclasses.

If the partition of the space of the instances is properly done, an instance will be more similar *in some profitable sense* to the instances belonging to the same cluster rather than to others. It is reasonable to expect in this case that the configuration selected for a given subclass will obtain on that subclass a better performance than the generic configuration selected for the whole class of instances: The collection of specialized configuration is therefore expected to produce better results than the generic configuration.

In this case the underlying model of how instances in the stream are generated is a *hierarchical* one, as the one represented in Figure 3.2. By adopting this model, we accept the working hypothesis that instances are generated in two steps:

1. At the top-level, possibly according to a random experiment, the selection is made of the subclass to which the instance to be generated will belong;

2. At the bottom-level, the instance is actually generated according to the probability measure defining the subclass selected at step 1. Within each subclass, instances are identically and independently distributed.

For each instance in the stream we observe the instance itself, together with the *indicator* of the subclass to which it belongs.

MARIO'S problem provides an example of how problem subclasses can be defined: We could expect *day-time* instances to be somehow different from *night-time* ones. Let's say that we expect, or we know on the basis of past experience, that night-time instances tends to be smaller in terms of number of customers to

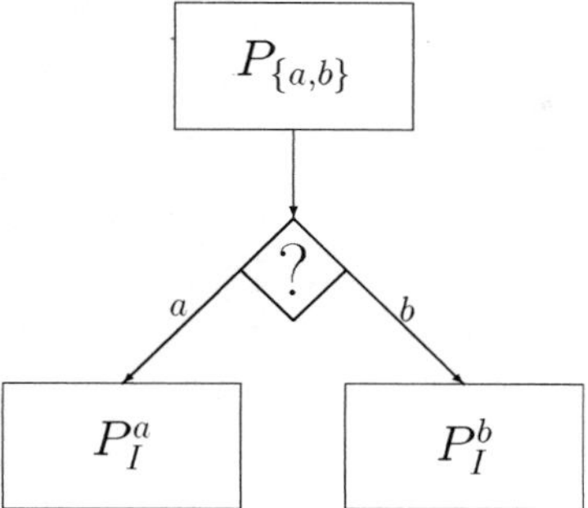

Figure 3.2: Graphical representation of a hierarchical model. At the top-level, a subclass is extracted; the actual instance is then extracted according to the probability measure characterizing the selected subclass.

be served, and are characterized by a larger number of calls from the university dorms. On the other hand, day-time instances are larger and customers tend to concentrate downtown, in the business area of the city, where streets are narrow and traffic jams are a standard. On the basis of this *a priori* information, we expect that rather than considering a single tuning problem we would better look for two configurations, each one specialized for one of the two subclasses of instances. A graphical representation of the decomposition of MARIO'S problem into two subproblems is given in Figure 3.3.

A further generalization of this issue is given in the Section 3.3.2.

3.3.2 Generic probabilistic models

In this thesis, we consider a simple model of how instances occur, namely, we assume that all instances in the stream are independent and identically distributed. In Section 3.3.1 a first possible extension is discussed. However, the assumption can also be removed by considering more complex models that allow temporal correlation in the characteristics of the instances.

The most general model that presents this feature is the **hidden Markov model** (Rabiner, 1989). By adopting this model, we accept the working hypothesis that an underlying *finite-state machine* evolves in time from state to state. At each state transition, an instance is generated by sampling an unknown distribution associated with the current state. For convenience, we distinguish here two cases: the one in which the underlying finite-state machine is deterministic and the more general case in which it is stochastic.

An hidden Markov model with an underlying deterministic process is graph-

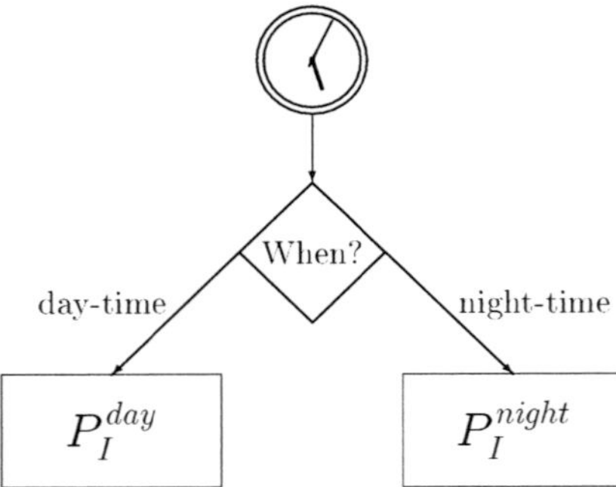

Figure 3.3: Graphical representation of the decomposition of MARIO'S problem into two subproblems. The *indicator*, in this case, is the time at which the instance emerged. Within each subclass, instances are identically and independently distributed. In order to decompose the problem, we made use of *a priori* knowledge about the temporal characterization of the instances.

ically represented in Figure 3.4. Figure 3.5 re-proposes the example, already discussed in Section 3.3.1, of the decomposition of MARIO'S problem into two subclasses. Here, the generation of instances is modeled as a hidden Markov model with an underlying deterministic state evolution.

On the other hand a graphical representation of a (4-state) hidden Markov model, characterized by nondeterministic state-transitions, is given in Figure 3.6. In this case, the underlying process can be described in probabilistic terms: A set of states

$$X = \{x_1, x_2, \dots, x_n\} \tag{3.3}$$

is given, together with the quantities

$$p_{vw} = P\big(x(k+1) = x_w \big| x(k) = x_v\big), \qquad \text{with } 1 \leq v, w \leq n, \tag{3.4}$$

representing the probability that the state at time $k+1$ will be x_w given that it is x_v at time k.[11]

Even if hidden Markov models with nondeterministic state-transitions are extremely powerful and capable of accurately model the most diverse streams of instances, their application to the problem of tuning metaheuristics appears, at

[11] We assume here that the state transition probabilities are time independent. The model can be further complicated by considering time-varying probabilities. This extension goes far beyond the aims of this thesis.

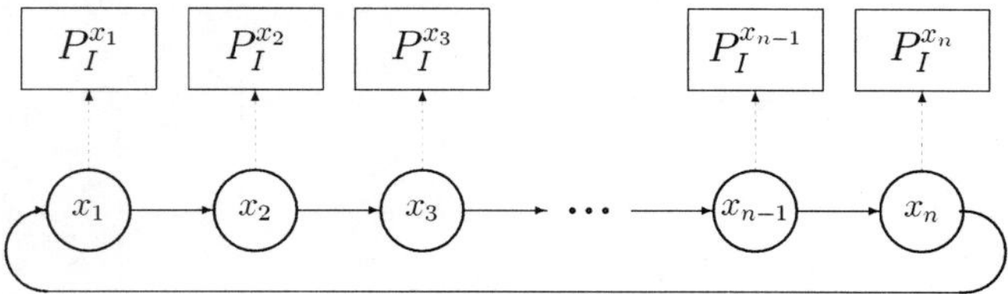

Figure 3.4: The generation of instances represented as a hidden Markov model. In this figure, the underlying finite-state machine is deterministic.

least at the current state, rather impractical. The downside of these models is precisely represented by their very generality and power that makes their practical application cumbersome: The adoption of a hidden Markov model with underlying nondeterministic state-transitions would requires to solve two different orders of difficulties:

- The state-transition probabilities have to be estimated. This is particularly difficult since we are given only sequences of instances that the process actually produces but we are not given the associated state transitions that occur. Unfortunately, no analytic method exist for solving this class of problems which are therefore tackled through iterative techniques such as the Baum-Welch algorithm or the EM algorithm—see Rabiner (1989) and references therein.

- Even once an estimate of the state-transition probabilities is available, the underlying state of the system cannot be directly observed. Some sort of filtering is necessary in order to determine the current state on the basis of the observed sequence of instances. This class of problems is usually solved through the Viterbi algorithm (Viterbi, 1967; Forney, 1973).

These two problems are far from being trivial.

It is our opinion that the use of simple hierarchical models, as those described in Section 3.3.1, or of hidden Markov models characterized by a small number of states and deterministic state-transition is perfectly viable and even advisable when *a priori* knowledge is available. On the other hand, given the difficulties outlined above, we expect that hidden Markov models with underlying nondeterministic state-transitions could be profitably adopted only in a restricted number of applications.

3.3.3 The single-instance case

In some applications, practitioners face the problem of solving one single instance rather than a stream. Clearly, the whole conceptual apparatus developed in this

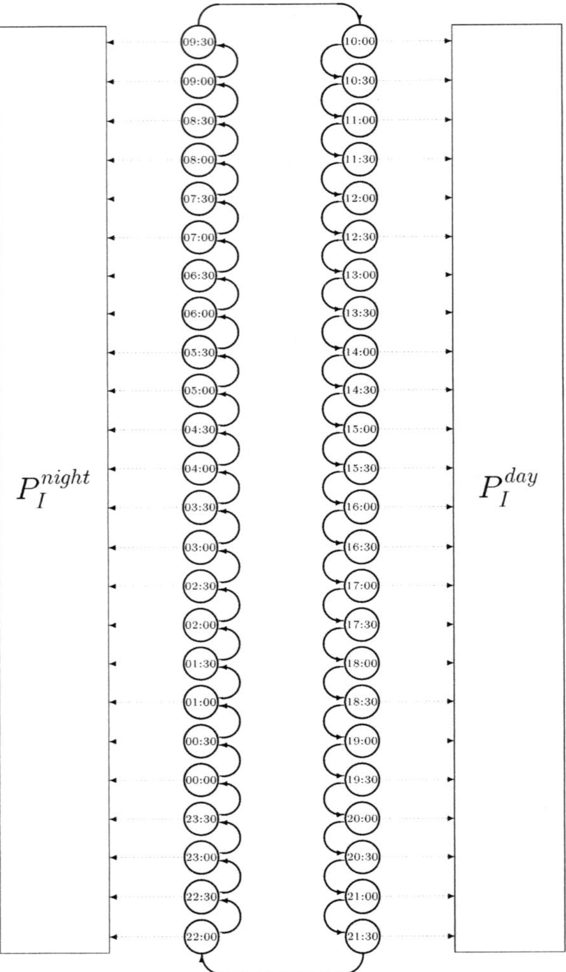

Figure 3.5: The decomposition of MARIO'S problem into two subproblems modeled here through a finite-state automaton: Every 30 minutes a new instance is generated and a state-transition occurs.

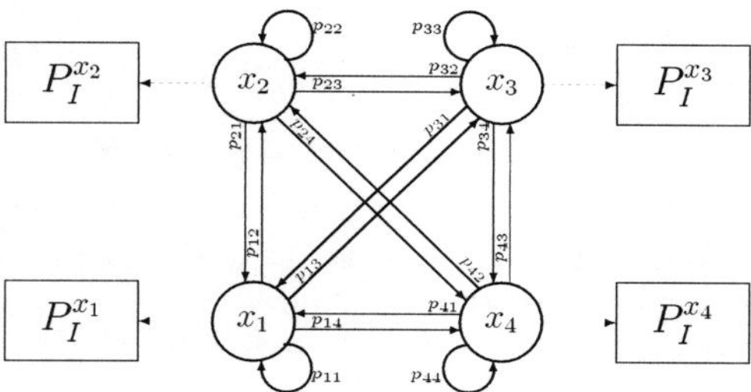

Figure 3.6: A graphical representation of a hidden Markov model with 4 states. When the process is in state x_v, an instance is generate according to the distribution $P_I^{x_v}$. From state x_v, a transition to state x_w might occur with probability p_{vw}. In this example, self-transitions are possible.

chapter does not apply to this case. Still, in some sense, also in the single-instance case some sort of tuning might be meaningful.

Before proceeding with this problem, some seemingly trivial issues need to be made clear to avoid possible misunderstandings:

1. Also in the single-instance case, a time constraint needs to be given. Otherwise we could, possibly in an extremely large amount of time, find the global optimum by exhaustive enumeration of the solutions.

2. The instance must be *large enough* to guarantee that no exact algorithm is able to find the provably optimal solution within the available time.

In such a context, a choice has to be made on whether to tackle the instance with one given configuration during the whole time available, or whether to try more configurations.

A typical solution—see for example McAllester *et al.* (1997)—that is often adopted in practice consists in splitting the available time in two segments: a tuning phase and an actual search. During the tuning phase, a selection is made among a number of different configurations on the basis of the results obtained on some short *pilot runs*. The selected configuration is then used in the actual search.

It is worth pointing out here that also in the selection based on pilot runs a sort of generalization is implied. The only difference is that, in this case, the generalization rests on the stronger hypothesis that what is observed on short runs extends to longer runs.

A part from this remarks, the main methods developed in Chapter 4 for tackling the problem defined in Section 3.2 can be adopted also for the tuning of metaheuristics through pilot runs.

3.3.4 The optimization of generic statistics

Rather than considering the optimization of the expected value, other statistics may be considered as well. As an example, the third interquartile or the median are known to be more robust statistics and in some application this property could be particularly appealing. The definition of the tuning problem given in Section 3.2 is not bound to the expected value and can be easily reformulated in terms of other statistics.

Nevertheless, while the expected value can be easily estimated on the basis of a sample, the estimation of other statistics might be problematic and data-inefficient: On the basis of a given finite sample, the estimate of the expected value is affected by a smaller variance compared with the estimate of other statistics.

The method we present in Chapter 4 is based on the optimization of the expected value but it can be possibly modified to handle different statistics. Research in this direction is currently ongoing.

3.3.5 Time versus cost

So far, we have considered the case in which the search time is *a priori* fixed, and a metaheuristic is evaluated on the basis of its ability in finding a low-cost solution within the given amount of time. For some applications, the dual problem is of interest: a given threshold cost is fixed, and a metaheuristic is evaluated on its ability in finding in a short time a solution whose cost is equal or smaller than the threshold. The formulation given in Section 3.2 can be easily modified to handle the optimization in the time-to-threshold sense.

Also here, as it is the case with the minimization of costs, the criterion to be optimized becomes infinite for a configuration θ, if an instance i with $P_I(i) > 0$ exists, for which the probability is non null that θ fails to reach the cost threshold in finite time. Also in this case, no major theoretical nor practical problem follows.

A further extension of the problem consists in formulating it as a bi-objective optimization in the Pareto sense. Research in this direction is currently ongoing.

3.4 Discussion

The cornerstone of the whole chapter, and possibly of the whole thesis, is the probability measure P_I. The notion of a probabilistic model for the generation of instances, previously missing in the literature, is of paramount importance for a precise definition of the tuning problem and for the development of algorithms to tackle it effectively.

The role played by the measure P_I is to define what are the "typical" instances for each of the different practical tuning problems that one has to solve. Thanks to P_I it is possible to give a meaning to the notion of expected behavior of a metaheuristic over the class of instances at hand, and therefore to select the most appropriate configuration for each application.

The current literature tends to focus the attention on "difficult" instances rather than on "typical" ones.[12] One could speculate that the reason of this tendency is a cultural legacy of the research on deterministic algorithms of the early days of operations research. Traditionally, operations research used to deal mostly with deterministic algorithms, exact or approximate, whose properties were usually studied through a formal worst-case analysis. Possibly due to such a legacy, when practitioners nowadays tune or assess their metaheuristics or, more in general, their stochastic algorithms, they tend to focus their tests on instances that are known to be particularly difficult. When interviewed on the issue,[13] they appear perfectly aware that the conclusions they might draw on "difficult" instances do not necessarily extend to "easy" ones; still, they follow this practice and try to justify it typically on the basis of the argument that on easy instances all algorithms—or all configurations in the case of a tuning problem—behave essentially the same, and possible differences are not easily observed.

An empirical analysis that focuses on what are considered difficult instances fails to attach a clear and well defined meaning to the outcome of the experiments. On the contrary, a methodology based on the notion of a probabilistic measure over the space of the instances provides such clear and well defined meaning: When referring to a probability measure P_I, the empirical mean of the performance on a sample of instances independently and identically distributed according to P_I is an **unbiased estimate** of the expected performance on any other sample of instances independently and identically distributed according to the same measure. In this precise sense, the conclusions drawn on the first sample **do** extend directly to any possible sample of instances extracted from P_I.

On the other hand, the typical criticism moved within the operations research community against the notion of probability measure P_I is that this probability is not available.[14] Indeed, as a rule, P_I is unknown but as we show in Chapter 4, the knowledge of this probability measure is not needed. Actually, to tackle the tuning problem we do not even need to model it explicitly. Nevertheless, in order

[12]See for example Monasson *et al.* (1999)—and references therein—for an outline of a research direction aiming at characterizing "difficult" instances. One of the explicitly declared goals of these studies is to define the classes of "difficult" instances on which research on search algorithm should focus.

[13]We report here the personal experience of the author of this thesis, gathered during some informal coffee-break discussions with colleagues. Clearly, what reported in the following does not have the value of a rigorous sociological study, and should be simply accepted as a, possibly debatable, sample of the attitude toward the issue within the operations research community.

[14]Also in this case we report the personal experience of the author: The same remark expressed in Note 13 holds here.

to give a meaning to the whole position and solution of the tuning problem, P_I **must** be *supposed*, even if no direct knowledge of it, nor an explicit model are needed: All the information we need about P_I is contained in the performance of the metaheuristic at hand on the samples we extract and the hypothesis of the existence of P_I is needed simply to guarantee that all subsequent samples will have the same statistical properties.

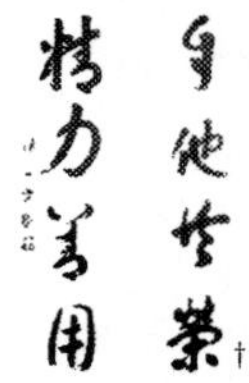

Jigoro Kano

Chapter 4

F-Race for tuning metaheuristics

This chapter is devoted to the definition of a number of algorithms for solving the tuning problem as posed in Section 3.2.

In the tuning problem, formally described by the tuple $\langle \Theta, I, P_I, P_C, t, \mathcal{C}, T \rangle$, a finite set Θ of candidate configurations is given together with a class I of instances. The instances appear sequentially and at each step an instance i is generated with a probability defined by the measure P_I. The cost of the best solution of i found by a candidate θ in a time $t(i)$ is a stochastic quantity described by the conditional measure P_C. The tuning problem consists in finding, within a time T, the best configuration according to the criterion $\mathcal{C}$, when the measures P_I and P_C are *unknown* but a sample of instances can be obtained on which to test the candidate configurations.

We assume in the following that the set Θ of configuration is finite. This assumption does not pose any problem in the case of categorical parameters and in the case of discrete parameters which are defined on a finite interval. On the other hand, continuous parameters need to be discretized in order to adopt the methods described in this thesis.[1]

For definiteness, in our treatment of the tuning problem we restrict our attention to the case in which the criterion $\mathcal{C}$ to be minimized is the expected cost μ of the solution found by a candidate θ on an instance. This expected cost, formally

---

†*Maximum-efficient use of power, mutual welfare and benefit.*

[1]The definition of a tuning method that handles continuous parameters directly, without the need of a preliminary discretization, is the subject of ongoing research. Such a method should result from an hybridization of the *racing* approach with the *response surface methodology* (Box & Draper, 1987; Myers & Montgomery, 2002).

expressed as the integral

$$\mu(\theta) = \int c \,\mathrm{d}P_C(c|\theta, i)\, \mathrm{d}P_I(i), \tag{4.1}$$

cannot be computed analytically for each candidate θ since the measures P_C and P_I are *unknown*.[2] Nonetheless, since we are able to *sample* observations according to these measures, the quantities $\mu(\theta)$, for $\theta \in \Theta$, can be estimated in a Monte Carlo fashion (Rubinstein, 1981). Indeed, with reference to the notion of *stream of instances* introduced in Chapter 3, any instance appearing in the stream in a random sample from P_I. On the other hand, any run of the given configuration θ on an instance i is a random sample from the conditional measure $P_C = P_C(c|\theta, i)$. On the basis of such samples, we can immediately obtain a Monte Carlo estimate $\hat{\mu}$ of the expected value.[3] More details on the definition of $\hat{\mu}$ are given in Section 4.1.1.

In the following, we treat for simplicity the case in which the computation time is constant for all instances, that is, $t(i) = t$ for all i.[4] In this case, the constraint imposing that the selection of the best configuration must be done within a time T is equivalent to a constraint on the maximum number of *experiments* we are allowed to perform, where an experiment consists in a single run of a given configuration on a given instance. Let us denote with $M = \lfloor T/t \rfloor$ the total number of experiments that we are allowed to perform.[5]

The most intuitive approach for solving the tuning problem is the *brute-force* approach consisting in allocating an equal share of computational power to each candidate configuration, that is, to perform the same number $N = \lfloor M/|\Theta| \rfloor$ of experiments on each of them. Section 4.2 formalizes ***Brutus***, a *brute-force* approach for tuning metaheuristics that serves in Chapter 5 as a baseline in our experimental analysis.

In order to define an algorithm implementing the *brute-force* approach, an important element has first to be discussed, notably how to estimate the expected performance of a candidate configuration using the finite number of experiments, say N, that have been allocated for its evaluation. In particular, the question concerns the number of instances that should be considered for its evaluation and, as a consequence the number of runs to be performed on each of these instances. Section 4.1 provides a formal answer to this question.

[2]See Section 3.2 for the formal definition of the tuning problem. The expected cost given in Equation 4.1 has been already introduced in Equation 3.2, page 73, and is reproduced here only for convenience.

[3]This is akin to the approximation of the *risk* functional by the *empirical risk* in machine learning. We refer the reader to Section 2.2.4 and in particular to Figure 2.4.

[4]This constraint is not strictly necessary and can be easily eliminated. We restrict to such case only for clarity since under this condition, the comparison results more intuitive and direct between the two classes of approaches to the tuning problem that we discuss: the *brute-force* approach and the *racing* approach described in Sections 4.2 and 4.3, respectively.

[5]The notation $\lfloor T/t \rfloor$ indicates the largest integer which does not exceed T/t.

The *brute-force* approach is possibly not the optimal solution to the tuning problem.[6] A more refined and efficient way of tuning metaheuristics can be obtained by streamlining the evaluation of the candidates and by dropping during the evaluation process those that appear less promising. This is the *racing* approach to tuning. Section 4.3 presents the main idea of *racing* for tuning metaheuristics and introduces the four *racing* algorithms we consider in our experimental evaluation. Section 4.4 gives more details on the most original of these algorithms, namely the *F-Race* algorithm.

Finally, the brief discussion proposed in Section 4.5 concludes the chapter.

4.1 How many instances, how man runs?

When it comes to defining an experimental setting for estimating the expected performance of a given configuration θ of a metaheuristic given that we can perform a maximum number N of runs, practitioners are often embarrassed.[7] The question is invariably: *How many instances, how many runs?* The answers typically cover a wide range. Often it is believed that some sort of trade-off is involved in the choice: If, given an instance, the configuration θ tends to be quite *erratic* and produces rather different results on subsequent runs, practitioners typically feel the need to perform more runs on each instance and are therefore inclined to *trade* instances for runs. On the other hand, if θ shows a quite stable behavior, they feel like considering less runs and more instances. In any case, most of them would be quite unhappy at the idea of performing one single run on each instance: They would argue that a metaheuristic is in any case a stochastic algorithm and that if you want your conclusions to be somehow meaningful, you need to average the results of more runs. They would probably add that it is pointless to average across more instances if the results you average, each concerning a different instance, are spoiled by a large margin of uncertainty.

The theorems presented in this section prove them wrong on the issue.[8]

4.1.1 Formal position of the estimation problem

The framework we consider is based on the concept of a *stream* of instances introduced in Chapter 3: An instance i is selected from a class I of instances. The given configuration θ is supposed to run for t seconds on i and return the best solution s found during the run; that is, the solution whose cost c is not

[6]Indeed it is not, as our experimental comparison presented in Chapter 5 indicates.

[7]We refer here to some *informal* conversations with colleagues. Nevertheless, also a number of published papers contain wrong statements and/or adopt some improper experimental setting that betrays a lack of understanding of the issues discussed in this section. See for example Yuan & Gallagher (2004).

[8]The results presented in this section were previously made available in Birattari (2004a).

larger than the cost associated to any other solution s' visited during the run. The process is then iterated *ad libitum*.

It is worth repeating here that we deal with the case in which instances belonging to I are *a priori* indistinguishable. In particular, if we are given 3 instances—say i_a, i_b, and i_c—prior to running the metaheuristic on them we are not able to predict if the cost of the best solution we will obtain for i_a will be closer to the one we will obtain for i_b or the one we will obtain for i_c. Such a hypothesis is not too restrictive. Indeed, in the case we are able to *a priori* distinguish among instances, we can consider a partition of I into disjoint subsets $I_1, I_2, \ldots, I_L$ within each of which instances are indistinguishable—See Section 3.3.1 for an example. The discussion we present here holds within each of the sets $I_1, I_2, \ldots, I_L$. The partition of the original set and the decomposition of the original estimation problem into subproblems is connected to the notion of *stratified sampling* which is a well known *variance reduction technique* adopted in Monte Carlo estimation—See for example Rubinstein (1981).[9]

Definition 1. We call a *scenario* for the estimation of the expected behavior of the configuration θ, the joint probability measure $P(c,i) = P_C(c|i)P_I(i)$.[10]

The estimation problem. *Estimate on the basis of N runs of the configuration θ its average behavior on the class I, that is, the expected value of the cost c with respect to the scenario $P(c,i) = P_C(c|i)P_I(i)$:*

$$\mu = E[c] = \int c \,\mathrm{d}P_C(c|i)\,\mathrm{d}P_I(i), \tag{4.2}$$

where the operator E denotes the expectation taken with respect to the joint probability $P(c,i)$.[11]

To this aim, we run a set J of experiments, with $|J| = N$. For each experiment $j \in J$ we observe a cost c_j. The quantity μ can be estimated by the estimator $\hat{\mu}$:

$$\hat{\mu} = \frac{1}{N}\sum_{j\in J} c_j.$$

[9] This issue, which goes beyond the aims of this thesis but is nonetheless its natural extension, is currently the subject of ongoing research.

[10] For the sake of an improved readability, in the whole Section 4.1 we drop from the notation the direct reference to the configuration θ at hand. This reference will remain implicit: we will therefore write $P_C(c|i)$ rather than $P_C(c|\theta,i)$, μ rather than $\mu(\theta)$, σ^2 rather than $\sigma^2(\theta)$, and so on. This should not generate any confusion since the whole section concerns the estimation of the expected performance of a *given* and *fixed* configuration θ. Starting from Section 4.2, where we compare the performance of different configurations, we will switch back to the full notation that makes explicit which configuration we refer to.

[11] Equation 4.2 is precisely Equation 4.1 where the reference to a specific configuration θ is implicit. See Note 10.

To be more precise, let us suppose we sample K distinct instances $i_1, i_2, \ldots, i_K$, with $K \leq N$, and we run the configuration θ for n_1 times on instance i_1, for n_2 times on instance i_2, and so on. This amounts to considering a set of experiments J which is partitioned in subsets $J_1, J_2, \ldots, J_K$, where $|J_k| = n_k$ and $\sum_k n_k = N$: each element j in the generic subset J_k is an experiment consisting in running θ once on instance i_k.

Definition 2. We call an *experimental setting*, or more simply a *setting*, the sequence of natural numbers $\mathcal{S}_N = (K, n_1, n_2, \ldots, n_K)$, that is, the specification of how many instances have to be considered, together with the number of runs to perform on each of them.

For convenience, we also introduce the following notation:

Definition 3. If K divides N, we denote with $\mathcal{H}_{K|N/K}$ the *homogeneous* setting, that is, $\mathcal{S}_N = (K, n_1, n_2, \ldots, n_K)$, where $n_k = N/K$ for all k. In particular, $\mathcal{H}_{N|1} = (N, n_1, n_2, \ldots, n_N)$, with $n_k = 1$ for all k, is the setting "N instances, one run per instance." Similarly, $\mathcal{H}_{1|N} = (1, N)$ is the setting "one instance, N runs."

Definition 4. In a given scenario $P(c, i) = P_C(c|i)P_I(i)$, and for a given experimental setting $\mathcal{S}_N = (K, n_1, n_2, \ldots, n_K)$, the estimator $\hat{\mu}_{\mathcal{S}_N}$ of the expected value μ of the cost c is given by:

$$\hat{\mu}_{\mathcal{S}_N} = \frac{1}{N} \sum_{k=1}^{K} \sum_{j \in J_k} c_j, \tag{4.3}$$

where $N = \sum_{k=1}^{K} |J_k|$, $|J_k| = n_k$, and instances i_k and costs c_j are extracted according to $P(c, i)$.

The following quantities are used in the following:

Definition 5. The expected value of the cost c within instance i is given by:

$$\mu_i = E[c|i] = \int c \, \mathrm{d}P_C(c|i).$$

Definition 6. The variance of the cost c within instance i is given by:

$$\sigma_i^2 = E\big[(c - \mu_i)^2 | i\big] = \int (c - \mu_i)^2 \, \mathrm{d}P_C(c|i).$$

Definition 7. The expected *within-instance* variance is:

$$\bar{\sigma}_{\mathrm{WI}}^2 = \int \sigma_i^2 \, \mathrm{d}P_I(i),$$

that is, the expected value with respect to the distribution of the instances of the variance of c within a same instance.

Definition 8. The *across-instance* variance is:

$$\sigma^2_{\mathrm{AI}} = \int (\mu_i - \mu)^2 \, \mathrm{d}P_I(i),$$

that is, the variance across the instances of the expected value of the cost for each instance.

4.1.2 First order analysis of the estimator $\hat{\mu}_{\mathcal{S}_N}$

Lemma 1. *In a given scenario $P(c,i) = P_C(c|,i)P_I(i)$, and for a given experimental setting $\mathcal{S}_N = (K, n_1, n_2, \dots, n_K)$, the probability of obtaining the specific instances $i_1, i_2, \dots, i_K$ and the specific results $c_1, c_2, \dots, c_N$ on which $\hat{\mu}_{\mathcal{S}_N}$ is based is given by:*

$$P(i_1, i_2, \dots, i_K, c_1, c_2, \dots, c_N) = \prod_{k=1}^{K} P_I(i_k) \prod_{j \in J_k} P_C(c_j|i_k),$$

where $P_I(i_k)$ is the probability of sampling instance i_k, and $P_C(c_j|i_k)$ is the probability of obtaining the cost c_j as best result in a run of the configuration θ on instance i_k.

Proof. The K instances are sampled independently according to the probability measure $P_I(i)$. Similarly, the costs c obtained on a given instance i are sampled independently according to $P_C(c|i)$. The joint probability is therefore the product of the terms. □

Theorem 1. *In all scenarios, irrespectively of the setting $\mathcal{S}_N$, that is, of how K and n_k with $k = 1 \dots K$ are selected, $\hat{\mu}_{\mathcal{S}_N}$ is an unbiased estimator of μ.*

Proof. The proof is immediate and is given only for the sake of completeness:[12]

$$\begin{aligned}\int \hat{\mu}_{\mathcal{S}_N} \, \mathrm{d}P(\hat{\mu}_{\mathcal{S}_N}) &= \int \frac{1}{N} \sum_{k=1}^{K} \sum_{j \in J_k} c_j \bigodot_{k=1}^{K} \mathrm{d}P_I(i_k) \bigodot_{j \in J_k} \mathrm{d}P_C(c_j|i_k) \\ &= \frac{1}{N} \sum_{k=1}^{K} \sum_{j \in J_k} \int c_j \, \mathrm{d}P_C(c_j|i_k) \, \mathrm{d}P_I(i_k) = \mu.\end{aligned}$$

□

[12] In the following, with the notation:

$$\int f(x_1, x_2, \dots, x_L) \bigodot_{l=1}^{L} \mathrm{d}P(x_l),$$

we denote the sequence of nested integrals

$$\iint \cdots \int f(x_1, x_2, \dots, x_L) \, \mathrm{d}P(x_1) \, \mathrm{d}P(x_2) \dots \mathrm{d}P(x_L).$$

In particular, $\hat{\mu}_{\mathcal{H}_{1|1}}$, based on a single run on a single instance, is an unbiased estimator of μ, irrespectively of which instance is considered, provided it is selected from I according to the *unknown* probability $P_I(i)$.[13] Similarly, the estimator $\hat{\mu}_{\mathcal{H}_{1|N}}$ based on N runs on one single instance is unbiased as well as $\hat{\mu}_{\mathcal{H}_{N/10|10}}$ which considers $N/10$ instances, 10 runs per instance.

4.1.3 Second order analysis of the estimator $\hat{\mu}_{\mathcal{S}_N}$

All possible estimators that can be written in the form given in Equation 4.3 are therefore equivalent for what concerns their expected behavior. Nonetheless, they differ for what concerns second order statistics. We are therefore interested here in finding the best *minimum-variance* estimator when the total number N of experiments is fixed. In simple words, we want to answer the question:

> *If I can run $N = 100$ experiments, should I consider (i) 1 instance and 100 runs; (ii) 10 instances and 10 runs on each; (iii) 100 instance and 1 single run on each; or what else?*

Lemma 2. *In a given scenario $P(c,i) = P_C(c|i)P_I(i)$, and for a given experimental setting $\mathcal{S}_N = (K, n_1, n_2, \dots, n_K)$, the variance of the estimator $\hat{\mu}_{\mathcal{S}_N}$ is given by:*

$$\int (\hat{\mu}_{\mathcal{S}_N} - \mu)^2 \,\mathrm{d}P(\hat{\mu}_{\mathcal{S}_N}) = \frac{1}{N}\,\bar{\sigma}^2_{\mathrm{WI}} + \frac{\sum_{k=1}^{K} n_k^2}{N^2}\,\sigma^2_{\mathrm{AI}}.$$

Proof. It results:

$$\int (\hat{\mu}_{\mathcal{S}_N} - \mu)^2 \,\mathrm{d}P(\hat{\mu}_{\mathcal{S}_N}) = \int \left(\frac{1}{N}\sum_{k=1}^{K}\sum_{j\in J_k} c_j - \mu\right)^2 \bigodot_{k=1}^{K} \mathrm{d}P_I(i_k) \bigodot_{j\in J_k} \mathrm{d}P_C(c_j|i_k) =$$

$$= \int \left(\frac{1}{N}\sum_{k=1}^{K}\sum_{j\in J_k} (c_j - \mu_{i_k} + \mu_{i_k} - \mu)\right)^2 \bigodot_{k=1}^{K} \mathrm{d}P_I(i_k) \bigodot_{j\in J_k} \mathrm{d}P_C(c_j|i_k),$$

It follows that:

$$\int (\hat{\mu}_{\mathcal{S}_N} - \mu)^2 \,\mathrm{d}P(\hat{\mu}_{\mathcal{S}_N}) =$$

$$= \frac{1}{N^2} \sum_{k,k'=1}^{K} \sum_{\substack{j\in J_k \\ j'\in J_{k'}}} \int (c_j - \mu_{i_k})(c_{j'} - \mu_{i_{k'}})\,\mathrm{d}P_C(c_j|i_k)\,\mathrm{d}P_I(i_k)\,\mathrm{d}P_C(c_{j'}|i_{k'})\,\mathrm{d}P_I(i_{k'}) + \tag{4.4a}$$

[13] The fact that $P_I(i)$ is unknown does not pose here any problem: in order to obtain an instance i extracted from I according to the unknown $P_I(i)$ it is sufficient to take randomly any of the instances that appear in the above described stream of instances: let's say the next one!

$$+\frac{1}{N^2}\sum_{k,k'=1}^{K}\sum_{\substack{j\in J_k\\ j'\in J_{k'}}}\int(\mu_{i_k}-\mu)(\mu_{i_{k'}}-\mu)\,\mathrm{d}P_I(i_k)\,\mathrm{d}P_I(i_{k'})+ \tag{4.4b}$$

$$+\frac{1}{N^2}\sum_{k,k'=1}^{K}\sum_{\substack{j\in J_k\\ j'\in J_{k'}}}2\int(c_j-\mu_{i_k})(\mu_{i_{k'}}-\mu)\,\mathrm{d}P_C(c_j|i_k)\,\mathrm{d}P_I(i_k)\,\mathrm{d}P_I(i_{k'}). \tag{4.4c}$$

Let us now consider one by one the three addends given in 4.4a, 4.4b, and 4.4c.

Addend 4.4a: if $k\neq k'$, it results:

$$\int(c_j-\mu_{i_k})(c_{j'}-\mu_{i_{k'}})\,\mathrm{d}P_C(c_j|i_k)\,\mathrm{d}P_I(i_k)\,\mathrm{d}P_C(c_{j'}|i_{k'})\,\mathrm{d}P_I(i_{k'})=$$
$$=\int\cancelto{0}{(c_j-\mu_{i_k})\,\mathrm{d}P_C(c_j|i_k)}\,\mathrm{d}P_I(i_k)\int\cancelto{0}{(c_{j'}-\mu_{i_{k'}})\,\mathrm{d}P_C(c_{j'}|i_{k'})}\,\mathrm{d}P_I(i_{k'})=0.$$

Similarly, if $k=k'$ but $j\neq j'$, it results:

$$\int(c_j-\mu_{i_k})(c_{j'}-\mu_{i_{k'}})\,\mathrm{d}P_C(c_j|i_k)\,\mathrm{d}P_I(i_k)\,\mathrm{d}P_C(c_{j'}|i_{k'})\,\mathrm{d}P_I(i_{k'})=$$
$$=\int\left(\int\cancelto{0}{(c_j-\mu_{i_k})\,\mathrm{d}P_C(c_j|i_k)}\int\cancelto{0}{(c_{j'}-\mu_{i_k})\,\mathrm{d}P_C(c_{j'}|i_k)}\right)\mathrm{d}P(i_k)=0.$$

On the other hand, if $k=k'$ and $j=j'$, it results:

$$\int(c_j-\mu_{i_k})(c_{j'}-\mu_{i_{k'}})\,\mathrm{d}P_C(c_j|i_k)\,\mathrm{d}P_I(i_k)\,\mathrm{d}P_C(c_{j'}|i_{k'})\,\mathrm{d}P_I(i_{k'})=$$
$$=\int(c_j-\mu_{i_k})^2\,\mathrm{d}P_C(c_j|i_k)\,\mathrm{d}P_I(i_k).$$

Thus, addend 4.4a amounts to:

$$\frac{1}{N^2}\sum_{k=1}^{K}\sum_{j\in J_k}\int(c_j-\mu_{i_k})^2\,\mathrm{d}P_C(c_j|i_k)\,\mathrm{d}P_I(i_k).$$

Addend 4.4b: since the integrand is independent from j and j', it results:

$$\frac{1}{N^2}\sum_{k,k'=1}^{K}\sum_{\substack{j\in J_k\\ j'\in J_{k'}}}\int(\mu_{i_k}-\mu)(\mu_{i_{k'}}-\mu)\,\mathrm{d}P_I(i_k)\,\mathrm{d}P_I(i_{k'})=$$
$$=\frac{1}{N^2}\sum_{k,k'=1}^{K}|J_k|\cdot|J_{k'}|\int(\mu_{i_k}-\mu)(\mu_{i_{k'}}-\mu)\,\mathrm{d}P_I(i_k)\,\mathrm{d}P_I(i_{k'}).$$

If $k \neq k'$, it results:

$$\int (\mu_{i_k} - \mu)(\mu_{i_{k'}} - \mu) \,\mathrm{d}P_I(i_k) \,\mathrm{d}P_I(i_{k'}) =$$

$$= \cancelto{0}{\int (\mu_{i_k} - \mu) \,\mathrm{d}P_I(i_k)} \cancelto{0}{\int (\mu_{i_{k'}} - \mu) \,\mathrm{d}P_I(i_{k'})} = 0.$$

Otherwise, if $k = k'$, it results:

$$\int (\mu_{i_k} - \mu)(\mu_{i_{k'}} - \mu) \,\mathrm{d}P_I(i_k) \,\mathrm{d}P_I(i_{k'}) = \int (\mu_{i_k} - \mu)^2 \,\mathrm{d}P_I(i_k).$$

Thus, addend 4.4b amounts to:

$$\frac{1}{N^2} \sum_{k=1}^{K} |J_k|^2 \int (\mu_{i_k} - \mu)^2 \,\mathrm{d}P_I(i_k).$$

Addend 4.4c: it results:

$$\int (c_j - \mu_{i_k})(\mu_{i_{k'}} - \mu) \,\mathrm{d}P_C(c_j|i_k) \,\mathrm{d}P_I(i_k) \,\mathrm{d}P_I(i_{k'}) =$$

$$= \int \left((\mu_{i_{k'}} - \mu) \cancelto{0}{\int (c_j - \mu_{i_k}) \,\mathrm{d}P_C(c_j|i_k)} \right) \mathrm{d}P_I(i_k) \,\mathrm{d}P_I(i_{k'}) = 0,$$

Thus, addend 4.4c is identically null.

It results therefore:

$$\int (\hat{\mu}_{\mathcal{S}_N} - \mu)^2 \,\mathrm{d}P(\hat{\mu}_{\mathcal{S}_N}) = \frac{1}{N^2} \sum_{k=1}^{K} \sum_{j \in J_k} \int (c_j - \mu_{i_k})^2 \,\mathrm{d}P_C(c_j|i_k) \,\mathrm{d}P_I(i_k) +$$

$$+ \frac{1}{N^2} \sum_{k=1}^{K} |J_k|^2 \int (\mu_{i_k} - \mu)^2 \,\mathrm{d}P_I(i_k).$$

On the basis of Definitions 7 and 8 we can write:

$$\int (\hat{\mu}_{\mathcal{S}_N} - \mu)^2 \,\mathrm{d}P(\hat{\mu}_{\mathcal{S}_N}) = \frac{1}{N^2} \sum_{k=1}^{K} |J_k| \,\bar{\sigma}^2_{\mathrm{WI}} + \frac{1}{N^2} \sum_{k=1}^{K} |J_k|^2 \,\sigma^2_{\mathrm{AI}}.$$

Remembering that $\sum_{k=1}^{K} |J_k| = N$ and that $|J_k| = n_k$, it results:

$$\int (\hat{\mu}_{\mathcal{S}_N} - \mu)^2 \,\mathrm{d}P(\hat{\mu}_{\mathcal{S}_N}) = \frac{1}{N} \,\bar{\sigma}^2_{\mathrm{WI}} + \frac{\sum_{k=1}^{K} n_k^2}{N^2} \,\sigma^2_{\mathrm{AI}}.$$

□

Let us go back to our original question: With the constraint that the total number of runs must be N, what is the optimal number of instances to consider and how many runs to perform on each?

Theorem 2. *The variance of $\hat{\mu}_{\mathcal{S}_N}$ is minimized by the experimental setting $\bar{\mathcal{S}}_N = \mathcal{H}_{N|1}$, that is, by the setting "N instances, one run per instance."*

Proof. According to Lemma 2, the variance of $\hat{\mu}_{\mathcal{S}_N}$ is:

$$\int (\hat{\mu}_{\mathcal{S}_N} - \mu)^2 \, \mathrm{d}P(\hat{\mu}_{\mathcal{S}_N}) = \frac{1}{N}\,\bar{\sigma}^2_{\mathrm{WI}} + \frac{\sum_{k=1}^{K} n_k^2}{N^2}\,\sigma^2_{\mathrm{AI}}.$$

Since the first addend does not depend on $\mathcal{S}_N = (K, n_1, \dots, n_K)$, we can focus on the minimization of the second. Moreover, since N is fixed and σ^2_{AI} is out of our control, we focus on the minimization of:

$$\mathcal{C}(\mathcal{S}_N) = \sum_{k=1}^{K} n_k^2, \qquad \text{under the constraint:} \quad \sum_{k=1}^{K} n_k = N.$$

Let us assume now, by way of contradiction, that an experimental setting $\mathcal{S}_N = (K, n_1, \dots, n_K)$ exists which is different form $\bar{\mathcal{S}}_N = \mathcal{H}_{N|1}$, satisfies the constraint, and which minimizes $\mathcal{C}$; that is, $\mathcal{S}_N$ is such that $\mathcal{C}(\mathcal{S}_N) \leq \mathcal{C}(\mathcal{S}'_N)$, for all $\mathcal{S}'_N$. Clearly, it must be $K \leq N$—otherwise the constraint would not be satisfied. Indeed, more precisely, it must be $K < N$ because otherwise it would be mandatory, in order to satisfy the constraint, to set $n_k = 1$ for all k and, in this case, we would fall back to the original statement to be proved. If $K < N$, in order to satisfy the constraint, there must exist at least an index q for which $n_q > 1$.

On the basis of the experimental setting $\mathcal{S}_N$ we can construct another setting $\mathcal{S}'_N = (K', n'_1, \dots, n'_{K'})$ where $K' = K + 1$, $n'_q = n_q - 1$, $n'_{K'} = 1$, and $n'_j = n_j$ otherwise. It is immediate to check that this second sequence satisfies the constraint if $\mathcal{S}_N$ does. Moreover, it results:

$$\mathcal{C}(\mathcal{S}'_N) = \sum_{k=1}^{K'} n'^2_k = \sum_{k=1}^{K} n_k^2 - n_q^2 + n'^2_q + 1 = \mathcal{C}(\mathcal{S}_N) - n_q^2 + (n_q - 1)^2 + 1 = \mathcal{C}(\mathcal{S}_N) - 2(n_q - 1).$$

Since $n_q > 1$, the term $2(n_q - 1)$ is strictly positive and the experimental setting $\mathcal{S}'_N$ is thus better that $\mathcal{S}_N$, which is a contradiction. □

Corollary 1. *The variance of the best estimator $\hat{\mu}_{\mathcal{H}_{N|1}}$ is:*

$$E\left[(\hat{\mu}_{\mathcal{H}_{N|1}} - \mu)^2\right] = \frac{1}{N}\left(\bar{\sigma}^2_{\mathrm{WI}} + \sigma^2_{\mathrm{AI}}\right).$$

Proof. It follows trivially from Lemma 2. □

Corollary 2. *$\hat{\mu}_{\mathcal{H}_{N|1}}$ is a consistent estimator of μ, that is, it converges in probability to μ:*

$$\lim_{N\to\infty} Prob\left\{|\hat{\mu}_{\mathcal{H}_{N|1}} - \mu| > \epsilon\right\} = 0, \quad \forall\epsilon > 0$$

Proof. The proof descends directly from Corollary 1. Indeed, $\hat{\mu}_{\mathcal{H}_{N|1}}$ converges to μ in the *mean square* sense: Provided that $\bar{\sigma}^2_{\mathrm{WI}}$ and σ^2_{AI} are finite, as N tends to infinity, $E\big[(\hat{\mu}_{N|1} - \mu)^2\big]$ converges to zero. The statement follows, since convergence in *mean square* implies convergence in *probability* (Papoulis, 1991). □

It is interesting to consider here a numerical example that compares the best estimator $\hat{\mu}_{\mathcal{H}_{N|1}}$ with other possible estimators of μ. For definiteness, let us assume in this example that the total number of runs is fixed to $N = 100$, and let us study the variance of the estimators that are obtained under the following three different experimental settings: (i) N instances, one run per instance, (ii) 10 instances, 10 runs per instance and, finally, (iii) one single instance, 100 runs. From Lemma 2 it results:

Setting 1: 100 instances, 1 run per instance—best estimator according to Theorem 2.

$$E\big[(\hat{\mu}_{\mathcal{H}_{100|1}} - \mu)^2\big] = \frac{1}{100}\,\bar{\sigma}^2_{\mathrm{WI}} + \frac{1}{100}\,\sigma^2_{\mathrm{AI}}.$$

Setting 2: 10 instances, 10 runs per instance.

$$E\big[(\hat{\mu}_{\mathcal{H}_{10|10}} - \mu)^2\big] = \frac{1}{100}\,\bar{\sigma}^2_{\mathrm{WI}} + \frac{1}{10}\,\sigma^2_{\mathrm{AI}}.$$

Setting 3: 1 instance, 100 runs.

$$E\big[(\hat{\mu}_{\mathcal{H}_{1|100}} - \mu)^2\big] = \frac{1}{100}\,\bar{\sigma}^2_{\mathrm{WI}} + \sigma^2_{\mathrm{AI}}.$$

While the three settings act in the same way on the coefficient of the first term, a difference emerges for what concerns the coefficient of the second term: Settings 2 and 3 fail to efficiently reduce the contribution of the *across-instance* variance. The variance yielded by the three settings is equal only in the trivial case in which the *across-instance* variance is null, that is, when all instances share the same expected cost $\mu = \mu_i$, for all $i \in I$.

Remark 1. Although the estimator $\hat{\mu}_{\mathcal{H}_{10|10}}$ considered in Setting 2 is less *data-efficient* than the best $\hat{\mu}_{\mathcal{H}_{100|1}}$ considered in Setting 1, it is nonetheless consistent. On the other hand, the estimator $\hat{\mu}_{\mathcal{H}_{1|100}}$ given in Setting 3 is not consistent—apart for the trivial case in which $\sigma^2_{\mathrm{AI}} = 0$.

Remark 2. It should be noticed that no scenario exists in which the estimator $\hat{\mu}_{\mathcal{H}_{N|1}}$ yields a higher variance than any other estimator $\hat{\mu}_{\mathcal{S}_N}$. That is, no better setting exists than "N instances, one run per instance," irrespectively of the measures P_I and P_C.

Corollary 3. *The variance of the cost c obtained by the given configuration θ on the whole class I of instances can be decomposed in two terms, the expected* within-instance *variance and the* across-instance *variance:*

$$\sigma^2 = E\big[(c-\mu)^2\big] = \bar{\sigma}^2_{\text{WI}} + \sigma^2_{\text{AI}}.$$

Proof. The result follows immediately Corollary 1 if we notice that the variance of the cost c is equal to the variance of an estimator $\hat{\mu}_{\mathcal{H}_{1|1}} = c$ based on a single sample. □

The expected *within-instance* variance $\bar{\sigma}^2_{\text{WI}}$ measures how different can be the costs c obtained by the configuration θ of the metaheuristic in different runs on the same instance; this quantity is averaged over all instance in I. On the other hand, the *across-instance* variance σ^2_{AI} measures how different the instances are one from the other for what concerns the expected value of the cost obtained by the given configuration θ.

Remark 3. Taken together, Corollaries 1 and 3 are just the statement, in a multivariate setting, of a basic and well known property of the variance of empirical estimates of univariate quantities: Given an univariate stochastic variable x with $E[x] = \mu$ and $E\big[(x-\mu)^2\big] = \sigma^2$, the variance of $\hat{\mu}_N = 1/N\sum_{j=1}^N x_j$, where x_j are independently realizations of x, is given by $E\big[(\hat{\mu}_N-\mu)^2\big] = \sigma^2/N$.

4.1.4 Yet another possible estimator

Somebody might wish to consider the *average* across different instances of the *averages* of the results obtained for each of the considered instances. Formally, this estimator is:

Definition 9. The estimator $\tilde{\mu}_{\mathcal{S}_N}$ is given by:

$$\tilde{\mu}_{\mathcal{S}_N} = \frac{1}{K}\sum_{k=1}^{K}\left(\frac{1}{n_k}\sum_{j\in J_k} c_j\right).$$

Remark 4. It can be immediately verified that if the experimental setting is homogeneous, that is, if $\mathcal{S}_N = \mathcal{H}_{K|N/K}$, then $\tilde{\mu}_{\mathcal{H}_{K|N/K}} = \hat{\mu}_{\mathcal{H}_{K|N/K}}$.

Theorem 3. *$\tilde{\mu}_{\mathcal{S}_N}$ is an unbiased estimator of μ.*

Proof. The proof is immediate and is given only for the sake of completeness:

$$\int \tilde{\mu}_{\mathcal{S}_N} \,\mathrm{d}P(\tilde{\mu}_{\mathcal{S}_N}) = \int \sum_{k=1}^{K} \sum_{j \in J_k} \frac{c_j}{n_k K} \bigodot_{k=1}^{K} \mathrm{d}P_I(i_k) \bigodot_{j \in J_k} \mathrm{d}P_C(c_j|i_k)$$
$$= \sum_{k=1}^{K} \sum_{j \in J_k} \frac{1}{n_k K} \int c_j \,\mathrm{d}P_C(c_j|i_k) \,\mathrm{d}P_I(i_k) = \mu.$$

□

Lemma 3. *In a given scenario $P(c,i) = P_C(c|i)P_I(i)$, and for a given experimental setting $\mathcal{S}_N = (K, n_1, n_2, \ldots, n_K)$, the variance of the estimator $\tilde{\mu}_{\mathcal{S}_N}$ is given by:*

$$\int (\tilde{\mu}_{\mathcal{S}_N} - \mu)^2 \,\mathrm{d}P(\hat{\mu}_{\mathcal{S}_N}) = \frac{1}{K^2} \sum_{k=1}^{K} \frac{1}{n_k} \,\bar{\sigma}^2_{\mathrm{WI}} + \frac{1}{K} \,\sigma^2_{\mathrm{AI}}.$$

Proof. It results:

$$\int (\tilde{\mu}_{\mathcal{S}_N} - \mu)^2 \,\mathrm{d}P(\tilde{\mu}_{\mathcal{S}_N}) = \int \left(\sum_{k=1}^{K} \left(\frac{1}{n_k K} \sum_{j \in J_k} c_j \right) - \mu \right)^2 \bigodot_{k=1}^{K} \mathrm{d}P_I(i_k) \bigodot_{j \in J_k} \mathrm{d}P_C(c_j|i_k) =$$
$$= \int \left(\sum_{k=1}^{K} \sum_{j \in J_k} \frac{c_j - \mu_{i_k} + \mu_{i_k} - \mu}{n_k K} \right)^2 \bigodot_{k=1}^{K} \mathrm{d}P_I(i_k) \bigodot_{j \in J_k} \mathrm{d}P_C(c_j|i_k).$$

It follows that:

$$\int (\tilde{\mu}_{\mathcal{S}_N} - \mu)^2 \,\mathrm{d}P(\tilde{\mu}_{\mathcal{S}_N}) =$$

$$= \sum_{k,k'=1}^{K} \sum_{\substack{j \in J_k \\ j' \in J_{k'}}} \int \frac{c_j - \mu_{i_k}}{n_k K} \frac{c_{j'} - \mu_{i_{k'}}}{n_{k'} K} \,\mathrm{d}P_C(c_j|i_k) \,\mathrm{d}P_I(i_k) \,\mathrm{d}P_C(c_{j'}|i_{k'}) \,\mathrm{d}P_I(i_{k'}) + \tag{4.5a}$$

$$+ \sum_{k,k'=1}^{K} \sum_{\substack{j \in J_k \\ j' \in J_{k'}}} \int \frac{\mu_{i_k} - \mu}{n_k K} \frac{\mu_{i_{k'}} - \mu}{n_{k'} K} \,\mathrm{d}P_I(i_k) \,\mathrm{d}P_I(i_{k'}) + \tag{4.5b}$$

$$+ \sum_{k,k'=1}^{K} \sum_{\substack{j \in J_k \\ j' \in J_{k'}}} 2 \int \frac{c_j - \mu_{i_k}}{n_k K} \frac{\mu_{i_{k'}} - \mu}{n_{k'} K} \,\mathrm{d}P_C(c_j|i_k) \,\mathrm{d}P_I(i_k) \,\mathrm{d}P_I(i_{k'}). \tag{4.5c}$$

Let us now consider one by one the three addends given in 4.5a, 4.5b, and 4.5c.

Addend 4.5a: if $k \neq k'$, it results:

$$\int \frac{c_j - \mu_{i_k}}{n_k K} \frac{c_{j'} - \mu_{i_{k'}}}{n_{k'} K} \,\mathrm{d}P_C(c_j|i_k)\,\mathrm{d}P_I(i_k)\,\mathrm{d}P_C(c_{j'}|i_{k'})\,\mathrm{d}P_I(i_{k'}) =$$

$$= \int \cancelto{0}{\frac{c_j - \mu_{i_k}}{n_k K} \,\mathrm{d}P_C(c_j|i_k)}\,\mathrm{d}P_I(i_k) \int \cancelto{0}{\frac{c_{j'} - \mu_{i_{k'}}}{n_{k'} K} \,\mathrm{d}P_C(c_{j'}|i_{k'})}\,\mathrm{d}P_I(i_{k'}) = 0.$$

Similarly, if $k = k'$ but $j \neq j'$, it results:

$$\int \frac{c_j - \mu_{i_k}}{n_k K} \frac{c_{j'} - \mu_{i_{k'}}}{n_{k'} K} \,\mathrm{d}P_C(c_j|i_k)\,\mathrm{d}P_I(i_k)\,\mathrm{d}P_C(c_{j'}|i_{k'})\,\mathrm{d}P_I(i_{k'}) =$$

$$= \int \left(\int \cancelto{0}{\frac{c_j - \mu_{i_k}}{n_k K} \,\mathrm{d}P_C(c_j|i_k)} \int \cancelto{0}{\frac{c_{j'} - \mu_{i_k}}{n_k K} \,\mathrm{d}P_C(c_{j'}|i_k)} \right) \mathrm{d}P(i_k) = 0.$$

On the other hand, if $k = k'$ and $j = j'$, it results:

$$\int \frac{c_j - \mu_{i_k}}{n_k K} \frac{c_{j'} - \mu_{i_{k'}}}{n_{k'} K} \,\mathrm{d}P_C(c_j|i_k)\,\mathrm{d}P_I(i_k)\,\mathrm{d}P_C(c_{j'}|i_{k'})\,\mathrm{d}P_I(i_{k'}) =$$

$$= \int \frac{(c_j - \mu_{i_k})^2}{(n_k K)^2} \,\mathrm{d}P_C(c_j|i_k)\,\mathrm{d}P_I(i_k).$$

Thus, addend 4.5a amounts to:

$$\frac{1}{K^2} \sum_{k=1}^{K} \left(\frac{1}{n_k^2} \sum_{j \in J_k} \int (c_j - \mu_{i_k})^2 \,\mathrm{d}P_C(c_j|i_k)\,\mathrm{d}P_I(i_k) \right).$$

Addend 4.5b: since the integrand is independent from j and j', it results:

$$\sum_{k,k'=1}^{K} \sum_{\substack{j \in J_k \\ j' \in J_{k'}}} \int \frac{\mu_{i_k} - \mu}{n_k K} \frac{\mu_{i_{k'}} - \mu}{n_{k'} K} \,\mathrm{d}P_I(i_k)\,\mathrm{d}P_I(i_{k'}) =$$

$$= \frac{1}{K^2} \sum_{k,k'=1}^{K} \int (\mu_{i_k} - \mu)(\mu_{i_{k'}} - \mu) \,\mathrm{d}P_I(i_k)\,\mathrm{d}P_I(i_{k'}).$$

If $k \neq k'$, it results:

$$\int (\mu_{i_k} - \mu)(\mu_{i_{k'}} - \mu) \,\mathrm{d}P_I(i_k)\,\mathrm{d}P_I(i_{k'}) =$$

$$= \int \cancelto{0}{(\mu_{i_k} - \mu) \,\mathrm{d}P_I(i_k)} \int \cancelto{0}{(\mu_{i_{k'}} - \mu) \,\mathrm{d}P_I(i_{k'})} = 0.$$

Otherwise, if $k = k'$, it results:

$$\int (\mu_{i_k} - \mu)(\mu_{i_{k'}} - \mu)\, \mathrm{d}P_I(i_k)\, \mathrm{d}P_I(i_{k'}) = \int (\mu_{i_k} - \mu)^2\, \mathrm{d}P_I(i_k).$$

Thus, addend 4.5b amounts to:

$$\frac{1}{K^2} \sum_{k=1}^{K} \int (\mu_{i_k} - \mu)^2\, \mathrm{d}P_I(i_k).$$

Addend 4.5c: it results:

$$\int \frac{c_j - \mu_{i_k}}{n_k K} \frac{\mu_{i_{k'}} - \mu}{n_{k'} K}\, \mathrm{d}P_C(c_j|i_k)\, \mathrm{d}P_I(i_k)\, \mathrm{d}P_I(i_{k'}) =$$

$$= \int \left(\frac{\mu_{i_{k'}} - \mu}{n_{k'} K} \int \frac{c_j - \mu_{i_k}}{n_k K}\, \mathrm{d}P_C(c_j|i_k) \right) \mathrm{d}P_I(i_k)\, \mathrm{d}P_I(i_{k'}) = 0.$$

Thus, addend 4.5c is identically null.

It results therefore:

$$\int (\tilde{\mu}_{\mathcal{S}_N} - \mu)^2\, \mathrm{d}P(\tilde{\mu}_{\mathcal{S}_N}) = \frac{1}{K^2} \sum_{k=1}^{K} \left(\frac{1}{n_k^2} \sum_{j \in J_k} \int (c_j - \mu_{i_k})^2\, \mathrm{d}P_C(c_j|i_k)\, \mathrm{d}P_I(i_k) \right) +$$

$$+ \frac{1}{K^2} \sum_{k=1}^{K} \int (\mu_{i_k} - \mu)^2\, \mathrm{d}P_I(i_k).$$

On the basis of Definitions 7 and 8 we can write:

$$\int (\tilde{\mu}_{\mathcal{S}_N} - \mu)^2\, \mathrm{d}P(\tilde{\mu}_{\mathcal{S}_N}) = \frac{1}{K^2} \sum_{k=1}^{K} \frac{1}{n_k}\, \bar{\sigma}_{\mathrm{WI}}^2 + \frac{1}{K}\, \sigma_{\mathrm{AI}}^2.$$

□

Let us consider the coefficient of the first term.

Lemma 4. *For a given $K < N$ and under the additive constraint $\sum_{k=1}^{K} n_k = N$, the quantity $\mathfrak{C}(\mathcal{S}_N) = \sum_{k=1}^{K}(1/n_k)$ is minimized if and only if $\max_k n_k - \min_k n_k \leq 1$, that is, $n_k = N/K\ \forall x$ when K divides N, or $n_v = n$ for $K - r$ distinct n_v and $n_w = n + 1$ for other r distinct n_w, where n and r are quotient and rest of the integer division of N by K, respectively. For the given K, the optimal value of the function $\mathfrak{C}$ is therefore*

$$\mathfrak{C}(\bar{\mathcal{S}}_N|K) = \frac{K - r}{n} + \frac{r}{n+1}.$$

Proof. In order to prove the statement, let us assume by way of contradiction, that the setting $\mathcal{S}_N = \{K, n_1, \dots, n_K\}$ with $\max_k n_k - \min_k n_k > 1$ minimizes $\mathcal{C}(\mathcal{S}_N)$ while satisfying the additive constraint. Let further $M = \arg\max_k n_k$ and $m = \arg\min_k n_k$, we have thus $n_M - n_m - 1 > 0$. We can generate a setting $\mathcal{S}'_N = \{K, n'_1, \dots, n'_K\}$ with $n'_m = n_m + 1$, $n'_M = n_M - 1$, and $n'_k = n_k$, otherwise. Clearly $\mathcal{S}_N$ satisfies the additive constraint. Moreover, it results:

$$\begin{aligned}\mathcal{C}(\mathcal{S}'_N) = \sum_{k=1}^{K} \frac{1}{n'_k} &= \mathcal{C}(\mathcal{S}_N) - \left(\frac{1}{n_m} + \frac{1}{n_M}\right) + \left(\frac{1}{n'_m} + \frac{1}{n'_M}\right) = \\ = \mathcal{C}(\mathcal{S}_N) - \frac{n_m + n_M}{n_m n_M} + \frac{n'_m + n'_M}{n'_m n'_M} &= \mathcal{C}(\mathcal{S}_N) - \frac{n_m + n_M}{n_m n_M} + \frac{n_m + 1 + n_M - 1}{(n_m + 1)(n_M - 1)} = \\ &= \mathcal{C}(\mathcal{S}_N) - \frac{n_m + n_M}{n_m n_M} + \frac{n_m + n_M}{n_m n_M + n_M - n_m - 1}.\end{aligned}$$

Since the $n_M - n_m - 1 > 0$, the second fraction is smaller than the first and thus $\mathcal{C}(\mathcal{S}'_N) < \mathcal{C}(\mathcal{S}_N)$, which is a contradiction. To conclude the prof we need to observe that for a given K, all possible settings for which $\max_k n_k - \min_k n_k \leq 1$ is satisfied are just permutations of the same set $\{n_1, n_2, \dots, n_K\}$, where the first r elements have value $n + 1$ and the other $K - r$ elements have value n. All such settings share therefore the same value of the function $\mathcal{C}$, which is clearly invariant under permutation of the addends, and thus all of them minimize it. The condition is therefore necessary and sufficient. The rest of the statement follows trivially. □

Lemma 5. *For any possible setting $\mathcal{S}_N = \{K, n_1, \dots, n_K\}$ that satisfies the additive constraint $\sum_k n_k = N$, it results:*

$$\frac{1}{K^2} \sum_{k=1}^{K} \frac{1}{n_k} \geq \frac{1}{Kn},$$

where n is the result of the integer division of N by K.

Proof. From Lemma 4 it follows that for any generic setting $\mathcal{S}_N$,

$$\frac{1}{K^2} \sum_{k=1}^{K} \frac{1}{n_k} \geq \frac{1}{K^2} \left(\frac{K - r}{n} + \frac{r}{n + 1}\right) = \frac{1}{K} \left(\frac{K - r}{K}\frac{1}{n} + \frac{r}{K}\frac{1}{n + 1}\right).$$

The two addends in parenthesis in the last term represent a weighted average of $1/n$ and $1/(n + 1)$, with weights $(K - r)/K$ and r/K, respectively. The value in parenthesis is therefore constrained to stay between $1/n$ and $1/(n + 1)$, thus:

$$\frac{1}{Kn} \leq \frac{1}{K} \left(\frac{K - r}{K}\frac{1}{n} + \frac{r}{K}\frac{1}{n + 1}\right) \leq \frac{1}{K(n + 1)}.$$

The statement follows. □

Theorem 4. *In any scenario $P(c,i) = P_C(c|i)P_I(i)$, for any given number of total runs N, the estimator $\tilde{\mu}_{\mathcal{S}_N}$ is not better than the estimator $\hat{\mu}_{\mathcal{H}_{N|1}}$ for what concerns the variance of the estimate.*

Proof. Let us recall that according to Corollary 1, the variance of $\hat{\mu}_{\mathcal{H}_{N|1}}$ is:

$$E\big[(\hat{\mu}_{\mathcal{H}_{N|1}} - \mu)^2\big] = \frac{1}{N}\,\bar{\sigma}^2_{\mathrm{WI}} + \frac{1}{N}\,\sigma^2_{\mathrm{AI}}.$$

According to Lemma 3, the variance of $\tilde{\mu}_{\mathcal{S}_N}$ is:

$$E\big[(\tilde{\mu}_{\mathcal{S}_N} - \mu)^2\big] = \frac{1}{K^2}\sum_{k=1}^{K}\frac{1}{n_k}\,\bar{\sigma}^2_{\mathrm{WI}} + \frac{1}{K}\,\sigma^2_{\mathrm{AI}}.$$

Let us compare the coefficients of σ^2_{WI} and σ^2_{AI} in the two equations. According to Lemma 5, $1/K^2 \sum_{k=1}^{K} 1/n_k \geq 1/Kn$, where n is the result of the integer division of N by K. Therefore $Kn \leq N$ and

$$\frac{1}{K^2}\sum_{k=1}^{K}\frac{1}{n_k} \geq \frac{1}{N}. \tag{4.6}$$

On the other hand, $K \leq N$ and therefore

$$\frac{1}{K} \geq \frac{1}{N}. \tag{4.7}$$

In both inequalities 4.6 and 4.7, the equal sign holds if and only if $\tilde{\mu}_{\mathcal{S}_N} = \hat{\mu}_{\mathcal{H}_{N|1}}$. □

4.1.5 Remarks

Concerning the problem of estimating on the basis of N runs the expected behavior of a given configuration θ of a metaheuristic on a class of instances, performing one single run on N different instances guarantees that the variance of the estimate is minimized. Any other experimental setting fails being efficient in terms of reduction of the variance. In particular, we have shown that the total variance can be decomposed in two terms: the expected *within-instance* variance and the *across-instance* variance. A suboptimal experimental setting fails to act on the latter.

Contrary to popular belief, there is no trade-off involved in the definition of the experimental setting when the total number of runs is fixed. The setting "N instances, one run per instance" is shown to be *uniformly* the best across all possible scenarios, that is, irrespectively of the ratio between expected *within-instance* variance and *across-instance* variance.

4.2 The *brute-force* approach

If the overall time available for tuning is T and each single experiment runs for a time t, the total number of experiments that can be performed is $M = \lfloor T/t \rfloor$. In a *brute-force* approach, the computational power is evenly allocated to the different candidates in Θ. Each of them is therefore tested $N = \lfloor M/|\Theta| \rfloor$ times in order to obtain the estimates $\hat{\mu}(\theta_1), \hat{\mu}(\theta_2), \ldots, \hat{\mu}(\theta_{|\Theta|})$ of their expected performance on the class I of instances. Following the theoretical results presented in Section 4.1, the optimal allocation of the allowed N experiments to be performed on each configuration consists in running each configuration once on N different instances sampled according to the unknown measure P_I.

On the basis of these elements, we can define ***Brutus***, the optimal algorithm in the sense defined in Section 4.1, implementing the *brute-force* approach. In ***Brutus***, N instances are randomly sampled according to the unknown distribution P_I. All given candidate configurations of the metaheuristic at hand are tested once on the selected instances. On the basis of the observed results, for each candidate θ an estimate $\hat{\mu}(\theta)$ of the expected performance $\mu(\theta)$ on the class I with respect to the underlying measure P_I is computed. The candidate $\tilde{\theta}$ for which the estimated expected performance is the best, is than selected. Figure 4.1 gives a description of the algorithm ***Brutus*** in pseudo-code.

It is worth noticing here that the memory requirements of ***Brutus*** are particularly limited. Since the only piece of information we need to retain about each candidate configuration is just an estimate of its expected performance—that is, the empirical mean of the results observed on N different instances—and since the mean of N values can be computed incrementally,[14] we simply need to store the current estimate for each candidate. An array of length $|\Theta|$ contains therefore the whole information on the ongoing computation.

Since the algorithm ***Brutus*** appears as the most direct, admittedly trivial, though perfectly legitimate and correct way of solving the tuning problem defined in Section 3.2, it will serve as a baseline in the experimental evaluation we propose in Chapter 5: Clearly, we cannot be satisfied with any tuning algorithm if it does not show to be able to outperform ***Brutus***. Always with the aim of measuring the relative efficiency of tuning algorithms with respect to the *brute-force* approach, we define the family ***Cheat*** as a collection of rather *unfair* algorithms. In particular, we consider ***Cheat2***, ***Cheat5***, and ***Cheat10*** which are simply the same algorithm ***Brutus*** but with a number of total experiments considered which is two, five, and ten times larger, respectively. The pseudo-code of these algorithms, though particularly trivial, is given for the sake of completeness in Figure 4.3.

[14] See the pseudo-code of the function **update_mean** given in Figure 4.2.

```
function Brutus(M)
  # Number of experiments for each candidate
  N = floor(M/|Θ|)

  # Allocate array for storing estimated
  # expected performance of candidates
  A = allocate_array(|Θ|)

  for (k = 1; k ≤ N; k++) do
    # Sample an instance according to P_I
    i = sample_instance()

    foreach θ in Θ do
      # Run candidate θ on instance i
      s = run_experiment(θ, i)

      # Evaluate obtained solution
      c = evaluate_solution(s)

      # Update estimate of expected
      # performance of candidate θ
      A[θ] = update_mean(A[θ], c, k)
    done
  done
  # Select best configuration
  θ̃ = which_min(A)
  return θ̃
```

Figure 4.1: Pseudo-code of the *Brutus* algorithm for tuning metaheuristics.

```
function update_mean(a, c, k)
  return (a * (k − 1) + c)/k
```

Figure 4.2: For the sake of completeness, we give here the definition of the function `update_mean`, notwithstanding its triviality.

function *Cheat2*(M)	**function** *Cheat5*(M)	**function** *Cheat10*(M)
return *Brutus*($2*M$)	**return** *Brutus*($5*M$)	**return** *Brutus*($10*M$)

Figure 4.3: The functions *Cheat2*, *Cheat5*, and *Cheat10* simply implement the *brute-force* approach in a rather "unfair" way: They indeed amount to a call to the function *Brutus* with a number of allowed experiments that is respectively 2, 5, and 10 times larger than M. These algorithms are considered in the experimental comparison presented in Chapter 5 for measuring the relative efficiency of the *racing* approach with respect to the *brute-force* approach.

4.3 The *racing* approach

This section introduces a family of algorithms for solving the problem of tuning metaheuristics as defined in Section 3.2: the family of *racing* approaches (Birattari *et al.*, 2002). These algorithms are inspired by the algorithm *Hoeffding race* introduced by Maron & Moore (1994) for solving the model selection problem in machine learning.[15]

The main idea underlying a *racing* approach is that the evaluation of the performance of a candidate configuration θ of the metaheuristic at hand can be performed incrementally. Indeed, the empirical mean

$$\hat{\mu}_k(\theta) = \sum_{j=1}^{k} c_j^\theta,$$

of the results obtained on any k experiments is an unbiased estimate of the criterion

$$\mu(\theta) = \int c \,\mathrm{d}P_C(c|\theta, i)\,\mathrm{d}P_I(i), \tag{4.8}$$

provided that the instances $i_1, i_2, \ldots, i_k$ which are considered are sampled according to the measure P_I, and the observed costs $c_1^\theta, c_2^\theta, \ldots, c_k^\theta$ of the best solutions found in a run of time t by the configuration θ of the metaheuristic at hand for these instances are a realization of stochastic variables described by the unknown conditional measures $P_C(c|\theta, i_1), P_C(c|\theta, i_2), \ldots, P_C(c|\theta, i_k)$, respectively. Both these conditions are satisfied by definition if we simply consider one after the other the instances that appear in the *stream* of instances described in Chapter 3, and on each of them we run once the configuration θ of the metaheuristic. Moreover, on the basis of the results given in Section 4.1, following such a procedure that prescribes to perform one single run on each instance,

[15]See Section 2.2.7 for a description of the original *racing* approaches as introduced in the machine learning literature, and more in general Section 2.2 for a brief presentation of the main issues in machine learning and supervised learning.

we are guaranteed that the estimate we obtain of the criterion given in Equation 4.8 is the one with the least variance possible. It can be further observed that, according to Corollary 1, page 92, the variance decreases with $1/k$.

On the basis of these elements, we can conclude that a sequence of unbiased estimates $\hat{\mu}_1(\theta), \hat{\mu}_2(\theta), \dots$ can be constructed where $\hat{\mu}_1(\theta) = c_1^\theta$ is simply the cost obtained by the configuration θ in a single run of time t on an instance i_1 sampled according to P_I, and the generic term $\hat{\mu}_k(\theta)$ of the sequence is given by

$$\hat{\mu}_k(\theta) = \frac{(k-1)\hat{\mu}_{k-1}(\theta) + c_k^\theta}{k},$$

where c_k^θ is the cost obtained by the configuration θ in a single run of time t on the k-th instance i_k appeared in the stream of instances, which is therefore sampled according to P_I, by definition. In other words, $\hat{\mu}_k(\theta)$ is the empirical mean of an array of observations

$$c^k(\theta) = (c_1^\theta, c_2^\theta, \dots, c_k^\theta),$$

and this array is obtained by appending the term c_k^θ to the array

$$c^{k-1}(\theta) = (c_1^\theta, c_2^\theta, \dots, c_{k-1}^\theta),$$

whose mean is the estimate $\hat{\mu}_{k-1}(\theta)$. The variance of this sequence of estimates decreases with $1/k$ and therefore the estimation of the performance of candidate θ gets sharper and sharper when k gets larger and converges to the true expectation $\mu(\theta)$.

Given the possibility of constructing the above described sequence of unbiased estimates $\hat{\mu}_1(\theta), \hat{\mu}_2(\theta), \dots$ for each candidate $\theta \in \Theta$, a *racing* algorithm can be defined that incrementally constructs in parallel such sequences for all candidates in Θ and, as soon as sufficient evidence is obtained that the criterion $\mu(\theta')$ for a given candidate θ' is larger that the criterion $\mu(\tilde{\theta})$ of some other candidate $\tilde{\theta}$, discards θ' from further evaluations.

A *racing* algorithm therefore generates a sequence of nested sets of candidate configurations:

$$\Theta_0 \supseteq \Theta_1 \supseteq \Theta_2 \supseteq \dots,$$

starting from $\Theta_0 = \Theta$. The step from a set Θ_{k-1} to Θ_k is obtained by possibly discarding some configurations that appear to be suboptimal on the basis of information available at step k.

At step k, when the set of candidates still in the race is Θ_{k-1}, a new instance i_k is considered. Each candidate $\theta \in \Theta_{k-1}$ is tested on i_k and each observed cost c_k^θ is appended to the respective array $c^{k-1}(\theta)$ to form the different arrays $c^k(\theta)$, one for each $\theta \in \Theta_{k-1}$. Step k terminates defining set Θ_k by dropping from Θ_{k-1} the configurations that appear to be suboptimal in the light of some statistical test that compares the arrays $c^k(\theta)$ for all $\theta \in \Theta_{k-1}$. The above described procedure is iterated and stops either when all configurations but one are discarded, or when a given maximum number of instance have been sampled, or finally when the predefined total number M of experiments has been performed. The pseudo-code of the generic *racing* algorithm is given in Figure 4.4.

The apparent advantage of the *racing* approach over *brute-force* is that it provides for a better allocation of computational resources among candidate configurations: Rather than waisting computing time to precisely estimate the performance of inferior candidates, the *racing* approach focuses on the most promising ones and obtains lower variance estimates for these latter. This allows for a more informed selection of the best candidate. Figure 4.5 proposes a graphical representation of the different strategies adopted by the two approaches for organizing the evaluation of the given candidate configurations.

Along the race, some *sufficient statistics* (Mendenhall *et al.*, 1986) of the results obtained by the surviving candidates has to be maintained. The amount of information to be stored depends on the specific statistical test to be used for deciding whether the observed differences in the performance of the candidates is significant or not. In the worst case, all observed results need to be stored for the surviving candidates. The memory requirement for a *racing* approach is therefore bounded by M times the amount of memory needed for storing the cost of the solution found in a single run of the metaheuristic.[16]

A variety of statistical tests can be considered in the implementation of a *racing* algorithm. In the context of our discussion, it is convenient to classify such statistical tests according to 3 different criteria:

Parametric vs. nonparametric tests: Parametric tests rely on some assumptions concerning the stochastic quantities at hand, namely their normality. On the other hand, nonparametric tests are *distribution independent.*

When the assumptions of a parametric test indeed match the reality, the parametric test is typically more *powerful* than his nonparametric counterpart; that is, the parametric test is able to detect significance on the basis of a set of observations that is smaller than the set needed by the nonparametric one. On the other hand, if the assumptions are not matched, the parametric test may lead to wrong conclusions (Siegel & Castellan, 1988).

Blocking vs. non-blocking design: In the context of the problem of tuning metaheuristics, the adoption of a blocking design (Dean & Voss, 1999; Montgomery, 2000) appears both natural and appealing.[17] Instances in I might be quite inhomogeneous and might present a quite large variability in the

[16] Typically much less, since the results obtained by the discarded configurations before elimination can be discarded ad well.

[17] For an example of the adoption of a blocking design, we refer the reader back to Note 60, page 64.

```
function generic_race(M, use_test)
  # Number of experiments performed so far
  experiments_soFar = 0

  # Number of instances considered so far
  instances_soFar = 0

  # Allocate array for storing observed
  # performance of candidates
  C = allocate_array(max_instances, |Θ|)

  # Surviving candidates
  S = Θ

  while(experiments_soFar + |S| ≤ M and
        instances_soFar + 1 ≤ max_instances) do
    # Sample an instance according to P_I
    i = sample_instance()
    instances_soFar += 1

    foreach θ in S do
      # Run candidate θ on instance i
      s = run_experiment(θ, i)
      experiments_soFar += 1

      # Evaluate solution and store result
      C[instances_soFar, θ] = evaluate_solution(s)
    done
    # Drop inferior candidates according to
    # the given statistical test
    S = drop_candidates(S, C, use_test)
  done
  # Select best surviving configuration
  θ̃ = select_best_survivor(S, C)
  return θ̃
```

Figure 4.4: Pseudo-code of a generic *racing* approach for tuning metaheuristics.

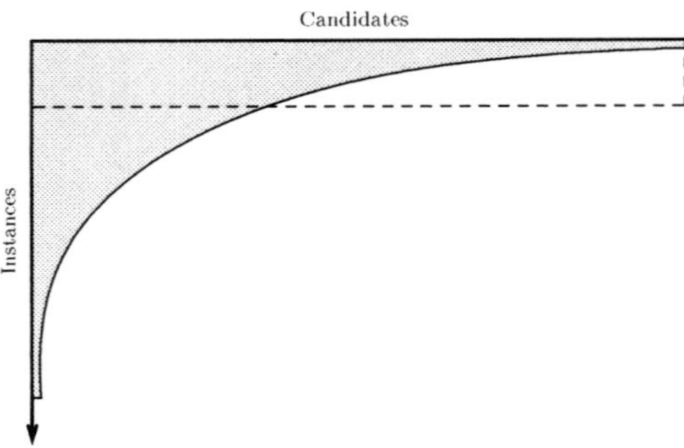

Figure 4.5: Graphical representation of the different ways adopted by the *racing* approach and by the *brute-force* approach of allocating computational power among the different candidates to be tested. In the *racing* approach, as soon as sufficient evidence is gathered that a candidate is suboptimal, such candidate is discarded from further evaluation. As the evaluation proceeds, the *racing* approach focuses thus more and more on the most promising candidates. On the other hand, the *brute-force* approach tests all given candidates on the same number of instances. The shadowed figure represents the computation performed by the *racing* approach, while the dashed rectangle the one of the *brute-force* approach. The two figures cover the same surface, that is, the two approaches are allowed to perform the same total number of experiments.

cost of their solutions.[18] In the terminology introduced in Section 4.1.1, we say that we are confronted with a large *across-instance* variance.

If not handled properly, such *across-instance* variance could *wash-out* the differences in the performance of the various configurations.

Family-wise vs. pair-wise tests: When comparing more than two candidates among them, two different approaches might be followed. In the *family-wise* approach one answers first the question whether all observed results, irrespectively of which candidate they belong to, might have been extracted from the same distribution. If, and only if, the answer to this question is negative, that is, if we have elements to believe that the candidates indeed differ, one can proceed to the so called *post-test* in which candidates are

[18] For definiteness, let us consider again MARIO'S PIZZA DELIVERY problem where the instances in I are instances of the TRAVELING SALESMAN problem representing delivery tours to be scheduled—see Section 3.1. Some of these instances could require visiting a small number of customers while other could be much larger. Clearly, the cost of the typical solutions of the small instance is smaller than the one of typical solutions of larger instances.

compared one with the others to tell which are better and which are worse.

On the other hand, in the *pair-wise* approach one infers a statement on the family-wise difference among candidates from their pair-wise comparison. When a *pair-wise* approach is adopted, a correction of the p-values has to be performed.[19]

In our treatment of the *racing* approach for tuning metaheuristics, we consider four different tests yielding each a specific implementation of a *racing* algorithm:

***tNo-Race*:** The statistical test adopted here is the classical **t-test** in its *paired* version. According to the taxonomy of statistical tests introduced above, this test is *parametric*, it implements a *blocking design*, and it is a *pair-wise* test that, in the form considered here does **not** consider any correction of the p-values for multiple comparisons. It should be noted that, in this context, the fact of not considering any correction for multiplicity is to be considered quite an *improper practice*, as it is pointed out in Note 19. The *tNo-Race* algorithm can be seen as the direct application to the problem of tuning metaheuristics of the *BRACE* algorithm for model selection described in Section 2.2.7.

[19] Details on the issue can be found in Sheskin (2000), Hsu (1996), or in any manual of probability theory such as, for example, Papoulis (1991). For the convenience of the readers who are not particularly familiar with statistical tests of significance, we briefly recall here some elements that are useful in our discussion. Let us consider the case in which two candidates θ_1 and θ_2 are given and the sets of observations $c(\theta_1)$ and $c(\theta_2)$ are available. We wish to conclude, for example, that θ_1 is better than θ_2 for what concerns the *central attitude*, that is, their mean (or median) performance. Let us say that indeed the observed mean value $\hat{\mu}(\theta_1)$ results smaller than $\hat{\mu}(\theta_2)$. The question is whether the observed difference is *significant* or is just to be ascribed to chance.

To answer this question, the *null hypothesis* H_0 is formulated that states that θ_1 and θ_2 are equivalent. Then the probability p is computed that under hypothesis H_0 one might obtain a difference between $\hat{\mu}(\theta_1)$ and $\hat{\mu}(\theta_2)$ which is *at least as large* as the observed one. If this value p, known as p-value, is smaller that a predefined α—typically $\alpha = 0.05$ in most applications—the null hypothesis H_0 is rejected and we are rather in favor of accepting that θ_1 and θ_2 differ. This procedure implies that when H_0 is true, we might reject it with probability α: Indeed, when we reject H_0, we state that we are *confident* with our conclusion at a degree of $1 - \alpha$.

In order to understand the reason why a correction of the p-values is needed when performing multiple simultaneous tests, let us consider the following example: $|\Theta|$ candidates $\theta_1, \theta_2, \ldots, \theta_{|\Theta|}$ are given which are *all* equivalent, that is, the corresponding observations gathered in the arrays $c(\theta_1), c(\theta_2), \ldots, c(\theta_{|\Theta|})$ are all extracted from the same population. If we perform all $L = |\Theta|(|\Theta| - 1)/2$ pair-wise tests on the given candidates, the probability that at least one of the p-values is less than α—and therefore the probability to reject the hypothesis that the candidates are equivalent—is $1 - (1 - \alpha)^L$. Since $1 - \alpha < 1$, such probability can be made arbitrarily close to 1 by increasing the number $|\Theta|$ of candidates. We conclude that the outlined procedure will reject with an arbitrarily high probability the hypothesis that a group of candidates are equivalent provided that the number of such candidates is sufficiently large. Hence, the necessity arises of rescaling the pair-wise p-values when multiple tests are performed.

***tBo-Race*:** Also in this case, the test adopted is the classical **t-test** in its *paired* version. Contrary to *tNo-Race*, in *tBo-Race* a Bonferroni's correction for multiplicity (Bonferroni, 1935, 1936) is adopted for rescaling the p-values of each of the pair-wise comparisons that are performed. Apart for the fact that here a proper correction of the p-values is adopted, *tBo-Race* is identical to *tNo-Race*.

***tHo-Race*:** Also in this case, the test adopted is the classical **t-test** in its *paired* version. As in *tBo-Race*, but contrary to *tNo-Race*, in *tHo-Race* a proper correction for multiplicity is adopted. In this case, the correction considered is the one proposed by Holm (1979). This correction is known to be less conservative than the one proposed by Bonferroni.

***F-Race*:** The statistical test adopted here is the **Friedman two-way analysis of variance by ranks**. This test is *nonparametric*, it implements a *blocking design*, and consists in the use of a *family-wise* test followed by some appropriate *post-tests*, if significance is detected by the former. Since *F-Race* is the most original of the four *racing* algorithm introduced in this thesis for tackling the problem of tuning metaheuristics, the full Section 4.4 is devoted to its description.

All the four aforementioned algorithms are described by the pseudo-code of the function `generic_race` given in Figure 4.4 and they differ only in the definition of the function `drop_candidates` whose pseudo-code is given in Figure 4.6. On the basis of `generic_race`, the definition of the four *racing* algorithms *tNo-Race*, *tBo-Race*, *tHo-Race*, and *F-Race* given in Figure 4.7 is immediate.

An implementation of these algorithms in R language[20] was made available in the public domain by the author (Birattari, 2003): The package race for R is available for free download from the official site of *The Comprehensive* R *Archive Network*.[21]

4.4 The peculiarities of *F-Race*

Though all four *racing* algorithms introduced in Section 4.3 are original in the context of the problem of tuning metaheuristics, *tNo-Race*, *tBo-Race*, and *tHo-Race* are fairly similar to the *BRACE* algorithm for model selection. In particular, similarly to *BRACE*, the three aforementioned algorithms all adopt some version of the t-test. The only difference lies in the fact that *tBo-Race* and *tHo-Race* adopt some sort of adjustment for multiplicity, namely those proposed by Bonferroni and Holm, respectively. On the other hand, *F-Race* (Birattari

[20] R is the free software implementation of the S language originally developed at AT&T Bell Labs, and it is similar to the commercial suite S-plus© of Mathsoft™.

[21] `http://cran.r-project.org/src/contrib/Descriptions/race.html`

```
function drop_candidates(S, C, use_test)
 switch(use_test)
   case friedman_test:
     if(is_significant(friedman_family_wise(S, C)))
       θ̃ = select_best_survivor(S, C)
       foreach θ in S do
         if(is_significant(friedman_post_test(θ̃, θ, C)))
           S = S \ {θ}
         end
       done
     end
   case t_test:
     θ̃ = select_best_survivor(S, C)
     foreach θ in S do
       # Paired t-test without any correction for multiplicity
       if(is_significant(t_test(θ̃, θ, C)))
         S = S \ {θ}
       end
     done
   case t_test_bonferroni:
     θ̃ = select_best_survivor(S, C)
     foreach θ in S do
       # Paired t-test with Bonferroni's correction for multiplicity
       if(is_significant(t_test_bonferroni(θ̃, θ, C)))
         S = S \ {θ}
       end
     done
   case t_test_holm:
     θ̃ = select_best_survivor(S, C)
     foreach θ in S do
       # Paired t-test with Holm's correction for multiplicity
       if(is_significant(t_test_holm(θ̃, θ, C)))
         S = S \ {θ}
       end
     done
 end
 return S
```

Figure 4.6: Pseudo-code of the function `drop_candidates`.

```
function F-Race(M)
  return generic_race(M, friedman_test)
```

```
function tNo-Race(M)
  return generic_race(M, t_test)
```

```
function tBo-Race(M)
  return generic_race(M, t_test_bonferroni)
```

```
function tHo-Race(M)
  return generic_race(M, t_test_holm)
```

Figure 4.7: The functions *F-Race*, *tNo-Race*, *tBo-Race*, and *tHo-Race* are simply a call to `generic_race(M, use_test)`, where `use_test` is the appropriate statistical test to be used for deciding whether some candidate configurations should be dropped from the race.

et al., 2002) is based on a statistical test that has never been adopted before in any *racing* algorithm: the **Friedman two-way analysis of variance by ranks**.

For giving a description of the test, let us assume that *F-Race* has reached step k, and $m = |\Theta_{k-1}|$ configurations are still in the race: $\theta_{v_1}, \theta_{v_2}, \ldots, \theta_{v_m}$. The Friedman test assumes that the costs observed so far for the configurations still in the race are the realization of k mutually independent m-variate random variables:

$$\begin{aligned}
b_1 &= \left(c_1^{\theta_{v_1}},\ c_1^{\theta_{v_2}},\ \ldots,\ c_1^{\theta_{v_m}}\right)\\
b_2 &= \left(c_2^{\theta_{v_1}},\ c_2^{\theta_{v_2}},\ \ldots,\ c_2^{\theta_{v_m}}\right)\\
\vdots & \qquad \vdots \qquad\quad \vdots \qquad\ \ddots \qquad \vdots\\
b_k &= \left(c_k^{\theta_{v_1}},\ c_k^{\theta_{v_2}},\ \ldots,\ c_k^{\theta_{v_m}}\right)
\end{aligned}$$

called *blocks*[22] where each block b_l corresponds to the computational results obtained on instance i_l by each configuration still in the race at step k. Within each block, the quantities c_l^{θ} are ranked from the smallest to the largest. Average ranks are used in case of ties. For each configuration $\theta_{v_j} \in \Theta_{k-1}$, let R_{lj} be the rank

[22] Note 60 at page 64, introduces with an example the main idea behind the *blocking* design. We refer the reader to Dean & Voss (1999) and Montgomery (2000) for more details on the issue.

of θ_{v_j} within block b_l, and $R_j = \sum_{l=1}^{k} R_{lj}$ the sum of the ranks concerning θ_{v_j}, over all instances i_l, with $1 \leq l \leq k$. The Friedman test considers the following statistic (Conover, 1999):

$$T = \frac{(m-1)\displaystyle\sum_{j=1}^{m}\left(R_j - \frac{k(m+1)}{2}\right)^2}{\displaystyle\sum_{l=1}^{k}\sum_{j=1}^{m} R_{lj}^2 - \frac{km(m+1)^2}{4}}.$$

Under the null hypothesis that all candidates are equivalent among them and therefore all possible rankings of the candidates themselves within each block are equally likely, T is approximatively distributed as χ^2 with $m-1$ degrees of freedom (Papoulis, 1991). If the observed T exceeds the $1-\alpha$ quantile of this distribution, the null hypothesis is rejected, at the approximate confidence level α, in favor of the idea that at least one candidate tends to yield a better performance than at least one of the others.[23]

If the null hypothesis is rejected in the above described *family-wise* test, we are justified in performing pairwise comparisons between individual candidates. In such *post-tests*, candidates θ_j and θ_h are considered different if

$$\frac{|R_j - R_h|}{\sqrt{\frac{2k\left(1-\frac{T}{k(m-1)}\right)\left(\sum_{l=1}^{k}\sum_{j=1}^{m} R_{lj}^2 - \frac{km(m+1)^2}{4}\right)}{(k-1)(m-1)}}} > t_{1-\alpha/2},$$

where $t_{1-\alpha/2}$ is the $1-\alpha/2$ quantile of the Student's t distribution (Conover, 1999).

In *F-Race*, if at step k the null hypothesis of the family-wise comparison is not rejected, all candidates in Θ_{k-1} pass to Θ_k. On the other hand, if the null hypothesis is rejected, pairwise comparisons are executed between the best candidate and each other one. All candidates that result significantly worse than the best are discarded and will not appear in Θ_k.

When only two candidates remain in the race, that is, if $|\Theta_k| = 2$; for some given k, the Friedman test reduces to the *binomial sign test for two dependent samples* (Sheskin, 2000). In the *F-Race* algorithm, as implemented in the package race for R which is considered for the experimental analysis proposed in Chapter 5, when only 2 candidates θ_{v1} and θ_{v2} remain in the race, the *Wilcoxon matched-pairs signed-ranks test* (Conover, 1999) is adopted instead. The main difference between the binomial sign test—or, alternatively, the Friedman test with only 2 candidates—and the Wilcoxon test rests in the fact that within each block b_l the former considers only the *sign* of the difference $c_l^{\theta_{v1}} - c_l^{\theta_{v2}}$, while the latter exploits

[23]All experimental results presented in this thesis where obtained with $\alpha = 0.05$: The adoption of a confidence level of 95% is rather typical in hypothesis testing.

also the knowledge of the *magnitude* of this difference. As a consequence, the Wilcoxon test is more powerful and data-efficient (Siegel & Castellan, 1988).[24]

The role of ranking in *F-Race*

In *F-Race*, ranking plays an important two-fold role. The first one is connected with the nonparametric nature of a test based on ranking. The main merit of nonparametric analysis is that it does not require to formulate hypotheses on the distribution of the observations. Discussions on the relative pros and cons of the parametric and nonparametric approaches can be found in most textbooks on statistics (Larson, 1982). For an organic presentation of the topic, we refer the reader, for example, to Conover (1999). Here we limit ourselves to mention some widely accepted facts about parametric and nonparametric hypothesis testing: When the hypotheses they formulate are met, parametric tests have a higher power than nonparametric ones and usually require much less computation. Further, when a large amount of data is available the hypotheses for the application of parametric tests tend to be met in virtue of the central limit theorem. Finally, it is well known that the t-test, the classical parametric test that is of interest here, is robust against departure from some of its hypotheses, namely the normality of data: When the hypothesis of normality is not strictly met, the t-test *gracefully* looses power.

For what concerns the problem of tuning metaheuristics, we are in a situation in which these arguments do not hold: First, since we wish to reduce as soon as possible the number of candidates, we deal with very small samples and it is exactly on these small samples, for which the central limit theorem cannot be advocated, that we wish to have the maximum power. Second, the computational cost of running the statistical test are not really relevant since in any case they are negligible compared to the computational cost of executing configurations of the metaheuristic in order to enlarge the available samples. Chapter 5 shows that the doubts expressed here find some evidential support in our experiments.

---

[24]Nevertheless it should be observed that, notwithstanding the theoretical superiority of the Wilcoxon test over the binomial sign test, the adoption of the former within *F-Race* does not have a major impact on the performance of the algorithm which is much more heavily influenced by the behavior of the Friedman test during the early phases of the race. Indeed, when the number of surviving candidates is reduced to two, the outcome of the race is already defined in its main traits and little can be determined by the adoption of one test rather than another: When only two candidates remain, data-efficiency is not really crucial since the cost of obtaining one further sample simply amounts to two runs of the metaheuristic at hand, one for each of the survivors. On the other hand, data-efficiency is a central issue in the early stages of the race when a large number of candidates are still under evaluation and the costs of a further sample is very large, that is, a run of the metaheuristic under consideration for each of the survivors.

For this reason, we present the adoption of the Wilcoxon test in *F-Race* simply as an implementation detail and we do not consecrate further attention to the analysis of its impact on the performance of the overall algorithm.

A second role played by ranking in *F-Race* is to implement in a natural way a blocking design (Dean & Voss, 1999; Montgomery, 2000). The variation in the observed costs c is due to different sources: Metaheuristics are intrinsically stochastic algorithms, the instances might be very different one from the other, and finally some configurations perform better than others. This last source of variation is the one that is of interest in the configuration problem while the others might be considered as disturbing elements. Blocking is an effective way for normalizing the costs observed on different instances. By focusing only on the ranking of the different configurations within each instance, blocking eliminates the risks that the variation due to the difference among instances washes out the variation due to the difference among configurations.

F-Race is openly and largely inspired by the *racing* algorithms proposed in the machine learning community for solving the model selection problem (Maron & Moore, 1994; Moore & Lee, 1994) but it is precisely in the adoption of a statistical test based on ranking that it diverges from previously published works. *Hoeffding race* (Maron & Moore, 1994) adopts a nonparametric approach but does not consider blocking. On the other hand, *BRACE* (Moore & Lee, 1994) adopts blocking but discards the nonparametric setting in favor of a Bayesian approach. Other relevant work was proposed by Gratch *et al.* (1993) and by Chien *et al.* (1995) who consider blocking in a parametric setting.

F-Race, to the best of our knowledge, is the first *racing* algorithm in which blocking is considered in a nonparametric setting. Further, in all the above mentioned *racing* algorithms, blocking was always implemented through multiple pairwise paired comparisons (Hsu, 1996), and only in the more recent one (Chien *et al.*, 1995) correction for multiple tests is considered. *F-Race* is the first *racing* algorithm to implement blocking through ranking and to adopt a family-wise test over all candidates, to be performed prior to any pairwise test.

4.5 Discussion

This chapter has presented a number of algorithms for solving the tuning problem defined in Chapter 3. All these algorithms rely on a Monte Carlo estimation of the expected performance of the candidate configurations since the latter cannot be calculate analytically given that the probability measures involved in the definition of the expectation are unknown.

Some important theoretical results were proposed in Section 4.1. In particular, it was shown that in the context defined in Chapter 3, among all possible estimators of the expected performance of a given configuration based on a fixed number N of experimental evaluations of the configuration itself, the best one, that is, the one of minimum variance, is obtained by averaging the results obtained in N runs of the configuration on N *different* instances, each independently sampled according to the measure P_I.

This result is exploited by all algorithms proposed in the chapter. In particular, we propose two classes of algorithms following two different approaches: the *brute-force* approach and the *racing* approach. The former is the most immediate way of tackling the problem of tuning metaheuristics. It is introduced here with the main goal of providing a baseline for the empirical analysis of the other algorithms proposed in the thesis. On the other hand, the *racing* approach is an innovative and particularly promising approach for the automatic tuning of metaheuristics. This class of algorithms is inspired by the original *Hoeffding race* algorithm (Maron & Moore, 1994) proposed within the machine learning community for solving the model selection problem. The main idea behind the *racing* approach is that the evaluation of the candidate configurations can be performed incrementally. Along the process inferior candidates can be dropped and not further evaluated, as soon as statistically sufficient evidence is gathered that they produce a worse performance that at least another candidate. By eliminating inferior candidates, the evaluation is speeded up and can focus on the most promising candidates of which a more accurate evaluation is performed. Among the *racing* algorithms for tuning metaheuristics that were presented in this chapter, the most innovative is *F-Race*. Indeed, *F-Race* is based on the **Friedman two-way analysis of variance by ranks**, a method for statistical testing of hypothesis that had never been adopted before in the context of *racing* algorithms. This test appears particularly appropriate for tuning metaheuristics given its *nonparametric* nature and the natural way in which it implements a *blocking* design.

It is worth noticing here that the development of all the algorithms presented in the chapter and of the theoretical results presented in Section 4.1 as well, were made possible by the formal definition of the tuning problem given in Chapter 3. In particular, they rest on the assumption that instances are independently extracted according to a *fixed* measure P_I, and that for a given instance and configuration of the metaheuristic, the observed cost is extracted independently according to a *fixed* conditional measure P_C. These measures are *unknown* and they are never explicitly modeled by the algorithms described in the chapter. Yet, they play the fundamental role of giving a meaning to the experiments performed with the given candidate configurations on the available instances, and to the averages of the observed results: Thanks to the hypothesis that instance and costs are *sampled* according to P_I and P_C, respectively, the average of the observed costs *becomes* an estimate of the expected cost, and thanks to the hypothesis that P_I and P_C are fixed, these estimate *becomes* a prediction of the cost we will observe on future instances. Since, as it was already observed in Section 3.1, the ultimate goal of tuning a metaheuristics is precisely to find the configuration that will provide the best performance on *future* instances, the central roles of the hypotheses concerning the measures P_I and P_C emerges distinctly.

Misura ciò che è misurabile, e rendi misurabile ciò che non lo è.[†]

Galileo Galilei

Chapter 5

Experiments and applications

In this chapter we provide some composite and extensive evidence of the effectiveness of the *racing* approach, and in particular of the *F-Race* algorithm, for tuning metaheuristics and more in general for tuning stochastic algorithms.

In particular, Section 5.1 proposes a formal empirical analysis of *F-Race* on the problem of tuning metaheuristics. In this analysis, the algorithm is compared against other *racing* algorithms and against the *brute-force* approach. The latter, being the most straightforward approach for tackling the tuning problem defined in Chapter 3, can be considered as the natural choice of a baseline algorithm for assessing the performance of tuning methods. In order to assess *F-Race*, two tuning problems are considered. In the first, proposed in Section 5.1.1, the metaheuristic to be tuned is *iterated local search* and the optimization problem considered is the QUADRATIC ASSIGNMENT problem. In the second, proposed in Section 5.1.2, the algorithm is *ant colony optimization* and the problem is the TRAVELING SALESMAN problem. On these problems, a formal empirical analysis is carried out: a number of algorithms, including indeed *F-Race*, are compared under controlled conditions, the differences in their performance are assessed through appropriate statistical tests of significance, and a number of graphs are proposed that help visualize and understand the characteristics of the algorithms under study. The experimental methodology followed in the analysis is heavily influenced by the one commonly adopted within the machine learning community. A discussion on the implications and on the opportunity of adopting this methodology is given in Chapter 6. A particularly valuable tool that has been employed is a so-called *re-sampling* method. This method, originally presented in the literature on nonparametric statistics, is rather well known by machine learning practitioners but, to the best of our knowledge, it has never been adopted before for what concerns the empirical analysis of metaheuristics: Its first application in the field is described in Birattari *et al.* (2002).

On the other hand, Section 5.2 gives examples of practical applications of

[†] *Measure what is measurable, and make measurable what is not so.*

F-Race and, more in general of related *racing* approachs. These examples do not provide any formal comparison with other methods and are of a *qualitative* rather than *quantitative* nature. Their goal is to show that the algorithms discussed in this thesis have the flexibility and usability that are necessary to make them appealing for practical applications. In particular, among the examples proposed in Section 5.2, it is worth mentioning here the adoption, discussed in Section 5.2.2, of a modified version of the *F-Race* algorithm for tuning the metaheuristic that was submitted by the author and co-workers to the *International Timetabling Competition* held in 2003. This metaheuristic outperformed all other submissions. Moreover, we wish to mention here a feasibility study that has been carried out in a joint research project by the German-based software company SAP and the INTELLEKTIK group of the Technische Universität Darmstadt, Germany. This study concerned the possible adoption of a *racing* algorithm for automatically tuning a critical component of a commercial products developed by SAP for vehicle routing and scheduling. The research is sketched in Section 5.2.4.

Sections 5.1 and 5.2 are therefore complementary: the former gives an academic analysis under controlled conditions, while the latter shows through some examples the actual applicability of the method in real-world applications. Section 5.3 concludes the chapter with a brief discussion.

5.1 Empirical analysis of *F-Race*

The experimental methodology adopted in this analysis contains many innovative elements that are to be considered as original contributions in themselves. The two most notable ones are the adoption of a re-sampling technique (Good, 2001) and a clear stand for what concerns the separation of the set of instances used for tuning the algorithm and those used for testing it. Both these elements are well known within the machine learning community. In particular, the separation between the training set and the test set is such an essential element of what is commonly considered a correct experimental practice, to be regarded almost as a commonplace. On the other hand, the separation between the set of instances used for tuning the parameters and the set of instances used for testing the selected configuration of the algorithm is sadly too often disregarded in scientific works in the optimization field. An introduction to these concepts for what concerns the supervised learning problem is given in Section 2.2.6. On the other hand, Chapter 6 discusses and proves with an example the relevance of these concepts also in the field of metaheuristics and optimization in general.

The rest of the section is devoted to the presentation of the abstract principles of the experimental methodology adopted and of the re-sampling strategy we implemented in practice. We provide also a brief description of the computing environment in which the experiments where performed and some guidelines on how to read and interpret the tables and graphs proposed in Sections 5.1.1 and 5.1.2.

The experimental methodology

The experimental methodology we adopted considers a *stream of instances* as described in Chapter 3: at each step a new instance is generated according to some *unknown but fixed* probability measure and the instances generated at different steps are independent. In the experiments we present here, the instances were artificially generated according to some distributions using some instance generators. No information on these distributions or on any other detail concerning the instance generators were used by the tuning algorithms under analysis: this reproduces the typical context in which metaheuristics are used in practice. Indeed, such information are clearly not available in real-world applications. A description of the instance generators adopted is given in Sections 5.1.1 and 5.1.2. The instances generated in the stream are employed for tuning the metaheuristic at hand using the different tuning algorithms considered in the study. In the following, we refer to these instances as *tuning instances*, and we call *tuning set* the set of these instances. The result of the tuning procedure is the selection of a candidate configuration for each of the tuning algorithms considered. The selected configurations are then tested on *new* instances that are also in this case extracted from the stream. We refer to these instances as *test instance* and to their set as *test set*. Here by *new* we mean that the test instances where not considered during the tuning phase and are therefore distinct from those appearing in the tuning set. The average performance of the selected configurations on the *new* instances is an *unbiased* estimate of their performance on the whole class of instances and can be therefore considered as an appropriate criterion for their comparison. Furthermore, since the set of candidate configurations out of which the selection has been operated is the same for all tuning algorithms considered, this criterion is appropriate also for comparing the performance of the tuning algorithms themselves.

With the aim of reducing the effects of chance on the observed results and of eliminating all nuisances that could wash out the differences in the performance of the tuning algorithms under analysis, we feed the *same* tuning instances to each of them and we assess the performance of the selected configuration on the *same* test instances. Moreover, in order to obtain some statistical relevance and to get rid of the possibles idiosyncrasies of a specific tuning set and test set pair, we repeat this procedure of *tuning & testing* a sufficiently large number of times, using different sets of tuning and test instances each time.

It is worth defining here some terminology that is consistently adopted in the following: We call a **run** a single execution of a given configuration on a given instance. Specifically, in the experiments proposed in Sections 5.1.1 and 5.1.2, each run lasts 10 s on the computers adopted for the analysis—See page 119 for a description of these machines. On the other hand, by **trial** we mean a complete execution of a *tuning & testing* procedure for the tuning algorithms under analysis.

The re-sampling approach

It is apparent that the above described procedure is particularly expensive from a computational point of view. In the case of the experiments proposed in Sections 5.1.1 and 5.1.2 each tuning algorithm is allowed to perform a total maximum number of runs of the given configurations equal to 6000 and 13680, respectively.[1] In both experiments, each run of the metaheuristics takes 10 s and for each of the 8 tuning algorithms studied, 1000 trials are considered for statistical significance. In each trial, the configuration selected by each tuning method is tested on 10 test instance, therefore each trial for each tuning methods involves 6010 and 13690 runs for each of the two experiments, respectively. This amounts to a total computation time of $(6010 + 13690) \times 1000 \times 8 \times 10\,\mathrm{s} \approx 1.6 \times 10^9\,\mathrm{s}$, that is, slightly less than 50 years of computation.[2]

The computational cost of such experimental analysis is apparently prohibitive. In order to deal with this problem, we adopted an experimental methodology based on re-sampling (Good, 2001).

For each of the two experimental studies, a number of instances are independently generated. Namely, 800 in the experiment proposed in Section 5.1.1 and 500 for the one proposed in Section 5.1.2. Each of the given candidate configurations is executed once on each of these instances and the cost of the best solution found in each of the considered 10 s runs is stored in a $\mathcal{K} \times |\Theta|$ two-dimensional array, where $\mathcal{K}$ is the number of instances generated—800 in the first experiment and 500 in the second—and $|\Theta|$ is, as usual, the number of configurations among which the selection of the best is to be performed. Once this array is filled with results for each instance/configuration pair, we are in the position of *simulating* a run of any of the given configurations on any of the given instances: we call a **pseudo-run** of configuration j on instance i the simulation of a run of configuration j on instance i, where such simulation simply consists in reading the value stored in position (i, j) of the above described array of results.

From the $\mathcal{K}$ available instances, we extract 1000 **pseudo-samples**, each of which has cardinality $\mathcal{K}$ and is obtained by randomly re-ordering the original sequence of instances. Each of these pseudo-samples is used for performing a **pseudo-trial**, that is, the simulation of a trial of the tuning algorithms under analysis. In particular, we adopt the convention that the last 10 instances in each pseudo-sample constitute the set of test instances for their respective pseudo-trial. Such instances are reserved for the evaluation of the configurations selected in

[1] In the experiments proposed here, each tuning algorithm may perform a number M of runs equal to 15 times the number of candidate configurations. In the experiment proposed in Section 5.1.1, the number of candidate configurations is 400. Hence, $M = 6000 = 15 \times 400$ is the number of total runs allowed. Similarly, in the experiment proposed in Section 5.1.2 the total number of runs allowed is $M = 13680 = 15 \times 912$ since the number of candidate configurations is 912.

[2] More details on the experiments are given in Sections 5.1.1 and 5.1.2. The data provided here serve solely the purpose of giving the reader a picture of the computational costs involved.

the tuning phase and are *never* used in the tuning itself. On the other hand, all other instances, that is, the first $\mathcal{K} - 10$ instances of each pseudo-sample, constitute the tuning set and are fed, in the specific sequence defined by the pseudo-sample, to the tuning algorithms under study. In other words, a **pseudo-stream** of instances is simulated by sampling *without replacement* from the set of $\mathcal{K}$ available instances. One after the other such instances are considered and are used by each of the tuning algorithms for selecting the best configuration among the available ones. Clearly, each tuning algorithm implements a different strategy for performing the selection of the best configuration and, in particular, each algorithm might consider a different number of instance among the given ones. In any case, all algorithms—with the notable exception of those belonging to the *cheat* family—will respect the constraint that no more than M pseudo-runs can be performed where $M = 6000$ in the experiment presented in Section 5.1.1 and $M = 13680$ in the one presented in Section 5.1.2. As already mentioned in Section 4.2, the members of the *cheat* family, which are *brute-force* approachs, will indeed cheat, that is, they will perform a larger number of runs before selecting from the set Θ the configuration that is deemed to be the best. This will let us draw some conclusions on the relative performance of *racing* algorithm with respect to the *brute-force* approach.

The computing environment

The experiments presented in Sections 5.1.1 and 5.1.2 where performed on 6 nodes of the cluster of personal computers available at IRIDIA, Université Libre de Bruxelles. This cluster, called *Polyphemus* (Labella & Birattari, 2004) was built, starting in 2002, with the aim of supporting in a first time and eventually replacing the older cluster *Beowulf* that has been serving the lab starting from 2000, and that is currently on its way to retire. *Polyphemus* is currently composed of a server and 25 disk-less clients living on a dedicated 1 gigabit Ethernet LAN. The server and 8 clients feature an AMD Athlon™ XP 2400+ processor, 7 clients an AMD Athlon™ XP 1400 processor, and the remaining 10 clients an AMD Athlon™ XP 2800+ processor. All machines have 512Mb of main memory, and the server features a RAID controller and 3 hard disks of 120 Gb each, managed in RAID Level 5, for a total available disk space of 225 Gb. The server and all clients run the GNU/Linux operating system as distributed by Debian. *Polyphemus* is currently serving the computation needs of two research project funded by the Commission of the European Communities and led by IRIDIA: The *Swarm-Bots Project* and the *Metaheuristics Network*.[3]

The 6 machines used for the experimental analysis presented in this thesis are the AMD Athlon™ XP 1400. As already mentioned in Section 4.3, all racing

[3]More information on these two research projects is available on their respective web sites: `http://www.swarm-bots.org/` and `http://www.metaheuristics.net/`. A brief presentation of the *Metaheuristics Network* is given at page 8.

algorithms considered in the analysis were implemented in R language by the author (Birattari, 2003) and are available for free download directly from the official site of *The Comprehensive* R *Archive Network*,[4] or from one of its mirrors.[5] The metaheuristics to be tuned were both designed and implemented in C language by Thomas Stützle.[6] The original source code were compiled and optimized for execution on *Polyphemus* using gcc, the GNU Compiler Collection of the Free Software Foundation, versions 3.2 and 3.3.

How to read tables and graphs

For each of the two experiments presented in Sections 5.1.1 and 5.1.2, the results are reported in the same format using tables and graphs.

Tables: Three tables are provided for each experiment at pages 129 and 142, respectively:

1. A table reproducing the results obtained on the *test instances* by each of the tuning algorithms under analysis. For each algorithm we present the minimum value obtained on the test instances, the 1st quartile, the median (2nd quartile), the mean, the 3rd quartile, and the maximum. These 6 quantities give a first picture of the distribution of the results over the test instances and are obtained based on a samples of size 10000, that is, 1000 pseudo-trials and 10 test instances for each of them.

2. A table reproducing the p-values of the pairwise comparisons between each pair of tuning algorithms under analysis. The statistical test adopted here is the *Wilcoxon matched-pairs signed-ranks test* (Conover, 1999). The p-values are corrected for multiplicity using Holm's method. The table features the names of the tuning algorithms under analysis both on its columns and on its rows. A number less than 0.05 at the crossing between the column associated with algorithm A and the row associated with algorithm B means that the null hypothesis that the observed performance of A and B are extracted from the same distribution is to be rejected at a confidence level of at least 95%.

3. A table reproducing the results obtained on the *tuning instances* by each of the tuning algorithms under analysis. The quantities reported for each algorithms are the same as in the table described at point 1: minimum, 1st quartile, median, mean, 3rd quartile, the maximum. These figures are reported only for the sake of completeness and **should not** be used for comparing the algorithms since the performance on the *tuning instances*

[4] `http://cran.r-project.org/src/contrib/Descriptions/race.html`

[5] `http://cran.r-project.org/mirrors.html`

[6] More details on the implementations of the algorithms are given in Sections 5.1.1 and 5.1.2.

is a biased measure of the performance on the whole class of instances.[7] For any comparative purpose, the figures in the tables described at point 1 should be used exclusively.

Box-plots: Moreover, two box-plots are provided for each experiment, at pages 130 and 143, respectively:

1. A box-plot of the costs obtained by each of the tuning algorithms under analysis on the *test instances*. Such box-plot provides a graphical representation of the information contained in the associated table described at point 1 in the previous list. The reader will observe that these plots fail at visualizing the differences in the performance of the tuning algorithms under analysis. This is due to the fact that the high variability in the instances washes out the existing differences. A possible solution is provided by the instance-per-instance normalization adopted in the box-plots described at point 2.

2. A box-plot of the costs obtained by each of the tuning algorithms under analysis on the *test instances* as at point 1 but with the difference that here the costs are normalized on an instance-per-instance basis.

Race profiles: For each of the two experiments—pages 131–132 and 144–145, respectively—a graph illustrating the typical race *profile* is provided for each of the four *racing* algorithms under analysis. These plots are akin to the one already presented in Figure 2.10, page 61. They feature the number of candidates still in the race along the horizontal axis, and the number of instances considered, along the vertical one. The latter, which points downwards, counts the steps the *racing* algorithm went through. The plot reads for each number of instances considered, that is, for each step of the tuning algorithm, the *average* number of candidates still in the race. Here the average is taken over the different pseudo-trials. On the plots, indicated by horizontal dotted lines the amounts of instances considered by *Brutus*, *Cheat2*, *Cheat5*, and *Cheat10* are reported. It should be noted that the surface comprised by each race profile represents the total number of runs of the underlying metaheuristic to be tuned that have been performed by the corresponding *racing* algorithm. This total amount is constrained to be less than or equal to 6000 runs in the first experiment and 13680 in the second—see Note 1, 118. Similarly, the surfaces of the nested rectangles delimited by the dotted lines represent the total number of runs on which the selection of the best is based for what concerns the algorithms implementing the *brute-force* approach: The inner rectangle refers to *Brutus* and has a surface equal to the one associated with the *racing* algorithm; the others refers to *Cheat2*, *Cheat5*, and *Cheat10*, in this order

[7] See Chapter 6 for a discussion of this issue.

from the inner rectangle to the outer one, and their surface is twice, five times and ten times, respectively, the one associated with the *racing* algorithm.

Frequencies: Finally, for each of the two experiments a number of histograms are provided—at pages 133–136 and 146–149, respectively—which illustrate the frequency with which each of the studied algorithm was able to select the best configurations. Each graph is composed of a main plot and a sub-plot. They are both histograms that illustrates the same issue, but they differentiate for what concerns the level of detail. In the main histogram, each bin refers to approximately one hundredth of the candidates—4 in the first experiments and 9 in the second. The first bar represents therefore the number of times the algorithm was able to select a candidates that rests among the best 1%, and so on. The histogram in the sub-plot is similar, with the only difference that it offers a more fine-grained representation since here each bin has size one. In other words, the first bar represents the number of times the tuning algorithm was able to select the very best candidate, the second bar, the second best, and so on. In both histogram, when we say *best* candidate, or equivalently that the candidate is among the *best* 1%, we refer to the expected performance of the candidates on the whole class of instances, as estimated on the basis of *all* the $\mathcal{K}$ instances originally sampled.

5.1.1 *Iterated local search* for QUADRATIC ASSIGNMENT

In this first experiment, the metaheuristic to be tuned is *iterated local search* and the combinatorial optimization problem addressed is the QUADRATIC ASSIGNMENT problem.

The metaheuristic to be tuned

Iterated local search is a simple and generally applicable metaheuristic that iteratively applies local search to perturbations of the current search point, leading to a randomized walk in the space of local optima (Lourenço *et al.*, 2002). To apply an *iterated local search* algorithm, four procedures have to be specified: `generate_initial_solution` generates the starting point of this walk, `perturbation` generates new starting points of the local search by perturbing some solution, the `acceptance_criterion` is used to decide from which solution the walk is continued, and the `local_search` procedure implements the local search and also defines (by the solutions it generates as its output) the space in which the walk actually takes place. Figure 5.1 gives an algorithmic scheme for *iterated local search*. The ***history*** component in `perturbation` and `acceptance_criterion` indicates that also the search history may influence the behavior of these procedures. Yet, often Markovian implementations

```
function iterated_local_search
  s_0 = generate_initial_solution
  s = local_search(s_0)
  while (termination condition not met) do
    s' = perturbation(s, history)
    s'' = local_search(s')
    s = acceptance_criterion(s, s'', history)
  end
```

Figure 5.1: Algorithmic outline of *iterated local search*.

of *iterated local search* are applied, that is, the output of `perturbation` and `acceptance_criterion` is independent of the search history.

Iterated local search is conceptually a rather simple metaheuristic. This is due to the simple underlying principle and to the fact that typically only few lines of code have to be added to an already existing local search procedure to implement an *iterated local search* algorithm. Despite its simplicity, it has shown very good computational results for some combinatorial optimization problems such as the TRAVELING SALESMAN problem (Martin *et al.*, 1991; Martin & Otto, 1996; Johnson & McGeoch, 1997), scheduling problems (Lourenço, 1995), *etc.*

To apply *iterated local search* to the QUADRATIC ASSIGNMENT problem, the four component procedures have to be defined; the following choices were considered here. For the initial solution we use a randomly generated assignment of items to locations, mainly because high performing construction heuristics for QUADRATIC ASSIGNMENT are not known.

For `local_search`, several different possibilities were considered, all based on the usual 2-opt neighborhood. The neighborhood $\mathcal{N}(s)$ of a solution s is defined by the set of permutations that can be obtained by exchanging two items at positions v and w, that is, $\mathcal{N}(s) = \{s' | \, s'_v = s_w, \, s'_w = s_v, \text{ and } s'_z = s_z \, \forall z \neq v, w\}$. In the experiment, we considered first- and best-improvement iterative descent algorithms and short runs (of length $p \cdot n$, where p is a parameter and n is the number of items in an instance) of a tabu search algorithm based on the *robust tabu search* of Taillard (1991). For the first-improvement iterative descent algorithm, additionally the technique of *don't look bits* (Bentley, 1992; Martin *et al.*, 1991) was adapted to QUADRATIC ASSIGNMENT.

The procedure `perturbation` exchanges k randomly chosen items, corresponding to a random move in the k-opt neighborhood. We use two fundamentally different ways of setting the parameter k. In the first approach, one value for k is held fixed throughout the algorithm's run; in the second approach, the value of k is adapted at computation time following the rules of basic *variable neighborhood search* (Hansen & Mladenović, 1999) using different settings of the minimum and maximum possible value k can take. That is, in the second approach, we vary k between two values k_{min} and k_{max} for different settings of k_{min} and k_{max}.

As acceptance criterion in our *iterated local search* algorithm we use four different possibilities:

1. Accept only better solutions;
2. Accept better solutions always, but accept worse solution with a probability of $\exp((f(s) - f(s''))/\mathsf{T})$ using a fixed value for parameter T. It should be noticed that this is the well-known Metropolis acceptance criterion from *simulated annealing*;
3. The same as at point 2, but here T is modified using an annealing schedule as known from *simulated annealing*;
4. Accept only better solutions, but restart from a new, randomly generated solution if for q iterations, where q is a parameter to be tuned, no improvement over the best solution is obtained.

The set of candidate configurations

The set of candidate configurations is given by all possible combinations of the following values of the parameters of the *iterated local search* algorithm:

local search	perturbation	strength	acceptance criterion
best	fix	1	better
first	vns	2	constTemp_low-med
firstDLB		3	constTemp_med-high
tabu2n		4	constTemp_randomwalk
tabu6n		5	LSMC_metanet
			restart_med
			restart_quick
			restart_slow

The total number of candidate configurations considered in this experimental analysis is therefore $8 \times 5 \times 2 \times 5 = 400$.

The class of instances

The QUADRATIC ASSIGNMENT problem has been the subject of an enormous amount of research efforts and, together with the TRAVELING SALESMAN problem, it is one of the most studied combinatorial optimization problems (Çela, 1998). QUADRATIC ASSIGNMENT can best be described as the problem of assigning facilities to a set of locations with given distances between the locations and given flows between the facilities; the flows, for example, correspond to the amount of materials or products to be exchanged between machines in a production environment. The goal is to assign the facilities to locations in such a way that the sum of the product between flows and distances is minimal.

Formally, a QUADRATIC ASSIGNMENT instance is specified by n facilities and n locations, where both facilities and locations are represented by integers from the set $\{1, \ldots, n\}$, and two $n \times n$ matrices A and B, where a_{vw} is the *distance* between locations v and w and $b_{v'w'}$ is the *flow* between facilities v' and w'; A and B are called *distance* and *flow matrix*, respectively. The goal is to find an optimal *assignment* of facilities to locations, that is, a permutation $s = \{s_1, s_2, \ldots, s_n\}$ of index set $\{1, 2, \ldots, n\}$ that minimizes the function:

$$f(s) = \sum_{v=1}^{n} \sum_{w=1}^{n} b_{vw} a_{s_v s_w}.$$

Here s_v denotes the location of facility v under assignment s and the term $b_{vw} a_{s_v s_w}$ intuitively represents the cost contribution of simultaneously assigning facility v to location s_v and facility w to location s_w.

For QUADRATIC ASSIGNMENT it is well known that the relative performance of different metaheuristics or, for one metaheuristic, the relative performance of different configurations, depends strongly on the particular class of instances (Stützle, 2003; Taillard, 1995; Hoos & Stützle, 2004). There are two main syntactical features to distinguish different classes of instances. They are (i) the *dominance* of the flow and of the distance, which are defined to be the coefficient of variation of the entries of the flow and of distance matrix, respectively; and (ii) the *sparsity* of the flow and of the distance matrix, defined as $sp = n_0/n^2$, where n_0 is the number of zero-entries in the given flow or distance matrix. For the empirical analysis of the *F-Race*, we consider two classes $C1$ and $C2$ of instances, each class comprising 400 instances. For both classes, the distance matrix is generated as follows. First, n points are generated, which are uniformly distributed in a square of side length 300. Then, each entry a_{vw} is defined to be the Euclidean distance between the v-th and the w-th point, rounded to the nearest integer.

The generation of the random flow matrix uses the following parameters:

- sp, with $0 \leq sp < 1$, indicates the sparsity of the flow matrix;
- A and B determine the flow values.

By varying the parameter sp, instances of arbitrary sparsity can be generate. The parameters A and B allow to modify the distribution of the matrix entries according to $y = (A \cdot x)^B$.

To generate the flow matrix of an instance from class $C1$, sp is assigned a random value uniformly distributed in $[0.0; 0.08]$ and the values of A and B are set to 100 and 1, respectively. For a class $C2$ instance, sp is chosen uniformly at

```
function flow_matrix_entry(A, B, sp)
 x = rand() # a random number in [0,1]
 if(x < sp)
   return 0
 else
   x = rand()
   return MAX(1, (A · x)^B)
 end
```

Figure 5.2: The function **flow_matrix_entry** is used for filling the flow matrix.

random from the interval [0.63; 0.71], and we have $A = 10$ and $B = 2.5$. Then, each flow matrix entry is generated by the routine given in Figure 5.2.

The result of this way of generating instances is that those of class $C2$ have a much larger sparsity than instances of $C1$ and, additionally, the distribution of the non-zero entries is different. The size of the instances is chosen uniformly at random from the set $\{65, 66, \ldots, 74\}$.

The results of the experiments

The first element that needs be observed is that the range of the numerical results obtained by all tuning methods under analysis is very large compared to the differences between the averages: In Table 5.1(a), the former is in the order of the millions while the latter of the thousands. If we had to base our empirical analysis of the tuning methods under study solely on the bare figures reproduced in Table 5.1(a), we would have to conclude that the algorithms are all equivalent and that the tiny differences in their mean behavior are just a matter of chance. Such conclusion would be clearly confirmed by the box-plot of the un-normalized costs given in Figure 5.3(top).

Nevertheless, a deeper analysis reveals that the large variations in the results obtained by each tuning algorithm is due mainly to a large difference among the instances adopted in the study. Apparently, such intrinsic diversity of the class of instances considered washes out the differences in the performance of the tuning algorithms under analysis. This hypothesis is confirmed by the box-plot of the normalized results given in Figure 5.3(bottom). In this second graph, the costs c obtained by the tuning algorithms on instance i are normalized between 0 and 1 according to the following *score* function:[8]

$$\acute{c}(c, i) = \frac{c - c_i^{min}}{c_i^{max} - c_i^{min}},$$

[8]See Section 6.1.1 for a discussion of several *score* functions that can be used for normalizing the observed costs on an instance-per-instance basis.

where c_i^{max} and c_i^{min} are, respectively, the maximum and the minimum cost obtained on instance i by the tuning algorithms under analysis.

Once the costs are normalized on an instance-per-instance basis, differences emerge clearly. Figure 5.3(bottom) shows that *F-Race* is clearly the best of the *racing* algorithms studied, and that *F-Race* and *tNo-Race* perform far better than *Brutus*. On the other hand, *tBo-Race* and *tHo-Race* are not able to improve over their *brute-force* opponent. Further, it should be observed that, as expected, the performance of the *brute-force* approachs considered in the study is ordered according to the amount of computation used: *Cheat10* is the best, while *Cheat5*, *Cheat2*, and *Brutus* follow in this order. *F-Race* results superior to *Brutus*, *Cheat2*, and *Cheat5*, and equivalent to *Cheat10*. This justifies the conclusion that, at least for what concerns this first experiment, the *racing* approach is about 10 times more efficient that the *brute-force* approach: Indeed, *brute-force* needs a computation time 10 times larger than *F-Race* in order to obtain an equivalent performance.

The conclusions drawn above are based on the reading of the box-plots of the normalized costs given in Figure 5.3(bottom). The same conclusions can be drawn in a more formal manner on the basis of the results of some statistical tests. Table 5.1(b) reproduces the p-values of the *Wilcoxon matched-pairs signed-ranks test* (Conover, 1999) performed between each pair of tuning algorithms, corrected for multiplicity using Holm's method: It appears that *F-Race* is significantly[9] better that all other *racing* algorithms and of *Brutus*, *Cheat2*, and *Cheat5*. On the other hand, no such conclusion can be drawn concerning *Cheat10*: The experimental results bring no evidence that one is better than the other. Moreover, the figures reproduced in Table 5.1(b) confirm that the differences that were already observed in Figure 5.3(bottom) between the four *brute-force* approachs of our study, are all statistically significant but that, on the basis of the results of the experiment, we are not authorized to reject the null hypothesis that the observations produced by *tHo-Race*, *tBo-Race*, and *Brutus* are all extracted from the same distribution.

A further insight on the results, and more specifically on the equivalence among *tHo-Race*, *tBo-Race*, and *Brutus*, can be obtained from the race profiles proposed in Figures 5.4 and 5.5. It can be observed that *tBo-Race* and *tHo-Race* are particularly conservative and discard very few candidates. As a result, they are not able to focus on the best candidates and they end up performing a final selection of the best that is substantially equivalent to the one performed by *Brutus*. This is confirmed also by a comparison of the histograms of the frequencies with which good candidates were selected. The histograms concerning *tHo-Race* and *tBo-Race*, see Figure 5.7, and the one concerning *Brutus*, see Figure 5.7(top), appear identical. On the other hand, the race profiles given in Figure 5.4 show that *F-Race* and *tNo-Race* are much bolder in discarding inferior candidates and

[9] At a confidence level of at least 95%.

in focusing on the most promising ones. This results in a higher probability of selecting a very good candidate, see Figure 5.6. Based on the frequency histograms, we could even conclude that *F-Race* performs better that *Cheat10*.[10]

A final remark concerns the comparison between *F-Race* and *tNo-Race*. The superiority of both algorithms with respect to *tHo-Race* and *tBo-Race* rests, as already observed, on their ability to discard inferior candidate and to focus on the best ones. Nevertheless, observing Figure 5.4, and taking into account that *F-Race* is significantly better than *tNo-Race*, see Table 5.1(b), we are led to the conclusion that *tNo-Race* is probably too aggressive at discarding candidates and that it gets therefore over-exposed to the risk of discarding the good ones in the early stages of the race. Clearly, a trade-off exists between the two extreme attitudes towards candidate elimination. The test of hypotheses adopted by *tNo-Race* does not consider any correction of the p-values in order to account for the multiplicity of the pairwise tests performed. This results in a relatively high probability of discarding candidates even if no statistically sufficient evidence exists against them.[11]

For the sake of completeness, a description of the best 20 configurations is given in Table 5.2. In this table, the configurations represented are those that on average obtained the smallest cost on the set of 800 instances on which the whole study was carried out.

[10]Compare the sub-plot of Figure 5.6(top) with the one of in Figure 5.9(bottom).

[11]It should be sufficient to notice here that if the confidence level is 95% and, say, 100 uncorrected t-tests are performed between samples *all* extracted from the same population, expectedly in 5 of such tests significance will be incorrectly detected.

Table 5.1: Tuning *iterated local search* for QUADRATIC ASSIGNMENT.

	Min.	1st Qu.	Median	Mean	3rd Qu.	Max.
F-Race	11894279	17138434	26214814	25174094	33141333	40792940
tNo-Race	11902235	17143118	26219483	25174869	33129746	40783681
tBo-Race	11894279	17157467	26219483	25180791	33125245	40826733
tHo-Race	11894279	17157467	26219483	25180821	33125245	40826733
Brutus	11894279	17157467	26219483	25180779	33125256	40826733
Cheat2	11890443	17153696	26219483	25178977	33125245	40792940
Cheat5	11894279	17145910	26219483	25176082	33125883	40783681
Cheat10	11902235	17138434	26214814	25174252	33129746	40755716

(a) Costs on the test instances.

	F-Race	*tNo-Race*	*tBo-Race*	*tHo-Race*	*Brutus*	*Cheat2*	*Cheat5*
tNo-Race	3.94E−06	—	—	—	—	—	—
tBo-Race	< 2E−16	< 2E−16	—	—	—	—	—
tHo-Race	< 2E−16	< 2E−16	3.65E−01	—	—	—	—
Brutus	< 2E−16	< 2E−16	1.00E+00	8.30E−01	—	—	—
Cheat2	< 2E−16	< 2E−16	8.89E−07	5.03E−07	9.07E−07	—	—
Cheat5	< 2E−16	2.31E−05	< 2E−16	< 2E−16	< 2E−16	< 2E−16	—
Cheat10	1.00E+00	2.34E−04	< 2E−16	< 2E−16	< 2E−16	< 2E−16	< 2E−16

(b) Pairwise comparisons using Wilcoxon test. P-value adjustment method: Holm's.

	Min.	1st Qu.	Median	Mean	3rd Qu.	Max.
F-Race	22709781	24835332	25106551	25099522	25365590	28288901
tNo-Race	21708438	24861445	25111952	25105230	25352345	29201166
tBo-Race	17266519	23521488	24956328	25021719	26627119	32238700
tHo-Race	17266519	23521488	24950148	25023912	26610051	32238700
Brutus	17036725	23458131	24927161	24987857	26610051	32292821
Cheat2	20839558	23996618	25137767	25092220	26173338	29480131
Cheat5	21937598	24487020	25163340	25144915	25794130	27796878
Cheat10	22959610	24701240	25129259	25115490	25562065	27182278

(c) Costs on the tuning instances.

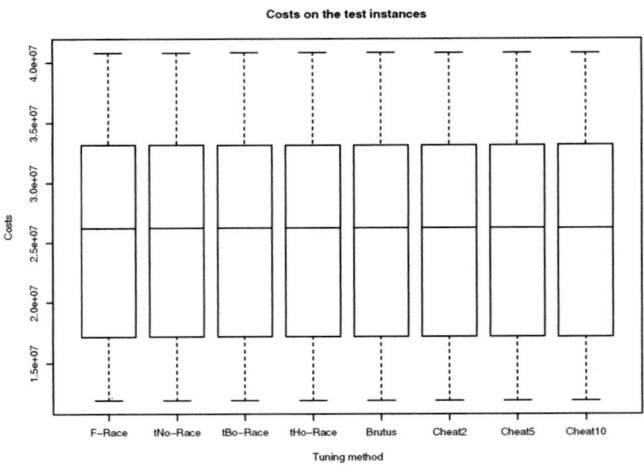

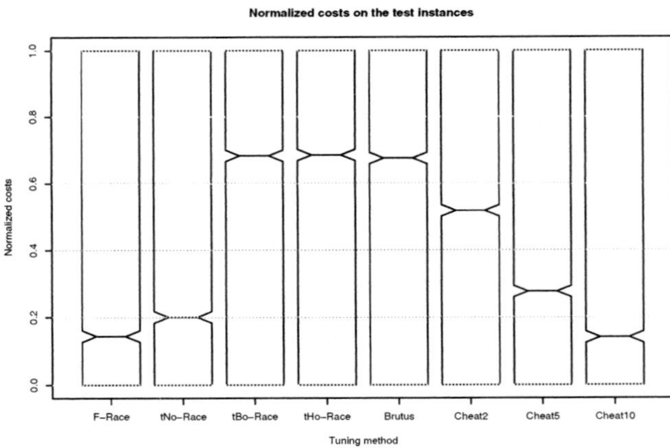

Figure 5.3: Box-plots. Tuning *iterated local search* for QUADRATIC ASSIGNMENT.

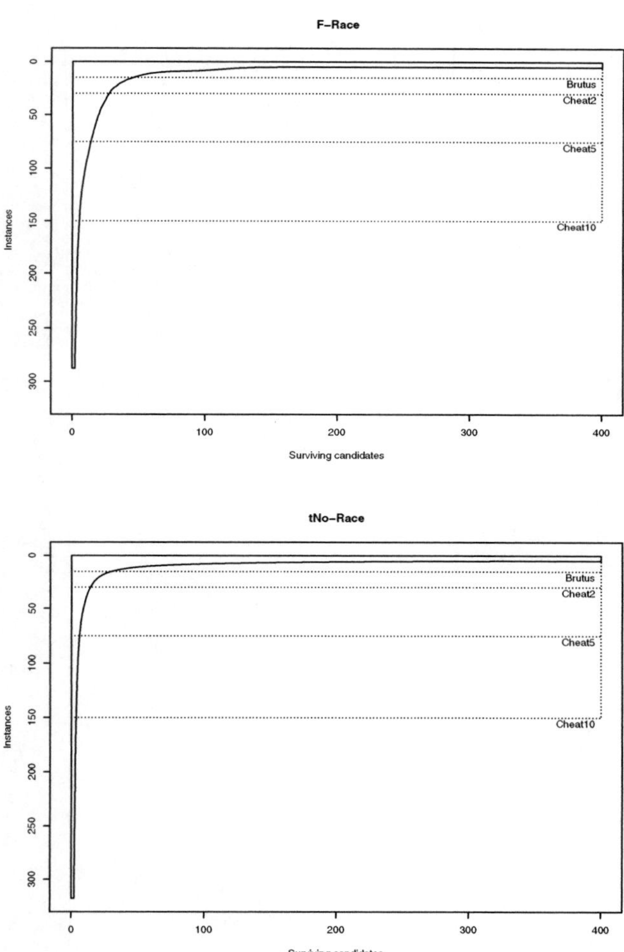

Figure 5.4: Race profiles. Profile of the races performed by *F-Race* and *tNo-Race*. The algorithm to be tuned is *iterated local search* and the problem is QUADRATIC ASSIGNMENT.

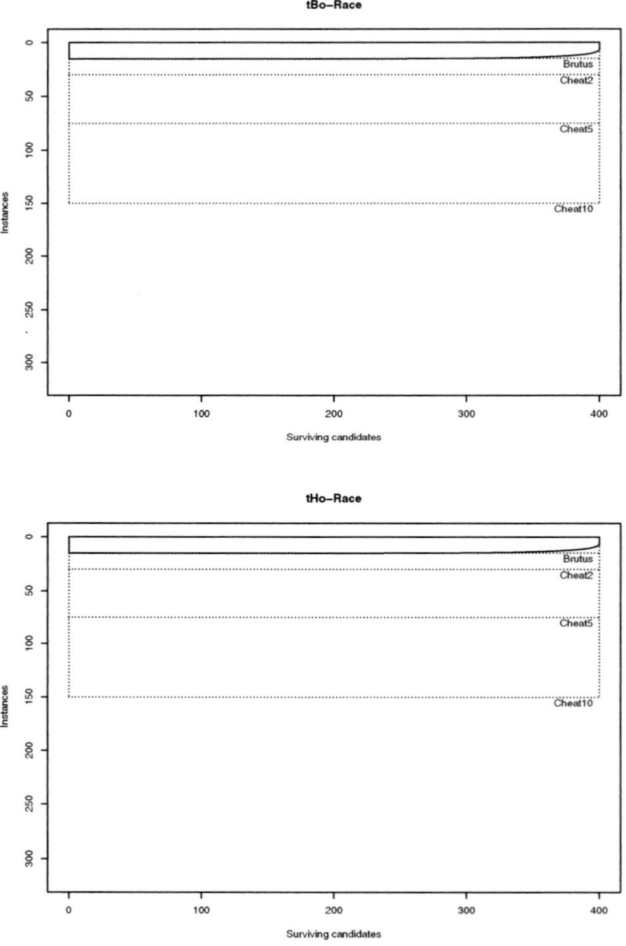

Figure 5.5: Race profiles. Profile of the races performed by *tBo-Race* and *tHo-Race*. The algorithm to be tuned is *iterated local search* and the problem is QUADRATIC ASSIGNMENT.

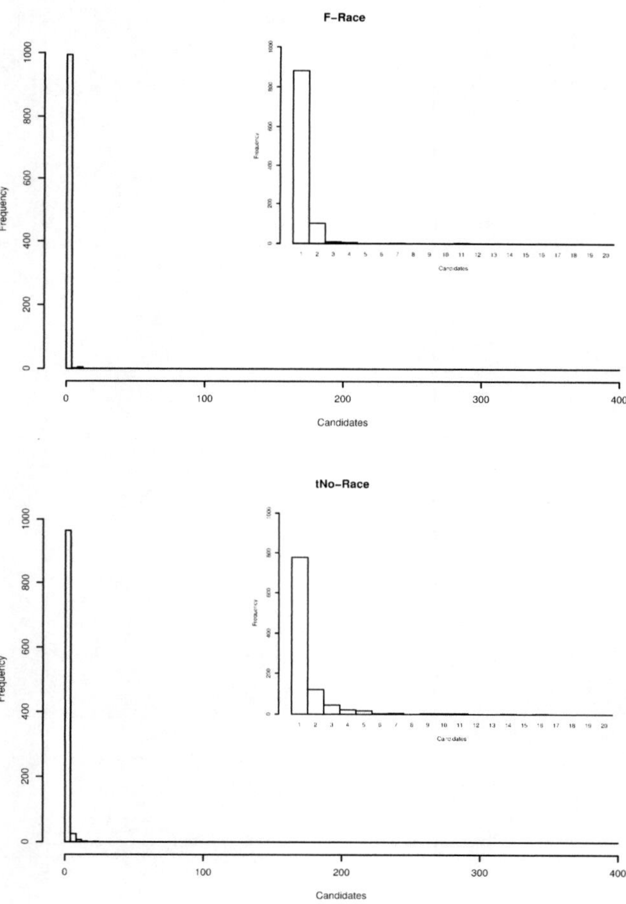

Figure 5.6: Frequencies. Results obtained by *F-Race* and *tNo-Race*. The algorithm to be tuned is *iterated local search* and the problem is QUADRATIC ASSIGNMENT.

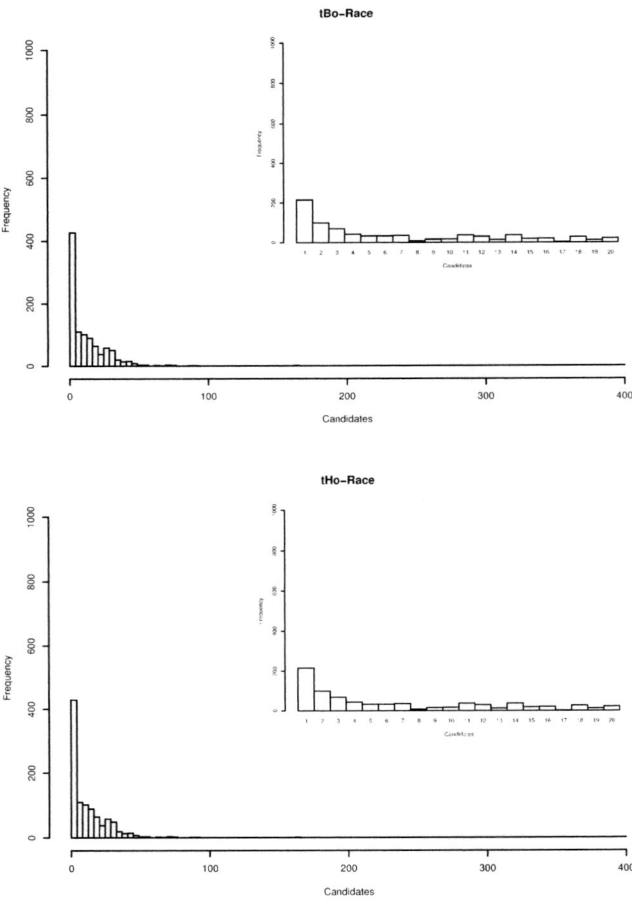

Figure 5.7: Frequencies. Results obtained by *tBo-Race* and *tHo-Race*. The algorithm to be tuned is *iterated local search* and the problem is QUADRATIC ASSIGNMENT.

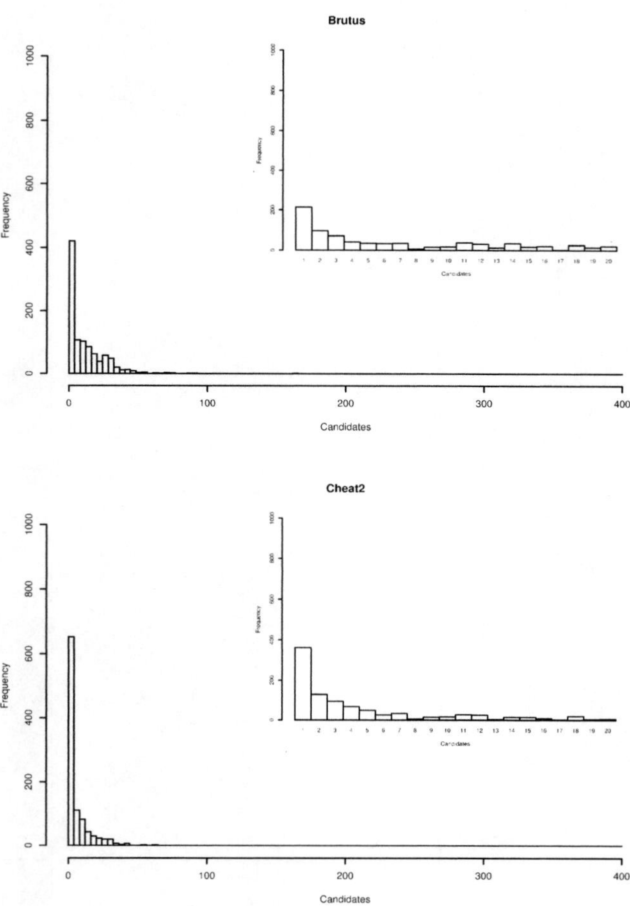

Figure 5.8: Frequencies Results obtained by ***Brutus*** and ***Cheat2***. The algorithm to be tuned is ***iterated local search*** and the problem is QUADRATIC ASSIGNMENT.

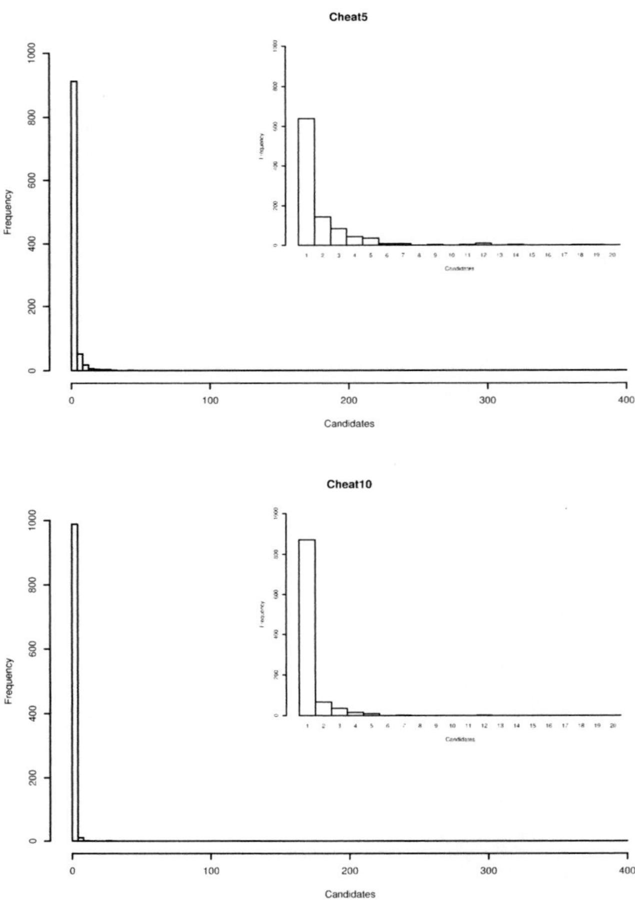

Figure 5.9: Frequencies. Results obtained by *Cheat5* and *Cheat10*. The algorithm to be tuned is *iterated local search* and the problem is QUADRATIC ASSIGNMENT.

Table 5.2: Parameters of the best 20 configurations and their performance.

acceptance	local search	prtb.	strg.	Min.	1st Qu.	Median	Mean	3rd Qu.	Max.
LSMC_metanet	firstDLB	fix	3	11902235	17126657	24347982	25116872	33021266	40755716
LSMC_metanet	firstDLB	fix	2	11894279	17143360	24340836	25120554	33034489	40783681
constTemp_med-high	firstDLB	fix	2	11920668	17161537	24364732	25121016	33010166	40750738
constTemp_randomwalk	firstDLB	fix	2	11890443	17122646	24356897	25121751	33034604	40783732
constTemp_med-high	firstDLB	fix	3	11946641	17155766	24378286	25121908	33021692	40765546
LSMC_metanet	best	fix	4	11923432	17173990	24403188	25123923	33026181	40753988
constTemp_low-med	firstDLB	fix	3	11893719	17125990	24342380	25124384	33006634	40792940
constTemp_randomwalk	firstDLB	fix	3	11932919	17156095	24355296	25124992	33012422	40758787
constTemp_randomwalk	firstDLB	fix	1	11917769	17112938	24375904	25125474	33034552	40753063
restart_quick	firstDLB	fix	3	11963948	17150091	24369924	25125815	33036602	40779742
LSMC_metanet	firstDLB	vns	5	11907630	17147492	24374658	25125947	33005214	40754091
constTemp_med-high	firstDLB	vns	2	11920341	17143168	24395296	25126327	33009558	40756424
constTemp_low-med	best	fix	4	11976441	17148629	24372962	25126830	33001854	40757001
constTemp_med-high	firstDLB	vns	5	11965831	17153459	24341222	25127068	33003711	40821582
constTemp_randomwalk	firstDLB	vns	5	11970960	17139092	24372818	25127150	33042062	40786958
constTemp_randomwalk	firstDLB	vns	2	11977769	17156575	24347804	25127153	33036811	40796674
constTemp_med-high	best	fix	4	11910446	17161500	24369186	25127567	33009656	40759799
constTemp_med-high	firstDLB	vns	3	11890735	17149246	24349520	25127694	33053502	40812190
constTemp_med-high	firstDLB	fix	1	11917997	17139182	24362010	25127764	33008914	40784939
constTemp_randomwalk	firstDLB	vns	3	11957289	17171313	24372938	25127974	33033138	40826733

5.1.2 *Ant colony optimization* for TRAVELING SALESMAN

In this second experiment, the metaheuristic to be tuned is *$\mathcal{MAX}$–$\mathcal{MIN}$ Ant System*, currently considered as one of the best performing metaheuristics belonging to the *ant colony optimization* family, and the optimization problem addressed is the well known TRAVELING SALESMAN problem in its symmetric version.

The metaheuristic to be tuned

Ant colony optimization (Dorigo *et al.*, 1996, 1999; Dorigo & Di Caro, 1999; Dorigo & Stützle, 2002, 2004) is a population-based approach inspired by the foraging behavior of ants for the solution of hard combinatorial optimization problems. In *ant colony optimization*, artificial ants implement stochastic construction procedures that are biased by pheromone trails and heuristic information on the problem being solved. The solutions obtained by the ants may then be improved by applying some local search routine. *Ant colony optimization* algorithms typically follow the high-level procedure given in Figure 5.10. *$\mathcal{MAX}$–$\mathcal{MIN}$ Ant System* (Stützle & Hoos, 1996, 1997, 2000) is currently one of the best performing *ant colony optimization* algorithms for the TRAVELING SALESMAN problem.

$\mathcal{MAX}$–$\mathcal{MIN}$ Ant System constructs tours as follows: Initially, each of the m ants is placed in some randomly chosen city. At each construction step, ant z applies a stochastic action choice rule. In particular, when being in city v, ant z chooses to go to a yet unvisited city w at the k-th iteration with a probability

$$p^z_{vw}(k) = \frac{[\tau_{vw}(k)]^\alpha \cdot [\eta_{vw}]^\beta}{\sum_{l \in \mathcal{N}^z_v} [\tau_{vl}(k)]^\alpha \cdot [\eta_{vl}]^\beta}, \qquad \text{if } w \in \mathcal{N}^z_v; \tag{5.1}$$

where $\eta_{vw} = 1/D_{vw}$ is an *a priori* available heuristic value, α and β are two parameters which determine the relative influence of the pheromone trail and the heuristic information, and $\mathcal{N}^z_v$ is the feasible neighborhood of ant z, that is, the set of cities which ant z has not visited yet; if $w \notin \mathcal{N}^z_v$, we have $P^z_{vw}(k) = 0$.

After all ants have constructed a solution, the pheromone trails are updated according to

$$\tau_{vw}(k) = (1-\rho) \cdot \tau_{vw}(k) + \Delta\tau^{best}_{vw}, \tag{5.2}$$

where $\Delta\tau^{best}_{vw} = 1/L^{best}$ if arc $(v, w) \in T^{best}$ and zero otherwise. Here T^{best} is either the *iteration-best* solution T^{ib}, or the *global-best* solution T^{gb} and L^{best} is the corresponding tour length. Experimental results showed that the best performance is obtained by gradually increasing the frequency of choosing T^{gb} for the pheromone trail update (Stützle & Hoos, 2000).

In *$\mathcal{MAX}$–$\mathcal{MIN}$ Ant System*, lower and upper limits τ_{min} and τ_{max} on the possible pheromone strengths on any arc are imposed to avoid search stagnation. The pheromone trails in *$\mathcal{MAX}$–$\mathcal{MIN}$ Ant System* are initialized to their upper pheromone trail limits τ_{max}, leading to an increased exploration of tours at the start of the algorithms. In our experiments each solution is improved by a local search procedure, either 2-opt, 3-opt, or 2.5-opt (Bentley, 1992).

```
function ant colony optimization
  Initialize pheromone and calculate heuristic
  while (termination condition not met) do
    p = ConstructSolutions(pheromone, heuristic)
    p = LocalSearch(p)     # optional
    UpdatePheromoneTrails(p)
  end
```

Figure 5.10: Algorithmic skeleton of *ant colony optimization* for static combinatorial optimization problems.

The set of candidate configurations

In our experimental study, we have chosen a number of configurations that differ in particular parameter settings for *MAX–MIN Ant System*. We focused on alternative settings for the main algorithm parameters as they were identified in earlier studies, in particular we considered values of α, β, ρ, m, and the kind of local search adopted for improving the quality of the solutions found by the ants.

The set of candidate configurations is the union of two subsets each of which is the set of all combinations of some given levels of the parameters of the algorithm. For what concerns the first subset, the levels of the parameters are:

α	β	ρ	m	ls
0.75	0	0.00	1	2-opt
1.00	1	0.10	5	2.5-opt
1.50	3	0.25	10	3-opt
	5	0.50	25	
		0.75		
		0.90		

The number of configurations in the first subset is therefore $3 \times 4 \times 4 \times 6 \times 3 = 864$. In the second subset, the levels of the parameters are:

α	β	ρ	m	ls
0	0	1.00	1	2-opt
	1		5	2.5-opt
	3		10	3-opt
	5		25	

The number of configurations in the second subset is therefore $1 \times 4 \times 4 \times 1 \times 3 = 48$. It should be noticed that the configurations in this second subset represent some *degenerate* version of *ant colony optimization* in which, since $\alpha = 0$, the pheromone does not play any role at all—see Equation 5.1. In such a setting, as it is immediately confirmed by an inspection of Equations 5.1 and 5.2, the evaporation parameter ρ becomes irrelevant. For definiteness, here it is set to 1, but it does not play any role.

Taking the two subsets together, the total number of candidate configuration is $864 + 48 = 912$.

The class of instances

Given a complete graph $G = (V, E, D)$ with V being the set of $n = |V|$ *vertices* or nodes, E being the set of *edges* or arcs fully connecting the nodes, and D being the weight function that assigns each edge $(v, w) \in E$ a length D_{vw}, the TRAVELING SALESMAN problem is the problem of finding a shortest closed tour visiting each node of G once. We assume the TRAVELING SALESMAN is symmetric, that is, we have $D_{vw} = D_{vw}$ for every pair of nodes v and w.

The TRAVELING SALESMAN problem is extensively studied in the literature and serves as a standard benchmark problem (Johnson & McGeoch, 1997; Lawler *et al.*, 1985; Reinelt, 1994). For our study we randomly generate Euclidean TRAVELING SALESMAN problem instances with a random distribution of city coordinates and a random number of cities. Euclidean TRAVELING SALESMAN problems were chosen because such instances are used in a large number of experimental researches on the TRAVELING SALESMAN problem (Johnson & McGeoch, 1997; Johnson *et al.*, 2001). In our case, city locations are randomly chosen according to a uniform distribution in a square of dimension 10.000×10.000, and the resulting distances are rounded to the nearest integer. The number of cities in each instance is chosen as an integer randomly sampled according to a uniform distribution in the interval $[300, 500]$. We generated a total number of 500 such instances for our experiments reported in Section 5.

The results of the experiments

Also in this second experiment, the range of the numerical results obtained by all tuning methods under analysis is very large compared to the differences between the averages: In Table 5.3(a), the former is in the order of the millions while the latter of the hundreds. Also in this case, the figures reproduced in Table 5.3(a) and the box-plot of the un-normalized costs given in Figure 5.11(top) are not very informative and do not show any difference between the algorithms.

Nevertheless, the tuning algorithms under analysis differ also on this second problem as confirmed by the box-plot of the normalized results given in Figure 5.11(bottom) and by Table 5.3(b) that reproduces the p-values of a *Wilcoxon matched-pairs signed-ranks test* (Conover, 1999) performed between each pair of tuning algorithms and corrected for multiplicity using Holm's method.

Once the costs are normalized on an instance-per-instance basis, differences emerge clearly. In this second experiment *F-Race* is still the best algorithm but in this case the difference between *F-Race* and *tNo-Race* is not significant. On the other hand both *F-Race* and *tNo-Race* are significantly better than *Cheat10*. Contrary to the first experiment, both *tBo-Race* and *tHo-Race* improve over *Brutus*.

The performance of the whole *racing* approach compared to the *brute-force* approach is even more satisfactory in this second experiment than it was in the first: All *racing* algorithms perform significantly better than *Brutus*, and *F-Race* is significantly better even than *Cheat10*. For what concerns this second experiment, we can therefore conclude that the *racing* approach is at least 10 times more efficient that the *brute-force* approach.

Further insight on these results can be obtained from the race profiles proposed in Figures 5.12 and 5.13. It can be observed that *tBo-Race* and *tHo-Race* are less conservative compared to the first experiment. They are able to discard a few candidates and this helps in improving over *Brutus*. This is confirmed also by a comparison of the histograms of the frequencies with which good candidates were selected. The histograms concerning *tHo-Race* and *tBo-Race*, see Figure 5.15, are in this case clearly better than the one concerning *Brutus*, see Figure 5.15(top).

The race profiles given in Figure 5.12 confirm that *F-Race* and *tNo-Race* are still much bolder than *tBo-Race* and *tHo-Race* in discarding inferior candidates and in focusing on the most promising ones. This explain their better performance. For what concerns the comparison between *F-Race* and *tNo-Race*, their race profiles are quite similar, with *tNo-Race* slightly more aggressive in the early stages. The histograms proposed in Figure 5.14 confirm that the two algorithms obtain substantially equivalent results, with *F-Race* having anyway a clearly higher probability of selecting the very best configuration[12]

Finally, a comparison of the histogram given in Figure 5.14(top) with the one in Figure 5.17(bottom), provides a clear evidence of the superiority of *F-Race* over *Cheat10*.

For the sake of completeness, a description of the best 20 configurations is given in Table 5.4. In this table, the configurations represented are those that on average obtained the smallest cost on the set of 500 instances on which the whole study was carried out.

[12]Compare the sub-plots in Figure 5.14.

Table 5.3: Tuning *ant colony optimization* for TRAVELING SALESMAN.

	Min.	1st Qu.	Median	Mean	3rd Qu.	Max.
F-Race	1456813	1537311	1577406	1574952	1611164	1690817
tNo-Race	1456252	1537458	1577406	1574964	1610494	1690817
tBo-Race	1456527	1537334	1577432	1575051	1610606	1690817
tHo-Race	1456252	1537334	1577469	1575041	1610540	1690817
Brutus	1455541	1537540	1577866	1575239	1610494	1694868
Cheat2	1455541	1537472	1577631	1575126	1610449	1691569
Cheat5	1456252	1537311	1577432	1575041	1610534	1690817
Cheat10	1455541	1537900	1577432	1575038	1610507	1690817

(a) Costs on the test instances.

	F-Race	*tNo-Race*	*tBo-Race*	*tHo-Race*	*Brutus*	*Cheat2*	*Cheat5*
tNo-Race	1.00E+00	—	—	—	—	—	—
tBo-Race	1.23E−04	2.74E−04	—	—	—	—	—
tHo-Race	2.70E−04	4.63E−04	1.00E+00	—	—	—	—
Brutus	< 2E−16	< 2E−16	1.69E−10	6.12E−12	—	—	—
Cheat2	1.05E−12	8.72E−13	1.61E−03	3.83E−04	3.83E−04	—	—
Cheat5	1.16E−03	9.97E−04	1.00E+00	1.00E+00	1.72E−12	3.48E−04	—
Cheat10	8.38E−04	1.63E−03	1.00E+00	1.00E+00	5.06E−12	3.48E−04	1.00E+00

(b) Pairwise comparisons using Wilcoxon test. P-value adjustment method: Holm's.

	Min.	1st Qu.	Median	Mean	3rd Qu.	Max.
F-Race	1565751	1574523	1574754	1574736	1574987	1578830
tNo-Race	1564873	1574501	1574774	1574767	1575035	1589207
tBo-Race	1555983	1571733	1574678	1574668	1577823	1590297
tHo-Race	1555785	1571610	1574616	1574602	1577439	1592108
Brutus	1537934	1566247	1575159	1574636	1582732	1617135
Cheat2	1550518	1569380	1574908	1574664	1580228	1601095
Cheat5	1557821	1571260	1574660	1574723	1578013	1592829
Cheat10	1560420	1572343	1574829	1574688	1576982	1585435

(c) Costs on the tuning instances.

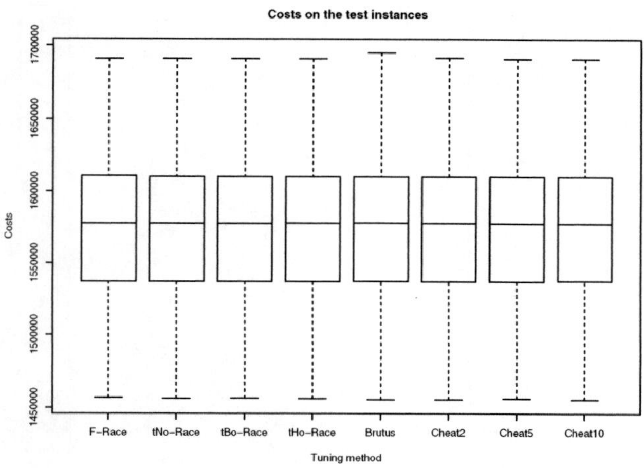

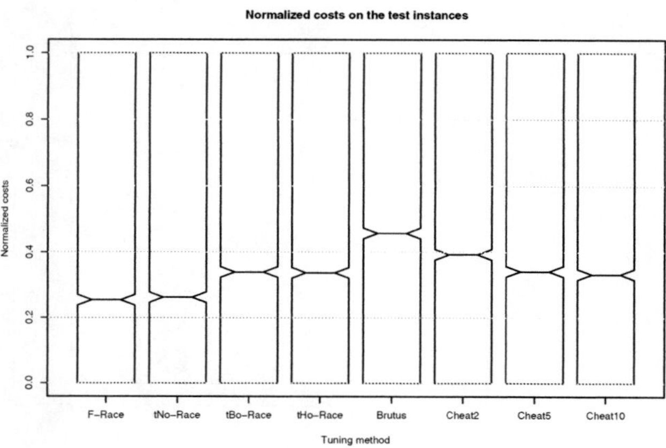

Figure 5.11: Box-plots. Tuning *ant colony optimization* for TRAVELING SALESMAN.

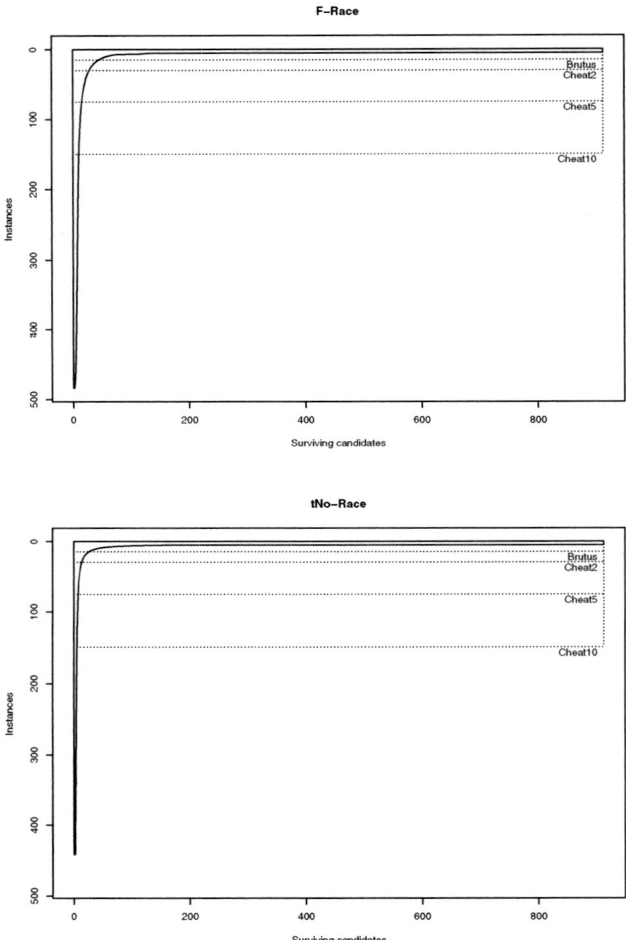

Figure 5.12: Race profiles. Profile of the races performed by *F-Race* and *tNo-Race*. The algorithm to be tuned is *ant colony optimization* and the problem is TRAVELING SALESMAN.

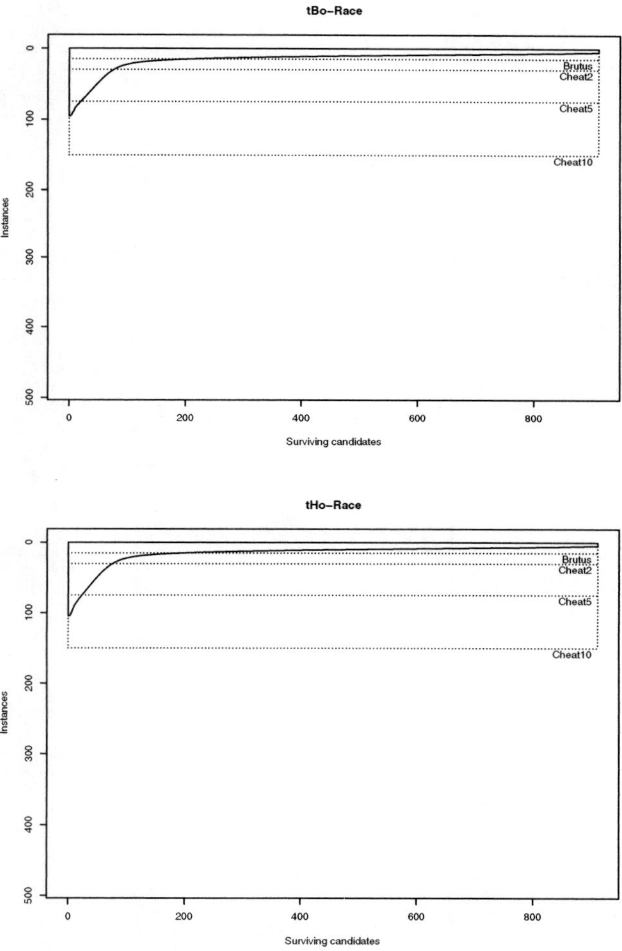

Figure 5.13: Race profiles. Profile of the races performed by *tBo-Race* and *tHo-Race*. The algorithm to be tuned is ***ant colony optimization*** and the problem is TRAVELING SALESMAN.

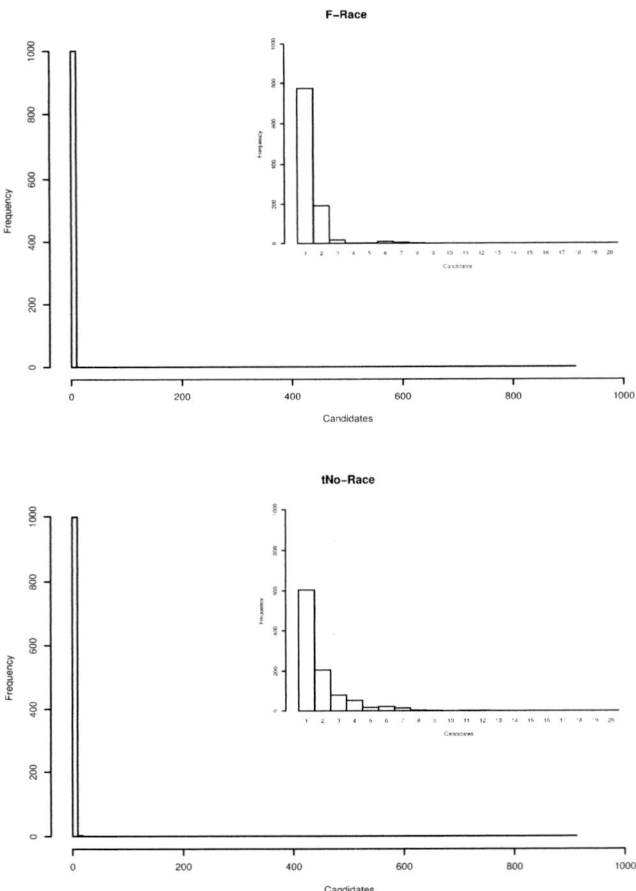

Figure 5.14: Frequencies. Results obtained by *F-Race* and *tNo-Race*. The algorithm to be tuned is ***ant colony optimization*** and the problem is TRAVELING SALESMAN.

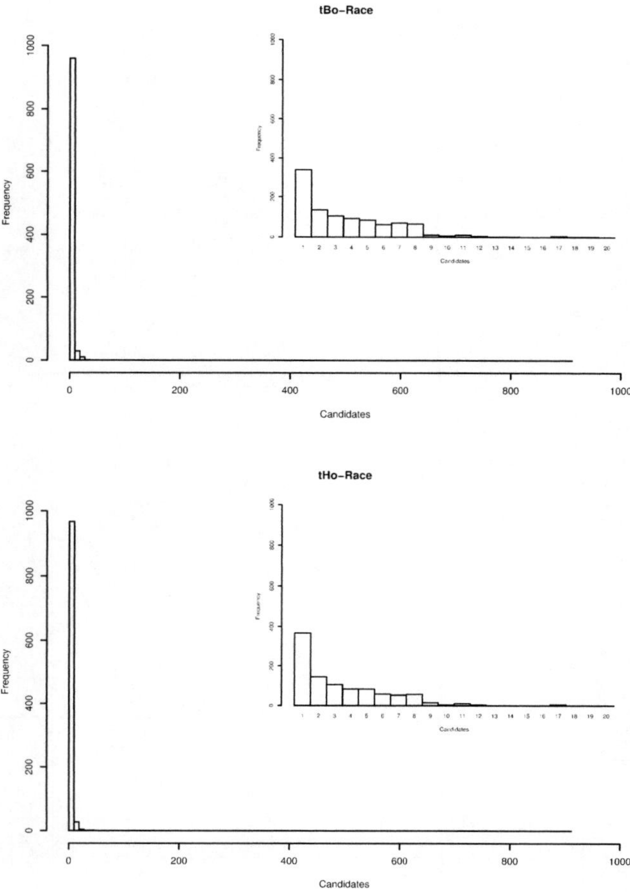

Figure 5.15: Frequencies. Results obtained by *tBo-Race* and *tHo-Race*. The algorithm to be tuned is *ant colony optimization* and the problem is TRAVELING SALESMAN.

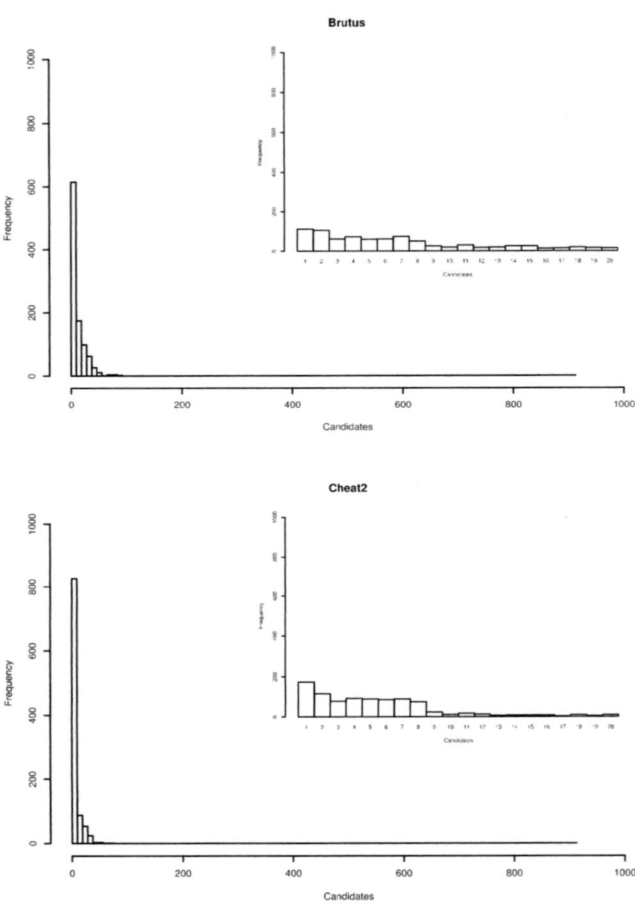

Figure 5.16: Frequencies. Results obtained by *Brutus* and *Cheat2*. The algorithm to be tuned is *ant colony optimization* and the problem is TRAVELING SALESMAN.

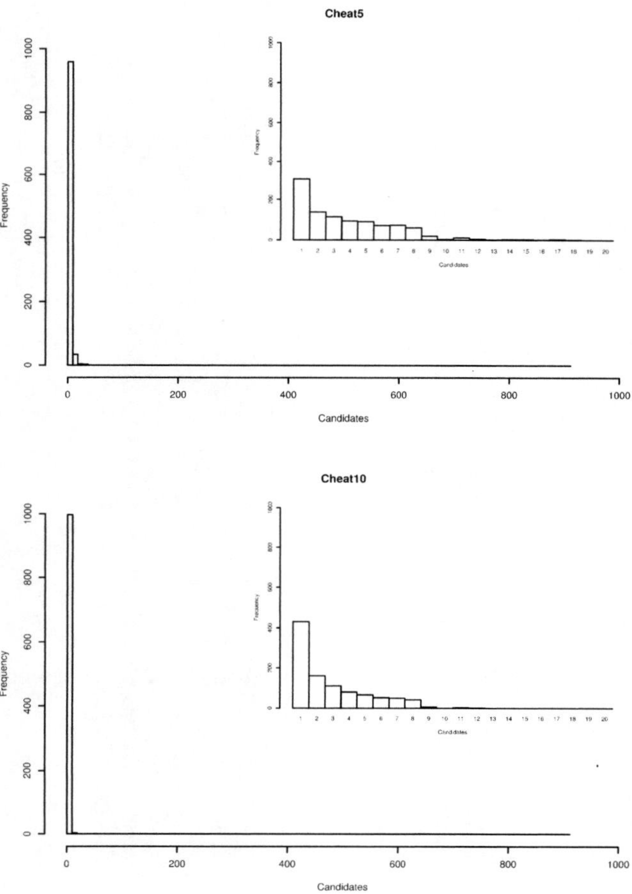

Figure 5.17: Frequencies. Results obtained by *Cheat5* and *Cheat10*. The algorithm to be tuned is *ant colony optimization* and the problem is TRAVELING SALESMAN.

Table 5.4: Parameters of the best 20 configurations and their performance.

α	β	m	ρ	ls	Min.	1st Qu.	Median	Mean	3rd Qu.	Max.
0.75	3	25	0.50	3-opt	1457329	1536314	1578178	1574743	1611220	1690817
0.75	5	25	0.50	3-opt	1456813	1535182	1577652	1574846	1611570	1686040
0.75	5	25	0.25	3-opt	1456252	1537300	1578500	1574866	1611378	1687182
0.75	3	10	0.50	3-opt	1457975	1536586	1579108	1574877	1611395	1686379
0.75	1	10	0.25	3-opt	1456527	1535564	1578354	1574917	1611204	1686813
0.75	5	10	0.25	3-opt	1456341	1537180	1578968	1574926	1610058	1690078
0.75	5	10	0.50	3-opt	1456853	1536781	1577846	1574930	1610500	1686529
0.75	1	25	0.25	3-opt	1455541	1535929	1578485	1574935	1610279	1687099
0.75	3	25	0.25	3-opt	1457522	1535789	1578726	1575127	1611128	1688760
1.00	1	25	0.50	3-opt	1456567	1536314	1579004	1575128	1612098	1687595
0.75	3	5	0.50	3-opt	1456252	1536237	1579042	1575140	1610824	1687348
1.00	5	25	0.50	3-opt	1456527	1536216	1578694	1575186	1611478	1688589
0.75	1	10	0.50	3-opt	1456209	1536555	1579286	1575246	1612002	1694868
0.75	1	25	0.10	3-opt	1457025	1536261	1578465	1575255	1611680	1690135
0.75	5	5	0.50	3-opt	1456341	1537318	1578734	1575295	1611060	1686022
1.00	0	25	0.25	3-opt	1456341	1537196	1578088	1575296	1611718	1686022
1.00	3	25	0.50	3-opt	1456341	1536242	1579668	1575299	1610291	1686206
0.75	5	25	0.10	3-opt	1456341	1536078	1578358	1575315	1611558	1686040
1.00	0	10	0.50	3-opt	1456341	1536466	1579836	1575329	1610781	1687096
0.75	1	5	0.25	3-opt	1455541	1536284	1579045	1575335	1610951	1689348

5.2 Some applications of the *racing* approach

This section gives a brief account of a number of successful applications of the *racing* algorithms introduced in the thesis and of some derived algorithms. As it has been already made clear, the aim of this section is not to provide quantitative results or to *formally* prove the superiority of one tuning algorithms over another. With the applications discussed here we wish instead to show that *F-Race*, and more generally the *racing* idea, are particularly flexible and manageable and that they can be profitably adopted in real-world (or at least real-world-*like*) situations.

The rest of the section is organized at follows: Section 5.2.1 illustrates the very first application of *F-Race*, the tuning of a number of metaheuristics developed by the *Metaheuristics Network* for the UNIVERSITY-COURSE TIMETABLING problem. Section 5.2.2 illustrates an approach to the design of hybrid metaheuristics that is derived from *F-Race*. This approach was adopted for designing and fine-tuning the algorithm submitted to the *International Timetabling Competition* by the author and co-workers. Section 5.2.3 illustrates a model selection application of *F-Race* for a supervised learning problem. Finally, Section 5.2.4 briefly mentions further works on *F-Race* that were carried out by other researchers.

5.2.1 Tuning metaheuristics for timetabling

The *F-Race* algorithm was developed by the author of the thesis while he was with the German node of the *Metaheuristics Network*, in Darmstadt. At that time, second half of the year 2001, the research focus of the *Metaheuristics Network* was on the UNIVERSITY-COURSE TIMETABLING problem, and the INTELLEKTIK group of the Technische Universität Darmstadt was in charge of the development of two metaheuristics for this problem: *simulated annealing* and *iterated local search*. For the research on the UNIVERSITY-COURSE TIMETABLING problem, the *Metaheuristics Network* has considered three classes of instances of increasing size and complexity denoted as *small*, *medium*, and *large*. A summary of the characteristics of these classes is given in Table 5.5. Instances from these three classes could be obtained in a straightforward way thanks to a parametric random instance generator developed by Ben Paechter.[13] For each class, a different time limit was defined: It was agreed that metaheuristics were to be evaluated on the basis of the quality of the best solution they could find within a run of 90 s for small instances, 900 s for medium instance, and 9000 s for large instances.

Moreover, it was agreed that for each metaheuristic to be studied, three different implementations could have been developed, one tailored for each of the classes of instances under analysis.

At INTELLEKTIK it was decided to develop one single generic version of

[13] `http://www.dcs.napier.ac.uk/~benp/`

	small	medium	large
number of events	100	400	400
number of rooms	5	10	10
number of features	5	5	10
features per room	3	3	5
percentage of features used	70	80	90
number of students	80	200	400
maximum number of events per student	20	20	20
maximum number of students per event	20	50	100

Table 5.5: Summary of the characteristics of the three classes of instances of the UNIVERSITY-COURSE TIMETABLING problem studied by the *Metaheuristics Network*.

the two metaheuristics we were supposed to implement, namely *simulated annealing* and *iterated local search*, and to automatically configure and fine-tune them for the different classes of instances. Marco Chiarandini[14] was in charge of the implementation of *simulated annealing*, and Luís Paquete[15] of *iterated local search*.

The *F-Race* algorithm was adopted for selecting the proper configuration of the two metaheuristics out of a set of 148 possible candidates for *iterated local search*, and 70 for *simulated annealing*. The *F-Race* algorithm that was adopted is exactly the one described in Chapter 4 in an implementation that was a pre-release version of the software package currently available for download from the R official repository.[16]

The selected configurations were submitted for an independent evaluation and comparison with the metaheuristics implemented by the other members of the *Metaheuristics Network*. The evaluation was performed by Michael Sampels[17] at IRIDIA, on a number of previously undisclosed instances.

The full set of the experimental results and their thorough statistical analysis is available in Sampels (2002). Here, we limit ourself to some considerations on the results obtained on the instances of class *medium* because on the class *small* most of the metaheuristics under analysis obtained similar results, and on the class *large* too few experiments were run for reaching some meaningful conclusions.

Figure 5.18 summarizes the results obtained on the 5 previously undisclosed *medium* instances adopted for the analysis. Each metaheuristic was run 50 times on each of these instances. In the plots, *iterated local search* is denoted by ILS and *simulated annealing* by SA. The other metaheuristics that were studied are *ant*

[14] `http://www.intellektik.informatik.tu-darmstadt.de/~machud`

[15] `http://www.intellektik.informatik.tu-darmstadt.de/~lpaquete`

[16] `http://cran.r-project.org/src/contrib/Descriptions/race.html`

[17] `http://iridia.ulb.ac.be/~msampels`

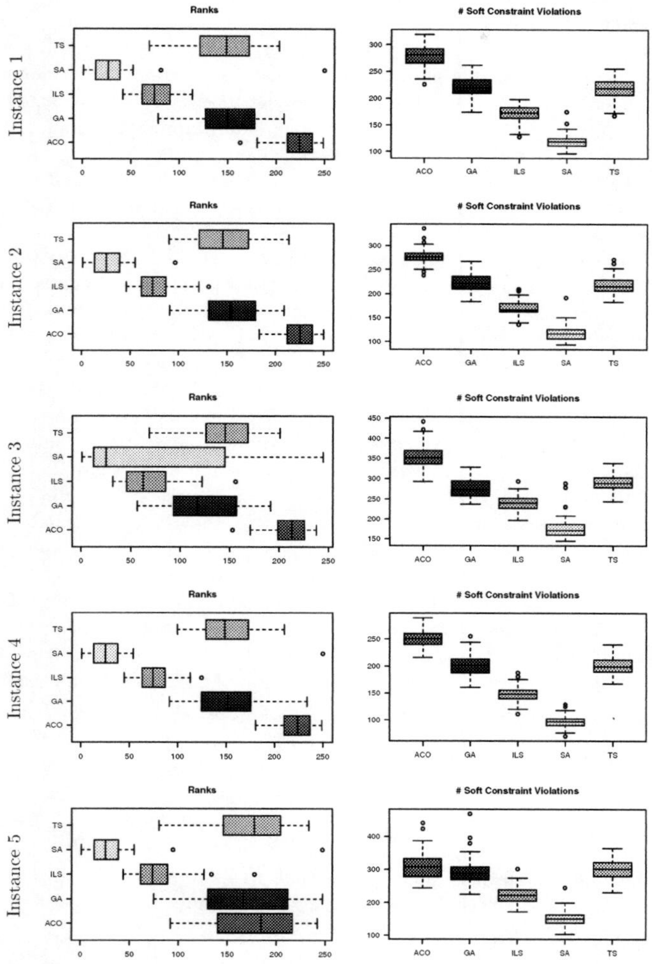

Figure 5.18: Results on UNIVERSITY-COURSE TIMETABLING instances of type *medium*: The plots on the left hand side give a ranking of the metaheuristics, those on the right hand side the optimal values found. The plots are obtained on the basis of 50 runs of 900 s for each metaheuristic on each of the 5 instances.

colony optimization, denoted by ACO, *genetic algorithm*, denoted by GA, and finally *tabu search*, denoted by TS. The plots in the right-hand column describe the number of soft constraint violations (the lower, the better) in the solution found by each metaheuristic. Those in the left-hand column, the ranking (the more on the left, the better) of the metaheuristics under analysis on the 50 runs. Therefore, the plots in the left-hand column bring a non-parametric version, scaled on an instance-by-instance basis, of the information contained in the corresponding plot in the right-hand column. It can be easily observed that *simulated annealing* is the best performing algorithm on all 5 instances, and that *iterated local search* is the second best.

It would be clearly improper to conclude from these results that the success of the implementations of *simulated annealing* and *iterated local search* developed by INTELLEKTIK is to be ascribed entirely to the fact that the *F-Race* algorithm was used for tuning their parameters. The ultimate reason of the success of these algorithms in the experiments proposed here cannot be extracted from the data themselves. Indeed, the whole experimental setting was designed with other goals in mind and did not aim at isolating the different contributions of the elements that might have concurred to obtain a given performance and, in particular, at isolating the contribution of the configuration algorithm.[18] Nevertheless, the results proposed in Figure 5.18 show the success of a complex cocktail of contributions including: the algorithmic ideas underlying *simulated annealing* and *iterated local search*, the skill of the implementers, the tuning algorithm, and possibly other elements that could not be identified and isolated.

In any case, the conclusion we can draw from this application of *F-Race* is that the algorithm has properly served the purpose and has been considered serviceable, reliable, and convenient by the researchers of INTELLEKTIK that have used it for finishing up the implementation of their metaheuristics.

In a later phase, also the *ant colony optimization* algorithm implemented at IRIDIA has been reconfigured using *F-Race*. The results of this research are given in Manfrin (2003).

5.2.2 The *International Timetabling Competition*

A method derived from *F-Race* was used by Chiarandini, Birattari, Socha & Rossi-Doria (2003; 2004) for designing and fine-tuning a high performing hybrid metaheuristic for the UNIVERSITY-COURSE TIMETABLING problem. The resulting algorithm was submitted to the *International Timetabling Competition* organized in 2003 by the *Metaheuristics Network* and sponsored by PATAT, the international series of conferences on the *Practice and Theory of Automated Timetabling*.

The algorithm was developed strictly following the competition guidelines and

[18] For an analysis of this kind, we refer the reader to Section 5.1.

was evaluated exactly as all other submitted algorithms but, according to the rules of the *International Timetabling Competition*, it was not allowed to win the prize since the authors were members of the *Metaheuristics Network*. The competition was eventually won by an algorithm developed by Philipp Kostuch (2003a; 2003b). Nevertheless, the algorithm submitted by Chiarandini, Birattari, Socha & Rossi-Doria and discussed here, outperformed, according to the evaluation criterion of the competition, the official winner which, in turn, outperformed by quite a large margin all the other entries.

This research has been carried out by the author of this thesis and co-workers during the third phase of the research activity of the *Metaheuristics Network* on the TIMETABLING problem.[19] During the second phase, a number of metaheuristics had been implemented in their most straight-forward version using common software libraries and data structures. This was done with the aim of comparing on a same basis the ideas underlying each metaheuristic and eventually understanding which search strategies were the most promising for the problem at hand. The metaheuristics considered during the second phase were *ant colony optimization*, *evolutionary computation*, *iterated local search*, *simulated annealing*, and *tabu search*.

In the third phase, other metaheuristics were included in the list of the algorithms to be considered:

- *Ant colony optimization* in its *MAX–MIN Ant System* variant (Stützle & Hoos, 1997, 2000). See Socha *et al.* (2003) and Socha (2003a) for a description of the implementation of *MAX–MIN Ant System* for the UNIVERSITY-COURSE TIMETABLING problem.

- The *heuristic memetic algorithm*, which is a metaheuristic belonging to the *evolutionary computation* family, that adopts construction heuristics for the initialization of the population and for the recombination of individuals, and local search for improving the quality of the generated solutions (Burke *et al.*, 1996; Moscato & Norman, 1992; Rossi-Doria & Paechter, 2003).

- An *iterated local search* that uses *variable neighborhood descent* as local search, *random moves* as perturbations, and *annealing* as acceptance criterion (Lourenço *et al.*, 2002).

- An *iterated greedy search* that is inspired by the research on the GRAPH COLORING problem (Culberson, 1992). This algorithm tries to escape from local optima by destructing part of the whole assignment and by then reconstructing it on the basis of construction heuristics.

[19] A brief description of the research methodology adopted by the *Metaheuristics Network* and, in particular, the definition of the three phases in which the study of each problem has been organized, are given in Chapter 1, at page 8.

Moreover, a number of hybrid metaheuristics were considered which are based on the following components:

Construction heuristics: More than 60 different construction heuristics were developed, which were inspired by the work on GRAPH COLORING and on other specific timetabling applications like those of Burke *et al.* (1995) and Newall (1999).

Local Search: A number of different local search algorithms were implemented, based on 7 different neighborhood structures and on various ways of exploring the neighborhood. The best alternatives are described in detail in Chiarandini *et al.* (2004), while other attempts are mentioned in Rossi-Doria *et al.* (2002).

Metaheuristics: A number of metaheuristics were considered. Among them, those that appeared being more effective in guiding the local search out of local optima and towards other promising regions were:

Variable neighborhood descent, which consists in a sequence of local search procedures in different neighborhood structures. The sequence is iteratively repeated until no further improvement is possible in none of the neighborhoods.

Tabu search, which is based on the idea of accepting also worsening solutions during local search provided that, in order to avoid cycles, already visited assignments are not re-visited. As suggested by the results of the first phase, tabu search is worth being used only for solving hard constraints.

Simulated annealing, which is based on the idea of accepting worsening solutions in the local search according to a probabilistic criterion inspired by the physical annealing process.

Taken together, and considering their possible combinations, the above mentioned algorithms define a quite large space of hybrid metaheuristics. In order to obtain a high-performing metaheuristic, this space was explored using an algorithms that is closely related to *F-Race*. Indeed, similarly to *F-Race*, the algorithm adopted sequentially evaluates a number of candidates and discards less promising ones, as soon as sufficient evidence is gathered against them. In time, the algorithm focuses on the best candidates and devotes to their evaluation more computational resources in order to obtain a more reliable assessment. On the other hand, contrary to *F-Race*, which is a fully automatic procedure, the algorithm adopted here relies on a human decision maker that at each stage is supposed to select the candidates that should be discarded. This decision is to be made on the basis of the information provided by the algorithm in the form of statistical tests and graphs. The reason for the adoption of such a semi-automatic procedure is that the race was not intended solely as a method for selecting the very best candidate but also as a method for gathering data on the performance of some classes of metaheuristics for further analysis. Therefore, some configurations, although apparently inferior, were not immediately discarded but were *artificially* kept alive with the aim of gaining a deeper understanding on their behavior. Moreover, the semi-automatic procedure gives the opportunity, at the end of each stage of the race, to analyze the performance of the candidates and possibly to include in the race other configurations on the basis of the partial results observed. This feature was indeed exploited in the race that led to the selection of the metaheuristic to be submitted to the competition: After the first stage of the race, it was understood that a subclass of candidates was particularly promising, namely those including a refinement of the assignment based on *simulated annealing*. On the basis of this observation, more configurations out of this subclass were included in the race. The candidate that won the race and that was eventually submitted to the competition is precisely one of those that were included in the race after the first stage of the race itself.

Figure 5.19 proposes a graphical representation of the race that led to the selection of the algorithm that was eventually submitted to the *International Timetabling Competition* by Chiarandini, Birattari, Socha & Rossi-Doria. It should be noted that, according to the rules of the competition, each algorithm to be submitted was required to solve 20 instances of the UNIVERSITY-COURSE TIMETABLING problem, published on the web by the organizers. These 20 instances were made available in two sets: **Set 1**, comprising 10 instances, was published on the competition site on October 1, 2002. **Set 2**, also comprising 10 instance, was published on March 17, 2003, that is, only two weeks before the deadline for the submission of algorithms to the competition, which was March 31, 2003.

The race considered an initial set of 879 candidates to which 306 further candidates were added after the first stage, for a total of 1185. The first stage was based only on the instances of the above mentioned Set 1. After the first stage, 200 candidates were retained and the other discarded. All evaluations of subsequent stages of the race were based on instances of both Set 1 and Set 2. The whole race took about one month of alternating phases of computation, analysis, and human decision. It involved up to a maximum of 30 personal computers physically located in Brussels, Edinburgh, and Darmstadt, all running the Linux operating system, with CPU clock ranging between 300 and 1800 MHz.

Giving a detailed description of the selected hybrid metaheuristic goes beyond the aims of this section. It will be sufficient to mention here that the algorithm it is based on *simulated annealing* and that it adopts a number of different construction heuristics for building a first assignment which is typically an unfeasible solution; this assignment is then modified by a procedure with the aim of obtaining a feasible solution; which, in turn, is finally optimized through local search. For a thorough description of the resulting algorithm we refer the interested reader to Chiarandini, Birattari, Socha & Rossi-Doria (2004).

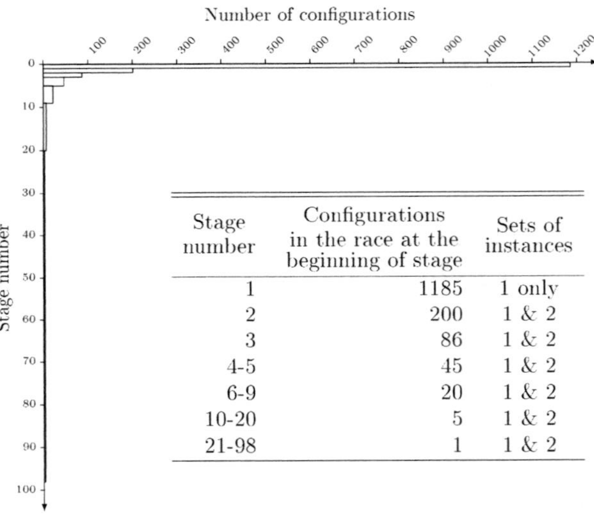

Stage number	Configurations in the race at the beginning of stage	Sets of instances
1	1185	1 only
2	200	1 & 2
3	86	1 & 2
4-5	45	1 & 2
6-9	20	1 & 2
10-20	5	1 & 2
21-98	1	1 & 2

Figure 5.19: A graphical description of the race. The race started with 879 configurations. The first stage consisted in testing the available configurations on the 10 instances composing the first set made available by the organizing committee. On the basis of the results observed during the first stage, another group of 306 configurations where added to the race for a total of 1185. Out of this set, 200 were kept and entered the second stage, while the others were discarded. Starting from the second stage on, each stage consisted in testing all surviving configurations on the 10 instances of the first set and on the 10 instances of the second set made available by the organizing committee.

Set 1	1	2	3	4	5	6	7	8	9	10
Competition winner	**45**	**25**	65	115	102	13	44	29	17	61
Chiarandini *et al.*	57	31	**61**	**112**	**86**	**3**	**5**	**4**	**16**	**54**

Set 2	11	12	13	14	15	16	17	18	19	20
Competition winner	44	107	78	52	24	22	86	31	44	7
Chiarandini *et al.*	**38**	**100**	**71**	**25**	**14**	**11**	**69**	**24**	**40**	**0**

Table 5.6: Results—the lower, the better—obtained on the two sets of instances of the *International Timetabling Competition* by the winner and by the algorithm discussed here which was submitted by Chiarandini, Birattari, Socha & Rossi-Doria. The algorithm submitted by Chiarandini *et al.* obtains a better result on 18 of the 20 instances, while the winner of the competition obtains a better result on the remaining 2 instances.

Table 5.6 reports the results obtained on the 20 instances of the *International Timetabling Competition* by the winning algorithm, submitted by Kostuch (2003a,b), and by the algorithm discussed here and submitted by Chiarandini *et al.* (2003; 2004).[20] The figures make clear that the algorithm of Chiarandini *et al.* outperforms the winner of the competition: on 18 instances out of 20, the former obtains a better result. However, for the sake of fairness, some elements have to be taken into account: First of all, it must be acknowledged that the algorithm of Chiarandini *et al.* could rely on much larger computational resources. Moreover, after the competition both algorithms have been further optimized and both obtained even better results (Chiarandini *et al.*, 2004; Kostuch, 2004).

Also in this case, as in the case of the application presented in Section 5.2.1, it is impossible to quantify the entity of the contribution given by the *racing* approach to the overall performance.[21] Nevertheless, the feeling shared by the people involved in this research is that the selection methodology adopted had a major impact on the results that were eventually obtained. The 1185 possible candidates out of which the best had to be selected, are hybrid metaheuristics proposed partly by Marco Chiarandini,[22] partly by Krzysztof Socha,[23], and partly by Olivia Rossi-Doria.[24] The author of this thesis has been in charge of designing the evaluation procedure and the selection strategy. Therefore, the application described in this section reproduces somehow a real-world situation in which the

[20] The results obtained by all algorithms submitted to the *International Timetabling Competition* can be found at `http://www.idsia.ch/Files/ttcomp2002/results.htm`

[21] See Section 5.1 for a formal empirical assessment of *F-Race*.

[22] `http://www.intellektik.informatik.tu-darmstadt.de/~machud`

[23] `http://iridia.ulb.ac.be/~ksocha`

[24] `http://www.soc.napier.ac.uk/people/op/onepeople/peopleid/10988`

racing approach is used on behalf of a third party. In a sense, this application has been a particularly illuminating experience in which Chiarandini, Socha, and Rossi-Doria have played the role of a *customer* requesting the service of a *racing* approach. From this experience we have learned, in particular, that a customer might not entirely trust, at least since the very beginning, a fully automatic procedure and wishes to *"know what is happening."* This attitude is often justified—and, indeed, it was fully justified in the application described here—because often the customer has some good understanding of the problem at hand and of the characteristics of the candidates among which a selection is to be performed. In such a case, his/her advice might be very useful at the moment of deciding which candidates should be retained and which discarded. Moreover, as it happened in this application, the customer can, on the basis of the analysis of the partial results of the race, understand if a particular subclass of candidates is particularly promising. In such case, he might suggest adding further candidates of that class, while the race is already in progress.

The application discussed in this section is a proper illustration of the flexibility of the *racing* approach presented in the thesis and of its adaptability to a real-world-*like* situation. In particular, it shows that with minor modifications, and without altering its characterizing features, the *F-Race* algorithm can be adopted as a powerful interactive tool for the incremental evaluation and selection of the best of a given number of alternatives.

5.2.3 *F-Race* for feature selection

The *F-Race* algorithm has been recently adopted by Bontempi, Birattari & Meyer (2004) for tackling the feature selection problem in a supervised learning setting. As it is made clear in Chapter 4, the source of inspiration for the development of *F-Race* have been the *Hoeffding race* and the *BRACE* algorithms that were originally proposed by Maron & Moore (1994) and Moore & Lee (1994), respectively, for tackling the model selection problem in supervised learning. Indeed, the first application of *BRACE* described in the literature was precisely a problem of feature selection (Moore & Lee, 1994)—See Section 2.2.7 for a brief description of *Hoeffding race* and *BRACE*.

Beside the adoption of a *racing* approach, another element of similarity between our work on feature selection and the work previously presented by Moore & Lee (1994), is that in both cases we deal with the same underlying learning approach, that is, *lazy learning* (Atkeson *et al.*, 1997; Birattari *et al.*, 1999)—See Section 2.2.6 for an introduction to a number of supervised learning methods, including *lazy learning*, and Annex B for a more detailed description of the original *lazy learning* algorithm developed by the author of this thesis.

In a sense, the application we present in this section brings back *F-Race* to the machine learning community: The *racing* idea was borrowed from the supervised learning literature and taken to the metaheuristics field where it was modified and improved, namely my adopting the Friedman test; with the application presented in this section, it is brought back to its original field.

However, in addition to the adoption of a different statistical test of hypothesis, another innovative element characterizes the feature selection algorithm that we propose here: The adoption of a *sub-sampling strategy* (John & Langley, 1996).

In the application that is proposed in this section, feature selection is performed using a *wrapper method* (Kohavi & John, 1997). The aim of feature selection is to find the subset of a given number of features that has the highest possible predictive power. In the wrapper approach, in order to evaluate the predictive power of a given subset, the feature selection algorithm uses an underlying learning method. The latter is *"wrapped"* in the sense that its details need not to be known by the feature selection algorithm: In other words, the underlying learning method is simply viewed as a black-box that is supposed to return, on the basis of a given subset of features, a prediction of the output together with an assessment of the quality of the prediction itself. Typically, such an assessment is obtained through cross-validation.[25]

Lazy learning, and local learning algorithms in general, are often deemed to be impractical when dealing with a high number of features and with large samples. A similar criticism is often moved to wrapper methods. Nonetheless, when lazy learning is adopted in the context of a wrapper method, these limitations can be overcome. Indeed, the peculiarity of *lazy learning* is that, contrary to other learning methods as for example neural networks, it does not require a time consuming training phase. This peculiarity is a great advantage in the context of wrapper-based feature selection. To be more explicit, let us consider the adoption of a neural network in the context of wrapper feature selection. In order to evaluate each single possible subset of features, the underlying neural network needs to be trained on these features and only after a typically lengthy training, an assessment of the predictive power of the subset of features under study can be eventually obtained. It is worth pointing out that the computational cost of the training is a *fixed* cost that is independent of the number of the evaluations of the neural network we need to perform. On the other hand, *lazy learning* does not require any training phase and the evaluation of the predictive power of a given subset of features can be immediately obtained: In other words, contrary to neural networks, *lazy learning* does not involve any *fixed* cost for the training but only a *marginal* cost for each evaluation. Admittedly, each single evaluation of the *lazy learning* algorithm is more expensive than a single evaluation of a neural network. Nevertheless, few evaluations are typically needed for assessing a subset of features and the difference between the two approaches regarding the evaluation phase can be neglected compared to the difference regarding the training phase.

In the feature selection algorithm developed by Bontempi, Birattari & Meyer

[25]For a definition of these concepts, we refer the reader to Section 2.2.

(2004), the rationale for the adoption of a sub-sampling strategy is precisely related to the fact that when *lazy learning* is adopted, only a *marginal* cost for each evaluation is incurred, and there is no *fixed* cost for training. In such a case, it make sense to reduce the number of evaluations performed. This reduction clearly increases the variance of the assessment of the predictive power of the set of features under study: We face therefore a trade-off accuracy/cost of an assessment. In the feature selection algorithm proposed by Bontempi *et al.* (2004) the trade-off is handled by scheduling the number of evaluations to be performed on each set of features: In a first phase, when a large number of candidate sets of features have to be screened, few evaluations are performed on each of them and a coarse selection is performed; later on, when fewer candidate sets of features are left, a more accurate assessment of each of them is considered on the basis of a larger number of evaluations. Clearly, the rationale behind the adoption of sub-sampling bears a strong similarity to the one behind the *racing* approach: In both cases, an incremental selection is performed on the basis of a criterion that is rather coarse at the beginning, when we have to deal with a large number of candidates, and that becomes finer and finer as the number of candidates is reduced. Quite naturally, in the *racing&sub-sampling* algorithm proposed by Bontempi, Birattari & Meyer (2004) the two ideas are combined.

Giving a fully detailed description of the *racing&sub-sampling* algorithm goes beyond the aims of this section. We refer therefore the interested reader to the original work of Bontempi *et al.* (2004). Here, it will be sufficient to summarize the main traits of the algorithm through the high-level pseudo-code description given in Figure 5.20.

In the following, we provide some evidence of the effectiveness of the algorithm. In particular, we summarize the results of two computational experiments.

Selection of relevant variables. In the first experiment, a functional relationship $f : X \to Y$ is considered, where $X \subset \mathbb{R}^{10}$ and $Y \subset \mathbb{R}$. We are given a set of examples,

$$\mathcal{Z} = \left\{(x_j^1, \dots, x_j^{10}, x_j^{11}, \dots, x_j^m, y_j)\right\}_{j=1}^N,$$

where $y_j = f(x_j^1, \dots, x_j^{10}) + \varepsilon_j$, being ε_j some random noise extracted from an unknown distribution, independently for each j. The variables $x_j^{11}, \dots, x_j^m$ are simply random noise uncorrelated from y_j. The goal is to select, out of the full set of variables $x^1, \dots, x^m$, only those that are indeed useful for predicting y, that is, $x^1, \dots, x^{10}$. In the specific experiment considered here, we have:

$$\begin{aligned} y = 10\sin(\pi x^1 x^2) + 20(x^3 - 1/2)^2 + 10x^4 + 5x^5 + \\ + 10\sin(\pi x^6 x^7) + 20(x^8 - 1/2)^2 + 10x^9 + 5x^{10} + \varepsilon, \end{aligned}$$

It should be noted that this feature selection problem is a somehow harder version of the problem proposed by Friedman (1991): (i) In the original problem, the

```
function racing&sub-sampling(M)
  # Number of assessments performed so far
  assessments_soFar = 0
  # Number of steps so far
  k = 0
  # Allocate array for storing results of assessments
  A = allocate_array(max_steps, |Θ|)
  # Surviving candidate subsets of features
  S = Θ
  while(assessments_soFar + |S| ≤ M and
          k + 1 ≤ max_steps) do
    # Sub-sample a training set and a test set
    # from the available dataset
    Tr = sample_training_set_of_size(N^k_Tr)
    Ts = sample_test_set_of_size(N^k_Ts)
    k += 1 # Increment number of steps so far
    foreach θ in S do
      # Assess candidate θ on Tr and Ts
      A[k, θ] = assess_candidate(θ, Tr, Ts)
      assessments_soFar += 1
    done
    # Drop inferior candidates
    S = drop_candidates(S, A, friedman_test)
  done
  # Select best surviving configuration
  θ̃ = select_best_survivor(S, A)
  return θ̃
```

Figure 5.20: Pseudo-code of the *racing&sub-sampling* algorithm for feature selection. The initial set of candidates Θ is composed of a number of possible subsets of features. The size of the training and test sets, N^k_{Tr} and N^k_{Tr}, respectively, are properly scheduled so that they increase in time for giving a more and more accurate assessment as the race converges to the most promising subsets of features. Formally: $N^{k+1}_{Tr} \geq N^k_{Tr}$ and $N^{k+1}_{Ts} \geq N^k_{Ts}$. The function `assess_candidate()` consists in a call to the underlying *wrapped* learning method; in this case, the *lazy learning* algorithm.

M/Init	*R&S*	*FS*	Model assessed	Training set	Test set
110/GS	92%	8%	7342 ± 572	259 ± 31	601 ± 307
110/RN	88%	8%	7054 ± 726	220 ± 21	213 ± 214
210/GS	88%	4%	7403 ± 595	265 ± 52	660 ± 522
210/RN	84%	4%	7017 ± 901	223 ± 37	240 ± 366

(a) *Racing&sub-sampling* (*R&S*) vs. *forward selection* (*FS*). In the first column, M is the total number of variables, while *Init* is the initialization procedure: GS is for *Gram-Schmidt* and RN for *random*.

	AILERON	POLE	ELEVATORS	TRIAZINES	WISCONSIN	CENSUS
LL-RS1	9.7E−05	3.1E+00	1.6E−03	2.1E−01	2.7E+01	1.7E−01
LL-RS2	9.0E−05	3.1E+00	1.5E−03	1.2E−01	2.7E+01	1.6E−01
SVM	1.3E−04	2.6E+01	1.9E−03	1.1E−01	2.9E+01	2.1E−01
RTREE	1.8E−04	8.8E+00	3.1E−03	1.1E−01	3.3E+01	1.7E−01

(b) Mean absolute error on the test set for 6 benchmarks.

Table 5.7: Summary of the results of the two experiments with the *racing&sub-sampling* algorithm.

number of relevant variables was 5, while in the version presented here it is 10; (ii) in the original version, the number of irrelevant variables was 5, while in the version presented here it is 100 in one of the settings and 200 in the other.

The *racing&sub-sampling* algorithm is compared with one of the simplest approaches to feature selection, namely *forward selection*, which consists in iteratively selecting variables starting from the most predictive one, adding then the one that, considered together with the already selected one, yields the most predictive pair, and so on; the process is repeated till when, by adding a further variable, the quality of the prediction does not improve anymore. In the experiment proposed here, both *racing&sub-sampling* and *forward selection* use *lazy learning* as the underlying *wrapped* learning algorithm.

We consider two different settings. In both of them, only 10 variables are relevant but, in the first, the total number of input variables is 110 and in the second it is 210. Moreover, in each of the settings we consider two ways of initializing the set of candidates Θ. The first is based on the Gram-Schmidt orthogonalization procedure[26] while the second relies on a simple random selection.

Table 5.7(a) summarizes the results of this first experiment. It can be observed that *racing&sub-sampling* is able to correctly select the right set of features from 84% to 92% of the times. On the other hand, *forward selection* obtains a much

[26] For more details, see Bontempi *et al.* (2004).

worse result: only a rate of 4% to 8% of correct selections. Beside the rate of success of the two algorithms, the following information is given in Table 5.7(a): (i) average and standard deviation of the number of candidate subsets of feature that have been assessed by *racing&sub-sampling* before delivering the selected one; (ii) average and standard deviation of the number of training examples needed by *racing&sub-sampling* for the assessment; (iii) average and standard deviation of the number of test examples needed by *racing&sub-sampling* for the assessment.

The experimental results show that the *racing&sub-sampling* algorithm is reasonably robust to the initialization procedure adopted and to the number of irrelevant variables.

Prediction accuracy. This second experiment proposes a comparison between the pair *lazy learning*/*racing&sub-sampling* and two state-of-the-art learning algorithms that perform an implicit and *embedded* feature selection: *support vector machines* and *regression trees*.[27]

The comparison is performed through a five-fold cross-validation on six real-world datasets of relatively high dimensionality that were gathered from various sources and made available for free download by Luís Torgo:[28]

AILERONS: This dataset addresses a control problem, namely flying an aircraft. The input variables describe the status of the airplane, while the output is the control action on the ailerons of the aircraft. The dataset consists of $N = 14308$ examples and the number of input variables is $m = 40$.

POLE: This is a commercial application described in Weiss & Indurkhya (1995). The data describe a telecommunication problem. The dataset consists of $N = 1500$ examples and the number of input variables is $m = 48$.

ELEVATORS: This dataset is obtained from the same control problem from which AILERON is obtained, but a different output variable and a different set of input variables are considered. In this case, the output variable is related to an action taken on the elevators of the aircraft. The dataset consists of $N = 16599$ examples and the number of input variables is $m = 18$.

TRIAZINES: This dataset generates in a biological application: the study of the inhibition of dihydrofolate reductase by triazines. The dataset consists of $N = 186$ examples and the number of input variables is $m = 60$.

WISCONSIN: This is a medical application concerning follow-up data for breast cancer cases. The dataset consists of $N = 194$ examples and the number of input variables is $m = 32$.

CENSUS: Collected as part of the 1990 US census. The dataset consists of $N = 22784$ examples and the number of input variables is $m = 137$.

[27] The experimental results proposed here are obtained using the implementations of this algorithms provided by the R packages `e1071` and `tree`, respectively.

[28] `http://www.liacc.up.pt/~ltorgo/Regression/DataSets.html`

Two version of the *racing&sub-sampling* algorithm are tested. In the first one, denoted in Table 5.7(b) by *LL-RS1*, the prediction returned by the algorithm is the one obtained by using the set of features selected by the *racing&sub-sampling* algorithm. In the second version, denoted in Table 5.7(b) by *LL-RS2*, the *racing&sub-sampling* algorithm does not return only the very best subset of features but rather the 5 best ones. The prediction returned by the algorithm is obtained by averaging the predictions obtained by using the 5 subsets of features proposed by *racing&sub-sampling*.

Table 5.7(b) summarizes the results. On the basis of an appropriate statistical test—see Bontempi *et al.* (2004) for the details—it can be stated that *LL-RS2* performs significantly better than *LL-RS1* on 3 datasets out of 6, and it is never significantly worse. Therefore, the idea of combining predictors yields a significant improvement. As far as the comparison with the state-of-the-art algorithms is concerned, *LL-RS2* is significantly better than the *support vector machine* on 5 datasets out of 6 and it is never significantly worse; finally, *LL-RS2* is significantly better than the *regression tree* on all 6 datasets.

With the application proposed in this section, we have brought *F-Race* back to the original domain of application of the *racing* approach, that is, model selection, and more specifically feature selection. Also this application highlights the flexibility of the *F-Race* algorithm and the possibility of combining it with other techniques as, in this specific case, a sub-sampling strategy for the evaluations of the candidates. Preliminary experimental results with the *racing&sub-sampling* algorithm are particularly encouraging.

5.2.4 Further applications

Beside the applications presented in the previous sections, which have involved the author of this thesis, the *F-Race* algorithm has been adopted by other researchers in a number of studies.

Academic studies

The *F-Race* algorithm was adopted for tuning the parameters of the implementation of *simulated annealing* for the UNIVERSITY-COURSE TIMETABLING problem that is analyzed in Chiarandini & Stützle (2002).

As already mentioned in Section 5.2.1, Manfrin (2003) has adopted the *F-Race* algorithm for tuning the parameters of his implementation of *ant colony optimization* for the UNIVERSITY-COURSE TIMETABLING problem.

The *F-Race* algorithm was adopted by Schiavinotto & Stützle for tuning an *iterated local search* algorithm and an *evolutionary computation* algorithm, more precisely a *memetic* algorithm,[29] for the LINEAR ORDERING problem (Schiavinotto & Stützle, 2004).

The *F-Race* algorithm was adopted by den Besten for tuning an *iterated local search* algorithm for deterministic scheduling problems with tardiness penalties (den Besten, 2004).

The *F-Race* algorithm is currently being adopted by Chiarandini for tuning the parameters of the algorithms for over-constrained combinatorial optimization problems that will be described in his Ph.D. thesis (Chiarandini, 2005).

Yuan & Gallagher (2004) discuss the use of *F-Race* for the empirical evaluation of *evolutionary algorithms*. Further, they introduce *A-Race*, a parametric instance of a *racing* approach based on the *analysis of variance* method. In the experiments they propose, both *racing* approachs perform particularly well, even if in one of the specific settings they consider *F-Race* obtains better results than *A-Race*.[30]

Thomas Stützle, Tommaso Schiavinotto, and Marco Chiarandini (2004) of INTELLEKTIK, Darmstadt, Germany, have used *F-Race* for fine-tuning the algorithm they submitted to the ROADEF'2005 challenge.[31]

Finally, in collaboration with IRIDIA, Université Libre de Bruxelles, Brussels, Belgium, three undergraduate students are currently working on the problem of tuning metaheuristics. Their research involves the use of the *F-Race* algorithm and the development of possible extensions (Lunghi, 2004; Boldrini, 2005; Denis, 2005).

An industrial application

F-Race has been considered in a feasibility study that aimed at optimizing an industrial computer program for vehicle routing and scheduling problems, developed by the German-based software company SAP. The study was conducted by Sven Becker (2004) under the guidance of Thomas Stützle and Jens Gottlieb.

Six different experimental setting were considered. Three of them concern the optimization of a specific parameter of the program under study, which determines the frequency of application of a critical operator. The other three concern the selection and fine-tuning of the metaheuristic on which the program under study should rely. In all experiments, *F-Race* was compared to a *discard-worst* strategy, which discards a fixed percentage of the worst candidate configurations after each iteration.

[29]See Section 2.1.7 and more specifically page 31, for a brief introduction to *evolutionary computation* and *memetic* algorithms, and for further references.

[30]Unfortunately, Yuan & Gallagher (2004) fail to understand the reason why we consider only one single run of each candidate on each instance—see Section 4.1 for a formal analysis of the issue.

[31]See `http://www.roadef.org`. The problem of the ROADEF'2005 challenge is a MULTIOBJECTIVE CAR SEQUENCING problem proposed by the French car manufacturer Renault.

This study has two peculiarities: The first is that, at each step of the races, all surviving candidate settings are tested once on all available instances of the problem. The reason for this is that only a limited number of instances are available and they are quite different one from the other. The second is that the instances considered are typically rather complex and therefore a run time of 10 minutes is allotted for a single run of each candidate setting on each instance. As a consequence, the overall time needed for completing a race is quite long.

The results of the experiments are mixed, mainly depending on the influence that the parameter to be optimized has on the overall performance of the program under analysis. As it might be expected, if the parameter has low influence, *F-Race* takes a rather long time, and a rather large set of candidates remains at the end of the race. On the other hand, if the parameter has high influence on the performance, inferior candidates are discarded very quickly and *F-Race* converges much faster and more reliably than the ***discard-worst*** strategy considered in this study.

On account of these results, the research group of SAP that followed this study currently considers *F-Race* as a promising tool for optimizing the parameters of future releases of their commercial product for vehicle routing and scheduling.

5.3 Discussion

This chapter has proposed a number of evidential elements to support the thesis that *F-Race*, and more in general the *racing* approach, are an effective and convenient way for tackling the problem of tuning metaheuristics.

The formal empirical analysis proposed in Section 5.1 compares, under controlled experimental conditions, the performance of various *racing* algorithms. This section has the main merit of somehow providing a *measure* of the performance of a tuning algorithm. This is done by adopting as a unit of measurement the performance of the most trivial, albeit perfectly legitimate and correct, of all selection method, namely, the *brute-force* approach. The section proposes two experiments. In the first one, in which *iterated local search* has been tuned for QUADRATIC ASSIGNMENT, the performance of *F-Race* is basically equivalent to the one of *Cheat10*, but it is significantly better than the one of *Cheat5*. Here, *Cheat10* and *Cheat5* are versions of the *brute-force* approach that are allowed a large amount of computation time: 10 and 5 times more than *F-Race*, respectively. Therefore, the results show that in this experiment the *brute-force* approach needs 10 times more time than *F-Race*—that is, 10 times the number of runs of the metaheuristic to be tuned that are needed by *F-Race*—for achieving the same results as obtained by *F-Race*. In the second experiment, in which *ant colony optimization* has been tuned for TRAVELING SALESMAN, the relative performance of *F-Race* with respect to the *brute-force* approach is even better: here, *F-Race* is even significantly better than *Cheat10*. From the results of these two experiments, we can conclude that F-Race is *at least* one order of magnitude more efficient than the *brute-force* approach in terms of the required number of runs of the metaheuristic to be tuned.

Concerning the comparisons within the *racing* family, the results clearly show that F-Race is always significantly better than tBo-Race and tHo-Race, where the latter two algorithms adopt a collection of pairwise t-tests with Bonferroni's and Holm's correction for multiplicity, respectively. This confirms the rationale for introducing the F-Race algorithm itself: In the context of *racing* algorithms, the *Friedman two-way analysis of variance by ranks* is a much more appropriate and powerful test of hypothesis than a collection of *pairwise t-tests*. On the other hand, a note of caution is needed in regard to the comparison between F-Race and tNo-Race, where the latter adopts a collection of pairwise t-tests *without* any correction for multiplicity. According to the results, the difference between the two is smaller and only in one of the two experiments it is significant. Nevertheless, we definitely favor F-Race over tNo-Race because, according to our experience in the application of *racing* algorithms, F-Race appears much more reliable and predictable in its behavior. In particular, we have observed that F-Race scales more reliably with the number of initial candidates in the race. We conjecture that the reason of the observed success of tNo-Race is due to a sort of *unstable equilibrium*: Indeed, the lack of a correction for multiplicity makes the algorithm more *bold and aggressive* in discarding candidates. This, because of some lucky circumstances, somehow compensates for the lack of power of the test. In other words, we believe that the tNo-Race algorithm can be uncontrollably too aggressive or too conservative in discarding candidates, and that the parameter on which the actual performance of the algorithm depends is the number of candidates in the race: For a *relatively* small number of candidates, the algorithm is too conservative, while for a *relatively* large number of candidates it becomes too aggressive. On the basis of the elements we have gathered so far, we have the feeling that a peak in the performance of tNo-Race is obtained when dealing with about a thousand candidates and that, at its peak performance, tNo-Race is roughly equivalent to F-Race. For the moment, these considerations are based only on casual observations: An experimental campaign is currently being designed, which will target this issue in a systematic way.

Before concluding the remarks concerning the experiments proposed in Section 5.1, we wish to point out once more the role played by the re-sampling strategy adopted. Without its service, it would have been simply impossible to obtain the results proposed. The adoption of a re-sampling method is particularly innovative in the metaheuristics community: To the best of our knowledge, Birattari *et al.* (2002) is the first work in which it has been adopted.

The second part of the chapter, that is, Section 5.2, has described a number of applications of F-Race and of derived algorithms. This second part is less formal and aims rather at showing with some example that the *racing* approach is particularly convenient to be used in practical applications and that it is sufficiently flexible for being modified and adapted to different settings. In particular, we have shown in Section 5.2.2 that *F-Race* can be turned into a powerful semi-automatic tool for designing hybrid metaheuristics. Such tool has been adopted by Chiarandini, Birattari, Socha & Rossi-Doria (2004) for designing and fine-tuning an algorithm that was submitted to the *International Timetabling Competition* and that obtained particularly brilliant results. Moreover, Section 5.2.3 has described the *racing&sub-sampling* algorithm for feature selection that is directly derived from *F-Race*. Finally, the interest shown by SAP for the *F-Race* algorithm is by itself an independent and quite authoritative assessment of its potential.

If you torture data sufficiently, it will confess to almost anything.

Statisticians' saying

Chapter 6

Some considerations on the experimental methodology

Throughout the thesis, a number of issues are raised that cast some shadow on the experimental methodology that is currently adopted in the vast majority of the works proposing an empirical evaluation of metaheuristics. Indeed, in the combinatorial optimization field it is common to encounter works in which some dubious procedure is adopted for assessing the algorithms under analysis and in which no clear statement is made on how the values of the parameters are obtained. Apparently, the need for a thorough revision of the research methodology in the optimization field is shared by many members of the research community as it is testified by the interest raised during the last years by a number of methodological articles appeared in the main journals of the community—the works by Barr *et al.* (1995), Hooker (1995), and Rardin & Uzsoy (2001) published in the *Journal of Heuristics* are just a representative sample. In this chapter, we intend to complement the existing literature with the analysis of some fundamental issues that remained so far under-explored. In particular, we focus on the problems connected with the tuning of metaheuristics. Indeed, tuning is a particularly critical element when metaheuristics are assessed and compared, being related with many different catches that might invalidate the results. Among them, we study the risks deriving from adopting the same set of instances for tuning a metaheuristic and for then assessing its performance. In the context of this study, we introduce the concept of *over-tuning* which is akin to *over-fitting* in supervised learning.

More generally, and consistently with the general framework of the thesis, the whole analysis we propose in this chapter of the experimental methodology in combinatorial optimization is inspired by the machine learning field. The chapter is structured as follows: Section 6.1 discusses some issues concerning the definition of an experimental methodology. Section 6.2 proposes a new approach to the empirical analysis of metaheuristics. Finally, Section 6.3 concludes the chapter with a summary of the issues discussed and with some final remarks.

6.1 Some fundamental methodological issues

In this section, a number of issues concerning the definition of a proper experimental methodology are analyzed. In particular, we highlight some elements in the current practice that deserve being revised.

The structure of this section is the following: Section 6.1.1 focuses on the definition of a measure of performance. Section 6.1.2 elaborates on the concept of *class of instances*. Section 6.1.3 discusses the intrinsic limitations of an experimental analysis and makes clear what kind of conclusions the latter can reach. Finally, Section 6.1.4 introduces the concept of *over-tuning* and illustrates it with an empirical analysis.

6.1.1 On some measures of performance

In the following, we restrict our attention to the framework defined in Section 3.2 and adopted in the rest of the thesis. We consider as a measure of performance of a metaheuristic the expected value of the cost of the best solution found within a given amount of time. As already stressed in Sections 3.3.4, variations are possible, which consider other statistics such as, for example, the median of the third interquartile. Advantages and disadvantages are associated with these alternative measures: On the one hand, they are more robust to outliers; on the other hand, they require more observations since their estimators are less data-efficient.

While remaining in the context of the analysis of the expectation, some alternatives exists to considering the bare expected cost.[1] In particular, some *score* functions can be considered. In the literature, the *absolute error* is often adopted:

$$\acute{c}(c, i) = c - \bar{c}_i,$$

where $\bar{c}_i$ is the cost of a (provably) optimal solution for instance i.[2] The *absolute error* has many obvious shortcomings—for example, it is not invariant under simple scaling of the cost function. Similarly, as noted in the seminal paper by Zemel (1981), also the more commonly used *relative approximation error*,

$$\acute{c}(c, i) = \frac{c - \bar{c}_i}{\bar{c}_i},$$

is not invariant with respect to some trivial transformation of the problem: For example, in the TRAVELING SALESMAN problem, an affine transformation of the distance between each pair of cities, while leaving the problem essentially the

[1]Similar considerations can be made if other statistics are adopted.

[2]In order to simplify the presentation, in the following we assume that the optimal value $\bar{c}_i$ for each instance i is known—see Rardin & Uzsoy (2001) for an excellent overview of different approaches for dealing with the situations where this does not hold.

same, changes the *relative approximation error* of solutions. As an alternative to the *relative approximation error*, Zemel (1981) proposes the adoption of

$$\acute{c}(c,i) = \frac{c - \bar{c}_i}{\check{c}_i - \bar{c}_i}, \tag{6.1}$$

where $\check{c}_i$ is the cost of a (provably) worst solution of instance i. The score given in Equation 6.1 is invariant under several trivial transformations of the problem. However, the problem with this score function, referred to in the literature as *differential approximation measure* (Demenage *et al.*, 1998) or *z-approximation* (Hassin & Khuller, 2001), is that it requires finding the worst possible cost $\check{c}_i$, which is often as difficult as finding $\bar{c}_i$. To overcome this problem, an alternative error measure was adopted in Zlochin & Dorigo (2002) and in Zlochin, Birattari & Dorigo (2004):

$$\acute{c}(c,i) = \frac{c - \bar{c}_i}{c_i^{rnd} - \bar{c}_i}, \tag{6.2}$$

where c_i^{rnd} is the expected cost of a *random* solution for instance i, selected according to the uniform distribution defined on the space S of the solutions of i. While remaining invariant under trivial problem transformations, the score function given in Equation 6.2 has two important advantages over the one given in 6.1. First, c_i^{rnd} can be computed efficiently for many problems. Second, under the score function given in 6.2, the expected error of a random solution is equal to 1, hence the proposed measure indicates how well the considered algorithm performs relatively to the most trivial one, that is, a random generator of solution. An additional useful consequence—holding also for the score function given in Equation 6.1—is that the error is automatically normalized across different problems.

To summarize, if a generic score function $\acute{c}$ is adopted and if the expected value of the cost of the best solution found within a given amount of time is the selected measure of performance, the proper criterion to be considered when comparing two or more metaheuristics is:

$$\mathcal{C}(\mathcal{M}) = \int \acute{c}(c,i)\,\mathrm{d}P_C(c|\mathcal{M},i)\,\mathrm{d}P_I(i), \tag{6.3}$$

where $\mathcal{M}$ is, in turn, each of the metaheuristics under analysis, and the integration is taken in the Lebesgue sense.[3]

Before concluding this brief digression on possible score functions, it is worth pointing out that in the empirical analysis proposed in Chapter 5, the bare-bone cost is considered rather than one of the more sophisticated score functions discussed above. The reason of this choice is that the conclusions we draw are mostly

[3]We refer the reader to Section 3.2 for a definition of the terms involved in the integration.

based on the use of a *Wilcoxon matched-pairs signed-ranks test* which, by virtue of its non-parametric nature and of its implicit use of a *blocking* design, produces results that are invariant with respect to adoption of the above mentioned scores. The use of a score function would have been just a useless complication. Nevertheless, for what concerns Figures 5.3(bottom) and 5.11(bottom), a per-instance normalization is considered[4] which, while enjoying most of the properties of invariance to simple transformations as the score functions given in Equation 6.1 and 6.2, is much easier to compute. A final remark concerns the possible adoption of a score function within a racing algorithm, that is, the use of a score function rather than directly the cost for selecting the most promising configuration of a metaheuristic. Similarly to the *Wilcoxon test*, the *Friedman two-way analysis of variance by ranks* is invariant to the adoption of the aforementioned score functions: *F-Race* therefore would not be affected. On the other hand, *tNo-Race*, *tHo-Race*, and *tNo-Race*, which are based on the t-test, could possibly yield unpredictably different results. The robustness, in this precise sense, of *F-Race* could be considered as a further reason for preferring it to its parametric counterparts.

6.1.2 On the concept of class of instances

The definition of a *class of instances* through a probability measure on the space of the instances is the single most valuable contribution of the thesis. From it, both the formal definition of the tuning problem and the proposed tuning algorithms proceed. In a rather different context and with different aims, a probabilistic description of the space of instances had been adopted previously by Wolpert & Macready in their seminal works on the *no free lunch* theorem (1996; 1997) but, apparently, it went unnoticed within the combinatorial optimization community since this device is not even mentioned in the following works on the subject—see for example Radcliffe & Surry (1995), Schumacher *et al.* (2001), Igel & Toussaint (2003), and Corne & Knowles (2003).

The implications of the adoption of a probabilistic model for defining a class of instances have been thoroughly analyzed in Chapter 3 and, more in particular, in Section 3.4. It should be sufficient to notice here that the probability measure defined on the space of the instances has a fundamental role in the evaluation of the performance of a metaheuristic and it is the very concept on which the definition of *expectation* rests: Without it, the notion of *expected* performance of the metaheuristics, or more loosely *average* or *mean* performance, could not be formally defined.

Another issue which is worth discussing here is related to the practical implication of the concept of class of instances as defined in the thesis. In practical applications, the class of instances and the associated underlying probability measure

[4] See also item 2 in the **Box-plots** section at page 121.

are given by the problem itself: Consider, as an example, MARIO'S problem as introduced in Section 3.1. In such cases, one can directly *sample* the space of the instances by simply collecting the instances as they appear. Such instances can be meaningfully used for assessing the performance of algorithms. On the other hand, in academic studies algorithms are tested on some *benchmark* problems. Two are the main approaches to defining a benchmark for testing and comparing algorithms. The first, by far the most common within the operations research community, consists in selecting a (typically small) number of instances. The second, consists in implementing an *instance generator*, that is, a computer program that can produce instances according to some underlying probability measure. Both kind of benchmarks can be cast in the framework of our definition of class of instances. This is clear for what concerns the second approach: An instance generator precisely realizes the concept of probability measure on the space of the instances. As far as the first approach is concerned, it should be observed that any given set of instances can be considered as a *sample* taken from some unknown and possibly extravagant distribution. Nevertheless, the first approach, due to the paucity of the instances that typically compose a benchmark, encourages some dangerous practice consisting in *"playing and playing"* with the same few instances until some good results are eventually obtained: Unfortunately, this approach produces algorithms that risk being over-specialized on the given instances and whose performance is possibly much lower on other (although only slightly different) instances. A thorough analysis of this problem is given in Section 6.1.4. For this reason, we definitely favor the use of an *instance generator* whenever a stream of real-world instances is not available.

6.1.3 On the empirical comparison of algorithms

As is has been already made clear by Hooker (1995), an empirical analysis should not be reduced to a sterile comparison between algorithms but should aim at highlighting the characteristics of the algorithms at hand, *explaining* the reason of their success or failure, and determining which factors have an impact on their performance. Nevertheless, the ability of properly and meaningfully comparing two algorithms remains central in any empirical analysis. This holds true also when all remarks expressed by Hooker (1995) are taken into account. Indeed, for example, in order to study the effects of a factor on the performance of an algorithm, one needs to *compare* two version of the algorithm itself: One that does include the factor of interest, and the other that does not. The following analysis on how to properly compare algorithms, remains therefore relevant also in the light of Hooker's considerations (1995).

When an empirical comparison is performed between two algorithms, say Alg_A and Alg_B, one might wish to reach a conclusion like:

Statement 1. *Algorithm Alg_A performs better than algorithm Alg_B.*

Or vice versa. Nevertheless, no matter how extensive the experimental campaign is, such a highly general and absolute conclusion cannot be drawn from empirical data. The generality of the statement that one might make is impaired on different grounds by a number of issues. Among them, with reference to the considerations presented in Sections 6.1.1 and 6.1.2, the superiority of one algorithm over the other can be stated only for what concerns:

1. the measure of performance and possibly the specific score function that were considered;

2. the specific class of instances at hand, that is, the underlying measure of probability defined over the space of the instances.

In the light of these issues, Statement 1 should be better reformulated as:

> **Statement 2.** *Under the given experimental conditions and on the given class of instances, Algorithm* Alg_A *performs better than algorithm* Alg_B.

Here, for convenience, with the generic expression *experimental conditions* we refer to the measure of performance and to the score function considered in the study.

A further issue that limits the generality of Statement 2, is directly related to the main topic of this thesis, that is, the tuning problem: As already pointed out in several methodologically-minded papers—see for example McGeoch (1996) and Johnson (2002)—any experimental study can only assess the performance of a *particular implementation* rather than a *general abstract algorithm*. However, we wish to stress here that a *particular implementation* is defined not only by structural decisions such as problem representation, data-structures, and so on, but also, especially for what concerns metaheuristics, by the *particular configuration* considered, that is, a certain selection of metaheuristic components and a certain set of values for their parameters. It should be emphasized at this point that we are only concerned here with *static parameters*, whose value is set *off-line* at design time. On the other hand, in case some parameters are set *on the fly* by the program itself, they are not considered to be part of the configuration—we are thinking here of the dichotomy *off-/on-line* tuning introduced in Section 2.1.8.

From this discussion, it follows that whenever the specific configuration of the algorithms to be compared are selected through some further unspecified procedure, performance evaluation and comparison are only meaningful with respect to the particular configurations considered. Therefore, unless specific reference is made to the procedure used for selecting the configurations to be tested, the only claim that can be formulated on the basis of an empirical comparison sounds like:

> **Statement 3.** *Under the given experimental conditions and on the given class of instances, the tested configuration of* Alg_A *performs better than the tested configuration of* Alg_B.

In order to compare Alg_A and Alg_B without restricting to particular configurations, the appropriate statement to be tested should be:

> **Statement 4'.** *Under the given experimental conditions and on the given class of instances, the pair $Alg_A/Conf_A$ performs better than the pair $Alg_B/Conf_B$.*

Where $Conf_A$ and $Conf_B$ are the two different tuning methods which are adopted for configuring Alg_A and Alg_B, respectively.

If one wishes to isolate the effects of the algorithmic ideas on the overall performance, one should use the same configuration procedure, say *Conf*, for both algorithms and compare therefore the pair $Alg_A/Conf$ against $Alg_B/Conf$. In this case, the conclusion of the experimental analysis could sound as:

> **Statement 4".** *Under the given experimental conditions, on the given class of instances and when both algorithms are tuned using Conf, Alg_A performs better than Alg_B.*

In this case, the superiority of one algorithm over the other can be assessed, with respect to the selected configuration procedure.

Unfortunately, this is not a common practice in the current literature and, in many papers involving comparisons of a newly proposed method against some "classical approaches," a better performance of the newer algorithm is often merely a result of a more careful tuning, that is, of a more sophisticated configuration procedure, rather than an indication of the superiority of the proposed algorithmic ideas. In light of this observation, the configuration problem becomes one of the central issues in the evaluation and comparison of metaheuristics. In fact, one can go as far as claiming that, unless the experimenter is only interested in a particular configuration of the algorithm, the configuration procedure becomes an inseparable part of the algorithm.

6.1.4 On the *over-tuning* phenomenon

In the supervised learning literature, the clear separation between the *training set* and the *test set* is an extremely deeply rooted practice which is almost considered as a commonplace. Indeed, machine learning researchers are well aware of the *over-fitting* problem, that is, the risk of overspecializing in the specific training set at hand following its accidental peculiarities—typically termed *noise*—rather than extracting the essential traits of the underlying input-output relation. As a result of over-fitting, the performance obtained on the training set is typically a biased estimate of the actual performance of a learning algorithm. Since this quantity can be *extremely* over-optimistic, it is never used in the empirical assessment and comparison of learning algorithms. It is customary, therefore, to have recourse to a second data set, the *test set*, that should have been independently drawn from the training set. The performance on this second set is an unbiased estimate of the performance of the learning algorithms at hand and is therefore well suited for being used in assessments and comparisons.

Unfortunately, a clear stand is missing in the metaheuristics literature for a separation between the *tuning set* and the *test set*, that is, between the set of instances used for tuning the metaheuristic on the one hand, and the set of instances used for the final assessment, on the other.

Nevertheless, when assessing the performance of metaheuristics, and more generally of stochastic algorithms whose parameters need to be tuned, a problem similar to over-fitting exists. In this thesis, we introduce the term *over-tuning* for indicating this problem.

Contrary to machine learning, where the *over-fitting* phenomenon is easy to spot and quantify, in the metaheuristics field *over-tuning* is admittedly slightly more difficult to illustrate. The difference derives, at least partially, from a different cultural background. Indeed, the empirical analysis of algorithms is a relatively recent acquisition in the operations research literature and therefore, as a cultural heritage, researchers and practitioners in the metaheuristics field do not typically have the same strong statistical background as their machine learning colleagues. Moreover, the analysis and the solution of the problem of tuning metaheuristics is still in its embryonic phase and, as it is shown in Section 2.1.8, very little literature exists on the issue.

In the following, we show that as the *tuning effort* increases, the performance of the metaheuristic at hand improves steadily on the instances that are used for tuning its parameters; whereas the performance on the whole class improves first, reaches an optimal value, and then deteriorates. Graphically, the kind of picture we want to show should look like the plot of the mean squared error on the training set and on the test set that is typically encountered in supervised learning—see for example Figure 2.9 at page 59.

In the sentence above, the expression *tuning effort* is italicized because the latter is indeed the critical element in this analysis, both for what concerns its conceptual definition and its practical measure. In the study we propose here, the *tuning effort* is measured by the *size* of the space of the parameters where the latter is the number of candidate configurations among which a selection is performed. This is somehow reminiscent of the supervised learning concepts of model complexity and VC-dimension discussed in Sections 2.2.5 and 2.2.6. To be more explicit, we consider a tuning set and a test set composed of one single instance each. Further, we consider the case in which tuning is reduced to an *exhaustive search* in a given space of configurations: Each configuration is tested once on the given tuning instance. The cost of the best solution found in such a single run by each configuration is, *a priori*, an unbiased estimate of the expected cost of the best solution that the given configuration can find: In this sense, the result found by the given configurations in one single run is an appropriate quantity to serve as a criterion for selecting the best among them.

Our reader should be aware from now that the catch hides exactly in the previous sentence, and more precisely in the apparently innocent expression "*a priori*". This is indeed the key for understanding the nature of the over-tuning phenomenon. Recalling here the following elementary fact, will give us the proper tools for framing the results presented in the rest of the section:

> Let us consider n independent random variables $\boldsymbol{x}_1, \boldsymbol{x}_2, \dots, \boldsymbol{x}_n$. If $x_1, x_2, \dots, x_n$ are a realization of these variables, each x_j is *a priori* an unbiased estimate of the expected value of the respective $\boldsymbol{x}_j$. More precisely, each x_j is to be considered as a realization of an *unbiased estimator* of the respective $\boldsymbol{x}_j$. Nevertheless, if we are told that $x_{j_m} \leq x_j, \forall j$, the previous statement does not typically hold anymore for x_{i_m}. Indeed, we should *a posteriori* consider x_{j_m} as a realization of another random variable, namely $\bar{\boldsymbol{x}} = \min_j \boldsymbol{x}_j$ which is an optimistically biased estimator of the expected value of $\boldsymbol{x}_{j_m}$. Formally: $E[\min_j \boldsymbol{x}_j] \leq \min_j E[\boldsymbol{x}_j] \leq E[\boldsymbol{x}_l]$, $\forall l$, and therefore also $E[\bar{\boldsymbol{x}}] \leq E[\boldsymbol{x}_{j_m}]$.[5]

With this in mind, let us proceed with our analysis. The kind of procedure one should implement in order to obtain an illustration of the over-tuning phenomenon is the following: Select a tuning instance and a test instance. For increasing values of the *tuning effort*, that is, for an increasing size of the space of configurations to be considered, select the configuration that obtains the best result on the tuning instance. Run it on the test instance. Record the results that the selected configuration obtained on the two instances. Repeat the procedure a large number of times for obtaining some significance and then average, for each value of the tuning effort, the results obtained on the tuning instances and those obtained on the test instances. For clarity, Figure 6.1 gives a pseudo-code description of the procedure.

Unfortunately, the above described procedure is *extremely* expensive from a computational point of view and it is not therefore a viable solution for showing the effects of over-tuning. Nevertheless, an alternative procedure can be designed that exploits a re-sampling method. Such procedure is akin to the one adopted in Chapter 5 for assessing the performance of *F-Race* and of the other tuning algorithms introduced in the thesis—see page 118 for an illustration of the re-sampling approach adopted in the thesis and for a definition of the re-sampling terminology.

The approach we adopt here consists of two phases. In the first one, a number of runs are performed with different configurations of the metaheuristic under analysis on some instances sampled from the distribution characterizing the class of instances of interest. The results of these runs are stored in a database. In the second phase, a procedure similar to the one given in Figure 6.1 is executed

[5] A formal treatment of the issue can be found in Appendix 6.A at page 192.

```
function overtuning_analysis(no_trials, max_conf)
  # Allocate arrays for storing results
  # observed on tuning and test instances
  TU = allocate_array(no_trials, max_conf)
  TE = allocate_array(no_trials, max_conf)
  for (j = 1; j ≤ no_trials; j++) do
    # Select a tuning and a test instance
    i_tu = sample_instance()
    i_te = sample_instance()
    for (k = 1; k ≤ max_conf; k++) do
      # Select a subset of k configurations
      Θ_k = generate_configuration_subset(k)
      # Select, out of Θ_k, the configuration
      # that obtains the best performance on i_tu
      θ = tune_on_instance(Θ_k, i_tu)
      # Evaluate θ on the tuning and on the test instance
      TU[j, k] = run_and_evaluate(θ, i_tu)
      TE[j, k] = run_and_evaluate(θ, i_te)
    done
  done
  # Average column-wise the results obtained
  graph_TU = column_mean(TU)
  graph_TE = column_mean(TE)
  # Plot the curves
  plot(graph_TU & graph_TE)
```

Figure 6.1: Algorithmic outline of the over-tuning analysis. Here, `no_trials` is the number of trials to be performed and `max_conf` is the maximum number of configurations to be considered, that is, the maximum tuning effort.

with the difference that: (i) tuning and test instances, rather than being sampled directly according to the underlying distribution, are re-sampled from the instances sampled in the first phase; (ii) all runs of the metaheuristic are replaced by *pseudo-runs*: rather than actually running a configuration of the metaheuristic on a re-sampled instance, the result obtained and stored in phase one is used. The curves given in Figure 6.2 are the result of the re-sampling methodology applied to the illustration of the over-tuning problem. In particular, the figure refers to the application of ***iterated local search*** to the QUADRATIC ASSIGNMENT problem. Both metaheuristic and class of instances are those that are used also in Section 5.1.1: In particular, 400 configurations are considered together with a sample of 800 instances—for a detailed description of the experimental setting, we refer the reader to Section 5.1.1. It should be noted that such an extreme smoothness for the two curves could be obtained only thanks to a very large number of pseudo-trials, 1×10^9, that allowed for a very precise approximation of the underlying regression function. Such precision would have been simply impossible without the adoption of re-sampling: As already noted in Chapter 1, the computation needed for producing the two curves, if actually performed, would have taken more than 8×10^{13} s, that is, more than 2.5 million years.

As far as the interpretation of Figure 6.2 is concerned, it clearly appears that the results obtained on the tuning instance are an over-optimistic estimate of the expected behavior of the metaheuristic: Irrespectively of the tuning effort, the curve concerning the tuning instance is always well below the one concerning the test instance where the latter, as already pointed out, is an unbiased estimate of the performance on the whole class of instances. But the real issue with the two curves represented in Figure 6.2 is that, as we wished to show, on the one hand, the curve concerning the tuning instance decreases monotonically with the tuning effort, that is, with the number of configurations among which the best one is selected by the tuning process; whereas, on the other hand, the curve concerning the test instance decreases until a minimum is reached, and then starts increasing again. This is precisely the same qualitative picture that illustrates the over-fitting problem in supervised learning: Compare Figure 6.2 with Figure 2.9, given at page 59. Our original idea is thus empirically confirmed that a problem similar to over-fitting, namely the *over-tuning* problem, affects the practice of tuning metaheuristics.

Before proceeding, a comment is needed on the fact that in the analysis that produced Figure 6.2, both tuning and test sets are composed of one single instance. As far as the test set is concerned, a larger number of instances would not have had any noticeable impact on the curves. Indeed it would have simply reduced the variance of the estimation of the curve describing the error on the test set but, as it can be observed, this curve is already particularly smooth thanks to the re-sampling technique adopted and considering a larger test set would have simply increased the computation time. On the other hand, the issue is much more complex for what concerns the tuning set. Indeed, a larger tuning set would

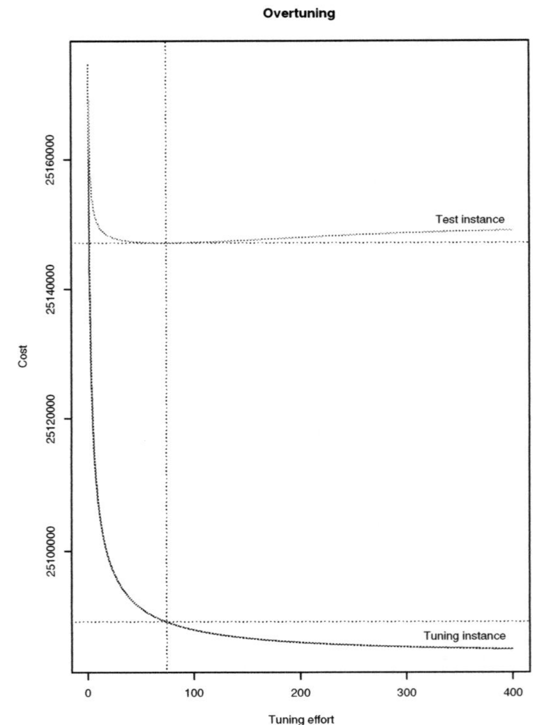

Figure 6.2: The over-tuning problem: As the *tuning effort* increases—the latter being measured here in terms of the number of configurations considered—the performance on the tuning instance improves steadily, whereas the performance on the test instance improve first, reaches an optimal value, and then deteriorates.

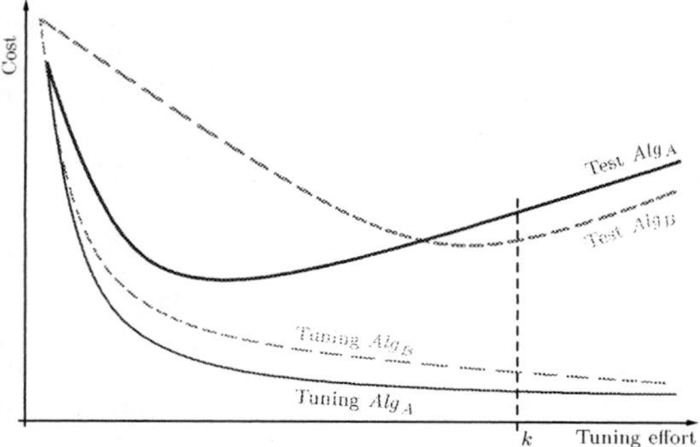

Figure 6.3: Implications of the *over-tuning* phenomenon: The performance on the tuning set should not be used for comparing algorithms. It might well be, as it is here illustrated, that even if Alg_A and Alg_B have received the same amount of tuning effort k, and even if the selected configuration of Alg_A performs better than the selected configuration of Alg_B over the tuning set, it is indeed the selected configuration of Alg_B that shows a better performance over the test set and therefore, on average, over the whole class of instances at hand.

have had a noticeable impact on the two curves, although the picture would have remained qualitatively unchanged. Informally, we could explain this by saying that a larger tuning set would have been *more representative* of the whole class of instances and, thus, the tuning procedure would have selected a less *specialized* and more *general* configuration. This would have effectively **reduced** the over-tuning problem, but it would have **not solved** it! In practice, a larger tuning set would have shifted to the right the minimum of the curve associated with the test set, but the latter would have preserved in any case its U-*like* shape. This shift to the right would have made our analysis even more expensive in terms of computation time, without adding much from a conceptual point of view.

Some major implications of over-tuning are worth being discussed here. In particular, the over-tuning problem should be seriously taken into account when assessing the performance of metaheuristics. Figure 6.2 makes clear that reporting the performance obtained by an algorithm on the instances used for tuning its parameters—or, more in general, used in pilot studies performed for guiding some design choices—is irrelevant and possibly misleading. Indeed, if the critical value of the tuning effort—that is, the value at which the test curve starts increasing—is passed, we are in the paradoxical situation in which:

> *The better the metaheuristic performs over the tuning instances, the worse it does over a generic other instance of the same class, and therefore, on average, over the whole class!*

In particular, if two metaheuristics are being compared, the comparison should be made on a set of fresh instances that have not been previously adopted in the design and tuning phase. Figure 6.3 shows a situation that might possibly arise in practice: Two metaheuristics Alg_A and Alg_B are tuned on the basis of a given tuning set extracted according to the probability measure that characterizes the class of instances under analysis. The same amount k of tuning effort is dedicated to both metaheuristics. Although the selected configuration of Alg_A performs better on the tuning set than the selected configuration of Alg_B, it is the latter that obtains a better performance on an independent test set, always extracted according to the same probability measure. Clearly, Alg_B is to be preferred to Alg_A since, on average, it is deemed to produces better results on the whole class of instances under analysis. If we had based our comparison on the results obtained on the tuning set, we would have mistakenly reached the opposite conclusion.

6.2 Towards a theory of practice

What is wrong with the current research in the metaheuristics field and, more generally, in combinatorial optimization? The problem is best illustrated by an old physicists' joke:

> *One chap, who was very fond of horses and horse races, decided to be scientific about it and asked his physicist friend to make a scientific prediction of the outcome of the next race. An hour before the race he called his friend, but the latter replied that he was still working on the problem. The same happened half an hour before the race ... and then five minutes before ... Only a week later the physicist, looking very proud of himself, showed up with a pile of papers, featuring a lot of diagrams and equations.*
>
> *Our race-fond chap glanced at the diagrams and the equations:*
>
> *"What does all that mean?"—he asked.*
>
> *"Well, so far I have managed to solve the problem for spherical horses racing in a vacuum."*

We fear that a similar joke could spread having as a main character a researcher of our own community: Indeed, at least in some sense, a non negligible part of operations research in the last two decades concerned spherical horses in vacuum! This claim will, perhaps, sound clearer once we consider the largely overlooked issue of *modeling* in operations research.

The main source of interest in operations research stems—or, at least, stemmed in the early days of the field—from the practical applications of its methods. Moreover, it is apparent, but possibly under emphasized, that the problems traditionally considered in operations research are *abstractions* of problems actually encountered in practice which, in turns, have often a huge economical relevance. In other words, the problems studied in operations research are *mathematical models* of real-world problems. Indeed, traditional operations research models are better understood as a *hierarchy of abstractions*:

1. At the lowest level of the hierarchy, we find straightforward *mathematical models* of some well defined practical problem. This first level is the one usually adopted by industrial researchers and practitioners: Their goal is to solve a specific problem instance rather than generalize their results and understand the properties of a whole class of instances.

2. At a second level of the hierarchy, we encounter classical problems such as the TRAVELING SALESMAN problem, the QUADRATIC ASSIGNMENT problem, and so on. Each of these problems is defined as a class of specific problem instances—as introduced at level 1—that share similar characteristics as, for example, the kind of constraints imposed on feasible solutions.

3. Ascending further on the hierarchy, we finally reach highly abstract problems such as, for example, NK landscapes (Kauffman, 1993) or deceptive problems (Goldberg, 1989).

These three levels should not be seen as an exhaustive description of the hierarchy of abstraction but just as the three main steps of the ladder. Indeed, a finer-grained analysis would reveal that other levels of the hierarchy should be considered which lie in between. As an example, let us consider the case of real-world stochastic and time-varying vehicle routing problems which are often cast into simpler and better understood TRAVELING SALESMAN problems. Model problem obtained in such a way lie indeed between the first and the second level of the hierarchy. Nonetheless, for the purposes of our discussion, it will be sufficient to restrict our attention to the three levels described above.

At this point, it seems beneficial to recall the reasons that led to the introduction of the various levels of the above described hierarchy of abstractions: The first *practical* reason is apparently the obvious aspiration to reduce the implementation effort in scientific research and applications. As an example, the very fact of having introduced the concept of TRAVELING SALESMAN problem let us refer to a large (infinite) number of specific problem instances all sharing the same structure and constraints: A single piece of software which is able to deal with such structure and constraints can be used for tackling all specific problem instances belonging to the class. A second reason, which is more *speculative* in nature, is the desire to spot and single out the characteristics of optimization problems that have the most significant impact on the performance of algorithms. This second issue is, in fact, the main motivation for the introduction of the highly abstract problems mentioned above at level 3 of the hierarchy.

Unfortunately, the understanding that all problems studied in operations research are but models, seemed to recede with time. This in turn resulted in a shift of the research focus which often became concentrated on the study of the model *per se*. At least in some sense, the development of the complexity theory, *NP*-completeness theory in particular (Garey & Johnson, 1979), is a result of such shift.[6] Although complexity theory represented a major breakthrough in the field of operations research, it should be emphasized that this theory is concerned only with the worst-case difficulty of a **whole class of model problems**, rather than with the **particular problem instances** actually encountered in practice or, more precisely, the simplified mathematical models of the latter. For example, the fact that TRAVELING SALESMAN is *NP*-hard, only means that, unless $NP = P$, there is no polynomial algorithm, which finds the optimal solution for **all** possible instances of the TRAVELING SALESMAN problem. This, however, does not imply anything about the difficulty of a particular class of real-life routing problems, or even of the corresponding subclass of TRAVELING SALESMAN problems which is used to model such routing problems.

There is, however, a particularly positive side to this development. The *NP*-completeness theory on one hand, and the non-dominance result of the *no free lunch* theorem (Wolpert & Macready, 1996, 1997) on the other,[7] made it clear that, without restricting the class of problems considered in the scientific research, it is impossible to predict the performance of algorithms on real-life problems. This led to an explosion of the amount of experimental work, especially concerning the highly flexible metaheuristics, for which the theoretical analysis seems particularly difficult. However, partly because the research on the models *per se* became a dominant approach by now, the experimental standards have little bearing to the actual design of algorithms in practice. This is not to say that the experimental research using abstract model problems has nothing to offer as far as practice is concerned. Insofar as the model manages to capture the essential characteristics of the practical problem, the experimental results with this abstract model can be very illuminating, **provided that** the whole experimental setting is properly designed to model the conditions under which algorithms are meant to be used in practice.

6.2.1 The real-life setting

As we have just pointed out, the main justification to the very existence of the combinatorial optimization field comes from the fact that traditional combinatorial optimization problems are abstract models of real-life problems encountered in practice. Consistently, it is commonly believed that the performance of an algorithm on such model problems is indicative as far as real-life performance is concerned. However, what is typically ignored is that, in order for studies conducted on models to be of any practical importance, it is absolutely necessary

[6] For an introduction to the *NP*-completeness theory, we refer the reader to Section 2.1.4.

[7] For an introduction to the *no free lunch* theorem, we refer the reader to Section 2.1.5.

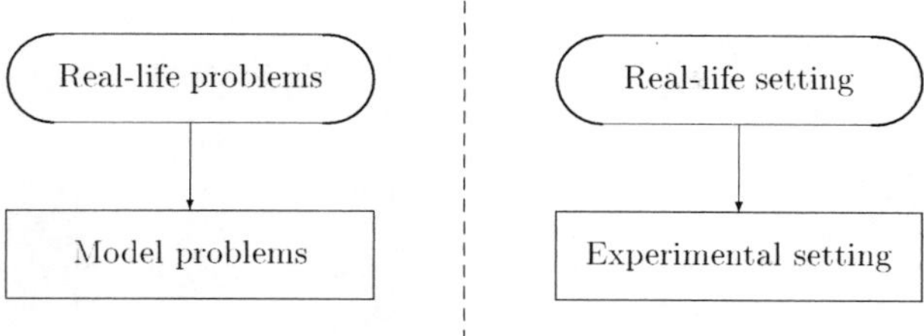

Figure 6.4: Model problems are abstractions of real-life problems. Similarly, the experimental setting should reproduce the real-life situations in which optimization algorithms are developed and practically employed.

to reproduce not only the problems characteristics, but also the whole *life-cycle* that optimization algorithms follow in practice. We borrow here the concept of product life-cycle commonly considered in manufacturing. Given the immaterial nature of optimization algorithms, such a concept assumes here the same connotations it assumes in the field of software engineering. For an organic presentation of this concept, we refer the reader to any manual of software engineering, for example, Sommerville (2001).

In the real-world, the life-cycle of optimization algorithms might be quite diverse. Different life-cycle models can be appropriate: linear, spiral, cascade, and so on. In the following, we implicitly consider a linear life-cycle model in which the algorithm undergoes a *development* phase for being finally employed in a *production* phase. Beside being the simplest, the linear life-cycle is also the building block composing more complex models. In this sense, the conclusions we draw referring to it immediately extend to the general case.

Obviously, there is no need to exactly mimic all the details of a life-cycle. Similarly to the problem modeling, an abstraction is needed, as suggested in Figure 6.4. Still, several aspects are absolutely essential. In the following, we examine the setting in which the optimization algorithms are employed in real-life applications and we extract several high-level characteristics that we consider essential.

We start by observing that, as a general rule, real-life optimization does not involve a single problem, but rather a class thereof, typically perceived by the practitioner as a *stream* of instances. As an example, consider the *stream* of instances characterizing MARIO'S PIZZA DELIVERY problem, as introduced in Section 3.1. The single-problem setting can be simply considered as a degenerate case, where the problem class has only one member—see Section 3.3.3 for a discussion on the single-instance case in the context of the definition of the tuning problem. Even in this case, the results on a particular problem instance are interesting only as far as they indicate some more general trend.

In general, the characteristics of the instances in the stream may change over time necessitating an adaptation of the optimization algorithm. In such cases, the life-cycle of an algorithm can be typically divided in stages, each properly described through a simple linear life-cycle model composed of (i) a *development* phase, consisting either in the development from scratch of an algorithm or in the modification of an already existing one; followed by (ii) the actual *production*, during which the problems to be solved are roughly homogeneous. It should be observed here that problem instances that are to be solved during the production phase are **not** available during the development phase! This implies the following rule that should be observed in any serious empirical study:

> **First experimental principle.** *Problem instances used for assessing the performance of an algorithm cannot be used during its development.*

The need of introducing this principle is clearly illustrated by the remarks on *over-tuning* proposed in Section 6.1.4. Nevertheless, we wish to add here a further *reductio ad absurdum* argumentation: Let us consider one single instance that we use both for tuning the parameters of an algorithm and then for assessing the performance of the selected configuration. Let us suppose further that the algorithm we consider accepts a parameter ranging in a space that coincides with the space of the possible solutions of the instance at hand. Moreover, let us imagine that our algorithm simply returns *immediately* the parameter it receives. In this case, provided we spend enough time in tuning the parameter, the algorithm with the selected parameter will be able to solve instantaneously and to the optimum the instance under analysis.

The aforementioned first experimental principle is rather obvious and might be even considered trivial by our reader; still, this basic principle is routinely violated in the current literature.

It should be emphasized that this principle does not imply that domain-specific knowledge cannot be used in the development of algorithms. Such knowledge can influence the development process in two ways. First, in case explicit knowledge is available, either based on domain theory or on the previous experience of the algorithm designer, it can clearly affect the design of the algorithm. Second, in many cases problems *similar to the ones used in production* are available, and pilot runs on these problems can be used to fine-tune the algorithm. These observations led us to a second principle, which is complementary to the first:

> **Second experimental principle.** *The designer can take into account any available domain-specific knowledge, as well as make use of pilot studies on similar problems.*

Finally, in real-life applications, the time available for the development of an algorithm is limited. Similarly, the maximum time available for obtaining a solution is typically a constraint given in the specifications of the algorithm to be designed: once operational in the production phase, the algorithm will be run for such given run-time. The existence of these time constraints is captured by a *fairness principle*, already advocated in Rardin & Uzsoy (2001):

> **Third experimental principle.** *When several algorithms are compared, all of them should make use of the available domain-specific knowledge and equal computational effort should be invested in all the pilot studies. Similarly, in the testing phase, all the algorithms should be compared on an equal time basis.*

Also this third experimental principle, although trivial, is unfortunately too often violated in the literature. It is common that researchers devote a large amount of time to the development of their favorite algorithm and then compare it against their quick-and-dirty implementations of state-of-the-art algorithms. Even worse, often researchers compare the results obtained by their algorithms against those published in the literature and possibly obtained years before on much slower computers.

The experimental methodology we describe in the next section is based on the three general principles given above.

6.2.2 The proposed methodology and some alternatives

Let us now summarize the general outline of the experimental design that, according to our analysis, should be used in the assessment and comparison of metaheuristics:

1. For every algorithm, the configuration space—that is, the space of all the allowed parameters combinations—should be specified. If some domain-specific knowledge can be used to narrow down the configuration space, it should be equally applied to all algorithms under analysis.

2. The same procedure should be used to choose the configuration of each algorithm under analysis. The selection should be based on the same tuning instances for all algorithms, and such instances should be extracted from the same problem class as the instances on which the algorithms are to be eventually tested. All algorithms should be given the same computational resources.

3. The selected configurations should be finally compared on the same instances. All algorithms should be given the same computational resources,

among them, computation time and memory. Whenever a comparison involves an algorithm with a well-defined stopping condition such as, for example, constructive algorithms or local search, an iterated version of such algorithms should be studied. These iterated versions should be allotted the same overall computation time as the other algorithms under analysis (Rardin & Uzsoy, 2001).

4. The results obtained should be used to calculate an empirical approximation of a criterion such as the expected performance on the class of instances considered as defined in Equation 6.3 in combination, possibly, with the score function defined in Equation 6.2.

In step 2, the configuration procedure can be based on *F-Race* or on some equivalent tuning algorithm. It could be argued that in some cases the tuning instances required by such procedures are not available. In such cases, the alternatives implicitly considered in the literature are either to use the test instances themselves for choosing the configurations to be tested or to choose the configuration based solely on the prior experience with the algorithm. Let us examine these two alternatives in more details.

The first approach, namely the use of the test instances, is commonly used in the current literature. In its *explicit* form, some sort of optimization of the average performance, typically based on some pilot studies, is used to tune the parameters. More often, the configuration problem is not addressed explicitly, but rather the results of the best performing configuration are reported for every instance. However, both the *explicit* and the *implicit* forms of this approach violates the first experimental principle from Section 6.2.1, which is based on the observation that *the problems to be solved during the production phase are not available during the development phase.* The results obtained with this approach are typically biased and not reliable.

Another alternative consists in not applying any configuration procedure at all, but rather using some configuration that was previously presented in the literature or that is known to be "good" from previous personal experience of the experimenter. This approach can be criticized on two grounds. First, the configurations reported in the literature are typically chosen following some pilot experimentation, in other words, also this approach amounts implicitly to using some empirical optimization procedure of the average performance. If the pilot studies were conducted using the same set of benchmark instances, then the experimenter is actually using (perhaps, without even being aware of it) the approach that we have just shown to be invalid, that is, the one in which tuning is based on test instances. If, on the other hand, a different set of benchmark instances was used for these pilot studies (or the experimental setting was different), then the employed configuration may be suboptimal for the problem at hand. In particular, this approach may easily introduce a bias towards some of the tested algorithms, due to uneven tuning effort: Clearly, more recent algorithms are often more carefully tuned than older ones, whose developers did not have access to today's computing power.

To summarize, most of the configuration procedures used in the literature are based, either explicitly or implicitly, on the empirical optimization of the average performance. However, unlike the systematic methodology advocated in this thesis, the existing approaches either involve some sort of *cheating*, in the form of using the test instances during the development phase, or, alternatively, do not guarantee that all the algorithms are configured equally well.

6.3 Discussion

This chapter has discussed a number of issues concerning the definition of a proper experimental methodology to be followed in the empirical assessment and comparison of metaheuristics. In particular, we have highlighted some common faults that can be encountered unfortunately way too often in the literature. Among them, it is worth mentioning here the fact that in many works the experimenter adopts the same instances both for configuring the metaheuristic under study and eventually for testing the resulting algorithm. In order to clearly frame this problem, we have introduced here the concept of *over-tuning* of which we give both a theoretical background and a practical illustration. The over-tuning problem is akin to *over-fitting* in supervised learning and we are sure that those of our reader who possess a formal training in machine learning have promptly framed the issue and have possibly found obvious and even *superfluous* our remarks on the need for a clear separation between a tuning set and a test set. On the other hand, we hope that our readers with a more classical operations research background can benefit from our discussion. For this class of readers we think that a practical illustration of over-tuning, as the one we give in our empirical study, is more convincing than a theoretical analysis based on machine learning concepts.

As far as the experimental methodology we propose in Section 6.2 is concerned, we think that its most characterizing element is the shift of attention from a specific configuration of a metaheuristic to its whole life-cycle, that is, to the process that starts from an abstract algorithmic idea and goes through a design and tuning phase for finally obtaining a fully configured algorithm that can be shipped out and effectively employed in production. In other words, what we promote with this methodological chapter is a sort of *cradle-to-grave* perspective in the research on metaheuristics. Indeed, flexibility is the main keyword when discussing metaheuristics. It should be always kept in mind that the very reason for the introduction of metaheuristics is the need of a *high-performing* and *problem-independent* approach to combinatorial optimization problems. Apparently, high-performance and generality are contrasting objectives and in order to achieve both, metaheuristics are devised to be general and to be easily *adapted* to the specific problem at hand for the best possible performance. For this reason, having parameters to be tuned is indeed so connatural to metaheuristics that they should not be, and indeed cannot be properly conceived other than jointly with the method adopted for tuning their parameters. In our view, a proper experimental methodology needs to reflect such indivisibility and handle the pair tuning method/metaheuristic as a whole.

As a final remark, we wish to point out that also with regard to the definition of an experimental methodology for assessing and comparing metaheuristics, the machine learning perspective adopted in the thesis has proved being particularly fruitful, further confirming therefore the general framework of the thesis itself.

Appendix

6.A Best is biased

We show here that if a realization of n random variables is given, the least of them is an ***optimistically biased*** estimate of its expected value. Formally, let us consider n independent random variables $\boldsymbol{x}_j$, with $j = 1, \dots, n$; each described by a cumulative distribution of probability $F_j(x) = \mathit{Prob}\{x_j \leq x\}$. Further, let $\bar{\boldsymbol{x}} = \min_j \boldsymbol{x}_j$ be the minimum of these variables, which is distributed according to

$$F(x) = 1 - \prod_j \left(1 - F_j(x)\right).$$

Indeed, this can be shown by observing that

$$\begin{aligned} F(x) &= \mathit{Prob}\{\bar{x} \leq x\} = \mathit{Prob}\left\{\bigvee_j x_j \leq x\right\} = 1 - \mathit{Prob}\left\{\bigwedge_j x_j > x\right\} \\ &= 1 - \prod_j \mathit{Prob}\{x_j > x\} = 1 - \prod_j \left(1 - \mathit{Prob}\{x_j \leq x\}\right) \\ &= 1 - \prod_j \left(1 - F_j(x)\right). \end{aligned}$$

It results that $F(x) \geq F_k(x)$, $\forall x \forall k$.[8] Indeed,

$$F(x) \geq F_k(x)$$

if and only if

$$1 - \prod_j \left(1 - F_j(x)\right) \geq F_k(x),$$

[8] In the decision theory literature, such a relation between two cumulative distributions is referred to as ***first-order stochastic dominance*** (Whitmore & Findlay, 1978).

which is equivalent to

$$1 - F_k(x) \geq \prod_j (1 - F_j(x)),$$

and ultimately to

$$1 - F_k(x) \geq (1 - F_k(x)) \prod_{j \neq k} (1 - F_j(x)), \quad \forall x \forall k. \tag{6.4}$$

Since $F_j(x) \geq 0$, $\forall x \forall j$, it follows that $1 - F_j(x) \leq 1$, $\forall x \forall j$, and therefore that

$$\prod_{j \neq k} (1 - F_j(x)) \leq 1, \quad \forall x \forall k.$$

This proves Inequality 6.4 and consequently the original statement:

$$F(x) \geq F_k(x), \quad \forall x \forall k.$$

It should be noticed that the equal sign could possibly hold only for the least, say $\boldsymbol{x}_m$, of the given random variables $\boldsymbol{x}_1, \ldots, \boldsymbol{x}_n$. Indeed, $F(x) \equiv F_m(x)$, if and only if $F_m(x)$ is such that

$$\prod_{j \neq m} (1 - F_j(x)) = 1, \quad \forall x : 1 - F_m(x) \neq 0.$$

In other words, for $F(x) \equiv F_m(x)$ to hold for a given F_m, there must exist an x' such that

$$Prob\,\{x_m \leq x'\} = 1 \quad \text{and} \quad Prob\,\{x_j \leq x'\} = 0, \quad \forall j \neq m;$$

that is, there must be no overlap between the *range* of the least variable and the *range* of any other one. See Figure 6.5 for a graphical illustration. This is a rather *trivial* case in which the stochasticity of the variables does not play any role in the selection of the least of them: A selection based on any realization $x_1, \ldots, x_n$ of the variables under analysis gives *deterministically* the variable that in any possible realizations is *deterministically* the least.

In all other cases, $F(x) \not\equiv F_k(x)$, $\forall k$, including $k = m$, and[9]

$$\int x \, \mathrm{d}F(x) < \int x \, \mathrm{d}F_k(x), \quad \forall k. \tag{6.5}$$

Indeed, if $F(x) \geq F_k(x)$, $\forall x$, there exists, for each k, a nonnegative function $\delta_k(x)$:

$$0 \leq \delta_k(x) = F(x) - F_k(x) \leq 1.$$

[9] In this section, all integrals are to be taken in the Riemann-Stieltjes sense. See, for example, Widder (1989) or Khuri (2003).

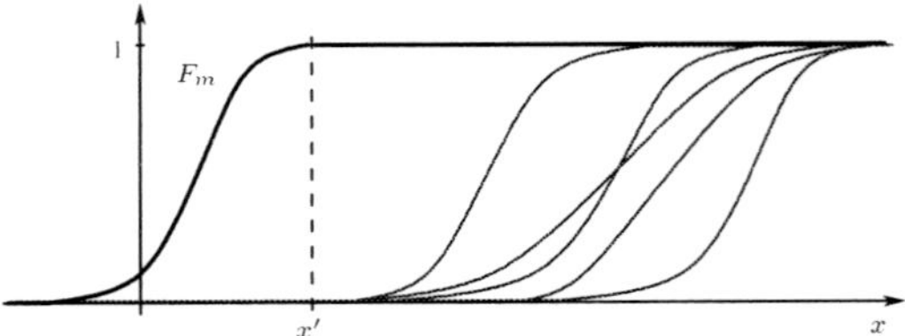

Figure 6.5: A *pathological* example of a set of n random variables: The range of one of them, namely $\boldsymbol{x}_m$, does not overlap with the range of any other one and is such that, for any possible realization $x_1, \dots, x_n$ of these variables, x_m is always smaller than any x_j with $j \neq m$. Clearly, in such a setting the problem of selecting the least of the given random variables looses all stochasticity and becomes trivial.

Since F and F_k, $\forall k$, are cumulative probability distributions, they are such that

$$\lim_{x \to -\infty} F(x) = 0, \qquad \lim_{x \to -\infty} F_k(x) = 0, \quad \forall k;$$
$$\lim_{x \to +\infty} F(x) = 1, \qquad \lim_{x \to +\infty} F_k(x) = 1, \quad \forall k.$$

It follows that

$$\lim_{x \to \pm\infty} \delta_k(x) = 0, \quad \forall k.$$

Actually, under the reasonable assumption that for all random variables under analysis the expectation exists, the functions $\delta_k(x)$ converge at a faster rate and in can be shown that

$$\lim_{x \to \pm\infty} x\delta_k(x) = 0, \quad \forall k. \tag{6.6}$$

Indeed, if the expectation exists for $\bar{\boldsymbol{x}}$ and for $\boldsymbol{x}_k$, $\forall k$, that is, if the integrals $\int x \, \mathrm{d}F(x)$ and $\int x \, \mathrm{d}F_k(x)$ converge $\forall k$, then it results that $\lim_{x \to -\infty} xF(x) = 0$, $\lim_{x \to +\infty} x\big(1 - F(x)\big) = 0$, $\lim_{x \to -\infty} xF_k(x) = 0$, and $\lim_{x \to +\infty} x\big(1 - F_k(x)\big) = 0$, $\forall k$.[10] The limit given in Equation 6.6 follows immediately.

Now, Inequality 6.5 can be written as

$$\int x \, \mathrm{d}F(x) - \int x \, \mathrm{d}F_k(x) < 0.$$

Integrating by parts both terms, we obtain

$$\left(xF(x)\Big|_{-\infty}^{+\infty} - \int F(x) \, \mathrm{d}x \right) - \left(xF_k(x)\Big|_{-\infty}^{+\infty} - \int F_k(x) \, \mathrm{d}x \right) < 0,$$

[10] See Birattari (2004b) or any manual of advanced calculus as, for example, Widder (1989) or Khuri (2003).

and therefore,

$$x\big(F(x) - F_k(x)\big)\Big|_{-\infty}^{+\infty} - \int \big(F(x) - F_k(x)\big)\,\mathrm{d}x < 0,$$

which in terms of δ_k is

$$x\delta_k(x)\Big|_{-\infty}^{+\infty} - \int \delta_k(x)\,\mathrm{d}x < 0.$$

The first term on the left-hand side is null according to Equation 6.6, while the integral of the second term on the left-hand side is positive since $\delta_k(x)$ is nonnegative. This proves the original statement.

Inequality 6.5 can be read as

$$E[\min_k \boldsymbol{x}_k] < \min_k E[\boldsymbol{x}_k], \tag{6.7}$$

whenever we are not in the trivial case described in Figure 6.5, otherwise the equality holds. The term on the left-hand side in Inequality 6.7 is simply the term on the left-hand side in Inequality 6.5:

$$E[\min_k \boldsymbol{x}_k] = \int x\,\mathrm{d}F(x);$$

while the one on the right-hand side is the minimum of the terms that appear on the right-hand side of Inequality 6.5 for the different values of k:

$$\min_k E[\boldsymbol{x}_k] = \min_k \int x\,\mathrm{d}F_k(x).$$

Since Inequality 6.5 holds for all k, it must hold also for the one that minimizes the expectation and Inequality 6.7 follows.

In particular, Inequality 6.5 holds for F_{j_m}, where j_m is the index of the variable $\boldsymbol{x}_{j_m}$ that in a given realization x_j, with $j = 1, \dots, n$, of the stochastic variables $\boldsymbol{x}_j$, results being the least; that is, $\bar{x} = x_{j_m} = \min_j x_j$ and $j_m = \arg\min_j x_j$. Unless we are in the trivial case described in Figure 6.5, it follows that x_{j_m} is a *optimistically biased* estimate of the expected value of $\boldsymbol{x}_{j_m}$. Indeed, *a priori*, that is, before knowing that $x_{j_m} = \min_j x_j$, we should assume that x_{j_m} is extracted from the distribution $F_{j_m}(x)$ and is therefore an unbiased estimate of $E[\boldsymbol{x}_{j_m}]$. On the other hand, *a posteriori*, that is, once we are told that $x_{j_m} = \min_j x_j$, we should consider x_{j_m} as extracted from the distribution $F(x)$ and, therefore, as an unbiased estimate of $E[\bar{\boldsymbol{x}}]$. Now, Inequality 6.5, or equivalently of Inequality 6.7, states that $E[\bar{\boldsymbol{x}}] < E[\boldsymbol{x}_k]$, $\forall k$, unless we are in the trivial case described in Figure 6.5. We should expect therefore that the specific realization x_{j_m} of the stochastic variable $\boldsymbol{x}_{j_m}$, for which $x_{j_m} = \min_j x_j$, is less than $E[\boldsymbol{x}_{j_m}]$.

Et j'espère que nos neveux me sauront gré, non seulement des choses que j'ai ici expliquées, mais aussi de celles que j'ai omises volontairement, afin de leur laisser le plaisir de les inventer.[†]

René Descartes

Chapter 7

Conclusions

Metaheuristics are a relatively novel but particularly promising approach for tackling combinatorial optimization problems. In the last decade, metaheuristics have been the focus of a significant amount of academic research and have been successfully employed in an increasing number of practical applications.[1] In particular, more and more companies rely on metaheuristics for solving complex optimization problems in various domains.[2] Indeed, the increasing availability of low-cost computing power starts convincing companies of any size that many aspects of their activities—including design, planning, manufacturing, inventory, distribution, management, *etc.*—would greatly profit from proper optimization. In this context, metaheuristics are a particularly appealing solution since their development costs are typically much lower than those of alternative approaches, such as, for example, *ad hoc* heuristics.

Indeed, the most notable strength of metaheuristics lies precisely in the fact

[†]*I hope that posterity will judge me kindly, not only as to the things which I have explained, but also to those which I have intentionally omitted so as to leave to others the pleasure of discovery.*

[1]See Corne *et al.* (1999), Glover & Kochenberger (2002), and Dréo *et al.* (2003) for extensive reviews. The MIC series of International conferences is entirely dedicated to metaheuristics (Hartl, 2005). Post-conference proceedings of past editions, which gather some of the most significant contributions to the metaheuristics field, were published in Osman & Kelly (1996), Voss *et al.* (1999), Ribeiro & Hansen (2001), Resende & Pinho de Sousa (2003), and Ibaraki *et al.* (2005).

[2]For example, metaheuristics are adopted in a number of commercial products developed by ILOG (`http://www.ilog.com`), SAP (`http://www.sap.com`), and NuTech Solutions (`http://www.nutechsolutions.com`). Moreover, some smaller consulting companies have made of the use of metaheuristics one of their characterizing traits. Among them, see the two companies that have participated in the research activities of the *Metaheuristics Network* : EuroBios (`http://www.eurobios.com`) and AntOptima (`http://www.antoptima.com`).

that they are relatively easy to implement and that, therefore, a quick-and-dirty version of a metaheuristic for a given class of problems to be solved can be produced by a practitioner in few days. Such quick-and-dirty implementations are typically capable of fair performance; nevertheless, when state-of-the-art results are at stake, careful design choices and an accurate tuning are needed. Although the centrality of tuning is acknowledged in the literature—see for example Barr *et al.* (1995)—the problem of tuning metaheuristics has received so far little attention and no well established methodology has been defined for tackling it effectively and efficiently. Indeed, tuning is still performed largely by hand and this entails a number of drawbacks such as, for example, little reproducibility of the process, low reliability, and high costs ... without mentioning that it involves a large amount of extremely boring clerical work.

It is our belief that the reason why the tuning problem has received little attention is to be ascribed to the fact that the intimate nature of the tuning problem has been so far misunderstood. In our opinion, the few scientific works that have been devoted to the development of tuning procedures fail to grasp the most characterizing features of the tuning problem.

In the thesis, we give a precise definition of the framework in which the tuning problem emerges:

> A *stream* of instances belonging to some (sub)class of instances of a combinatorial optimization problem is considered. The stream is to be conceived as an infinite sequence of instances appearing in time, one after the other, which are to be solved. Moreover, a metaheuristic—or more precisely a finite set of configurations thereof—is given which can be used for tackling such instances.
>
> We assume that a metaheuristic undergoes a *life-cycle* composed of a *development phase* and a *production phase*: In the development phase, some limited amount of time is available for selecting one of the configurations of the metaheuristic at hand. Then, once the development phase is accomplished, the metaheuristic, in its selected configuration, leaves the workshop and eventually enters into production where it has to solve the instances that will appear in the stream. During the development, we might have recourse to a number of instances sampled from the stream but, clearly, not those that will appear in the stream in a future time and, in particular, not those that the metaheuristic will have to face once in production.

A careful analysis of this framework led us to put forward the idea that the tuning problem could be profitably looked at from a machine learning point of view. Indeed, by taking inspiration from a number of machine learning concepts and methods, in the thesis (i) we give a formal definition of the tuning problem, (ii) we propose the *F-Race* algorithm for effectively tackling it, (iii) we adopt an experimental methodology for assessing in an unbiased way the performance of a tuning algorithm, (iv) we take advantage of a re-sampling method for dramatically reducing the computation time needed for obtaining such an assessment, and finally (v) we introduce the concept of *over-tuning* for framing some catches that are connatural with the practice of tuning metaheuristics.

Nevertheless, in our personal opinion, the single most important contribution of the whole thesis, the one on which all the aforementioned others rest, is the understanding that the proper way of formalizing the concept of class of instances (or subclass thereof), and therefore of characterizing a stream of instances that defines a specific tuning problem, is through the definition of a probability measure P_I defined over the space of all instances of the problem at hand.

Although we have developed the idea of such a probability measure in a totally independent way, we have later on realized that the same concept had been previously adopted by Wolpert & Macready (1996, 1997), although in a quite different context and with different goals. Apparently, this idea did not have much following in the years and, nowadays, it is not easily accepted by researchers in the field. According to our experience, gathered in informal discussions with researchers active in the metaheuristic domain, the idea of considering a probability measure defined over the space of the instances is regarded as unnatural, impractical, an somehow *weird.*

The typical objection raised against this idea is that such probability measure is not, in most practically relevant situations, available. This criticism is dangling in many respects. We discuss here two issues. The first one is simply an epistemological clarification: The probability measure we discuss is just a probabilistic *model* of the mechanism underlying the stream of instances at hand. As all models, it is to be intended as a *possible description* of a phenomenon and not as some entity that *necessarily exists* in Nature. In this sense, a model is *always* available ... indeed infinite models might be produced at will: The point is, when a model is needed, how to select one that serves a specific purpose.[3]

On the other hand, the second issue we wish to discuss here is more technical and is directly related to the practical use that is made, in the context of this thesis, of the notion of probability measure defined over the space of the instances. The knowledge of this probability measure P_I needs not be made explicit neither at any stage of our theoretical development, nor at any moment in the execution of the tuning algorithms we propose in the thesis: As we have shown in Chapter 4, we simply need to have access to a number of instances from the aforementioned stream, which we need to be ready to *assume* as indeed independently sampled according to P_I. These instances are sufficient for estimating directly the expected performance of the different candidate configurations of the metaheuristic to be tuned, and eventually for selecting the best one. It is worth further stressing

[3]We consider particularly illuminating the statement on the issue that is attributed to G. E. P. Box: *All models are wrong; some are useful.* His point is made clear in Box (1976).

that the estimation of the expected performance of the candidates can be done *directly* on the basis of the given instances, and does not require the intermediate step of obtaining an explicit estimation of P_I.

Nevertheless, although neither P_I nor any explicit model of it is used in *F-Race* or in any of the other tuning algorithms we discuss in the thesis, this probability measure plays a fundamental role. It is indeed on the basis of P_I that we are able to give a meaning to the very notion of *expected* (or average) performance of the metaheuristic at hand or, more precisely, of one of its configurations: Without reference to a probability measure, the concept of expectation cannot be defined. Since tuning amounts to selecting the best configuration according to a criterion of performance, and since the *expected* performance on the instances of the problem at hand is a meaningful, convenient, and particularly natural criterion, the key importance of the role played by P_I in the thesis emerges clearly.

Moreover, it is in the terms of the measure P_I that we are able to formulate another hypothesis that is of paramount importance, namely, the *regularity* of Nature. In particular, in the context of tuning metaheuristics, we need to formulate the hypothesis that the aforementioned stream of instances preserves in time *some* of its characteristics: Typically, we cannot expect that the stream will keep producing the same instances over and over. In this case, the whole setting would be trivial and such repeating instances could be solved once for all: The best solution of each instance could be stored, and re-used at each occurrence of the instance itself. Nevertheless, although such an extreme form of regularity should not be expected, we need to postulate that *something* in the stream remains unchanged in time. This *element of regularity* is what would justify the whole tuning process: Indeed, it is what would entitle us to assume that a configuration that obtained a good performance on some tuning instances will eventually obtain a good performance also on the instances it will encounter once in production. In the framework we have developed in the thesis, this *element of regularity* is precisely postulated in term of the measure P_I: We postulate indeed a probabilistic time-invariance of the stream of instances by requiring that P_I remain constant in time.[4] In other words, we postulate that the instances used for tuning and those that will be encountered once in production, although different, share the property of being extracted according to the *same* probability measure P_I. To summarize, tuning entails a *generalization* and this generalization rests on the assumption that the measure P_I remains unchanged in time. Whether an explicit representation of P_I is available or not does not play any role.

Once the notion is established of a probability measure P_I defined over the space of the instances, tuning is reduced to the problem of estimating the expected performance for a number of candidate configurations—where the expectation is taken with respect to P_I—and then selecting the one presenting the best expected

[4]The possibility and the opportunity of considering more complex models is discussed in Section 3.3.

performance. The estimation of these expectations can be performed in a Monte Carlo fashion, on the basis of a number of instances that are supposed being independently extracted according to P_I.

Beside the trivial *brute-force* approach to the so-defined tuning problem, the thesis proposes a class of *racing* algorithms, which consist in estimating the expected performance of the candidate configurations in an incremental way, and in discarding the worst ones as soon as sufficient evidence is gathered against them. This allows a better allocation of computing power: Rather than wasting time in the evaluation of low-performance configurations, the algorithm focuses on the assessment of the best ones. As a result, more data is gathered concerning the configurations that are deemed yielding the best results, and eventually a more informed and sharper selection is performed among them.

Racing algorithms had been previously proposed within the machine learning community for solving model selection tasks. Beside using for the first time this class of algorithms for tuning metaheuristics, we propose in the thesis another important novel element, namely, the adoption of the *Friedman two-way analysis of variance by ranks* as a statistical test for deciding whether configurations should be discarded or kept in the race on the basis of their performance observed incrementally: The Friedman test, which appears as particularly appropriate in the design of *racing* algorithms, had never been employed before in this context.

Summary of main contributions

The following is a summary of the main contributions proposed in the thesis:

The framework: The thesis defines the framework in which the tuning problem emerges: A *stream* of instances is considered and the tuning task consists in selecting a configuration of the metaheuristic to be tuned that is deemed to produce the best possible performance on the instances of the stream. This framework refers to a life-cycle model in which a metaheuristic undergoes a *development* phase, during which it is implemented and tuned, and then enters in a *production* phase.

Tuning as a learning problem: The thesis unveils the true nature of tuning. Tuning is indeed a *generalization* problem which rests on a hypothesis of *regularity* of the aforementioned stream of instances. The performance of the metaheuristic, or of a configuration thereof, on a number of instances sampled from the stream *informs* on its performance on future instances that will appear in the stream itself.

Formal position of the tuning problem: The thesis gives a formal definition of the tuning problem in which the key role is played by the notion of a probability measure P_I defined over the space of the instances. In terms of P_I, it is possible to formally define a criterion for selecting the best configuration of the metaheuristic to be tuned, namely the *expected* performance.

Formal analysis of the evaluation problem: The thesis proposes a formal analysis of the Monte Carlo estimation of the performance of a metaheuristic on the basis of a number of observations. Different estimators are considered in the analysis, and the one that uniformly yields the least variance is singled out. This analysis has a major impact on the definition of the tuning algorithms proposed in the thesis and on the definition of the experimental methodology adopted for their empirical assessment.

Definition of tuning algorithms: The thesis introduces a number of tuning algorithms. Beside the trivial *brute-force* approach, the class of *racing* algorithms for tuning is introduced. Among them, the thesis proposes *F-Race*, a *racing* approach that adopts the *Friedman two-way analysis of variance by ranks*; this test appears particularly appropriate in the context of the definition of *racing* algorithms.

The race package for R has been implemented and is distributed in the public domain under the GNU General Public License. The race package is available for free download from the official site of *The Comprehensive* R *Archive Network*.

Empirical analysis: The experimental methodology adopted in the thesis has been accurately designed and contains a number of novel elements. In particular, it explicitly separates the set of instances that are used for tuning a metaheuristic, from those that are used for assessing the selected configuration. This guarantees an unbiased evaluation of the latter. A number of *brute-force* approachs are included in the analysis and are used as a yardstick for measuring the performance of the *racing* algorithms proposed in the thesis. Moreover, a re-sampling methodology is adopted that allows obtaining results that would have been simply out of reach if all computation were to be actually performed.

Practical applications: The thesis illustrates a number of successful applications of *F-Race* and of related algorithms. Among them, it discusses the use of a *racing* algorithm for designing a hybrid metaheuristic that outperformed all competitors in the *International Timetabling Competition* organized in 2003 by the *Metaheuristics Network* and sponsored by PATAT, the international series of conferences on the *Practice and Theory of Automated Timetabling*. Moreover, the thesis sketches a feasibility study that has been carried out by INTELLEKTIK, Technischen Universität Darmstadt, Darmstadt, Germany, in collaboration with the German-based software company SAP. This study concerned the possible use of *F-Race* for automatically tuning a critical component of a commercial computer program produced by SAP for vehicle routing and scheduling problems.

Experimental methodology: The thesis discusses a number of issues concerning the definition of an appropriate experimental methodology to be adopted in the empirical analysis of metaheuristics. In particular, some catches are analyzed that are related to the practice of tuning. The notion of *over-tuning* is introduced that parallels the already well understood machine learning concept of *over-fitting*.

Moreover, the following contributions are contained in the Annexes:

Analysis of *ant colony optimization*: An original analysis of *ant colony optimization* is given from the machine learning point of view. In particular, a description of *ant colony optimization* is proposed in the terms of reinforcement learning, optimal control, and dynamic programming. Moreover, the model-based search framework is introduced which accommodates a number of combinatorial optimization methods including *ant colony optimization*.

***Lazy learning* for local regression:** An original *lazy learning* algorithm is described and some evidence is provided that it can be an effective alternative to state-of-the-art supervised learning methods for tackling the regression problem.
The lazy package for R has been implemented and is distributed in the public domain under the GNU General Public License. The lazy package is available for free download from the official site of *The Comprehensive* R *Archive Network*.

Future developments

The research described in the thesis is currently being further developed along a number of directions:

The race package: Since its first *alpha* version, back in 2002, the race package for R has already had a number of applications. At the moment of writing, October 2004, the race package is fairly stable and it is about 6 month that it has been available for general download from the official site of *The Comprehensive* R *Archive Network* and from its mirrors. Since the package starts being used in independent researches, we expect new users to adapt it to their specific needs and to contribute their modifications and improvements. As an example, the current version 0.1-49 of race adopts the *parallel virtual machine* (PVM) protocol for parallel computation; Schiavinotto (2004) has modified race and has added support for the *message passing interface* (MPI). These modifications will be included in future releases of the package.

Beside this *physiological* evolution of the package, we plan to extend the functionality of race with the final aim of implementing a general tool for tuning metaheuristics. Such tool will have the form of a collection of R packages—a *bundle* in R's terminology—implementing different algorithms for stochastic optimization that might prove useful for tuning parameters of metaheuristics in the sense defined in this thesis. In particular, we are considering methods for handling continuous parameters directly, that is, without prior discretization, namely the *response surface methodology*, and some form of hybrid approach based on the latter in conjunction with F-Race. Preliminary research in this direction is currently ongoing (Lunghi, 2004; Boldrini, 2005; Denis, 2005).

Theoretical work on F-Race: Further theoretical work on F-Race will be devoted to the problem of defining bounds on the probability of discarding the best candidate configuration at some stage of the race. It is in the nature of the algorithm to provide such a bound for each stage of the race: The adoption of a statistical test of hypothesis, namely the Friedman test, imposes indeed a bound of $\alpha = 0.05$ to the probability of discarding the very best candidate *at each stage* of the race. Expressing a *global* bound is far from being a trivial issue since tests performed in subsequent stages of the race are not independent, being (at least partially) based on the same pieces of evidence. Further research is needed in this direction.

Variance reduction: The Monte Carlo estimation adopted by F-Race and by the other tuning algorithms presented in the thesis might be made more efficient by adopting some variance reduction method. A preliminary discussion of the issue is already given in Sections 3.3.1 and 4.1.1. Research on the use of *stratified sampling* (Rubinstein, 1981) in the context of racing algorithms is currently ongoing.

Connections with other fields: Future research will explore connections with other research fields. In particular, we recently became aware of possible connections with a corpus of related work in the simulation field—see for example Goldsman & Nelson (2001), Nelson *et al.* (2001), and Pichitlamken & Nelson (2001).

Empirical analysis of F-Race: Also thanks to the *Metaheuristics Network*, that provided the general framework in which this research was carried out, a number of researchers working on metaheuristics became aware of the research presented in this thesis and of the possibility offered by F-Race. The latter enjoyed, as a consequence, much attention and was adopted in a fairly large number of applications. This allowed gathering an insight on its properties that we could not have possibly reached if we were not working within a large and active research group such as the *Metaheuristics Network*.

Now that the activities of the *Metaheuristics Network* are formally accomplished, we keep *"promoting"* the F-Race algorithm and the race package by collaborating with a number of researchers: In particular, we provide assistance in the application of F-Race to different tuning tasks with the final goal of gathering first-hand experience on all practical issues that are possibly encountered when tackling a tuning problem.

Moreover, the issues that are discussed in the Annexes are currently the focus of further research:

Analysis of *ant colony optimization*: Further research is currently being carried out on the concepts framed by *ant programming* and on their possible practical relevance in the design of algorithms (Darquennes, 2005). Moreover, we are currently evaluating the possibility of adopting an approach akin to the model-based search for tuning metaheuristics in the sense defined in the thesis.

***Lazy learning* for local regression:** The research on *lazy learning* is particularly active at the moment, and it is heading in different directions including system identification and control, process monitoring, and data mining for the analysis of massive datasets, possibly in distributed computing environment.

Concluding statement

The work presented in this thesis is relevant for the development of the whole metaheuristics field, both for what concerns academic studies and for practical applications. Given the very nature of metaheuristics, tuning is to be considered as an integral part of their development: Indeed, a metaheuristic is best conceived as a template for conveniently crafting optimization algorithms for tackling some given class of problems. Typically, even a quick-and-dirty version of such algorithms can obtain a fair performance but when state-of-the-art results are sought, a careful tuning process is essential.

In this thesis, an inherently interdisciplinary approach proved to be extremely fruitful: The problem of tuning metaheuristics has been profitably formalized and analyzed on the basis of machine learning concepts, and it has been effectively tackled using algorithms derived from machine learning methods.

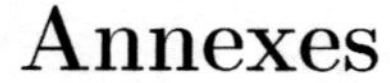
Annexes

None preaches better than the ant, and she says nothing.

Benjamin Franklin

Annex A

A machine learning point of view on *ant colony optimization*

In the last decade, a number of algorithms inspired by the foraging behavior of ant colonies have been introduced for the approximate solution of combinatorial optimization problems—see Dorigo & Di Caro (1999), Dorigo *et al.* (1999), and Dorigo & Stützle (2004) for extensive reviews. The framework of *ant colony optimization* (Dorigo & Di Caro, 1999; Dorigo *et al.*, 1999) recently gave a first unifying description of (most of) these algorithms.

Ant colony optimization has been successfully applied to a number of different problems.[1] Nevertheless, a complete theoretical analysis of the algorithms of this class is not available yet. Only recently some works have been devoted to the theory of *ant colony optimization*. They have moved along two main lines: On the one hand, the issue of the convergence of the algorithm has been explored (Gutjahr, 2000, 2002; Stützle & Dorigo, 2002). On the other hand, the relations existing between *ant colony optimization* and other approaches have been highlighted (Birattari *et al.*, 2002; Meuleau & Dorigo, 2002; Zlochin *et al.*, 2004). For an organic presentation of the *ant colony optimization* theory, we refer the reader to Dorigo & Stützle (2004). Here, we focus on the studies that addressed the relationship between *ant colony optimization* and other approaches: Birattari *et al.* (2000, 2002) and Birattari (2001) gave a description of *ant colony optimization* in the language of dynamic programming (Bellman, 1957) and optimal

[1]See Dorigo & Di Caro (1999), Dorigo *et al.* (1999), Dorigo *et al.* (2000), and Dorigo & Stützle (2004) for lists and descriptions of implementations of *ant colony optimization* for a variety of combinatorial optimization problems like, among others, traveling salesman, quadratic assignment, and graph coloring. See also the proceedings of the International series of conferences ANTS, held bi-annually in Brussels (Dorigo, 1998; Dorigo *et al.*, 2000, 2002, 2004), which are entirely dedicated to the advancements in *ant colony optimization* and related algorithms. Additionally, overviews of algorithms inspired by the behavior of real ants but not strictly falling in the *ant colony optimization* class, are reported in Bonabeau *et al.* (1999), Bonabeau *et al.* (2000), and Dorigo *et al.* (2000).

control (Bertsekas, 1995a). This point of view has been further explored in Di Caro (2004). Meuleau & Dorigo (2002) proposed a description of *ant colony optimization* in terms of stochastic gradient descent and *model-free* reinforcement learning (Sutton & Barto, 1998). Finally, Zlochin, Birattari, Meuleau & Dorigo (2004) proposed the general framework of *model-based search* for combinatorial optimization that accommodates a number of algorithms including *ant colony optimization*.

The remaining of the chapter is structured as follows: Section A.1 presents the work of Birattari *et al.* (2002) on the relation between *ant colony optimization* and optimal control, while Section A.2 presents the model-based search framework proposed by Zlochin *et al.* (2004). The latter, includes also a section on the stochastic gradient method and therefore brings some elements of the work of Meuleau & Dorigo (2002).

A.1 Formal foundation of ant programming†

Loosely speaking, *ant colony optimization* presents the following features. A graph is defined in a way that each solution of the combinatorial problem corresponds to at least one path on the graph itself. The weights associated to the edges are such that the cost of a path equals the cost of the associated solution. In this sense, the goal of *ant colony optimization* is to find a path of minimum cost. To this end, a number of paths are incrementally generated in a Monte Carlo fashion, and the observed costs are used to bias the generation of further paths. This process is iterated with the aim of gathering information on the graph and of eventually producing a path of minimum cost. In *ant colony optimization*, the above described algorithm is visualized in terms of a metaphor in which the generation of a path is represented as the walk of an *ant* that, at each node, stochastically selects the following one on the basis of local information called *pheromone trail* (Beckers *et al.*, 1992). In turn, the *pheromone trail* is modified by the *ants* in order to bias the generation of future paths toward better solutions.

The very possibility of obtaining better solutions by exploiting memory about solutions generated so far is the basic assumption of *ant colony optimization*. A further implicit assumption concerns what this memory should consist in. In spite of the key role played in all implementations of *ant colony optimization*, this assumption was never critically discussed before: The formal definition of *ant colony optimization* (Dorigo & Di Caro, 1999) envisages, for each optimization problem, a unique way of defining the memory. To clarify this issue, let us consider an optimization problem whose solutions are expressed by *ant colony optimization* as a sequence of components. *Ant colony optimization* generates so-

†This section is based on Birattari *et al.* (2002) which is, in turn, an abridged version of Birattari *et al.* (2000). The issues discussed here have been further elaborated in Birattari (2001) and in Di Caro (2004).

lutions in the form of paths in the space of such components. Memory is kept of all the observed transitions between components. A degree of desirability is associated to each transition depending on the quality of the solutions in which it occurred so far. While a new solution is being incrementally generated, a component y is included with a probability that is proportional to the desirability of the transition between the last component included and y itself. Even if it seems natural that memory should be associated with pairs of solution components, as assumed by *ant colony optimization*, in our treatment of the subject, we maintain that such an assumption is just a matter of choice. Indeed, this is only one of the possible *representations* of the solution generation process that can be adopted for framing information about solutions previously observed. As it will be clear in the following, this representation is neither optimal nor the most natural, provided that a correct analysis of the problem at hand is given. Our analysis will be based on a clear understanding of the concept of state of the process of incremental solution construction.

Here, we propose a novel formal description of the combinatorial optimization problems to which *ant colony optimization* applies, and we analyze the implication of adopting a generic solution strategy based on the incremental Monte Carlo construction of solutions biased by a memory. In this section we present *ant programming* as an abstract class of algorithms which presents the characterizing features of *ant colony optimization* but which is more amenable to theoretical analysis for what concerns the concepts of representation and state. In particular, *ant programming* bridges the terminological gap between *ant colony optimization* and the fields of optimal control (Bertsekas, 1995a) and reinforcement learning (Sutton & Barto, 1998). Accordingly, the name *ant programming* was chosen for its assonance with *dynamic programming*, with which *ant programming* has in common the stress on the concept of state and the related idea of reformulating an optimization problem as a multi-stage decision problem and then searching for a good (hopefully optimal) decision *policy* for the latter. Both in dynamic programming and in *ant programming*, such a reformulation is not trivial and requires an *ad hoc* analysis of the optimization problem under consideration. These concepts, being among the main issues in this research, will be discussed in detail in the rest of the section: Section A.1.1 shows how to reformulate a discrete optimization problem into a discrete-time optimal control problem and then into a shortest path problem. Section A.1.2 introduces the concepts of *graph of the representation*, *phantasma* and *sequential decision process* under incomplete information. Section A.1.3 introduces and discusses the *ant programming* abstract class of algorithms. Section A.1.4 discusses the main issues and describes the future developments of this research.

A.1.1 Optimization, optimal control, and shortest paths

Let us consider a discrete optimization problem defined by a finite set S of feasible solutions and by a cost function f. The set S is:

$$S = \{s_1, s_2, \ldots, s_|S|\}, \quad |S| \in \mathbb{N}, \quad |S| < \infty, \tag{A.1}$$

where each solution s_l is a n_l-tuple

$$s_l = (s_l^0, s_l^1, \ldots, s_l^{n_l-1}), \quad n_l \in \mathbb{N}, \quad n_l \leq n < \infty, \tag{A.2}$$

with $n = \max n_l$, and $s_l^j \in Y$, where Y is a finite set of *components*. The cost function $f : S \to \mathbb{R}$ assigns a cost to each feasible solution s_l. The optimization problem is therefore the problem of finding the element $\bar{s} \in S$ which minimizes the function f:

$$\bar{s} = \arg\min_{s \in S} f(s). \tag{A.3}$$

Being the set S finite, the minimum of f on S indeed exists. If such minimum is attained for more than one element of S, it is a matter of indifference which one is considered.

A feasible solution in S can be built incrementally starting from the 0-tuple $x_0 = ()$, and adding one-at-a-time a component. The generic iteration can be described as:

$$x_j = (u_0, \ldots, u_{j-1}) \to x_{j+1} = (u_0, \ldots, u_{j-1}, u_j), \quad \text{with } u_j \in Y, \tag{A.4}$$

where x_j is a *partial solution* of length j. A partial solution x_j is called *feasible* if it can be completed into a feasible solution $s_l \in S$, that is, if at least one feasible solution $s_l \in S$ exists, of which x_j is the initial sub-tuple of length j. It is understood that a process generating a sequence of feasible partial solutions necessarily ends up into a feasible solution. For each feasible partial solution x_j, we define the set $U(x_j) \in Y$ of all the possible new components u_j that can be appended to x_j giving in turn a feasible (partial) solution x_{j+1}.

Now, the set X of all feasible tuples x_j is finite since both the set S and the length of each feasible solution s_l are finite. Moreover, it can be shown that $S \subset X$, since all the solutions s_l are composed of a finite number of components, all belonging to Y.

Since a feasible solution can be obtained incrementally, the original optimization problem can be reformulated as a *multi-stage decision process* in which the optimal solution $\bar{s}$ is obtained by a sequence of decisions concerning the set Y of the components. Such a way of proceeding results particularly natural when the cost $f(s_l)$ of a solution s_l is expressed as a sum of contributions c_{j+1}, each related to the fact that a particular component u_j is included in the solution s_l itself after a sequence of components described by the tuple x_j. Formally, a function

$C : X \setminus \{x_0\} \rightarrow \mathbb{R}$ must be conveniently defined, which associates a cost c_{j+1} to each tuple x_{j+1}.[2]

The finite-horizon multi-stage decision process described above can be thoroughly seen as a deterministic *discrete-time optimal control problem* (Boltyanskii, 1978). The tuple x_j can be seen as the *state* at time $t = j$ of a discrete-time dynamic system whose state-transition application is such that the state at time $t + 1$ is obtained by appending the current control action $u_t \in U(x_t)$ to the state x_t:

$$\begin{cases} x_{t+1} = [x_t, u_t], \\ y_{t+1} = u_t, \end{cases} \tag{A.5}$$

The set of the feasible actions, given the current state, is a subset of the range of the output: $U(x_t) \subset Y$.

Now, let $\mathcal{U}$ be the set of all the admissible control sequences that bring the system from the initial state x_0 to a terminal state belonging to S: The generic element of $\mathcal{U}$, $u = \langle u_0, u_1, \ldots, u_{\tau-1} \rangle$, is such that the corresponding state trajectory, which is unique, is $\langle x_0, x_1, \ldots, x_\tau \rangle$, with $x_\tau \in S$, and $u_t \in U(x_t)$, for $0 \leq t < \tau$. In this sense, the dynamic system defines a mapping $\mathcal{S} : \mathcal{U} \rightarrow S$ which assigns to each admissible control sequence $u \in \mathcal{U}$ a final state $s = \mathcal{S}(u) \in S$.

The problem of optimal control consists in finding the sequence $\bar{u} \in \mathcal{U}$ for which the sum f of the costs c_t, incurred along the state trajectory, is minimized:

$$\bar{u} = \arg\min_{u \in \mathcal{U}} f\big(\mathcal{S}(u)\big), \tag{A.6}$$

where with "arg min" we denote the element of $\mathcal{U}$ for which the minimum of the composed function $f \circ S$ is attained. If such a minimum is attained for more than one element of $\mathcal{U}$, it is a matter of indifference which one is considered.

It is apparent that the solution of the problem of optimal control stated in Equation A.6 is equivalent to the solution of the original optimization problem given in Equation A.3, and that the optimal sequence of control actions $\bar{u}$ for the optimal control problem determines uniquely the optimal solution $\bar{s}$ of the original optimization problem. Since the set X is discrete and finite, together with all the sets $U(x_t)$, for all $x_t \in X$, and since trajectories have a fixed maximum length n, all the possible state trajectories of the system given in Equation A.5 can be conveniently represented through a weighted and oriented graph with a finite number of nodes. Let $\mathcal{G}(X, U)$ be such a graph, where X is the set of nodes and U is the set of edges, and let $C : U \rightarrow \mathbb{R}$ be a function that associates a weight to each edge. In terms of the system described in Equation A.5, each node of the graph $\mathcal{G}(X, U)$ represents a state x_t of the system. The set $U \subset X \times X$

[2]Given the rule defined in Equation A.4, the tuple x_{j+1} determines uniquely the tuple x_j and the component u_j, and is in turn determined uniquely by them. Therefore, the function C could be equivalently defined as a function mapping on the real line an ordered pair $\langle x_j, u_j \rangle$, a transition $\langle x_j, x_{j+1} \rangle$, or even the triplet $\langle x_j, u_j, x_{j+1} \rangle$.

is the set of the edges $\langle x_t, x_{t+1}\rangle$. Each of the edges departing from a given node x_t represents one of the actions $u_t \in U(x_t)$, feasible when the system is in state x_t. Finally, the function C is defined in terms of the function C. Namely, $c_{t+1} = C(\langle x_t, x_{t+1}\rangle) = \mathsf{C}(x_{t+1})$ is the cost of the edge $\langle x_t, x_{t+1}\rangle$. Furthermore, on the graph $\mathcal{G}(X, U)$ we can single out the initial state x_0, as the only state with no incoming edges, and the set S of the terminal nodes from which no edges depart. In terms of the graph $\mathcal{G}(X, U)$ and of the function C, the optimal control problem defined in Equation A.6 can be stated as the problem of finding the *path of minimal cost* from the initial node x_0 to any of the terminal nodes in S.

As already mentioned, the solution strategy of *ant colony optimization* is based on the iterated generation of multiple paths on a graph that encodes the optimization problem under consideration. As it will be defined in the following, this graph is obtained as a transformation of the graph $\mathcal{G}$ consisting in an aggregation of nodes. In previous works on *ant colony optimization*, the graph resulting from such a transformation was the only graph taken into consideration explicitly. In the treatment of the issue that we propose here, we move the focus on the original graph $\mathcal{G}$ and on the properties of the transformation.

A.1.2 Markov and non-Markov representations

Consistently with the optimal control literature, we have called *state* each node of the graph $\mathcal{G}(X, U)$ and, by extension, we call *state graph* the graph $\mathcal{G}$ itself. In the following, the properties of the state graph will be discussed in the perspective of the solution of the problem given in Equation A.3, and in relation to the solution strategy of *ant colony optimization*. The ant metaphor will be used to visualize abstract concepts. In particular, we will picture the state evolution of the system given in Equation A.5, and therefore the incremental construction of a solution, as the walk of an *ant* on the state graph $\mathcal{G}$. In the following, the state x_t at time t will be called interchangeably the "partial solution," the "state of the system," or, by extension, the "state of the ant."

The state of a stochastic or deterministic dynamic system can be informally thought of as the piece of information that gives the most predictive description possible of the system at a given time instant.[3] Since what is known in the literature as *Markov property* is related precisely to the concept of state, it is clear that the state, when correctly conceived, is *always* a state in the Markov sense: When described in terms of its state, any discrete-time system is *intrinsically* Markov.[4] It is therefore of dubious utility to state the Markov property with

[3]A detailed analysis of the concept of state in the context of *ant colony optimization* can be found in Birattari *et al.* (2000). A general analysis of the concept of state is given in the classical literature on linear system theory (Zadeh & Desoer, 1963), dynamic programming (Bellman, 1957), and optimal control (Bertsekas, 1995a).

[4]For a discrete Markov decision process, the following holds by definition: $P(x_{t+1}|x^t, u^t) = P(x_{t+1}|x_t, u_t)$, where $x^t = (x_t, x_{t-1}, x_{t-2}, \dots)$ and $u^t = (u_t, u_{t-1}, u_{t-2}, \dots)$ indicate the past

respect to a dynamic system *tout court*. Of much greater significance, it is to assert the Markov property of a *representation*. Informally, we call a representation the structure in which an agent[5] frames experience: an agent refers to a representation for describing the state of the system, for possibly keeping memory of observed trajectories, and for performing predictions or control actions. In the limit, a representation might bear the same information as the state. In this case the Markov property holds for such representation. In the more general case, a representation is of non-Markov type, that is, it gives less information than the state. Being non-Markov is therefore a characteristic of the interaction system-agent and is related to the fact that the agent describes the system in terms of a representation that brings less information than a state description. In general, such a shortcoming of the representation can be ascribed to the inability of the agent to obtain information on the system, or to the deliberate choice of reducing the amount of information to be handled. In this second case, we are facing a *quality-complexity dilemma*.

In the context of *ant colony optimization*, as already pointed out, the basic assumption is that better solutions can be obtained by exploiting memory about previously generated ones. In this context, the discussion proposed above entails two major issues. First, for most combinatorial optimization problems of interest for which the state space grows exponentially with the size of the problem itself, it is clear that it is infeasible to gather and use memory about solutions in terms of a state description: it is very unlikely that a trajectory has exploitable superpositions with previously generated ones. Therefore, in *ant colony optimization* it is necessary to refer to a representation that reduces the information retained

history of x and u, respectively. Now, let us consider a time-varying system whose state dynamic is given by $x_{t+1} = F_t(x_t, u_t, \xi_t)$ where x_t and u_t are respectively state and input at time t, and the state disturbance $\xi_t \sim P(\xi)$ is a white noise independent of the state and the input in the following sense: $P(\xi_t|x^t, u^t) = P(\xi_t)$. Clearly, x_{t+1} is a random variable whose distribution is $P(x_{t+1}|x_t, u_t) = P(\Xi_{x_{t+1}})$ where $\Xi_{x_{t+1}} = \{\xi : F_t(x_t, u_t, \xi) = x_{t+1}\}$ is the set of the values ξ that, for the given x_t and u_t, map to x_{t+1}, and $P(\Xi_{x_{t+1}})$ indicates the probability of observing a ξ belonging to such a set. The Markov property holds when the above introduced time-varying system is seen as a decision process. In particular:

$$P(x_{t+1}|x^t, u^t) = \sum_{\Xi_{x_{t+1}}} P(\xi|x^t, u^t) = \sum_{\Xi_{x_{t+1}}} P(\xi) = P(\Xi_{x_{t+1}}) = P(x_{t+1}|x_t, u_t).$$

The treatment given above assumes that ξ is a discrete variable. Thought the property holds also for continuous ξ, the proof for the general case involves a more complex notation and goes beyond the scope of this footnote.

Conversely, any discrete Markov decision process is a state description of a system in the Kalman sense. It is straightforward to verify that any $x_{t+1} \sim P(x_{t+1}|x_t, u_t)$ can be written in the form $x_{t+1} = F_t(x_t, u_t, \xi_t)$ where the dependence on time t accounts for the fact that in the definition of the Markov property the distributions at different temporal instants need not be the same. Since $x_{t+1} = F_t(x_t, u_t, \xi_t)$ is the classical form in which the state dynamic of a generic time-varying system can be given, the assertion is proved.

[5]By *agent* we mean any entity acting on or observing purposely the system at hand.

about the current state. This determines some sort of *aliasing* of distinct states which induces a criterion for *generalizing* previous experience. Second, as it will be made clear in the following, since a generic representation is non-Markov, it is not possible to generate feasible solutions on the basis of the sole representation. Therefore, it is necessary to refer to a state description in order to insure that a feasible solution be generated. These two issues, taken together, force to devise a strategy for the incremental generation of solution that on the one hand refers to a state description for guaranteeing feasibility, and on the other hand refers to a representation for optimizing the quality of the generated solution. The characteristics of the representation to be adopted reflect the design choice regarding the trade-off associated with the *quality-complexity dilemma*. *Ant programming* makes explicit the necessity to refer both to a representation and to a state description. Every step in the incremental construction of a solution consists of two sub-steps: first, a set of feasible candidate actions is defined on the basis of information pertaining to the state description; second, one of such candidates is selected on the basis of its desirability expressed in terms of the representation. In this sense, *ant programming* introduces the categories needed for understanding some mechanisms already adopted in *ant colony optimization* such as, for instance, keeping and updating at each step the list of the components whose inclusion into the solution under construction would make the latter unfeasible. Such a list implicitly brings information about the state of the solution construction process.

For the class of problems discussed here, a formal definition of a representation can be given with reference to the state graph $\mathcal{G}(X, U)$. We define the *representation graph* as the graph $\mathcal{G}_r(Z_r, U_r)$, where Z_r is the set of the nodes and U_r is the set of the edges. Furthermore, we call *generating function of the representation* the function $r : X \rightarrow Z_r$ that maps the set X of the states onto the set Z_r. The function r associates therefore to every elements of X an element in Z_r: every element $z_t \in Z_r$ has *at least* one preimage in X, but generally the preimage is not unique. The notation $r^{-1}(\{z_t\}) = \{x_\tau | r(x_\tau) = z_t\}$ indicates the set of states x_τ whose image under r is z_t. The function r induces an equivalence relation on X: Two states x_l and x_j are *equivalent* according to the representation defined by r, if and only if $r(x_l) = r(x_j)$. In this sense, a representation can be seen as a *partition* of the set X.

In the following, we will call each $z_t \in Z_r$ a *phantasma*, adopting the term used by Aristotle with the meaning of *mental image*.[6] With such a term we want to stress that, from the point of view of an agent that observes the system through the representation r, z_t plays the role of the *phenomenal perception*, that is, what is retained about the system at time t for optimization purposes.[7]

[6]Aristotle (384–322 BC) *De Anima*: "The soul never thinks without a mental image." The term *phantasma* [Gr. φάντασμα, vision or mental image] was re-introduced in Medieval epistemology by Thomas Aquinas (1225–1274) in *Summa Theologiae*.

[7]As an example, let us consider the case in which the set Z_r coincides with the set of

Thanks to the notion of *phantasma*, we can give a precise interpretation to the concept of representation in the context of the control problem given in Equation A.6. As we pointed out before, the state evolution of the system given in Equation A.5, can be described as the walk of an *ant* on $\mathcal{G}(X, U)$. Let us assume now that the *ant* visits in sequence the nodes $x_0, x_1, \ldots, x_n$. The same sequence, under the representation induced by r, appears as a sequence $z_0, z_1, \ldots, z_n$ where for each l, with $0 \leq l \leq n$, z_l is the *phantasma* of the state x_l, that is, $z_l = r(x_l)$. In the *ant* metaphor, we say that the *ant*, though moving on the state graph $\mathcal{G}(X, U)$, *represents* its movement on the representation graph $\mathcal{G}_r(Z_r, U_r)$. In control theory, the process that carries the state into what we call a *phantasma*, is related to the concept of *state-space reduction*.[8]

In the same spirit of the definition of the set Z_r, also the set of the edges U_r can be defined in terms of the generating function r. The set $U_r \subset Z_r \times Z_r$ is the set of the edges $\langle z_l, z_j \rangle$ for which an edge $\langle x_l, x_j \rangle \in U$ exists on the state graph such that x_l and x_j are the preimages under r of z_l and z_j, respectively. Formally:

$$U_r = \Big\{ \langle z_l, z_j \rangle \mid \exists \langle x_l, x_j \rangle \in U : z_l = r(x_l),\ z_j = r(x_j) \Big\}.$$

When the system is described through a generic representation r, the subset $U_r(t) \subset U_r$ of the admissible control actions at time t cannot usually be described in terms of the *phantasma* z_t alone, but needs for its definition the knowledge of the underlying state x_t. In other words, for the generic generating function r, the *phantasma* z_t does not bring the same information as the state x_t and therefore the corresponding representation is non-Markov. The adoption of a non-Markov representation is by no means free from complications. While on the graph $\mathcal{G}$ every (partial) path is a (partial) feasible solution and *vice versa*, on $\mathcal{G}_r$ this property does not hold anymore. As far as the construction of feasible solutions is concerned, $\mathcal{G}$ is not therefore superseded by $\mathcal{G}_r$: As anticipated before, the graph $\mathcal{G}_r$ and the information stored on it are used for optimizing the construction of a solution while the graph $\mathcal{G}$ is used for guaranteeing feasibility. In any case, because of the loss of topological information induced by the transformation from $\mathcal{G}$ to $\mathcal{G}_r$ and since the optimization process is based on $\mathcal{G}_r$, in the general case only sub-optimal solutions will be obtained.

---

solution components Y and $r : [x_t, u_t] \mapsto u_t$. This is the typical transformation adopted in the applications of *ant colony optimization* to the traveling salesman problem and to other combinatorial optimization problems. For this reason, such a transformation will be denoted in the following as r_{aco}.

[8]Yet, the result of a *state-space reduction* does not have a standard name in control theory and the various terms used always bring a direct reference to the concept of state: for example, *reduced state*. It is just in order to underline the important qualitative difference between the properties of the state and those of the result of a *state-space reduction*, that we introduce here the term *phantasma* to denote the latter.

The parallel of the weight function C of $\mathcal{G}$ for the graph $\mathcal{G}_r$ cannot be defined in a straightforward manner for a generic r. Moreover, it results more useful to define the weights of the edges of the graph $\mathcal{G}_r(Z_r, U_r)$ so that they describe the quantity that in *ant colony optimization* is called *pheromone trail*. The function $T : U_r \to \mathbb{R}$ will be used in the process of selecting an action by an *ant* when perceiving a given *phantasma*, and will be iteratively modified in order to improve the quality of the solutions generated. The definition of the function T will be given in Section A.1.3.

A.1.3 Ant programming

In this section we introduce *ant programming* as a new class of algorithms that deal with the optimization problems defined in Equation A.3 under the form described by Equation A.6. *Ant programming* is inspired by *ant colony optimization*, and from the latter it inherits the essential features, the terminology and the underlying philosophy. The aim of this section is mostly speculative: we do not describe a specific algorithm, but rather a class of algorithms, in the sense that we define a general resolution strategy and an algorithmic structure where some components are functionally specified but left uninstantiated.

The three phases of ant programming

Two are the essential features of *ant programming*. The first is the incremental Monte Carlo generation of complete paths over the state graph $\mathcal{G}$, on the basis of desirability information provided by the function T associated with the representation graph $\mathcal{G}_r$. The second is the update of the desirability information in $\mathcal{G}_r$ on the basis of the cost of the generated solutions and the use of such information to bias subsequent generations. These two features are described in terms of the three *phases* that, when properly iterated, constitute *ant programming*. At each iteration, a new set of *ants*, hereafter called a *cohort*, is considered. Each *ant* in the *cohort* undergoes a *forward* phase that determines the generation of a path, and a *backward* phase that states how the costs experienced along such a path should influence the generation of future paths. Finally, each iteration is concluded by a *merge* phase that combines the contribution of all the *ants* of the *cohort*. The three phases *forward*, *backward*, and *merge* are in turn characterized by the three *operators* π, ν, and σ respectively.

The forward phase. Using the terminology of *ant colony optimization* and in the light of the formalization given in Section A.1.2, *ant programming* metaphorically describes each Monte Carlo run as the walk of an *ant* over the graph $\mathcal{G}(X, U)$, where at each node a random experiment determines the following node. In the ant metaphor, the random experiment is depicted as a *decision* taken by the *ant* on the basis of a probabilistic policy parameterized in terms of the function

T, usually called the *pheromone trail*, defined on the set of edges of the graph $\mathcal{G}_r(Z_r, U_r)$.

The *forward* phase can be described as follows: Let us suppose that after t decision steps the partial solution built so far is $(u_0, \ldots, u_{t-1})$. The state of the solution generation process is therefore $x_t = (u_0, \ldots, u_{t-1})$. In the ant metaphor, this fact is visualized as an *ant* being in the node x_t of $\mathcal{G}(X, U)$. The *ant* perceives the state x_t in terms of the *phantasma* $z_t = r(x_t)$. In the general case, it is not possible to express the set $U_r(t)$ of admissible actions available to the *ant* when in z_t only in terms of z_t itself, and of the information given by $\mathcal{G}_r$. The set $U_r(t)$ of the admissible actions at time t is indeed:

$$U_r(t)=U_r(z_t|x_t)=\Big\{\langle z_t, z_{t+1}\rangle \in U_r \;\Big|\; z_t = r(x_t), \exists u \in U(x_t) : z_{t+1} = r([x_t, u])\Big\}.$$

The decision of the *ant* consists in the selection of one element from the set $U_r(z_t|x_t)$ of the available transitions, as described at the level of the graph $\mathcal{G}_r$. Once an element, say $\langle z_t, z_{t+1}\rangle$, is selected, the partial solution is transformed according to Equation A.4 and Equation A.5: $x_{t+1} = [x_t, u_t] = (u_0, \ldots, u_{t-1}, u_t)$, where $x_{t+1} \in r^{-1}(\{z_{t+1}\})$ is one of the preimages of the *phantasma* z_{t+1}. In terms of the metaphor, this state transition is described as a movement of the *ant* to the node x_{t+1} of $\mathcal{G}$ which in turn is perceived by the *ant* as a movement to the *phantasma* $z_{t+1} = r(x_t)$ on $\mathcal{G}_r$.

The decision among the elements of $U_r(z_t|x_t)$ is taken according to the first operator of **ant programming**: the *stochastic policy* π. Given the current *phantasma* and the set of admissible actions $U_r(z_t|x_t)$, the policy selects an element of $U_r(z_t|x_t)$ as the outcome of a random experiment whose parameters are defined by the weights $T(\langle z_t, z_{t+1}\rangle)$ associated with the edges $U_r(z_t|x_t)$ of the graph $\mathcal{G}_r(Z_r, U_r)$. Accordingly we will adopt the following notation to denote the stochastic policy:

$$\pi\big(z_t, U_r(z_t|x_t); T|_{U_r(z_t|x_t)}\big). \tag{A.7}$$

With the notation $T|_{U_r(z_t|x_t)}$ we want to suggest that, when in z_t, the full knowledge of the function T is not strictly needed to select an element of the set $U_r(z_t|x_t)$. Indeed it is sufficient to know the restriction of T to the subset $U_r(z_t|x_t)$ of the domain U_r.[9] The function T plays the role of parameter of the policy π: changing T will change the policy itself.

In relation to the definition of the policy π, it is worth noticing here how the decision process uses the information contained in the two graphs $\mathcal{G}$ and $\mathcal{G}_r$: The decision is taken on the basis of information pertaining to the graph $\mathcal{G}_r$, restricted by the knowledge of the actual state x_t which in turn is a piece of information pertaining to the graph $\mathcal{G}$.

[9] This fact is the expression of one of the feature of **ant programming**, namely the *locality* of the information needed by the *ant* in order to take each elementary decision. Such a feature plays and important role in the implementation, allowing a *distribution* of the information on the graph of the representation $\mathcal{G}_r$.

Given the abstract definition proposed in Equation A.7, of the policy π, the *forward* phase can be defined as the sequence of steps that take one *ant* from the initial state x_0, to a solution, say $s = x_\tau$, of the original combinatorial problem defined in Equation A.3. Each of such steps is composed of three operations: first define, on the basis of the current state x_t, the set $U_r(z_t|x_t)$ of the available transitions; second select a transition on $\mathcal{G}_r$; and third move on $\mathcal{G}$ from the current node x_t to the neighboring node x_{t+1}. Formally, the single *forward* step is described as:

$$\begin{aligned} \langle z_t, z'_{t+1} \rangle &= \pi\big(z_t, U_r(z_t|x_t); T|_{U_r(z_t|x_t)}\big); \\ x_{t+1} &= \mathcal{F}\big(x_t, \langle z_t, z'_{t+1} \rangle\big); \\ z_{t+1} &= r(x_{t+1}), \end{aligned} \tag{A.8}$$

where the operator π is the stochastic policy that indicates the transition to be executed as seen on the graph $\mathcal{G}_r$, and where with the operator $\mathcal{F}$ we denote the operation of selecting one preimage x_{t+1} of z'_{t+1} and moving to it on the graph $\mathcal{G}$ from the current state x_t. Such a movement on $\mathcal{G}$ will be indeed "perceived" by the *ant* as a movement to the *phantasma* $z_{t+1} = r(x_{t+1}) = z'_{t+1}$, as requested by the policy π.

The backward phase. The ultimate goal of *ant programming* is to find a policy $\bar{\pi}$, not necessarily stochastic, such that a sequence of decisions taken according to $\bar{\pi}$ leads an *ant* to define the solution $\bar{s}$ which minimizes the cost function f of the original optimization problem given in Equation A.3.

Since the generic policy given in A.7 is described parametrically in terms of the function T, that is, in terms of the weights associated to the edges of the graph $\mathcal{G}_r$, a search in the space of the policies amounts to a search in the space of the possible weights of the graph $\mathcal{G}_r$ itself. From a conceptual point of view, the function T is to be related to Hamilton's *principal function* of the calculus of variations, and to the *cost-to-go* and *value function* of dynamic programming and reinforcement learning. More precisely, the function T can be closely related to the function that in the reinforcement learning literature is known as "*state*-action value function," and that is customarily denoted by the letter Q. In fact, $T(\langle z_t, z_{t+1} \rangle)$ determines, as to Equation A.7, the probability of selecting the action "go to *phantasma* z_{t+1}" when the current *phantasma* is z_t. It therefore associates to the *phantasma*-action pair, a number which represents the *desirability* of performing such an action in the given *phantasma*. In this respect, it is clear the similarity with the role of the function Q in reinforcement learning.[10] The value of $T(\langle z_t, z_{t+1} \rangle)$ is generally given as a *statistic* of the observed cost of paths containing the transition $\langle z_t, z_{t+1} \rangle$. It therefore brings information on the quality of the solution that can be obtained by "going to z_{t+1}" when in z_t.

[10] An important difference is precisely that the function Q supposes a direct knowledge of the state, while T refers to the *phantasma*. In reinforcement learning, the situation in which more states are not perceived as distinct is termed *perceptual aliasing* (Whitehead & Ballard, 1991).

Also in this respect, it can be stated a parallel with the function Q which indeed informs on the long-term cost of a given action, provided that future actions are selected optimally. In *ant programming*, as generally in reinforcement learning, the search in the space of the policies is performed through some form of *generalized policy iteration* (Sutton & Barto, 1998). Starting from some arbitrary initial policy, *ant programming* iteratively generates a number of paths in order to *evaluate* the current policy and then *improves* it on the basis of the result of the evaluation. At each iteration, therefore, a *cohort* of *ants* is considered, each generating a solution through a *forward* phase. Once the solution is completed, each *ant* traces back its path proposing at each visited *phantasma* an update of the local values of the function T on the basis of the costs experienced in the forward movement. This phase is denoted in the terminology of *ant programming* as the *backward* phase of the given *ant*. The actual new value of T is obtained by some combination of the values proposed by the *ants* of the *cohort*. This phase is denoted as the *merge* phase.

Let us now see in detail the *backward* phase for a given single *ant*. Let us consider a complete path $x = \langle x_0, x_1, \ldots, x_\tau \rangle$ over the graph $\mathcal{G}$. If $z = \langle z_0, z_1, \ldots, z_\tau \rangle$ is the complete forward path as seen under r, and $c = \langle c_1, \ldots, c_\tau \rangle$ is the experienced sequence of costs, then the single step of the *backward* phase is:

$$\begin{aligned} z_t &= \mathcal{B}(z_{t+1}, z), \\ T'(\langle z_t, z_{t+1} \rangle) &= \nu(c, T), \end{aligned} \tag{A.9}$$

where the operator $\mathcal{B}$ indicates a single step backward on $\mathcal{G}_r$, along the forward trajectory z. The operator ν is the key element of the *backward* phase. It has the role of proposing a new value for the weight associated to each visited edge $\langle z_t, z_{t+1} \rangle$, on the basis of the sequence of costs experimented during the *forward* phase, and of the current values of the function T. Hence, in our pictorial description of *ant programming*, this phase is pictured through an *ant* that "traces back" its forward path and leaves on such a path some information. From a logical point of view, the different strategies for propagating the information gathered along a path are to be related to the different *update* strategies in reinforcement learning. In particular, to propose values of T' only for the visited transitions and on the basis of the cost of the associated solution, is equivalent to what in reinforcement learning is called *Monte Carlo update* (Sutton & Barto, 1998). On the other hand, it is equivalent to a *Q-learning update* (Watkins, 1989) to propose a value of T' for a visited transition on the basis of the experienced cost for the transition itself and of the minimum of the current values that T assumes on the edges departing from the node to which the considered transition leads. The details of the definition of the *backward* phase, and in particular of the operator ν are not given as part of the description of *ant programming* and are left uninstantiated.

The merge phase. In the same spirit, we leave here undefined in its details also the *merge* phase which combines the different functions T' proposed by the individual *ants* of the same *cohort*. At this level of our description it will be sufficient to note that, for every transition $\langle z_t, z_{t+1}\rangle \in U_r$, the actual new value of $T(\langle z_t, z_{t+1}\rangle)$ will be some linear or nonlinear function of the current value of $T(\langle z_t, z_{t+1}\rangle)$, and of the different $T'_j(\langle z_t, z_{t+1}\rangle)$, where j is the index ranging over the *ants* of the *cohort*. The *merge* phase will be therefore characterized by the operator σ:

$$T(\langle z_t, z_{t+1}\rangle) = \sigma\big(T(\langle z_t, z_{t+1}\rangle), T'_1(\langle z_t, z_{t+1}\rangle), T'_2(\langle z_t, z_{t+1}\rangle), \ldots\big). \tag{A.10}$$

Different possible instances of the operators ν and σ will be discussed in a future work.

The algorithm and the metaphor

The abstract definition of *ant programming* was given in previous sections in terms of the operators π, ν, and σ. In order to define an instance of the *ant programming* class, such operators need to be instantiated. Together with the operators π, ν, and σ, the other key element in the definition of an instance of the class, is the generating function r that defines the relation between the state graph $\mathcal{G}$ and the representation $\mathcal{G}_r$. We will therefore denote an instance of *ant programming* with the 4-tuple $\mathcal{I} = \langle r, \pi, \nu, \sigma\rangle$. Indeed, other elements are to be instantiated as, for example, the number of ants composing a *cohort* and the way of initializing the function T. Anyway, such elements are either less relevant, or are to be defined as a more or less direct consequence of the definition of $\mathcal{I}$.

In particular, the 4-tuple $\mathcal{I}$ gives an operative definition of the function T. As seen in the previous sections, the generating function r, together with the graph $\mathcal{G}$, gives the topology of the graph $\mathcal{G}_r$ and determines therefore the domain of the function T. The operator π defines how the values of T are used in the decision process, while the operators ν and σ define how the function T is to be modified on the basis of the quality of the solutions obtained. According to the pictorial description of *ant programming*, the function T is called *pheromone trail* and defines the policy π followed by the *ant* during the forward walk. Once a solution s is completed, the *ant* traces back its forward path and *deposits its pheromone* to update the function T. The role of the *pheromone trails* T is therefore to make available the information gathered on a particular path by one *ant* belonging to one given *cohort*, to other *ants* of a future *cohort*; it is therefore a form of *inter-cohort* communication mediated by the graph $\mathcal{G}_r$. From the terminology adopted in the studies on social insects (Grassé, 1959), it is customary to refer to such indirect communication with the term *stigmergy* (Dorigo *et al.*, 2000).

At this point, having defined the 4-tuple $\mathcal{I}$, we have completed the definition of the elements that are necessary to handle the complexity of the combinatorial problem given in Equation A.3 in the spirit of the solution strategy originally suggested by *ant colony optimization*.

A.1.4 Discussion

Further research is needed on *ant programming*, In particular, it is of paramount importance to gain a full understanding of the impact of the choice of r, the *generating function of the representation*, on the resulting algorithms. Such a function associates a *phantasma* to the current state and therefore can be informally thought of as the "lens" under which the process of incremental construction of a solution is seen. In this sense, "the *ant* never thinks without a *phantasma*" and, as far as the decision process is concerned, this is to be understood as "the *ant* takes decisions on the basis of the *phantasma*." The generating function determines therefore the information on the basis of which decisions will be taken. At the extreme, the generating function might be a one-to-one mapping. In this case, only one state is associated to a *phantasma*, and *vice versa*. As a consequence, the state graph $\mathcal{G}$ and the representation graph $\mathcal{G}_r$ have the same topological structure and, therefore, the representation enjoys the Markov property. Accordingly, we refer to this extreme instance of the *ant programming* class with the name of *Markov ants*. *Markov ants* face directly the exponential explosion of the number of edges of the graph $\mathcal{G}$. Nevertheless, since r is a one-to-one mapping, no two states are *aliased* in the representation. As a consequence, the policy that according to Equation A.7, selects the action on the basis of the current *phantasma*, indeed implicitly bases the choice on the actual underlying state. From this fact, different appealing properties follow. It can be shown, for instance, that an optimal policy exists, and that it is deterministic. The performance of *Markov ants* can be improved if the pheromone trails T and the operator ν are designed in such a way that the Markov property of the representation is fully exploited. This can be done by defining T as a costs-to-go function, and by allowing the operator ν to *bootstrap* (Sutton & Barto, 1998). In this way *Markov ants* would reduce to an algorithm of the *temporal difference* class (Sutton & Barto, 1998). Anyway, *Markov ants* are not meant to be implemented. The focus of *ant programming* is indeed on problems whose Markov representation is computationally intractable and, in such situations, *Markov ants* are ruled out by their very own nature. Still, *Markov ants* remain of great theoretical interest.

Another class of instances of *ant programming* is of much greater practical interest. These instances are characterized by the function r_{aco}, as in Note 7, that associates a *phantasma* with one and only one of the possible solution components. The function r_{aco} generates the representation used in almost all the implementations of *ant colony optimization* since the first "template" instance developed by Marco Dorigo and colleagues (Dorigo *et al.*, 1991; Dorigo, 1992) back in 1991. Accordingly, we call *Marco's ants* the instances of this class. Thanks to the concepts introduced with the definition of *ant programming*, it becomes apparent that the representation graph generated by r_{aco} is much more compact than the state graph. In order to compensate this drastic loss of information, most of the instances of *ant colony optimization* adopt some additional device both to guarantee the feasibility and to improve the quality of the solutions being built. As far as feasibility is concerned, all instances of *ant colony optimization* use an implicit description of the state graph usually in the form of a list of components already included into the solution under construction. As far as quality is concerned, two major approaches have been followed. In the first approach, some additional *a priori* knowledge about the problem at hand, has been combined to the estimate of the function T for the definition of the decision policy. In the second approach, local optimization procedures, *ad hoc* tailored on the problem at hand, have been used in order to improve the quality of the solutions generated by the *ants*. Some of the resulting implementations have been shown to be comparable to or better than state-of-the-art techniques on several NP-hard problems. Moreover, under "reasonable" assumptions on the characteristics of the other components of the algorithm, *ant colony optimization* has been proved to asymptotically converge in probability to the optimal solution (Gutjahr, 2000; Stützle & Dorigo, 2002).

Ongoing research (Darquennes, 2005) is focusing on the possibility of designing other instances of *ant programming* that, on the one hand, keep an eye on the practical implementation, as *Marco's ants* do, and that, on the other, try to preserve as much as possible the properties of a state-space representation, going therefore in the direction of *Markov ants*.

A.2 Model-based search‡

The necessity to solve *NP*-hard optimization problems, for which the existence of efficient exact algorithms is highly unlikely, has led to a wide range of heuristic algorithms that implement some sort of search in the solution space. These heuristic algorithms can be classified, similarly to what is done in the machine learning field (Quinlan, 1993a), as being either *instance-based* or *model-based*. Most of the classical search methods may be considered instance-based, since they generate new candidate solutions using solely the current solution or the current "population" of solutions. Typical representatives of this class are genetic algorithms (Holland, 1975) or local search and its variants, such as, for example, *simulated annealing* and iterated local search (Aarts & Lenstra, 1997). On the other hand, in the last decade several new methods, which may be classified as *model-based search* algorithms, have been proposed. In model-based search algorithms, candidate solutions are generated using a parameterized probabilistic

‡This section is based on Zlochin, Birattari, Meuleau & Dorigo (2004).

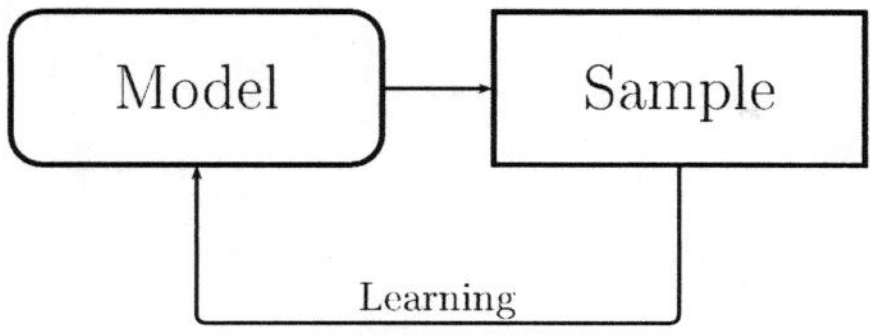

Figure A.1: Schematic description of the model-based search approach.

model that is updated using the previously seen solutions in such a way that the search will concentrate in the regions containing high quality solutions. In order to avoid any terminological confusion, we would like to emphasize that the term "model" is used here to denote an adaptive stochastic mechanism for generating candidate solutions, and not an approximate description of the environment, as done, for example, in reinforcement learning (Sutton & Barto, 1998).[11] The general approach is described schematically in Figure A.1. Some of the early works exploiting the model-based approach, such as ***ant colony optimization*** (Dorigo, 1992; Dorigo *et al.*, 1996; Dorigo & Di Caro, 1999; Dorigo & Stützle, 2004) and ***population-based incremental learning*** (Baluja & Caruana, 1995), do not provide an explicit description of the model-based idea. The first explicit description of a solution process consisting in a series of suitably updated probability distributions on the solution space was given by De Bonet *et al.* (1997). More recently, on the basis of concepts borrowed from the stochastic simulation field and, in particular, from rare events estimation, Rubinstein (1999a) re-proposed the ideas of De Bonet *et al.* and provided an extensive analysis of many details (de Boer *et al.*, 2005).

While the behavior of classical instance-based search methods has been thoroughly investigated and is relatively well understood, the model-based search field is still little more than a collection of independently developed heuristic techniques, without solid theoretical foundations. The goal of this research is to provide a unifying framework that accommodates all these seemingly unrelated methods and to analyze their similarities as well as their distinctive features. The analysis of these methods within a common framework allows to discriminate between the essential elements of the algorithm and those that appear only for historical reasons.

A well-established approach that belongs to the model-based search framework is the ***ant colony optimization*** metaheuristic (Dorigo, 1992; Dorigo *et al.*,

[11]There is, however, a rather close connection between these two usages of the term "model", as the model adaptation in combinatorial optimization may be considered as an attempt to model (in the reinforcement learning sense) the structure of the "promising" solutions.

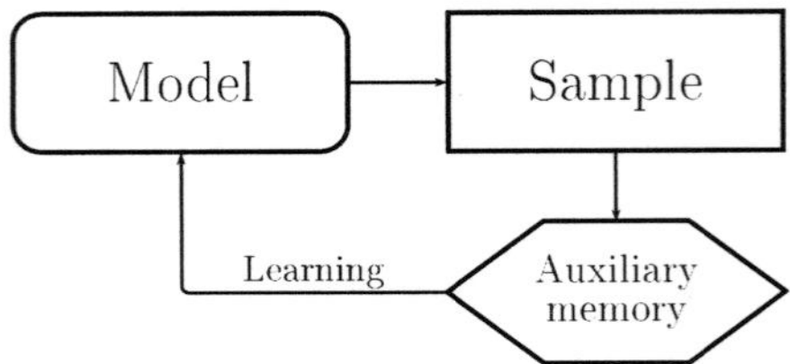

Figure A.2: The model-based search with auxiliary memory.

1996; Dorigo & Di Caro, 1999; Dorigo & Stützle, 2004). The distinctive feature of *ant colony optimization* is a particular type of probabilistic model, in which a structure called *construction graph* is coupled with a set of stochastic procedures called *artificial ants*. *Ants* have a two-fold function—they both generate solutions and update the model's parameters. Various model update rules have been proposed within the *ant colony optimization* framework, but they are all of a somewhat heuristic nature and are lacking a theoretical justification.

On the other hand, the *stochastic gradient ascent* (Robbins & Monro, 1951; Bertsekas, 1995b) and the *cross-entropy* (Rubinstein, 1999a) methods provide a systematic way for the derivation of model update rules in the model-based search framework, without being restricted to a particular type of probabilistic model. As we show in the following, both the stochastic gradient ascent and the cross-entropy methods can be cast into the *ant colony optimization* framework, and, in fact, in some cases the cross-entropy method leads to the same update rule as does stochastic gradient ascent. Moreover, quite unexpectedly, some existing *ant colony optimization* updates are re-derived as a particular implementation of the cross-entropy method.

It should be noted that Figure A.1 describes the model-based search approach in its "pure" form, where the model update is based solely on the current solutions' sample. However, many model-based search algorithms update the model using not only the current sample, but also some additional information gathered during the search and stored in the auxiliary memory, as described in Figure A.2. In particular, a recently developed class of evolutionary algorithms called *estimation of distribution algorithms* (Pelikan *et al.*, 1999; Larrañaga & Lozano, 2001) may be considered a particular realization of model-based search with an auxiliary memory that stores high-quality solutions encountered during the search. Not only all these algorithms belong to the model-based search approach, but many of them are actually closely related to the *ant colony optimization* and cross-entropy frameworks, as we show in the following.

The remaining of the section is structured as follows. In Section A.2.1 we describe model-based search in general terms and present stochastic gradient ascent and cross-entropy as particular realizations of the model-based search approach. The relationship between the two methods is also discussed in that section.

Section A.2.2 presents the ***ant colony optimization*** metaheuristic and discusses the implementation of the cross-entropy and the stochastic gradient ascent methods using the ***ant colony optimization***-type construction mechanism as a model.

In Section A.2.3 the ***estimation of distribution algorithms*** are presented as a particular realization of model-based search with auxiliary memory. An overview of existing ***estimation of distribution algorithms*** is given and their relations to the ***ant colony optimization*** framework and the cross-entropy method are discussed.

Section A.2.4 draws some conclusions and outlines several interesting future research directions.

A.2.1 The model-based search framework

Let us consider a minimization problem[12] (S, f), where S is the *set of feasible solutions*, f is the *objective function*, which assigns to each solution $s \in S$ a cost value $f(s)$. The goal of the minimization problem is to find an optimal solution $\bar{s}$, that is, a feasible solution of minimum cost. The set of all optimal solutions is denoted by $\bar{S}$.

At a very general level, the model-based search approach attempts to solve this minimization problem by repeating the following two steps:

- Candidate solutions are constructed using some parameterized probabilistic model, that is, a parameterized probability distributions defined over the solution space.
- The candidate solutions are used to modify the model[13] in a way that is deemed to bias future sampling toward low cost solutions.

As it has been already mentioned, one may also use an auxiliary memory, in which some important information collected during the search is stored. The memory, which may store, for example, information on the distribution of the cost values or a collection of high-quality solutions, can be later used for the model update. Moreover, in some cases we may wish to build a new model at every iteration, rather than to iteratively update the same one.

For any algorithm belonging to this general scheme, two components, corresponding to the two steps above, need to be instantiated:

- A probabilistic model allowing an efficient generation of candidate solutions.
- An update rule for the model's parameters and/or structure.

[12]The obvious changes must be done if a maximization problem is considered.

[13]The structure of the model may be fixed in advance, with solely its parameters being updated, or alternatively, the structure of the model may be allowed to change as well.

In the remainder of this section we discuss two systematic approaches within the model-based search framework, namely the stochastic gradient ascent method and the cross-entropy method, which might be used in order to define the second component, that is, the update rule for the model. We show that, although having a completely different motivation, the two approaches are closely related. In fact, we show that a particular version of the cross-entropy method produces the same updates as the stochastic gradient ascent method does.

Throughout the remainder of this section we assume that a space $\mathcal{M}$ of possible probabilistic models is given and that it is expressive enough. Specifically, we need to assume that for every possible solution s, the distribution δ_s (defined as $\delta_s(s') = 1$, if $s' = s$, and $\delta_s(s') = 0$ otherwise) belongs to $\mathcal{M}$. This condition may actually be relaxed by assuming instead that δ_s is in the closure of $\mathcal{M}$, that is, that there exists a sequence $P_l \in \mathcal{M}$ for which $\lim_{l \to \infty} P_l = \delta_s$. This "expressiveness" assumption is needed in order to insure that the sampling can concentrate in the proximity of any solution, the optimal solution in particular.

The stochastic gradient ascent method

Let us assume that the model structure is fixed, and the model space, $\mathcal{M}$, is smoothly parameterized by $\mathcal{T} \in \Phi \subset \mathbb{R}^m$, where Φ is an m-dimensional parameter space. In other words, $\mathcal{M} = \{P_\mathcal{T} | \mathcal{T} \in \Phi\}$ and for any $s \in S$ the function $P_\mathcal{T}(s)$ is smooth[14] with respect to $\mathcal{T}$.

The original optimization problem may be replaced with the following equivalent continuous *maximization problem*:

$$\bar{\mathcal{T}} = \arg\max_{\mathcal{T}} \mathcal{E}(\mathcal{T}), \tag{A.11}$$

where $\mathcal{E}(\mathcal{T}) = E_\mathcal{T} Q_f(s)$, $E_\mathcal{T}$ denotes expectation with respect to $P_\mathcal{T}$, and $Q_f(s)$ is a fixed *quality function*, which is strictly decreasing with respect to f, that is, $Q_f(s_1) < Q_f(s_2) \Leftrightarrow f(s_1) > f(s_2)$.

It may be easily verified that, under the "expressiveness" assumption we made about the model space, the support of $P_{\bar{\mathcal{T}}}$ (that is, the set $\{s | P_{\bar{\mathcal{T}}}(s) > 0\}$) is necessarily contained in $\bar{S}$. This implies that solving problem (A.11) is equivalent to solving the original combinatorial optimization problem.

One may then search for an optimum (possibly a local one) of the problem given in Equation A.11 using a gradient ascent method—in other words, gradient ascent may be used as a heuristic to change $\mathcal{T}$ with the goal of solving A.11:

- Start from some initial guess $\mathcal{T}^0$.
- At stage t, calculate the gradient $\nabla\mathcal{E}(\mathcal{T}^t)$ and update $\mathcal{T}^{t+1}$ to be $\mathcal{T}^t + \alpha_t \nabla\mathcal{E}(\mathcal{T}^t)$, where α_t is a step-size parameter.

[14]Technically, the smoothness assumption means that the function is continuously differentiable.

The gradient can be calculated, bearing in mind that $\nabla \ln f = \frac{\nabla f}{f}$, as follows:

$$\begin{aligned}\nabla \mathcal{E} &= \nabla E_{\mathcal{T}} Q_f(s) = \nabla \sum_s Q_f(s) P_{\mathcal{T}}(s) = \sum_s Q_f(s) \nabla P_{\mathcal{T}}(s) \\ &= \sum_s P_{\mathcal{T}}(s) Q_f(s) \frac{\nabla P_{\mathcal{T}}(s)}{P_{\mathcal{T}}(s)} = \sum_s P_{\mathcal{T}}(s) Q_f(s) \nabla \ln P_{\mathcal{T}}(s) \\ &= E_{\mathcal{T}} Q_f(s) \nabla \ln P_{\mathcal{T}}(s). \end{aligned} \tag{A.12}$$

However, the gradient ascent algorithm cannot be implemented in practice, as for its evaluation a summation over the whole search space is needed. A more practical alternative would be to use stochastic gradient ascent (Robbins & Monro, 1951; Bertsekas, 1995b), which replaces the expectation in Equation A.12 by an empirical mean of a sample generated from $P_{\mathcal{T}}$.

The update rule for the stochastic gradient is:

$$\mathcal{T}^{t+1} = \mathcal{T}^t + \alpha_t \sum_{s \in S_t} Q_f(s) \nabla \ln P_{\mathcal{T}^t}(s), \tag{A.13}$$

where S_t is the sample at iteration t.

In order to derive a practical algorithm from the stochastic gradient ascent approach, we need a model for which the derivatives of $\ln P_{\mathcal{T}}$ can be calculated efficiently. In Section A.2.2 we show how this can be done in the context of the iterative construction scheme used in the *ant colony optimization* metaheuristic.

The cross-entropy method

The basic ideas behind the cross-entropy method for combinatorial optimization can be already found in De Bonet *et al.* (1997). However, the full development of the method was given in the works of Rubinstein and co-workers, who have initially proposed this method as a tool for rare events estimation in stochastic simulation (Rubinstein, 1999b; Lieber, 1999) and have later adapted it to the field of combinatorial optimization (Rubinstein, 1999a, 2001). In this overview we focus on the central idea of cross-entropy and we propose a presentation of the main concepts without reference to rare events estimation. This presentation should appear more straightforward to the operations research community.[15]

Starting from some initial distribution $P_0 \in \mathcal{M}$, the cross-entropy method inductively builds a series of distributions $P_t \in \mathcal{M}$, in an attempt to increase the probability of generating low-cost solutions after each iteration. A tentative way to achieve this goal is to set P_{t+1} equal to

$$\hat{P} \propto P_t Q_f, \tag{A.14}$$

[15]For the treatment of further details, we refer the interested reader to the original works of Rubinstein (1999a).

where Q_f is, again, some quality function, depending on the cost value.

If this were possible, then, for time independent quality functions,[16] after n iteration we would obtain $P_n \propto P_0(Q_f)^n$. Consequently, as $n \to \infty$, P_n would converge to a probability distribution restricted to $\bar{S}$. Unfortunately, even if the distribution P_t belongs to the family $\mathcal{M}$, the distribution $\hat{P}$ as defined by Equation A.14 does not necessarily remain in $\mathcal{M}$,[17] hence some sort of projection is needed.

Accordingly, a natural candidate for P_{t+1} is the distribution $P \in \mathcal{M}$ that minimizes the *Kullback-Leibler divergence* (Kullback, 1959), which is a commonly used measure of misfit between two distributions:

$$D(\hat{P}\|P) = \sum_s \hat{P}(s) \ln \frac{\hat{P}(s)}{P(s)},$$

or equivalently the cross-entropy:

$$-\sum_s \hat{P}(s) \ln P(s).$$

Since $\hat{P} \propto P_t Q_f$, the cross-entropy minimization is equivalent to the following maximization problem:

$$P_{t+1} = \arg\max_{P \in \mathcal{M}} \sum_s P_t(s) Q_f(s) \ln P(s). \tag{A.15}$$

It should be noted that in the cross-entropy method, differently from what done by stochastic gradient ascent, the quality function is only required to be non-increasing with respect to the cost and may also be time-dependent, either deterministically or stochastically. For example, it might depend on the points sampled so far. One common choice is $Q_f^t(s) = I(f(s) < f_t)$, where I is an indicator function, and f_t is, for example, some quantile (for example, lower 10%) of the cost distribution during the last iteration.[18] Another quality function considered in Rubinstein (1999a) is a Boltzmann function $Q_f(s) = \exp(-f(s)/\gamma)$, where γ is changed adaptively based on the sample.

Similarly to the gradient ascent algorithm, the maximization problem given in Equation A.15 cannot be solved in practice, as the evaluation of the function $\sum_s P_t(s) Q_f(s) \ln P(s)$ requires summation over the whole solution space, and once again a finite sample approximation is used instead:

$$P_{t+1} = \arg\max_{P \in \mathcal{M}} \sum_{s \in S_t} Q_f(s) \ln P(s), \tag{A.16}$$

[16] Similar result can be shown for many time-dependent quality functions.

[17] As a simple example, consider the case where $\mathcal{M}$ contains all distributions over the binary variables x, y such that x and y are independent, and the quality function is $Q(x, y) = 2$, if $x = y = 0$, and 1 otherwise. If, for example, P_0 is the uniform distribution (hence in $\mathcal{M}$), then $\hat{P}(x, y) = \frac{2}{5}$, if $x = y = 0$, and $\frac{1}{5}$ otherwise, and it can be easily verified that $\hat{P}_1$ is not in $\mathcal{M}$.

[18] This kind of quality function was also used in De Bonet *et al.* (1997).

where S_t is a sample from P_t.

Note that if the quality function is of the form $I(f(s) < c)$, then Equation A.16 defines a *maximum-likelihood* model, with the sample used for estimation being restricted to the top-quality solutions. With other quality functions, Equation A.16 may be interpreted as defining a weighted maximum-likelihood estimate.

In some relatively simple cases, some of which are discussed in Sections A.2.2 and A.2.3, the problem given in Equation A.16 can be solved exactly. In general, however, the analytical solution is unavailable. Still, even if the exact solution is not known, some iterative methods for solving this optimization problem may be used.

A natural candidate for the iterative solution of the maximization problem given in Equation A.16, is gradient ascent:

- Start with $\mathcal{T}' = \mathcal{T}^t$. Other starting points are possible, but this is the most natural one, since we may expect $\mathcal{T}^{t+1}$ to be close to $\mathcal{T}^t$.
- Repeat:

  $\mathcal{T}' \leftarrow \mathcal{T}' + \alpha \sum_{s \in S_t} Q_f(s) \nabla \ln P_{\mathcal{T}'}(s)$,

  where α is a step-size parameter

  Until some stopping criterion is satisfied.
- Set $\mathcal{T}^{t+1} = \mathcal{T}'$.

It should be noted that, since the new vector $\mathcal{T}^{t+1}$ is a random variable, depending on a sample, there is no use in running the gradient ascent process till full convergence. Instead, in order to obtain some robustness against sampling noise, we may use a fixed number of gradient ascent updates. One particular choice, which is of special interest, is the use of a single gradient ascent update, leading to the updating rule:

$$\mathcal{T}^{t+1} = \mathcal{T}^t + \alpha_t \sum_{s \in S_t} Q_f(s) \nabla \ln P_{\mathcal{T}^t}(s), \tag{A.17}$$

which is identical to the stochastic gradient ascent update given in Equation A.13. However, as it was already mentioned earlier, the cross-entropy method imposes less restrictions on the quality function (for example, allowing it to change over time), hence the resulting algorithm may be seen as a generalization of stochastic gradient ascent.

As with stochastic gradient ascent, in order to have an efficient algorithm, a model is needed for which the calculation of the derivatives can be carried out in reasonable time. In the next section, we show that this is indeed possible for the models typically used in *ant colony optimization*.

A.2.2 *Ant colony optimization*

So far, we have limited our discussion to the generic approaches for updating the model. However, this is only one out of the two components needed in any model-based search algorithm. In order to complete the description of a model-based search algorithm, a probabilistic model needs to be specified.

In this section we describe the *ant colony optimization* metaheuristic (Dorigo, 1992; Dorigo *et al.*, 1996; Dorigo & Di Caro, 1999; Dorigo & Stützle, 2004) that employs a particular type of probabilistic model in which a structure called *construction graph* is coupled with a set of stochastic procedures called *artificial ants*. The artificial ants build solutions in an iterative manner using local information stored in the construction graph.[19] After describing the probabilistic model, we present several updates that were suggested in the past within the *ant colony optimization* framework as well as the ones derived from the stochastic gradient ascent algorithm and the cross-entropy method.

Ant colony optimization—The probabilistic model

We assume that the combinatorial optimization problem (S, f) is mapped on a problem that can be characterized by the following list of items:[20]

- A finite set $\mathcal{C} = \{c_1, c_2, \ldots, c_{N_\mathcal{C}}\}$ of *components*.
- A finite set $\mathcal{X}$ of *states* of the problem, defined in terms of all the possible sequences $x = \langle c_i, c_j, \ldots, c_k, \ldots \rangle$ over the elements of $\mathcal{C}$. The length of a sequence x, that is, the number of components in the sequence, is expressed by $|x|$. The maximum length of a sequence is bounded by a positive constant $n < +\infty$.
- The set of (candidate) solutions S is a subset of $\mathcal{X}$, that is, $S \subseteq \mathcal{X}$.
- A set of feasible states $\tilde{\mathcal{X}}$, with $\tilde{\mathcal{X}} \subseteq \mathcal{X}$, defined via a set of *constraints* Ω.
- A non-empty set $\bar{S}$ of optimal solutions, with $\bar{S} \subseteq \tilde{\mathcal{X}}$ and $\bar{S} \subseteq S$.

Given the above formulation, *ants* build candidate solutions by performing randomized walks on the completely connected, weighted graph $\mathcal{G} = (\mathcal{C}, \mathcal{L}, \mathcal{T})$, where the vertices are the components $\mathcal{C}$, the set $\mathcal{L}$ fully connects the components $\mathcal{C}$,

[19] It should be noted that the same type of model was later (although independently) used in the cross-entropy framework under the name *associated stochastic network* (Rubinstein, 1999a, 2001).

[20] How this mapping can be done in practice has been described in a number of earlier works on the *ant colony optimization* metaheuristic. See, for example, Dorigo & Di Caro (1999), Dorigo *et al.* (1999), or Dorigo & Stützle (2004).

and $\mathcal{T}$ is a vector gathering so-called *pheromone trails* τ.[21] The graph $\mathcal{G}$ is called *construction graph*.

Each *ant* is put on a randomly chosen vertex of the graph and then it performs a randomized walk by moving at each step from vertex to vertex in the graph in such a way that the next vertex is chosen stochastically according to the strength of the pheromone currently on the arcs. While moving from one node to another of the graph $\mathcal{G}$, constraints Ω may be used to prevent ants from building infeasible solutions. Formally, the solution construction behavior of a generic ant can be described as follows:

`ant_solution_construction`

- for each ant:
  - select a start node c_1 according to some problem dependent criterion,
  - set $k = 1$ and $x_k = \langle c_1 \rangle$.
- While $x_k = \langle c_1, c_2, \ldots, c_k \rangle \in \tilde{\mathcal{X}}$ and $x_k \notin S$ and $J_{x_k} \neq \emptyset$ do:
  at each step k, after building the sequence x_k, select the next node (component) c_{k+1} randomly following

$$P_{\mathcal{T}}(c_{k+1} = c | x_k) = \begin{cases} \dfrac{F_{(c_k,c)}\Big(\tau(c_k, c)\Big)}{\sum\limits_{(c_k,y)\in J_{x_k}} F_{(c_k,y)}\Big(\tau(c_k, y)\Big)} & \text{if } (c_k, c) \in J_{x_k}, \\ 0 & \text{otherwise;} \end{cases} \tag{A.18}$$

where a connection (c_k, y) belongs to J_{x_k} if and only if the sequence $x_{k+1} = \langle c_1, \ldots, c_k, y \rangle$ satisfies the constraints Ω (that is, if $x_{k+1} \in \tilde{\mathcal{X}}$) and $F_{(l,j)}(z)$ is some monotonic function—most commonly, $z^\alpha \eta(l, j)^\beta$, where $\alpha, \beta > 0$ and η are heuristic "visibility" values (Dorigo *et al.*, 1996). If at some stage $x_k \notin S$ and $J_{x_k} = \emptyset$, that is, the construction process has reached a dead-end, the current state x_k is discarded.[22]

For certain problems, one may find useful to use a more general scheme, where F depends on the pheromone values of several "related" connections, rather than just a single one. Moreover, instead of the *random-proportional rule* above, different selection schemes, such as the *pseudo-random-proportional rule* (Dorigo & Gambardella, 1997), may be considered.

[21] Pheromone trails can be associated to components, connections, or both. In the following, unless stated otherwise, we assume that the pheromone trails are associated to connections, so that $\tau(l, j)$ is the pheromone associated to the connection between components l and j. It is straightforward to extend the algorithms to the other cases.

[22] This situation may be prevented by allowing *ants* to build infeasible solutions as well. In such a case an infeasibility penalty term is usually added to the cost function. However, it should be noted that in most settings *ant colony optimization* was applied to, the dead-end situation does not occur.

The probabilistic rule given in Equation A.18, together with the underlying construction graph, implicitly defines a first component of the model-based search algorithm—the probabilistic model. Having chosen the probabilistic model, the next step is to choose the parameter update mechanism. In the following, we describe several updates that were suggested in the past within the *ant colony optimization* framework as well as the ones derived from the stochastic gradient ascent algorithm and the cross-entropy method.

Ant colony optimization–The pheromone updates

Many different schemes for pheromone update have been proposed within the *ant colony optimization* framework. For an extensive overview, see Dorigo & Di Caro (1999), Dorigo & Stützle (2002), and Dorigo & Stützle (2004). Most pheromone updates can be described using the following generic scheme:

`Generic_AntColonyOptimization_Update`

- $\forall s \in \hat{S}_t, \forall (l,j) \in s: \ \tau(l,j) \leftarrow \tau(l,j) + Q_f(s|S_1,\ldots,S_t)$
- $\forall (l,j): \ \tau(l,j) \leftarrow (1-\rho)\cdot\tau(l,j)$, where S_l is the sample in the l-th iteration, ρ, $0 \leq \rho < 1$, is the evaporation rate, and $Q_f(s|S_1,\ldots,S_t)$ is some "quality function", which is typically required to be non-increasing with respect to f and is defined over the "reference set" $\hat{S}_t$.

Different *ant colony optimization* algorithms may use different quality functions and reference sets. For example, in the very first *ant colony optimization* algorithm, *Ant System* (Dorigo *et al.*, 1991, 1996), the quality function was simply $1/f(s)$ and the reference set $\hat{S}_t = S_t$. In a more recently proposed scheme, called *iteration best update* (Dorigo & Gambardella, 1997), the reference set was a singleton containing the best solution within S_t—if there were several iteration-best solutions, one of them was chosen randomly. For the *global-best update* (Stützle & Hoos, 1997; Dorigo & Gambardella, 1997), the reference set contained the best among all the iteration-best solutions—and if there were more than one global-best solution, the earliest one was chosen.

In Dorigo *et al.* (1996) an *elitist* strategy was introduced, in which the update was a combination of the previous two.

In case a good lower bound on the optimal solution cost is available, one may use the following quality function (Maniezzo, 1999):

$$Q_f(s|S_1,\ldots,S_t) = \tau_0\left(1 - \frac{f(s)-LB}{\bar{f}-LB}\right) = \tau_0\,\frac{\bar{f}-f(s)}{\bar{f}-LB},$$

where $\bar{f}$ is the average of the costs of the last k solutions and LB is the lower bound on the optimal solution cost. With this quality function, the solutions are evaluated by comparing their cost to the average cost of the other recent solutions, rather than by using the absolute cost values. In addition, the quality function is automatically scaled based on the proximity of the average cost to the lower bound.

A pheromone update, which slightly differs from the generic update described above, was used in *ant colony system* (Dorigo & Gambardella, 1997). There the pheromones are evaporated by the ants online during the solution construction, hence only the pheromones involved in the construction evaporate.

Two additional modifications of the generic update were described in the literature. In the first, *$\mathcal{MAX}$–$\mathcal{MIN}$ Ant System* (Stützle & Hoos, 1997), maximum and minimum pheromone trail limits were introduced. With this modification, the probability to generate any particular solution is kept above some positive threshold, which helps preventing search stagnation and premature convergence to suboptimal solutions.

The second modification, proposed under the name ***hyper-cube ant colony optimization*** (Blum *et al.*, 2001; Blum, 2004) in the context of combinatorial problems with binary coded solutions, is to normalize the quality function, hence obtaining an automatic scaling of the pheromone values:

$$\tau_l \leftarrow (1-\rho)\tau_l + \rho \frac{\sum_{s\in S_t} Q_f(s)s_l}{\sum_{s\in S_t} Q_f(s)}.$$

While all the updates described above are of a somewhat heuristic nature, the stochastic gradient ascent and the cross-entropy methods allow to derive parameters update rules in a more systematic manner, as we show in the next two subsections.

The stochastic gradient ascent update

In Section A.2.1 an update rule for the stochastic gradient was derived:

$$\mathcal{T}^{t+1} = \mathcal{T}^t + \alpha_t \sum_{s\in S_t} Q_f(s)\nabla \ln P_{\mathcal{T}^t}(s),$$

where S_t is the sample at stage t.

As shown in Meuleau & Dorigo (2002), in case the distribution is implicitly defined by an *ant colony optimization*-type construction process, parameterized by the vector of the pheromone values, $\mathcal{T}$, the gradient $\nabla \ln P_{\mathcal{T}}(s)$ can be efficiently calculated. The following calculation is a generalization of the one in Meuleau & Dorigo (2002).

From the definition of `ant_solution_construction`, it follows that, for $s = \langle c_1, c_2, \ldots\rangle$,

$$P_{\mathcal{T}}(s) = \prod_{k=1}^{|s|-1} P_{\mathcal{T}}\Big(c_{k+1}\Big|\mathrm{pref}_k(s)\Big),$$

where $\mathrm{pref}_k(s)$ is the k-prefix of s, and consequently

$$\nabla \ln P_{\mathcal{T}}(s) = \sum_{k=1}^{|s|-1} \nabla \ln P_{\mathcal{T}}\Big(c_{k+1}\Big|\mathrm{pref}_k(s)\Big).$$

Finally, given a pair of components $(l, j) \in \mathcal{C}^2$, using Equation A.18 and assuming differentiability of F, it is easy to verify that:

- If $l = c_k$ and $j = c_{k+1}$ then

$$\frac{\partial}{\partial\tau(l,j)}\Big\{\ln P_{\mathcal{T}}\Big(c_{k+1}\Big|\mathrm{pref}_k(s)\Big)\Big\} =$$

$$\frac{\partial}{\partial\tau(l,j)}\left\{\ln\left(F\Big(\tau(l,j)\Big)\Big/\sum_{(l,y)\in J_{x_k}} F\Big(\tau(l,y)\Big)\right)\right\} =$$

$$\frac{\partial}{\partial\tau(l,j)}\Big\{\ln F\Big(\tau(l,j)\Big) - \ln\sum_{(l,y)\in J_{x_k}} F\Big(\tau(l,y)\Big)\Big\} =$$

$$F'\Big(\tau(l,j)\Big)\Big/F\Big(\tau(l,j)\Big) - F'\Big(\tau(l,j)\Big)\Big/\sum_{(l,y)\in J_{x_k}} F\Big(\tau(l,y)\Big) =$$

$$\left\{1 - F\Big(\tau(l,j)\Big)\Big/\sum_{(l,y)\in J_{x_k}} F\Big(\tau(l,y)\Big)\right\}\frac{F'\Big(\tau(l,j)\Big)}{F\Big(\tau(l,j)\Big)} =$$

$$\Big\{1 - P_{\mathcal{T}}\Big(j\Big|\mathrm{pref}_k(s)\Big)\Big\}G\Big(\tau(l,j)\Big),$$

where $G = F'/F$, and the subscript of F was omitted for the clarity of presentation.

- If $l = c_k$ and $j \neq c_{k+1}$ then (by a similar argument)

$$\frac{\partial \ln\Big(P_{\mathcal{T}}\Big(c_{k+1}\Big|\mathrm{pref}_k(s)\Big)\Big)}{\partial\tau(l,j)} = -P_{\mathcal{T}}\Big(j\Big|\mathrm{pref}_k(s)\Big)G\Big(\tau(l,j)\Big),$$

- if $l \neq c_k$, then $P_{\mathcal{T}}(c_{k+1}|\mathrm{pref}_k(s))$ is independent of $\tau(l, j)$ and

$$\frac{\partial \ln\Big(P_{\mathcal{T}}(c_{k+1}\Big|\mathrm{pref}_k(s))\Big)}{\partial\tau(l,j)} = 0.$$

By combining these results, the following pheromone update rule is derived:

`StochasticGradientAscent_Update`

- $\forall s \in S_t, \forall (l,j) \in s : \tau(l,j) \leftarrow \tau(l,j) + \alpha_t Q_f(s) G(\tau(l,j))$,
- $\forall s = \langle c_1, \ldots, c_k, \ldots \rangle \in S_t, \forall l = c_k$, with $1 \leq k < |s|, \forall j$:
  $\tau(l,j) \leftarrow \tau(l,j) - \alpha_t Q_f(s) P_{\mathcal{T}}(j|\mathsf{pref}_k(s)) G(\tau(l,j))$.

Hence any connection (l,j) used in the construction of a solution is reinforced by an amount $\alpha_t Q_f(s) G(\tau(l,j))$, and any connection *considered* during the construction has its pheromone values evaporated by an amount

$$\alpha_t Q_f(s) P_{\mathcal{T}}(j|\ \mathrm{pref}_k(s)) G(\tau(l,j)).$$

Note that, if the solutions are allowed to contain loops, a connection may be updated more than once for the same solution.

In order to guarantee stability of the resulting algorithm, it is desirable to have a bounded gradient $\nabla \ln P_{\mathcal{T}}(s)$. This means that a function F, for which $G = F'/F$ is bounded, should be used. Meuleau & Dorigo (2002) suggest using $F(\cdot) = \exp(\cdot)$, which leads to $G \equiv 1$. It should be further noted that if, in addition, $Q_f = 1/f$ and $\alpha_t = 1$, the reinforcement part becomes $1/f$ as in the original *Ant System* proposed by Dorigo *et al.* (1996).

The cross-entropy update

As we have shown in Section A.2.1, the cross-entropy approach requires solving the following intermediate problem:

$$P_{t+1} = \arg\max_{P \in \mathcal{M}} \sum_{s \in S_t} Q_f(s) \ln P(s).$$

Let us now consider this problem in more details when a probabilistic model of the *ant colony optimization*-type is adopted.

Since at the maximum the gradient must be zero, we have:

$$\sum_{s \in S_t} Q_f(s) \nabla \ln P_{\mathcal{T}}(s) = 0. \tag{A.19}$$

In some relatively simple cases, for example when the solution s is represented by an unconstrained string of bits of length n, $(s_1, \ldots, s_n)$, and there is a single parameter τ_l for the l-th position in the string, such that $P_{\mathcal{T}}(s) = \prod_l p_{\tau_l}(s_l)$, the system of Equations A.19 reduces to a set of independent equations:

$$\frac{d \ln p_{\tau_l}}{d\tau_l} \sum_{\substack{s \in S_t \\ s_l = 1}} Q_f(s) = -\frac{d \ln(1 - p_{\tau_l})}{d\tau_l} \sum_{\substack{s \in S_t \\ s_l = 0}} Q_f(s), \quad l = 1, \ldots, n \tag{A.20}$$

which may often be solved analytically. For example, for $p_{\mathcal{T}_l} = \mathcal{T}_l$ it can be verified that the solution of Equation A.20 is simply

$$p_{\mathcal{T}_l} = \mathcal{T}_l = \frac{\sum_{s \in S_t} Q_f(s) s_l}{\sum_{s \in S_t} Q_f(s)}. \tag{A.21}$$

and, in fact, a similar solution also applies to a more general class of Markov chain models (Rubinstein, 2001).

Now, since the pheromone trails $\mathcal{T}_l$ in Equation A.21 are random variables, whose values depend on the particular sample, we may wish to make our algorithm more robust by introducing some conservatism into the update. For example, rather than discarding the old pheromone values, the new values may be taken to be a convex combination of the old values and the solution of Equation A.21:

$$\mathcal{T}_l \leftarrow (1-\rho)\mathcal{T}_l + \rho \frac{\sum_{s \in S_t} Q_f(s) s_l}{\sum_{s \in S_t} Q_f(s)}. \tag{A.22}$$

The resulting update is identical to the one used in the *hyper-cube ant colony optimization* (Blum *et al.*, 2001; Blum, 2004).

However, for many cases of interest, Equations A.19 are coupled and an analytical solution is unavailable. Nevertheless, in the actual implementations of the cross-entropy method (Rubinstein, 2001), the update was of the form given in Equation A.21—with some brief remarks about using Equation A.22—which may be considered as an approximation to the exact solution of the cross-entropy minimization problem given in Equation A.16.

Since, in general, the exact solution is not available, an iterative scheme such as gradient descent could be employed, as described in Section A.2.1. As we have shown in the previous section, the gradient of the log-probability may be calculated as follows:

- If $l = c_k$ and $j = c_{k+1}$, then

$$\frac{\partial \ln\Big(P_{\mathcal{T}}\big(c_{k+1}\big|\mathrm{pref}_k(s)\big)\Big)}{\partial \tau(l,j)} = \Big(1 - P_{\mathcal{T}}\big(j\big|\mathrm{pref}_k(s)\big)\Big) G(\tau(l,j));$$

- If $l = c_k$ and $j \neq c_{k+1}$, then

$$\frac{\partial \ln\Big(P_{\mathcal{T}}\big(c_{k+1}\big|\mathrm{pref}_k(s)\big)\Big)}{\partial \tau(l,j)} = -P_{\mathcal{T}}\big(j\big|\mathrm{pref}_k(s)\big) G\big(\tau(l,j)\big);$$

- If $l \neq c_k$,then

$$\frac{\partial \ln\Big(P_{\mathcal{T}}(c_{k+1}\big|\mathrm{pref}_k(s))\Big)}{\partial \tau(l,j)} = 0.$$

and these values may be plugged into any general iterative solution scheme of the cross-entropy minimization problem, for example, the one described by Equation A.17.

To conclude, we have shown that if we use A.21 as a (possibly approximate) solution of Equation A.16, the *hyper-cube ant colony optimization* algorithm is derived. If otherwise we use a single-step gradient ascent for solving A.16, we obtain a generalization of the stochastic gradient ascent update, in which the quality function is allowed to change over time.

A.2.3 Model-based genetic algorithms

In the "pure" model-based search, as it was described in the introduction, the parameterized model is iteratively updated, using the information extracted from the sample. However, if the whole search history is compressed into a single vector of model's parameters, a lot of useful information may be lost. In order to make a better use of the previous samples, many existing model-based search algorithms use an auxiliary memory, in which they store some additional information collected during the search. This information is then used together with the latest sample for updating the model. For example, as we have seen in Section A.2.2, some existing *ant colony optimization* algorithms store the cost of the best-so-far solution or the average of the costs of the recent solutions. Another alternative would be to store several high-quality solutions encountered during the search. This is exactly what is being done in the majority of *estimation of distribution algorithms* , recently developed within the evolutionary computation community.

In the following we give a brief overview of some existing *estimation of distribution algorithms* and discuss their relations to the model-based search algorithms described in the previous sections.

Estimation of distribution algorithms

As already mentioned, the classical *genetic algorithm* can be considered to be an example of the instance-based approach, in which the search is carried out by evolving the population of candidate solutions (typically represented by a string of bits) using selection, crossover and mutation operators (Holland, 1975).

The classical *genetic algorithm* approach relies heavily on the assumption that there are some *building blocks*, from which a good solution can be constructed. Moreover, it is assumed that with a proper choice of the crossover operator, these blocks will be (implicitly) detected and maintained in the population, while the selection operator will bias the search towards low-cost solutions. However, in practice, finding an appropriate crossover operator turns out to be a difficult task, while using some "general purpose" crossover operators often leads to poor performance. Another problem is the existence of *genetic drift* (Goldberg &

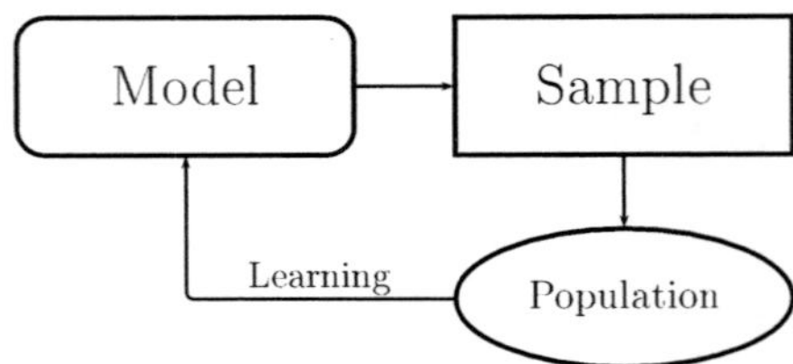

Figure A.3: Graphic description of the *estimation of distribution algorithms*.

Segrest, 1987), that is, a loss of population diversity due to the finite population size, and, as a result, a premature convergence to sub-optimal solutions.

In order to cope with the finite-population effects and also as an attempt to find an efficient alternative to the crossover/mutation operators, the *estimation of distribution algorithms* (Mühlenbein *et al.*, 1996) were proposed. These algorithms generate new solutions using probabilistic models, instead of crossover and mutation, and may be described using the following generic scheme:

`EstimationOfDistribution_Iteration`

- Generate new solutions using the current probabilistic model.
- Replace (some of) the old solutions by the new ones.
- Modify the model using the new population.

This scheme, which may be seen as a particular type of model-based search with auxiliary memory, is represented graphically in Figure A.3.

Different *estimation of distribution algorithms* use different methods for construction/modification of the probabilistic model. However, most of them use the same method for estimating model parameters—a (possibly weighted) maximum-likelihood estimation. In this respect they are all closely related to the cross-entropy method described earlier and, as we show in the following, some of them employ particular forms of cross-entropy-type update.

In the remainder of this section we give an overview of existing *estimation of distribution algorithms* and discuss their relations with the algorithms presented in the previous sections. We consider two major classes of *estimation of distribution algorithms*. The first class contains the algorithms that use a fixed simple model, which assumes that there are no interactions between the different string positions, that is, that the assignments to the different positions are independent. We observe that this is a particular kind of *ant colony optimization*-type model and show that all these algorithms lead to particular forms of *ant colony optimization*-type updates. The algorithms in the second class allow for dependencies between the positions, and, consequently, try to infer both the model structure and the model's parameters. Unlike the first group, both the models and the update mechanisms used by the algorithms in the second group are different from the ones used in the *ant colony optimization* framework.

It should be noted that all of the following algorithms were originally formulated for maximization problems, hence the obvious changes were done in order to translate them into the minimization setting that we consider in the following.

Assuming independence between string positions. All the algorithms presented in this section create the new solutions, coded as binary vectors, by independently generating assignments for every position, with the l-th position having probability p_l to take value 1. This may be considered a particularly simple *ant colony optimization*-type model, in which the components correspond to bit assignments, pheromone trails are associated with components, and there are no constraints.

The idea was initially proposed in Syswerda (1993), where the necessary probabilities were calculated as weighted frequencies over the population and randomly perturbed in order to simulate mutation. Apart from the mutation component, which seems to be an historical artifact borrowed from the classical *genetic algorithm* and absent in later algorithms, this method is clearly an instance of model-based search with auxiliary memory in the form of the solution population, which uses the *hyper-cube ant colony optimization*-type (or, equivalently, cross-entropy-type) update with learning rate $\rho = 1$ for constructing the probabilistic model.

A similar approach was used in the *univariate marginal distribution* algorithm (Mühlenbein *et al.*, 1996), the only difference being that in the *univariate marginal distribution* algorithm explicit classical selection procedures were used instead of giving weights to the solutions.

This idea is pushed even further in the *population-based incremental learning* algorithm (Baluja, 1994; Baluja & Caruana, 1995), where the population is completely replaced by a probability vector,[23] p, with all p_l's initially set to 0.5. At every iteration a sample S is generated using the probability vector and then the probability vector is updated as follows:

```
PopulationBasedIncrementalLearning_Update
```

- $S_{best} \leftarrow$ a fixed number of lowest cost solutions from S,
- for every $s \in S_{best}$, $p_l \leftarrow (1-\rho)p_l + \rho s_l$,

where ρ is the learning rate.

[23] In this sense, the *population-based incremental learning* algorithm belongs to the model-based search approach in its "pure" form and is, in fact, the first published algorithm belonging to the model-based search approach.

As it can be easily seen, this update is virtually identical to the *hyper-cube ant colony optimization* update with the quality function being the indicator for the lowest cost solutions. In particular, if only the best solution is used for the update, *hyper-cube ant colony optimization* with iteration-best update is obtained.

Finally, the *compact genetic algorithm* (Harik *et al.*, 1999) was proposed as a modification of *population-based incremental learning*, intended to represent more faithfully the dynamics of the real genetic algorithm. Specifically, the *compact genetic algorithm* simulates a genetic algorithm, with population size n and steady-state binary tournament selection, in the following way. At every iteration two solutions, a and b, are generated using the probability vector, and then the probability vector is updated as follows (assuming, without loss of generality, that a has lower cost):

`CompactGeneticAlgorithm_Update`

- when $a_l \neq b_l$, if $a_l = 1$ then $p_l \leftarrow p_l + 1/n$, otherwise $p_l \leftarrow p_l - 1/n$.

This basic scheme can be extended to larger samples. Two variants were proposed in Harik *et al.* (1999). In the first variant, intended to simulate tournaments of size m, a sample S of size m is generated and the basic update above is used for every pair in the set $\{(s^{best}, b) | b \in S, b \neq s^{best}\}$. In the second variant, a "round-robin tournament" is simulated, that is, the basic update is used for every pair of solutions from the sample.

Note that the basic *compact genetic algorithm* update can also be written in *ant colony optimization*-like form as:

$$p_l \leftarrow p_l + \frac{1}{n}(a_l - b_l).$$

Consequently, it can be shown that the update for "tournament of size m" *compact genetic algorithm* can be written as:

$$p_l \leftarrow p_l + \rho \sum_{s \in S} Q(s) s_l - \frac{\rho}{m} \sum_{s \in S} s_l, \tag{A.23}$$

where $\rho = m/n$ and

$$Q(s) = \begin{cases} 1 \ , & s = s^{best} \\ 0 \ , & \text{otherwise.} \end{cases}$$

For the "round-robin tournament" *compact genetic algorithm*, it can be shown that the update can also be described by Equation A.23, with $\rho = m(m+1)/n$ and

$$Q(s) = \frac{2 \cdot \text{rank}(s)}{m(m+1)},$$

where the highest rank, m, is assigned to s^{best}.

It can be easily verified that these two updates are virtually identical to the *hyper-cube ant colony optimization* iteration-best and rank-based updates respectively. The only difference between the *compact genetic algorithm* and *hyper-cube ant colony optimization* is in the form of the evaporation factor. In the *compact genetic algorithm* it is equal to $\frac{\rho}{m}\sum_{s\in S} s_l$, whereas in *hyper-cube ant colony optimization* it is equal to ρp_l, which is simply the expected value of the former.

Modeling dependencies between string positions. All the algorithms described in the previous section, assumed a fixed model for the solutions' distribution, namely independence between assignments at different positions, and proposed different rules for calculating the parameters of the model. However, it may well happen that certain components produce good solutions only in conjunction with others, hence there may be strong dependencies within the population distribution.

Once the algorithm tries to model these *a priori* unknown dependencies between the solution constituents, the simple fixed structure has to be abandoned and the correct structure needs to be inferred together with the model's parameters.[24]

In the first *estimation of distribution algorithms* that abandoned the independence assumption, only pairwise interactions were covered. The *MIMIC* algorithm, *mutual-information-maximizing input clustering*, (De Bonet *et al.*, 1997), which was already mentioned earlier in the context of the cross-entropy method, maintains a population of the best solutions seen so far and constructs a chain distribution as a model of population by minimizing the Kullback-Liebler divergence between the model and the population distribution. Since finding the optimal chain distribution is an *NP*-hard problem, *MIMIC* uses a greedy search procedure for constructing the chain. For a given structure, the conditional probabilities (which are the parameters of the model) are estimated using the sample frequencies.

Baluja & Davies (1997) extend *MIMIC* in two important respects. First, they use a broader class of dependency trees instead of chain distributions, and, consequently, they are able to present an exact polynomial algorithm, rather than a greedy approximation. Second, instead of explicitly storing the population, the algorithm's history is summarized in a matrix of pairwise joint frequencies (with more weight given to recent instances), which are later used for optimal tree construction.

A somewhat more heuristic approach is taken in the *bivariate marginal distribution* algorithm (Pelikan & Mühlenbein, 1999), where the population is modeled

[24]Note, however, that in *ant colony optimization* models, pairwise dependencies may be learned implicitly, when the pheromone trails are associated with the connections between the components. Hence *ant colony optimization* provides an alternative way of learning pairwise dependencies, while still maintaining a fixed-structure model.

using a forest, that is, a set of mutually independent dependency trees.[25] The model structure is determined using a Pearson's χ-square test (Marascuilo & McSweeney, 1977) for detecting dependencies.

The attempt to obtain yet more general models led to two different approaches. The first, the *extended compact genetic algorithm* (Harik, 1999), is a brute-force generalization of the *univariate marginal distribution* algorithm, with the population modeled using a marginal product model. In the marginal product model the variables are divided into a number of independent clusters, while within a cluster any distribution is permitted. The cluster structure is determined by greedily optimizing the minimum description length metric (Mitchell, 1997) and the inter-cluster distributions are estimated using the population frequencies. The second approach, which is a generalization of ideas behind the tree-based algorithms described earlier, is to use a Bayesian network for modeling the population (Pelikan *et al.*, 1999; Etxeberria & Larrañaga, 1999), with the network structure determined using some standard techniques for Bayesian network learning (Heckerman, 1995).

To summarize, all the algorithms described in this section use probabilistic models that are different from the one employed in *ant colony optimization*. Various criteria are used for choosing the model structure, but in all these algorithms a (weighted) maximum-likelihood (or, equivalently, minimal cross-entropy) method is used for estimating the model's parameters.

A.2.4 Discussion

During the last decade a new approach for solving combinatorial optimization problems has been emerging. This approach, which we refer to as model-based search, tackles the combinatorial problem by sampling the solution space using a probabilistic model, which is adaptively modified as the search proceeds.

We observe that any successful algorithm belonging to the model-based search framework is characterized by two components: a probabilistic model, which should allow an efficient generation of the candidate solutions, and a model update rule, which allows to concentrate the sampling in the high-quality regions. Accordingly, we describe two general approaches, the stochastic gradient ascent and the cross-entropy methods, for updating model's parameters and we observe some previously unknown relationships between the two methods. Further, we demonstrate how the stochastic gradient ascent and the cross-entropy methods can be applied in the context of *ant colony optimization*, which is a typical representative of the model-based search approach. Moreover, we also show that in some cases the resulting updates coincide with existing *ant colony optimization* updates. Finally, we show that *estimation of distribution algorithms*, proposed in

[25]While seemingly more general, this class is in fact equivalent to the class of dependency trees, as any forest can be represented using a tree with degenerate links.

the field of genetic algorithms, also fall into the model-based search framework, and that they are closely related to the other algorithms considered here.

While sharing a lot of similar traits, each of the methods considered here has some distinctive characteristics. Consequently, many interesting questions arise as to whether these peculiarities are contributing to the algorithm's performance.

For example, some of the *estimation of distribution algorithms*, which are the subject of Section A.2.3, contain at least one of the two following important components, absent in other approaches considered in our discussion. The first is a population of solutions, which evolves throughout the search process and is used for constructing the probabilistic model. The other is the use of a flexible model structure, which is determined using an appropriate learning algorithm. However, it is still unclear whether either of these components gives any advantage in solving real-life problems. In addition, to the best of our knowledge, all the dependency-learning *estimation of distribution algorithms* described in Section **modeling dependencies between string positions**, page 243, have been applied only to unconstrained optimization problems, which is a rather atypical situation in combinatorial optimization.[26] It remains to be seen whether similar algorithms can be designed for a more general setting. It should be further noted that, if a flexible model structure is shown to be beneficial in model-based search, some new model-selection rules should probably be used. The use of general purpose model-selection rules, borrowed from the machine learning field, seems to be inappropriate in the optimization context, since complex models are usually computationally more expensive, hence a stronger (than in generic learning) bias toward simpler models should probably be imposed.

Another interesting research direction, suggested by the approach presented in Baluja & Davies (1997), is to use a collection of sufficient statistics rather than a population, for the construction of the probabilistic model. This can be seen as a kind of two-stage learning procedure, where the statistics are learned incrementally, in a manner similar to *ant colony optimization*, but the actual (second-stage) model is re-constructed in every iteration using the first-stage statistics instead of raw samples.

Finally, the choice of the quality function, which provides a link between the original cost function and the model update rule, clearly has a crucial effect on the algorithms' dynamics. Some of the algorithms described here, use iteration-independent quality functions, while others adapt the quality function based on the search history. However, the issue of appropriate quality function choice is still poorly understood and is clearly an interesting future research direction.

Evaluating the utility of the different characteristics of the model-based search algorithms clearly requires a serious experimental work. A first step in this di-

[26] Although for some problems sophisticated schemes for coding the solutions as unconstrained binary strings have been devised—see Baluja (1994) for an example—all the useful dependencies between the solution components may be hidden by these coding schemes.

rection was made in Zlochin & Dorigo (2002), where several model-based search algorithms were rigorously compared over a class of MAXIMUM SATISFIABILITY problems.

To conclude, considering all these algorithms within a common general framework provides a better understanding of what are the important parts of the algorithm and what is just an historical artifact due to a particular background of its proponents. Hopefully, the results presented above will facilitate cross-fertilization between the considered model-based search methods and, perhaps, provide useful guidelines for designing new efficient optimization algorithms.

The quick brown fox jumps over the lazy dog.
Sentence for testing typewriters

Annex B

Lazy learning for local regression

Lazy learning (Aha, 1997) is a memory-based techniques for supervised learning that postpones all computation until an explicit request for a prediction is received. The request is fulfilled by interpolating locally a number of examples that are considered relevant according to a given distance metric.

In this chapter we present an original *lazy learning* algorithm developed by the authors and co-workers. In particular, Section B.1 discusses a general algorithm for local polynomial regression, while Section B.2 focuses on a more efficient method that is specifically devised for local polynomials of order zero, that is, for local constant models. Section B.3 concludes the chapter with a list of practical applications of the proposed *lazy learning* algorithm.

B.1 Lazy learning and recursive least squares†

In the *lazy learning* approach, no preliminary computation is performed on the available dataset and all computation is postponed until an explicit request for a prediction is received. When this happens, a local model is built by interpolating locally a number of examples that are considered relevant according to a given distance metric. Each prediction requires therefore a local modeling procedure that can be seen as composed of a *structural* and of a *parametric* identification. The parametric identification consists in the optimization of the parameters of the local approximator. On the other hand, structural identification involves, among other things, the selection of a family of local approximators, the selection of a metric to evaluate which examples are more relevant, and the selection of the *bandwidth* which indicates the size of the region in which the data are correctly modeled by members of the chosen family of approximators. For a comprehensive tutorial on local learning and for further references see Atkeson *et al.* (1997).

As far as the problem of bandwidth selection is concerned, different approaches

†This section is based on Birattari *et al.* (1999). Some of the experimental results presented were previously published in Bontempi *et al.* (2000).

exist. The choice of the bandwidth may be performed either based on some *a priori* assumption or on the data themselves. A further sub-classification of data-driven approaches is of interest here. On the one hand, a constant bandwidth may be used; in this case it is set by a global optimization that minimizes an error criterion over the available dataset. On the other hand, the bandwidth may be selected locally and tailored for each query point.

In this chapter, we propose a method that belongs to the latter class of local data-driven approaches. Assuming a given fixed metric and local linear approximators, the method we introduce selects the bandwidth on a query-by-query basis by means of a local leave-one-out cross-validation. The problem of bandwidth selection is reduced to the selection of the number k of neighboring examples which are given a non-zero weight in the local modeling procedure. Each time a prediction is required for a specific query point, a set of local models is identified, each including a different number of neighbors. The generalization ability of each model is then assessed through a local cross-validation procedure. Finally, a prediction is obtained either combining or selecting the different models on the basis of some statistic of their cross-validation errors.

The main reason to favor a query-by-query bandwidth selection is that it allows better adaptation to the local characteristics of the problem at hand. Moreover, this approach is able to handle directly the case in which the database is updated on-line (Bontempi *et al.*, 1999b). On the other hand, a globally optimized bandwidth approach would, in principle, require the global optimization to be repeated each time the distribution of the examples changes.

The major contribution of this research consists in the adoption of the *recursive least squares* algorithm in the context of *lazy learning*. This is an appealing and efficient solution to the intrinsically incremental problem of identifying and validating a sequence of local linear models centered in the query point, each including a growing number of neighbors. It is worth noticing here that a leave-one-out cross-validation of each model considered does not involve any significant computational overload, since it is obtained though the PRESS statistic (Myers, 1994) which simply uses partial results returned by the recursive least squares algorithm. Schaal & Atkeson (1994) used already the recursive least squares algorithm for the incremental update of a set of local models. The work proposed here presents an original (Birattari *et al.*, 1999) algorithm in which, for the first time, the recursive least squares algorithm is adopted in a query-by-query perspective as an effective way to explore the neighborhood of each query point.

As a second contribution, we propose a comparison, on a local scale, between a *competitive* and a *cooperative* approach to model selection. On the problem of extracting a final prediction from a set of alternatives, we compared a *winner-takes-all* strategy with a strategy based on the *combination of estimators* (Wolpert, 1992).

In Section B.1.4 an experimental analysis of the recursive algorithm for local identification and validation is presented. The algorithm proposed, used in conjunction with different strategies for model selection or combination, is compared experimentally with a *feed-forward neural network* and with *Cubist*, the rule-based tool developed by Ross Quinlan for generating piecewise-linear models.[1]

B.1.1 Local weighted regression

Given two variables $x \in \mathbb{R}^d$ and $y \in \mathbb{R}$, let us consider the mapping f: $\mathbb{R}^d \rightarrow \mathbb{R}$, known only through a set of N examples $\{(x_j, y_j)\}_{j=1}^N$ obtained as follows:

$$y_j = f(x_j) + \varepsilon_j,$$

where $\forall j$, ε_j is a random variable such that $E[\varepsilon_j] = 0$ and $E[\varepsilon_j \varepsilon_l] = 0$, $\forall l \neq j$, and such that $E[\varepsilon_j^m] = \mu_m(x_j)$, $\forall m \geq 2$, where $\mu_m(\cdot)$ is the unknown m-th moment of the distribution of ε_j and is defined as a function of x_j. In particular for $m = 2$, the last of the above mentioned properties implies that no assumption of global homoscedasticity is made.

The problem of local regression can be stated as the problem of estimating the value that the regression function $f(x) = E[y|x]$ assumes for a specific query point x, using information pertaining only to a neighborhood of x.

Given a query point x_q, and under the hypothesis of a local homoscedasticity of ε_j, the parameter β of a local linear approximation of f in a neighborhood of x_q can be obtained solving the local polynomial regression:

$$\sum_{j=1}^{N} \left\{ (y_j - x_j'\beta)^2 \mathcal{K}\left(\frac{D(x_j, x_q)}{h}\right) \right\}, \tag{B.1}$$

where, given a metric on the space $\mathbb{R}^d$, $D(x_j, x_q)$ is the distance from the query point to the j-th example, $\mathcal{K}$ is a weight function, h is the bandwidth, and where a constant value 1 has been appended to each vector x_j in order to consider a constant term in the regression.

In matrix notation, the solution of the above stated weighted least squares problem is given by:

$$\hat{\beta} = (X'W'WX)^{-1}X'W'Wy = (Z'Z)^{-1}Z'v = PZ'v,$$

where X is a matrix whose j-th row is x_j', y is a vector whose j-th element is y_j, W is a diagonal matrix whose j-th diagonal element is $w_{jj} = \sqrt{\mathcal{K}\left(D(x_j, x_q)/h\right)}$, $Z = WX$, $v = Wy$, and the matrix $X'W'WX = Z'Z$ is assumed to be non-singular so that its inverse $P = (Z'Z)^{-1}$ is defined.

Once obtained the local linear polynomial approximation, a prediction of $y_q = f(x_q)$, is finally given by:

$$\hat{y}_q = x_q'\hat{\beta}.$$

[1] Details on *Cubist* are available at `http://www.rulequest.com`

Moreover, exploiting the linearity of the local approximator, a leave-one-out cross-validation estimation of the error variance $E[(y_q - \hat{y}_q)^2]$ can be obtained without any significant overload. In fact, using the PRESS statistic (Myers, 1994), it is possible to calculate the error $\varepsilon_l^{cv} = y_l - x_l'\hat{\beta}_{-l}$, without explicitly identifying the parameters $\hat{\beta}_{-l}$ from the examples available with the l-th removed. The formulation of the PRESS statistic for the case at hand is the following:

$$\varepsilon_l^{cv} = y_l - x_l'\hat{\beta}_{-l} = \frac{y_l - x_l'PZ'v}{1 - z_l'Pz_l} = \frac{y_l - x_l'\hat{\beta}}{1 - h_{ll}}, \tag{B.2}$$

where z_l'.is the l-th row of Z and therefore $z_l = w_{ll}x_l$, and where h_{ll} is the l-th diagonal element of the *Hat matrix* $H = ZPZ' = Z(Z'Z)^{-1}Z'$.

B.1.2 Recursive local regression

In what follows, for the sake of simplicity, we will focus on linear approximator. An extension to generic polynomial approximators of any degree is straightforward. We will assume also that a metric on the space $\mathbb{R}^d$ is given. All the attention will be thus centered on the problem of bandwidth selection.

If as a weight function $\mathcal{K}$ the indicator function

$$\mathcal{K}\left(\frac{D(x_j, x_q)}{h}\right) = \begin{cases} 1 & \text{if } D(x_j, x_q) \leq h, \\ 0 & \text{otherwise;} \end{cases} \tag{B.3}$$

is adopted, the optimization of the parameter h can be conveniently reduced to the optimization of the number k of neighbors to which a unitary weight is assigned in the local regression evaluation. In other words, we reduce the problem of bandwidth selection to a search in the space of $h(k) = D(x(k), x_q)$, where $x(k)$ is the k-th nearest neighbor of the query point.

The main advantage deriving from the adoption of the weight function defined in Equation B.3, is that, simply by updating the parameter $\hat{\beta}(k)$ of the model identified using the k nearest neighbors, it is straightforward and inexpensive to obtain $\hat{\beta}(k+1)$. In fact, performing a step of the standard recursive least squares algorithm (Bierman, 1977), we have:

$$\begin{cases} P(k+1) & = P(k) - \dfrac{P(k)x(k+1)x'(k+1)P(k)}{1 + x'(k+1)P(k)x(k+1)} \\ \gamma(k+1) & = P(k+1)x(k+1) \\ e(k+1) & = y(k+1) - x'(k+1)\hat{\beta}(k) \\ \hat{\beta}(k+1) & = \hat{\beta}(k) + \gamma(k+1)e(k+1) \end{cases} \tag{B.4}$$

where $P(k) = (Z'Z)^{-1}$ when $h = h(k)$, and where $x(k+1)$ is the $(k+1)$-th nearest neighbor of the query point.

Moreover, once the matrix $P(k+1)$ is available, the leave-one-out cross-validation errors can be directly calculated without the need of any further model identification:

$$\varepsilon_l^{cv}(k+1) = \frac{y_l - x_l'\hat{\beta}(k+1)}{1 - x_l'P(k+1)x_l}, \qquad \forall l : D(x_l, x_q) \leq h(k+1). \tag{B.5}$$

It will be useful in the following to define for each value of k the $[k \times 1]$ vector $e^{cv}(k)$ that contains all the leave-one-out errors associated to the model $\hat{\beta}(k)$.

Once an initialization $\hat{\beta}(0) = \tilde{\beta}$ and $P(0) = \tilde{P}$ is given, Equation B.4 and Equation B.5 recursively evaluate for different values of k a local approximation of the regression function f, a prediction of the value of the regression function in the query point, and the vector of leave-one-out errors from which it is possible to extract an estimate of the variance of the prediction error. Notice that $\tilde{\beta}$ is an *a priori* estimate of the parameter and $\tilde{P}$ is the covariance matrix that reflects the reliability of $\tilde{\beta}$ (Bierman, 1977). For non-reliable initialization, the following is usually adopted: $\tilde{P} = \lambda I$, with λ large and where I is the identity matrix.

B.1.3 Local model selection and combination

The recursive algorithm described by Equation B.4 and Equation B.5 returns for a given query point x_q, a set of predictions $\hat{y}_q(k) = x_q'\hat{\beta}(k)$, together with a set of associated leave-one-out error vectors $e^{cv}(k)$.

From the information available, a final prediction $\hat{y}_q$ of the value of the regression function can be obtained in different ways. Two main paradigms deserve to be considered: the first is based on the selection of the *best* approximator according to a given criterion, while the second returns a prediction as a combination of more local models.

If the selection paradigm, frequently called *winner-takes-all*, is adopted, the most natural way to extract a final prediction $\hat{y}_q$, consists in comparing the prediction obtained for each value of k on the basis of the classical *mean square error* criterion:

$$\hat{y}_q = x_q'\hat{\beta}(\hat{k}), \quad \text{with } \hat{k} = \arg\min_k \text{MSE}(k) = \arg\min_k \frac{\sum_{j=1}^k \omega_j \left(e_j^{cv}(k)\right)^2}{\sum_{j=1}^k \omega_j};$$

where ω_j are weights than can be conveniently used to discount each error according to the distance from the query point to the point to which the error corresponds (Atkeson *et al.*, 1997).

As an alternative to the *winner-takes-all* paradigm, we explored also the effectiveness of local combinations of estimates (Wolpert, 1992). Adopting also in this case the *mean square error* criterion, the final prediction of the value y_q is obtained as a weighted average of the best b models, where b is a parameter of the algorithm. Suppose the predictions $\hat{y}_q(k)$ and the error vectors $e^{cv}(k)$ have

	HOUSING	CPU	PRICES	MPG	SERVO	OZONE
Number of examples	506	209	159	392	167	330
Number of regressors	13	6	16	7	8	8

Table B.1: A summary of the characteristics of the datasets considered.

been ordered creating a sequence of integers $\{k_j\}$ so that $\text{MSE}(k_j) \leq \text{MSE}(k_l)$, $\forall j < l$. The prediction of $\hat{y}_q$ is given by

$$\hat{y}_q = \frac{\sum_{j=1}^{b} \zeta_j \hat{y}_q(k_j)}{\sum_{j=1}^{b} \zeta_j}, \tag{B.6}$$

where the weights are the inverse of the mean square errors: $\zeta_j = 1/\text{MSE}(k_j)$. This is an example of the *generalized ensemble method* (Perrone & Cooper, 1993).

B.1.4 Experiments and results

The experimental evaluation of the incremental local identification and validation algorithm was performed on six datasets. The first five, described by Quinlan (1993a), were obtained from the UCI Repository of machine learning databases (Blake & Merz, 1998), while the last one, OZONE, was provided by Leo Breiman. A summary of the characteristics of each dataset is presented in Table B.1.

The methods compared adopt the recursive identification and validation algorithm, combined with different strategies for model selection or combination. We considered also two approaches in which k is selected globally:

***lb1*:** Local bandwidth selection for linear local models. The number of neighbors is selected on a query-by-query basis and the prediction returned is the one of the best model according to the mean square error criterion.

***lb0*:** Local bandwidth selection for constant local models. The algorithm for constant models is derived directly from the recursive method described in Equation B.4 and Equation B.5. The best model is selected according to the mean square error criterion.

***lbC*:** Local combination of estimators. This is an example of the method described in Equation B.6. On the datasets proposed, for each query the best 2 linear local models and the best 2 constant models are combined.

***gb1*:** Global bandwidth selection for linear local models. The value of k is obtained minimizing the prediction error in 20-fold cross-validation on the dataset available. This value is then used for all the query points.

	HOUSING	CPU	PRICES	MPG	SERVO	OZONE
lb1	2.21	28.38	1509	1.94	0.48	3.52
lb0	2.60	31.54	1627	1.97	0.32	3.33
lbC	2.12	26.79	1488	1.83	0.29	3.31
gb1	2.30	28.69	1492	1.92	0.52	3.46
gb0	2.59	32.19	1639	1.99	0.34	3.19
Cubist	2.17	28.37	1331	1.90	0.36	3.15
nnet	2.33	31.18	2092	2.05	0.38	3.32

Table B.2: Mean absolute error on unseen cases.

	HOUSING	CPU	PRICES	MPG	SERVO	OZONE
lb1	12.63	9.20	15.87	12.65	28.66	35.25
lb0	18.06	20.37	22.19	12.64	22.04	31.11
lbC	12.35	9.29	17.62	11.82	19.72	30.28
gb1	13.47	9.93	15.95	12.83	30.46	32.58
gb0	17.99	21.43	22.29	13.48	24.30	28.21
Cubist	16.02	12.71	11.67	12.57	18.53	26.59
nnet	14.06	14.40	32.17	12.65	22.47	30.06

Table B.3: Relative error (%) on unseen cases.

gb0: Global bandwidth selection for constant local models. As in ***gb1***, the value of k is optimized globally and kept constant for all the queries.

As far as the metric is concerned, we adopted a global Euclidean metric based on the relative influence (*relevance*) of the regressors (Friedman, 1994). We are confident that the adoption of a local metric could improve the performance of our *lazy learning* method.

The results of the methods introduced are compared with those we obtained, in the same experimental settings, with a ***feed-forward neural network*** and with ***Cubist***, the rule-based tool developed by Quinlan for generating piecewise-linear models. While ***Cubist*** is an integrated tool which performs an automatic model selection and returns the best expected prediction, a fair comparison with a ***feed-forward neural network*** should require a state-of-the-art selection procedure for determining the most appropriate number of neuron the hidden layer should comprise. In order to avoid possible criticisms on the issue, we consider here several different two-layer networks with sigmoidal activation function in the first layer, and linear in the second, and where the number of neuron in the hidden layer ranges between 2 and 12. Each of these network is trained using the Levenberg-Marquardt algorithm on each of the dataset. The result we report is the best *a posteriori* on the test set. Therefore, we are here clearly *cheating* in favor of the *feed-forward neural network*.

Each approach was tested on each dataset using the same 10-fold cross-validation strategy. Each dataset was divided randomly into 10 groups of nearly equal size. In turn, each of these groups was used as a testing set while the remaining ones together were providing the examples. Thus all the methods performed a prediction on the same unseen cases, using for each of them the same set of examples. In Table B.2 we present the results obtained by all the methods, and averaged on the 10 cross-validation groups. Since the methods were compared on the same examples in exactly the same conditions, the sensitive one-tailed paired test of significance can be used. In what follows, by "significantly better" we mean better at least at a 5% significance level.

The first consideration about the results concerns the local combination of estimators. According to Table B.2, the method *lbC* performs in average always better than the *winner-takes-all* linear and constant. On two dataset *lbC* is significantly better than both *lb1* and *lb0*; and on three dataset it is significantly better than one of the two, and better in average than the other.

The second consideration is about the comparison between our query-by-query bandwidth selection and a global optimization of the number of neighbors: in average *lb1* and *lb0* performs better than their counterparts *gb1* and *gb0*. On two datasets *lb1* is significantly better than *gb1*, while is about the same on the other four. On one dataset *lb0* is significantly better than *gb0*.

As far as the comparison with *Cubist* is concerned, the recursive *lazy learning* identification and validation proposed obtains results comparable with those obtained by the state-of-the-art method implemented in *Cubist*. On the six datasets, *lbC* performs one time significantly better than *Cubist*, and one time significantly worse.

As far as the comparison with the *feed-forward neural network* is concerned, the proposed *lazy learning* method *lbC* obtains results that are significantly better on five datasets notwithstanding the particularly favorable setting in which the neural network has been operated.

The second index of performance we investigated is the *relative error*, defined as the mean square error on unseen cases, normalized by the variance of the test set. The relative errors are presented in Table B.3 and show a similar picture to Table B.2, although the mean square errors considered here penalize larger absolute errors.

A further experimental evaluation of the *lazy learning* algorithm presented here is given in Bontempi (1999) where a larger number of datasets are considered and other state-of-the-art approaches are included in the analysis.

The experimental results confirm that the recursive least squares algorithm can be effectively used in a local context. Despite the trivial metric adopted, the local combination of estimators, identified and validated recursively, showed to be able to compete with a state-of-the-art approach.

B.2 Constant models in a local setting[‡]

The *lazy learning* algorithm presented in Section B.1 can be used to recursively identify and validate local models of any degree and then, in principle, also for constant models, that is, for polynomials of degree zero.

Anyway a far more efficient implementation is possible which fully exploits properties peculiar to constant models. In this section we focus on the derivation of such an algorithm for recursive identification and recursive leave-one-out validation of local polynomial approximators of degree zero. We take for granted that an appropriate metric has been defined in the input space $\mathbb{R}^d$, that a rectangular weighting kernel has been adopted, and that an algorithm has been chosen to (efficiently) retrieve from the original dataset the K-nearest-neighbors of a given query point x_q. We assume also that it is valuable to obtain a sequence of prediction yielded by constant models, each identified on the basis of a growing number of nearest-neighbors of the query point, together with their respective mean square error in cross-validation. In other words, we suppose that a method has been defined in order to extract a final prediction starting from a sequence of approximators of degree zero, and from their leave-one-out assessment, and in case from equivalent sequences of higher degree approximators identified and validated through an appropriate algorithm.

B.2.1 Local constant models and local assessment

We suppose that a subset of K nearest-neighbors of the query point x_q at hand has been selected. The sequence $\{(x_j, y_j)\}_{j=1}^K$ will be, from here on, the sequence of the K-nearest-neighbors ordered so that $D(x_j, x_q) \leq D(x_l, x_q)$, $\forall j \leq l$, where D is an appropriate distance function in the space $\mathbb{R}^d$.

A generic local constant model identified on the first k nearest neighbors is the classical *sample average* (Papoulis, 1991) of the output associated to the nearest k examples:

$$\hat{y}(k) = \frac{1}{k}\sum_{j=1}^{k} y_j = \hat{\mu}(k). \tag{B.7}$$

A leave-one-out mean square error of this model is obtain as follows:

$$mse^{cv}(k) = \frac{1}{k}\sum_{l=1}^{k}\left(\varepsilon_l^{cv}(k)\right)^2, \tag{B.8}$$

where $\varepsilon_l^{cv}(k)$ is the error in the prediction of the l-th neighbor, yielded by the

[‡]This section is based on Birattari & Bontempi (1999a).

model identified on the k nearest-neighbors with the l-th removed:

$$
\begin{aligned}
\varepsilon_l^{cv}(k) &= y_l - \hat{y}_{-l}(k) = y_l - \frac{\sum_{\substack{j=1 \\ j\neq l}}^{k} y_j}{k-1} \\
&= y_l - \frac{\sum_{j=1}^{k} y_j}{k-1} = y_l - \frac{k\frac{\sum_{j=1}^{k} y_j}{k} - y_l}{k-1} \\
&= y_l - \frac{k\hat{\mu}(k) - y_l}{k-1} \frac{ky_l - k\hat{\mu}(k)}{k-1} \\
&= \frac{k}{k-1}(y_l - \hat{\mu}(k)) = \frac{k}{k-1}(y_l - \hat{y}(k)) \\
&= \frac{k}{k-1}\varepsilon_l(k).
\end{aligned}
\tag{B.9}
$$

Equation B.9 shows that the leave-one-out error for the l-th neighbor is a linear function of the re-substitution error and does not depend on x_l. From Equations B.8 and B.9, it follows that:

$$
\begin{aligned}
mse^{cv}(k) &= \frac{\sum_{l=1}^{k}\left(\frac{k}{k-1}\varepsilon_l(k)\right)^2}{k} = \frac{\frac{k^2}{(k-1)^2}\sum_{l=1}^{k}\left(y_l - \hat{\mu}(k)\right)^2}{k} \\
&= \frac{k}{k-1}\frac{\sum_{l=1}^{k}\left(y_l - \hat{\mu}(k)\right)^2}{k-1} = \frac{k}{k-1}\hat{\sigma}^2(k),
\end{aligned}
\tag{B.10}
$$

where $\hat{\sigma}^2(k)$ is the *sample variance* (Papoulis, 1991) of the output associated to the nearest k examples.

B.2.2 The recursive algorithm

In Section B.2.1 we have defined the local prediction and the leave-one-out mean square error obtained from the first k nearest-neighbors for a generic value of k.

In this section we derive a recursive formulation of Equations B.7 and B.10, that is, we will make explicit the equations that allow the computation of $\hat{y}(k)$ and $mse^{cv}(k)$ starting from $\hat{y}(k-1)$, $mse^{cv}(k-1)$, and the k-th nearest-neighbor y_k.

The recursive formulation of the prediction $\hat{y}(k)$ can be easily obtained observing that:

$$
\begin{aligned}
\hat{\mu}(k) &= \frac{1}{k}\sum_{j=1}^{k} y_j = \frac{\sum_{j=1}^{k-1} y_j + y_k}{k} \\
&= \frac{(k-1)\frac{\sum_{j=1}^{k-1} y_j}{k-1} + y_k}{k} = \frac{(k-1)\hat{\mu}(k-1) + y_k}{k} \\
&= \frac{k-1}{k}\hat{\mu}(k-1) + \frac{1}{k}y_k.
\end{aligned}
\tag{B.11}
$$

From Equations B.7 and B.11, it follows directly that:

$$\hat{y}(k) = \frac{k-1}{k}\hat{y}(k-1) + \frac{1}{k}y_k. \tag{B.12}$$

As far as the recursive formulation of the leave-one-out mean square error is concerned, a slightly longer demonstration is needed. The basis of the recursive computation of the sample variance can be obtained from the following:

$$\begin{aligned}
\hat{\sigma}^2(k) &= \frac{\sum_{l=1}^{k}\left(y_l - \hat{\mu}(k)\right)^2}{k-1} \\
&= \frac{1}{k-1}\sum_{l=1}^{k}\left(y_l - \frac{(k-1)\hat{\mu}(k-1) + y_k}{k}\right)^2 \\
&= \frac{1}{k-1}\sum_{l=1}^{k}\left(y_l - \frac{k\hat{\mu}(k-1) - \hat{\mu}(k-1) + y_k}{k}\right)^2 \\
&= \frac{1}{k-1}\sum_{l=1}^{k}\left(\left(y_l - \hat{\mu}(k-1)\right) - \frac{y_k - \hat{\mu}(k-1)}{k}\right)^2 \\
&= \frac{1}{k-1}\sum_{l=1}^{k}\left(\left(y_l - \hat{\mu}(k-1)\right)^2 + \left(\frac{y_k - \hat{\mu}(k-1)}{k}\right)^2\right. \\
&\qquad \left. - 2\left(y_l - \hat{\mu}(k-1)\right)\frac{y_k - \hat{\mu}(k-1)}{k}\right) \\
&= \frac{1}{k-1}\sum_{l=1}^{k}\left(y_l - \hat{\mu}(k-1)\right)^2 + \frac{1}{k-1}\sum_{l=1}^{k}\left(\frac{y_k - \hat{\mu}(k-1)}{k}\right)^2 \\
&\qquad - 2\frac{1}{k-1}\sum_{l=1}^{k}\left(\left(y_l - \hat{\mu}(k-1)\right)\frac{\left(y_k - \hat{\mu}(k-1)\right)}{k}\right) \\
&= \frac{1}{k-1}\left(\sum_{l=1}^{k-1}\left(y_l - \hat{\mu}(k-1)\right)^2 + \left(y_k - \hat{\mu}(k-1)\right)^2\right) \\
&\qquad + \frac{1}{k-1}k\left(\frac{y_k - \hat{\mu}(k-1)}{k}\right)^2 \\
&\qquad - \frac{2}{k-1}\frac{\left(y_k - \hat{\mu}(k-1)\right)}{k}\left(\sum_{l=1}^{k} y_l - k\hat{\mu}(k-1)\right) \\
&= \frac{k-2}{k-1}\frac{\sum_{l=1}^{k-1}\left(y_l - \hat{\mu}(k-1)\right)^2}{k-2} + \frac{1}{k-1}\left(y_k - \hat{\mu}(k-1)\right)^2 \\
&\qquad + \frac{1}{k(k-1)}\left(y_k - \hat{\mu}(k-1)\right)^2
\end{aligned}$$

$$
\begin{aligned}
&- \frac{2}{k(k-1)} \left(y_k - \hat{\mu}(k-1)\right) \left(\sum_{l=1}^{k-1} y_l + y_k - k\hat{\mu}(k-1) \right) \\
&= \frac{k-2}{k-1}\hat{\sigma}^2(k-1) + \frac{k+1}{k(k-1)} \left(y_k - \hat{\mu}(k-1)\right)^2 \\
&\quad - \frac{2}{k(k-1)} \left(y_k - \hat{\mu}(k-1)\right) \left((k-1)\hat{\mu}(k-1) + y_k - k\hat{\mu}(k-1)\right) \\
&= \frac{k-2}{k-1}\hat{\sigma}^2(k-1) + \frac{k+1}{k(k-1)} \left(y_k - \hat{\mu}(k-1)\right)^2 - \frac{2}{k(k-1)} \left(y_k - \hat{\mu}(k-1)\right)^2 \\
&= \frac{k-2}{k-1}\hat{\sigma}^2(k-1) + \frac{1}{k} \left(y_k - \hat{\mu}(k-1)\right)^2.
\end{aligned}
$$

Remembering now the result of Equation B.10, we obtain the recursive formulation of the leave-one-out mean square error:

$$
mse^{cv}(k) = \frac{k(k-2)^2}{(k-1)^3} mse^{cv}(k-1) + \frac{1}{k-1} \left(y_k - \hat{\mu}(k-1)\right)^2. \tag{B.13}
$$

B.2.3 Discussion

The algorithm described in Section B.2.2 computes, for a given query, the sequence of the predictions and the sequence of the mean square errors when a growing number of nearest-neighbors is used as local training subset.

The recursion in Equation B.12 is initialized for $k = 1$ with $\hat{y}(1) = y_1$, that is, with the output associated with the nearest-neighbor. On the contrary, the recursion on the mean square error is started for $k = 2$ since a leave-one-out error cannot be defined for less than two examples. Furthermore, it is worth noticing here as a detail, that $mse^{cv}(1)$ does not need to be explicitly initialized since for $k = 2$ the first term in Equation B.13 equals zero because of the numerator of its coefficient.

In figure B.1 we propose a comparison between the recursive algorithm described by Equations B.12 and B.13 and its non-recursive counterpart obtained from the direct implementation of Equations B.7 and B.8. For a given query, and once the neighbors have been retrieved, the plot shows the time needed by the two methods in order to fit and assess all the constant models which consider a number of neighbors in the range between 2 and K, for values of K between 3 and 50.[2] Figure B.1 visually confirms that the time needed by the recursive algorithm grows linearly with K, as it could be expected from the nature of Equations B.12 and B.13.

A comparison is of interest here between the algorithm developed in Section B.2.2 and the *lazy learning* algorithm described in Section B.1, which adopts

[2] The experiments were performed on a Pentium 400MHz CPU.

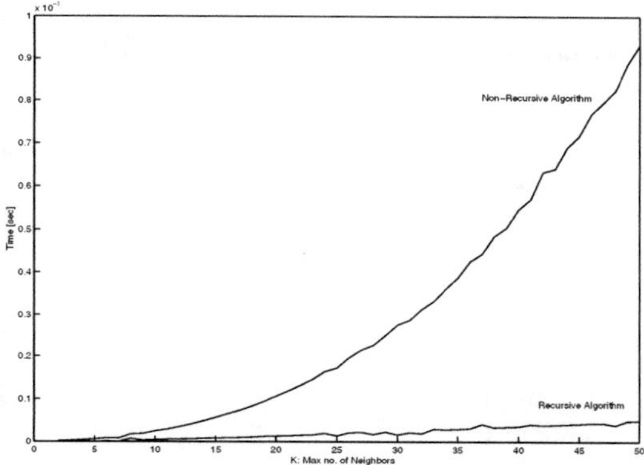

Figure B.1: Time of computation needed to fit and asses all the models which consider a number of neighbors in the range between 2 and K.

the recursive least squares algorithms for the identification of generic linear models.

The recursive least square, as described in Section B.1, does not return for every value of k the "exact" model that would be obtained by solving off-line the corresponding least square problem on the first k neighbors. The returned model is rather the model that would be obtained by solving off-line a *ridge regression* (Draper & Smith, 1981). This implicit effect of regularization is obtained through the conventional initialization of the variance/covariance matrix (Bierman, 1977), and prevents problems due to a nearly singular local data matrix.

Local constant models do not suffer from this kind of problems: the single parameter that needs to be identified is, for a given query and for a given value of k, a function only of the output y_j and not of the input x_j of the k-nearest-neighbors. Therefore, the position of the nearest-neighbors in the input space is not relevant, and it is not necessary to adopt any regularization method. From this, it follows that the predictions return by Equation B.12 and the mean square errors returned by Equation B.13 are "exact," that is, they are identical to the values that would be obtained by their off-line counterparts.

B.3 The lazy package and its applications

The *lazy learning* algorithm described in Sections B.1 and B.2 has been implemented by the author in the lazy package for R (Birattari & Bontempi, 2003). This package is currently available for free download from the R official repository.[3] Previously, an implementation for Matlab™ of the *lazy learning* algorithm (Birattari & Bontempi, 1999b) had been made available by the author.[4] The lazy package is part of a larger IRIDIA project, whose goal is the implementation of a set of local modeling approaches for data analysis and regression. In the same context, also a tool for neuro-fuzzy identification and data analysis, described in Bontempi & Birattari (1999), has been released.[5]

The lazy has been adopted in a number of research works and industrial applications. The following is a non-exhaustive list:

Financial prediction of stock markets. *Lazy learning* has been adopted in a joint project involving IRIDIA and the research center of Masterfood, for the prediction of some market indices (Birattari, 1997). Another application of local learning techniques to the prediction of stock markets is described in Bontempi, Bertolissi & Birattari (2000).

Prediction of chaotic time series. The algorithm for time series prediction based on *lazy learning* and described in Bontempi, Birattari & Bersini (1998, 1999c), ranked second among 17 participants in the International Competition on Time Series organized by the *International Workshop on Advanced Black-box techniques for nonlinear modeling* in Leuven, Belgium (Suykens & Vandewalle, 1998).

Nonlinear control and identification. The *lazy learning* method was used to implement adaptive control strategies based on the extension of linear control techniques to the nonlinear setting. This research is described in Bontempi, Birattari & Bersini (1999c). The method has been studied (Bontempi *et al.*, 2001) within the Esprit project FAMIMO—Fuzzy algorithms for multi-input multi-output processes—funded by the Commission of the European Communities. A comparison of the lazy and fuzzy approaches for non linear control is given in Bertolissi, Birattari, Bontempi, Duchâteau & Bersini (2000a,b, 2002). A survey on local linear techniques for nonlinear control is given in Bontempi & Birattari (2005)

Modeling of industrial processes. The *lazy learning* technique has been employed to model the rolling steel mill process of the FaFer Usinor steel company in Charleroi, Belgium (Birattari, 1999). It is also the subject of an active collaboration of IRIDIA with the Honeywell Technology Center in Minneapolis, MI, USA.

Electric load forecasting. A joint project of IRIDIA and Tractebel Belgium is adopting *lazy learning* techniques for the forecasting of electrical loads.

[3] `http://cran.r-project.org/src/contrib/Descriptions/lazy.html`

[4] `http://iridia.ulb.ac.be/ lazy`

[5] `http://iridia.ulb.ac.be/ gbonte/software/Local/FIS.html`

Prediction of economic variables. A joint project of IRIDIA and Dieteren, the first Belgian car dealer, is studying the adoption of *lazy learning* techniques to predict the annual amount of sales on the basis of historical data.

Design and optimization of embedded systems. The *lazy learning* algorithm has been adopted in Bontempi & Kruijtzer (2004) for modeling the performance of multimedia applications running on an embedded microprocessor.

Quality of service in multimedia. Bontempi & Lafruit (2002) have used the lazy package in a study on quality of service methods in multimedia applications.

Power system monitoring. The *Lazy learning* algorithm has been used by Villacci, Bontempi, Vaccaro & Birattari (2004) for predicting the hot-spot temperature of a mineral-oil-immersed transformer under heavy loads. The method is applied in (Bontempi *et al.*, 2004) to a specific case study concerning a system of power cables.

I am tired, I am weary
I could sleep for a thousand years

Lou Reed

References

Aarts, E. H. L. & Lenstra, J. K. (1997). *Local Search in Combinatorial Optimization*. John Wiley & Sons. Chichester, United Kingdom.

Adenso-Díaz, B. & Laguna, M. (2002). Fine-tuning of algorithms using fractional experimental designs and local search. Unpublished. Available from: `http://www-bus.colorado.edu/Faculty/Laguna/articles/finetune.html`.

Aha, D. W. (1997). Editorial. *Artificial Intelligence Review*, *11*(1–5):1–6. *Special Issue on Lazy Learning*.

Alexéev, V., Tikhomirov, V., & Fomine, S. (1982). *Commande Optimale*. Éditions MIR. Moscow, Soviet Union. In French.

Allen, J. A. & Minton, S. (1996). Selecting the right heuristic algorithm: Runtime performance predictors. In McCalla, G. (Ed.), *Advances in Artificial Intelligence: The Eleventh Biennial Conference of the Canadian Society for Computational Studies of Intelligence*, volume 1081 of *LNCS*, pp. 41–53, Springer-Verlag. Berlin, Germany.

Aquinas, T. (ca. 1270). *Summa Theologiae*.

Aristotle (ca. 350 BC). *De Anima*.

Atkeson, C. G., Moore, A. W., & Schaal, S. (1997). Locally weighted learning. *Artificial Intelligence Review*, *11*(1–5):11–73.

Baluja, S. (1994). Population-based incremental learning: A method for integrating genetic search based function optimization and competitive learning. Technical Report CMU-CS-94-163, School of Computer Science, Carnegie Mellon, Pittsburgh, PA, USA.

Baluja, S. & Caruana, R. (1995). Removing the genetics from the standard genetic algorithm. In Prieditis, A. & Russel, S. (Eds.), *Proceedings of the Twelfth International Conference on Machine Learning*, pp. 38–46, Morgan Kaufmann. San Francisco, CA, USA.

Baluja, S. & Davies, S. (1997). Using optimal dependency-trees for combinatorial optimization: Learning the structure of the search space. In Jr., D. H. F. (Ed.), *Proceedings of the Fourteenth International Conference on Machine Learning*, pp. 30–38, Morgan Kaufmann. San Francisco, CA, USA.

Barnett, V. (1999). *Comparative Statistical Inference.* Third edition. John Wiley & Sons. New York, NY, USA.

Barr, R. S., Golden, B. L., Kelly, J. P., Resende, M. G. C., & Stewart, W. R. (1995). Designing and reporting computational experiments with heuristic methods. *Journal of Heuristics, 1*(1):9–32.

Battiti, R. (1996). Reactive search: Toward self–tuning heuristics. In Rayward-Smith, V. J., Osman, I. H., Reeves, C. R., & Smith, G. D. (Eds.), *Modern Heuristic Search Methods*, pp. 61–83. John Wiley & Sons. Chichester, United Kingdom.

Battiti, R. & Tecchiolli, G. (1994). The reactive tabu search. *ORSA Journal on Computing, 6*(2):126–140.

Becker, S. (2004). Racing-Verfahren für Tourenplanungsprobleme. Diplomarbeit, Technische Universität Darmstadt, Darmstadt, Germany.

Beckers, R., Deneubourg, J. L., & Goss, S. (1992). Trails and U-turns in the selection of the shortest path by the ant Lasius Niger. *Journal of Theoretical Biology, 159*:397–415.

Bellman, R. (1957). *Dynamic Programming.* Princeton University Press. Princeton, NJ, USA.

Bellman, R. E. (1961). *Adaptive Control Processes.* Princeton University Press. Princeton, NJ, USA.

Bentley, J. L. (1992). Fast algorithms for geometric traveling salesman problems. *ORSA Journal on Computing, 4*(4):387–411.

Bernoulli, J. (1696). Problema novum ad cuius solutionem mathematici invitantur. *Acta Eruditorum, 15*:264–269.

Bertolissi, E., Birattari, M., Bontempi, G., Duchâteau, A., & Bersini, H. (2000a). Data-driven techniques for divide and conquer adaptive control. In Zakharov, V. (Ed.), *Control Applications of Optimization. Proceedings of the 11th IFAC International Workshop, CAO 2000*, Pergamon Press/Elsevier. Oxford, United Kingdom.

Bertolissi, E., Birattari, M., Bontempi, G., Duchâteau, A., & Bersini, H. (2000b). Multiple models for adaptive control: The lazy and the fuzzy approach. In Smith, R. (Ed.), *System Identification. A Proceedings volume from the 12th IFAC Symposium on System Identification. SYSID 2000*, Pergamon Press/Elsevier. Oxford, United Kingdom.

Bertolissi, E., Birattari, M., Bontempi, G., Duchâteau, A., & Bersini, H. (2002). Data-driven techniques for direct adaptive control: The lazy and the fuzzy approaches. *Fuzzy Sets and Systems*, *128*(1):3–14.

Bertsekas, D. P. (1995a). *Dynamic Programming and Optimal Control.* Athena Scientific. Belmont, MA, USA. Vols. I and II.

Bertsekas, D. P. (1995b). *Nonlinear Programming.* Athena Scientific. Belmont, MA, USA.

Bianchi, L., Birattari, M., Chiarandini, M., Manfrin, M., Mastrolilli, M., Paquete, L., Rossi-Doria, O., & Schiavinotto, T. (2004). Metaheuristics for the vehicle routing problem with stochastic demands. In Yao, X., Burke, E., Lozano, J. A., Smith, J., Merelo-Guervós, J. J., Bullinaria, J. A., Rowe, J., Tino, P., Kabán, A., & Schwefel, H.-P. (Eds.), *Parallel Problem Solving from Nature, 8th International Conference, PPSN VIII*, volume 3242 of *LNCS*, pp. 450–460, Springer-Verlag. Berlin, Germany.

Bierman, G. J. (1977). *Factorization Methods for Discrete Sequential Estimation.* Academic Press. New York, NY, USA.

Billings, S. A. & Voon, W. S. G. (1987). Piecewise linear identification of non-linear systems. *International Journal of Control*, *46*:215–235.

Billingsley, P. (1986). *Probability and Measure.* Second edition. John Wiley & Sons. New York, NY, USA.

Birattari, M. (1997). Modelli locali per l'apprendimento: dall'approccio neuro-fuzzy al lazy learning. Tesi di Laurea, Politecnico di Milano, Milano, Italy.

Birattari, M. (1999). First project: IRIDIA and FaFer. Technical Report TR/IRIDIA/1999-13, IRIDIA, Université Libre de Bruxelles, Brussels, Belgium.

Birattari, M. (2001). On the formal foundation of ant programming. Mémoire de DEA, Université Libre de Bruxelles, Brussels, Belgium.

Birattari, M. (2003). The race package for R. Racing methods for the selection of the best. Technical Report TR/IRIDIA/2003-37, IRIDIA, Université Libre de Bruxelles, Brussels, Belgium. Package available at: `http://cran.r-project.org/src/contrib/Descriptions/race.html`.

Birattari, M. (2004a). On the estimation of the expected performance of a metaheuristic on a class of instances. How many instances, how many runs? Technical Report TR/IRIDIA/2004-01, IRIDIA, Université Libre de Bruxelles, Brussels, Belgium.

Birattari, M. (2004b). Notes on the existence of the expected value. Technical Report TR/IRIDIA/2004-20, IRIDIA, Université Libre de Bruxelles, Brussels, Belgium.

Birattari, M. & Bontempi, G. (1999a). Lazy learning vs. Speedy Gonzales: A fast algorithm for recursive identification and recursive validation of local constant models. Technical Report TR/IRIDIA/1999-6, IRIDIA, Université Libre de Bruxelles, Brussels, Belgium.

Birattari, M. & Bontempi, G. (1999b). The lazy learning toolbox. For use with Matlab. Technical Report TR/IRIDIA/1999-7, IRIDIA, Université Libre de Bruxelles, Brussels, Belgium.

Birattari, M. & Bontempi, G. (2003). The lazy package for R. Lazy learning for local regression. Technical Report TR/IRIDIA/2003-38, IRIDIA, Université Libre de Bruxelles, Brussels, Belgium. Package available at: `http://cran.r-project.org/src/contrib/Descriptions/lazy.html`.

Birattari, M., Bontempi, G., & Bersini, H. (1999). Lazy learning meets the recursive least-squares algorithm. In Kearns, M. S., Solla, S. A., & Cohn, D. A. (Eds.), *Advances in Neural Information Processing Systems 11*, pp. 375–381, MIT Press. Cambridge, MA, USA.

Birattari, M., Di Caro, G., & Dorigo, M. (2000). For a formal foundation of the Ant Programming approach to combinatorial optimization. Part 1: The problem, the representation, and the genearl solution strategy. Technical Report TR-H-301, ATR-Human Information Processing Labs, Kyoto, Japan.

Birattari, M., Di Caro, G., & Dorigo, M. (2002). Toward the formal foundation of ant programming. In Dorigo, M., Di Caro, G., & Sampels, M. (Eds.), *Ant Algorithms, 3rd International Workshop, ANTS 2002*, volume 2463 of *LNCS*, pp. 188–201, Springer-Verlag. Berlin, Germany.

Birattari, M., Stützle, T., Paquete, L., & Varrentrapp, K. (2002). A racing algorithm for configuring metaheuristics. In Langdon, W. B., Cantú-Paz, E., Mathias, K., Roy, R., Davis, D., Poli, R., Balakrishnan, K., Honavar, V., Rudolph, G., Wegener, J., Bull, L., Potter, M. A., Schultz, A. C., Miller, J. F., Burke, E., & Jonoska, N. (Eds.), *Proceedings of the Genetic and Evolutionary Computation Conference*, pp. 11–18, Morgan Kaufmann. San Francisco, CA, USA.

Birkendorf, A. & Simon, H.-U. (1998). Using computational learning strategies as a tool for combinatorial optimization. *Annals of Mathematics and Artificial Intelligence*, *22*(3/4):237–257.

Bishop, C. M. (1995). *Neural Networks for Pattern Recognition*. Clarendon Press. Oxford, United Kingdom.

Blake, C. L. & Merz, C. J. (1998). UCI repository of machine learning databases. `http://www.ics.uci.edu/~mlearn/MLRepository.html`.

Blum, C. (2004). *Theoretical and Practical Aspects of Ant Colony Optimization*. PhD thesis, Université Libre de Bruxelles, Brussels, Belgium.

Blum, C. & Roli, A. (2003). Metaheuristics in combinatorial optimization: Overview and conceptual comparison. *ACM Computing Surveys*, *35*(3):268–308.

Blum, C., Roli, A., & Dorigo, M. (2001). HC–ACO: The hyper-cube framework for Ant Colony Optimization. In Pinho de Sousa, J. (Ed.), *Proceedings of the 4th Metaheuristics International Conference*, volume 2, pp. 399–403. Porto, Portugal.

Boldrini, F. (2005). Costruzione di modelli locali nel metodo della superficie di risposta per la configurazione di una metaeuristica. Tesi di Laurea, Università degli Studi di Ferrara, Ferrara, Italy. Tentative title. In preparation.

Boltyanskii, V. (1978). *Optimal Control of Discrete Systems*. John Wiley & Sons. New York, NY, USA.

Bonabeau, E., Dorigo, M., & Theraulaz, G. (1999). *Swarm Intelligence: From Natural to Artificial Systems*. Oxford University Press. New York, NY, USA.

Bonabeau, E., Dorigo, M., & Theraulaz, G. (2000). Inspiration for optimization from social insect behavior. *Nature*, *406*:39–42.

Bonferroni, C. E. (1935). Il calcolo delle assicurazioni su gruppi di teste. In *Studi in Onore del Professore Salvatore Ortu Carboni*, pp. 13–60. Roma, Italy.

Bonferroni, C. E. (1936). Teoria statistica delle classi e calcolo delle probabilità. *Pubblicazioni del Regio Istituto Superiore di Scienze Economiche e Commerciali di Firenze*, *8*:3–62.

Bontempi, G. (1999). *Local Learning Techniques for Modeling, Prediction and Control*. PhD thesis, Université Libre de Bruxelles, Brussels, Belgium.

Bontempi, G., Bersini, H., & Birattari, M. (2001). The local paradigm for modeling and control: From neuro-fuzzy to lazy learning. *Fuzzy Sets and Systems*, *121*(1):59–72.

Bontempi, G., Bertolissi, E., & Birattari, M. (2000). Predicting stock markets in boundary conditions with local models. In Birge, J., Marshall, J., & Yager, R. R. (Eds.), *Proceedings of the IEEE/IAFE/INFORMS Conference on Computational Intelligence for Financial Engineering, CIFEr 2000*, pp. 158–161, IEEE Publications. Piscataway, NJ, USA.

Bontempi, G. & Birattari, M. (1999). Toolbox for neuro-fuzzy identification and data analysis. For use with Matlab. Technical Report TR/IRIDIA/1999-9, IRIDIA, Université Libre de Bruxelles, Brussels, Belgium.

Bontempi, G. & Birattari, M. (2005). From linearization to lazy learning: A survey of divide-and-conquer techniques for nonlinear control. *International Journal of Computational Cognition*, *3*(1):56–73.

Bontempi, G., Birattari, M., & Bersini, H. (1998). Lazy learning for iterated time-series prediction. In Suykens, J. A. K. & Vandewalle, J. (Eds.), *International Workshop on Advanced Black-Box Techniques for Nonlinear Modeling*, pp. 62–68, Katholieke Universiteit Leuven. Leuven, Belgium.

Bontempi, G., Birattari, M., & Bersini, H. (1999a). Lazy learners at work: The lazy learning toolbox. In *EUFIT'99: The 7th European Congress on Intelligent Techniques and Soft Computing, Abstract Booklet with CD Rom*, ELITE Foundation. Aachen, Germany.

Bontempi, G., Birattari, M., & Bersini, H. (1999b). Lazy learning for local modeling and control design. *International Journal of Control*, *72*(7/8):643–658.

Bontempi, G., Birattari, M., & Bersini, H. (1999c). Local learning for iterated time-series prediction. In Bradko, I. & Dzeroski, S. (Eds.), *Proceedings of the Sixteenth International Conference on Machine Learning*, pp. 32–38, Morgan Kaufmann. San Francisco, CA, USA.

Bontempi, G., Birattari, M., & Bersini, H. (2000). A model selection approach for local learning. *AI Communications*, *13*:41–47.

Bontempi, G., Birattari, M., & Meyer, P. E. (2004). Combining lazy learning, racing and subsampling for effective feature selection. Technical Report 527, Département d'Informatique, Université Libre de Bruxelles, Brussels, Belgium. Submitted for publication.

Bontempi, G. & Kruijtzer, W. (2004). The use of intelligent data analysis techniques for system-level design: a software estimation example. *Soft Computing Journal*, *8*(7):477–490.

Bontempi, G. & Lafruit, G. (2002). Enabling multimedia QoS control with black-box modeling. In Bustard, D., Liu, W., & Sterritt, R. (Eds.), *Soft-Ware 2002: Computing in an Imperfect World*, volume 2311 of *LNCS*, pp. 46–59, Springer-Verlag. Berlin, Germany.

Bontempi, G., Vaccaro, A., & Villacci, D. (2004). A semi-physical modelling architecture for dynamic assessment of power components loading capability. *IEE Proceedings of Generation Transmission and Distribution*, *151*(4):533–542.

Box, G. E. P. (1976). Science and statistics. *Journal of the American Statistical Association*, *71*(356):791–799.

Box, G. E. P. & Draper, N. R. (1987). *Empirical Model-Building and Response Surfaces*. John Wiley & Sons. New York, NY, USA.

Box, G. E. P., Hunter, W. G., & Hunter, J. S. (1978). *Statistics for Experimenters*. John Wiley & Sons. New York, NY, USA.

Boyan, J. & Moore, A. (1997). Using prediction to improve combinatorial optimization search. In *Proceedings of the Sixth International Workshop on Artificial Intelligence and Statistics*.

Boyan, J. & Moore, A. (2000). Learning evaluation functions to improve optimization by local search. *Journal of Machine Learning Research*, *1*:77–112.

Brady, R. M. (1985). Optimization strategies gleaned from biological evolution. *Nature*, *317*:804–806.

Breiman, L., Friedman, J. H., Olshen, R. A., & Stone, C. J. (1984). *Classification and Regression Trees*. Waldsforth. Belmont, MA, USA.

Brel, J. (1968). Vesoul. In *J'arrive*. Barclay.

Burke, E. K., Elliman, D. G., & Weare, R. F. (1994). A university timetabling system based on graph colouring and constraint manipulation. *Journal of Research on Computing in Education*, *27*(1):1–18.

Burke, E. K., Elliman, D. G., & Weare, R. F. (1995). Specialised recombinative operators for timetabling problems. In Fogarty, T. C. (Ed.), *Evolutionary Computing, AISB Workshop*, volume 993 of *LNCS*, pp. 75–85, Springer-Verlag. Berlin, Germany.

Burke, E. K., Newall, J. P., & Weare, R. F. (1995). A memetic algorithm for university exam timetabling. In Burke, E. K. & Ross, P. (Eds.), *Practice and Theory of Automated Timetabling, 1st International Conference, PATAT 1995*, volume 1153 of *LNCS*, pp. 241–251, Springer-Verlag. Berlin, Germany.

Burke, E. K., Newall, J. P., & Weare, R. F. (1996). A memetic algorithm for university exam timetabling. In Burke, E. & Ross, P. (Eds.), *Practice and Theory of Automated Timetabling, First International Conference*, volume 1153 of *LNCS*, pp. 241–250, Springer-Verlag. Berlin, Germany.

Byrne, D. & Taguchi, S. (1987). The Taguchi approach to parameter design. *Quality Progress, 20*(12):19–26.

Cameron, J. (1984). The Terminator. Orion Pictures Corporation.

Campbell, Y., Lo, A. W., & MacKinlay, A. C. (1997). *The Econometrics of Financial Markets*. Princeton University Press. Princeton, NJ, USA.

Capek, K. (1920). *Rossum's Universal Robots*.

Carbonell, J., editor. (1990). *Machine Learning. Paradigms and Methods*. MIT Press. Cambridge, MA, USA.

Çela, E. (1998). *The Quadratic Assignment Problem: Theory and Algorithms*. Kluwer Academic Publisher. Dordrecht, The Netherlands.

Cerny, V. (1985). A thermodynamical approach to the traveling salesman problem: an efficient simulation algorithm. *Journal of Optimization Theory and Applications, 45*:41–51.

Chiarandini, M. (2004). Personal communication.

Chiarandini, M. (2005). *Stochastic local search for overconstrained problems*. PhD thesis, Technische Universität Darmstadt, Darmstadt, Germany. In preparation.

Chiarandini, M., Birattari, M., Socha, K., & Rossi-Doria, O. (2004). An effective hybrid approach for the university course timetabling problem. *Journal of Scheduling*. Accepted for publication.

Chiarandini, M., Socha, K., Birattari, M., & Rossi-Doria, O. (2003). International timetabling competition. a hybrid approach. Technical Report AIDA-03-04, FG Intellektik, FB Informatik, Technische Universität Darmstadt, Darmstadt, Germany.

Chiarandini, M. & Stützle, T. (2002). Experimental evaluation of course timetabling algorithms. Technical Report AIDA-02-05, FG Intellektik, FB Informatik, Technische Universität Darmstadt, Darmstadt, Germany.

Chien, S., Gratch, J., & Burl, M. (1995). On the efficient allocation of resources for hypothesis evaluation: A statistical approach. *IEEE Transactions on Pattern Analysis and Machine Intelligence, 17*(7):652–665.

Clarke, R. (1993). Asimov's laws of robotics: Implications for information technology. Part 1. *Computer, 37*(1):53–61.

Clarke, R. (1994). Asimov's laws of robotics: Implications for information technology. Part 2. *Computer, 36*(12):57–66.

Collodi (1883). *Pinocchio.*

Conover, W. J. (1999). *Practical Nonparametric Statistics.* Third edition. John Wiley & Sons. New York, NY, USA.

Cook, S. A. (1971). The complexity of theorem-proving procedures. In *Proceedings of the 3rd Annual ACM Symposium on Theory of Computing*, pp. 151–158. New York, NY, USA.

Cooper, T. B. & Kingston, J. H. (1995). The complexity of timetable construction problems. In Burke, E. K. & Ross, P. (Eds.), *Practice and Theory of Automated Timetabling, 1st International Conference, PATAT 1995*, volume 1153 of *LNCS*, pp. 283–295, Springer-Verlag. Berlin, Germany.

Corne, D., Dorigo, M., & Glover, F., editors. (1999). *The Ant Colony Optimization Meta-Heuristic.* McGraw-Hill. New York, NY, USA.

Corne, D. W. & Knowles, J. D. (2003). No free lunch and free leftovers theorems for multiobjective optimization problems. In Fonseca, C. M., Fleming, P. J., Zitzler, E., Deb, K., & Thiele, L. (Eds.), *Evolutionary Multi-Criterion Optimization, Second International Conference, EMO 2003*, volume 2632 of *LNCS*, pp. 327–341, Springer-Verlag. Berlin, Germany.

Coy, S. P., Golden, B. L., Runger, G. C., & Wasil, E. A. (2001). Using experimental design to find effective parameter settings for heuristics. *Journal of Heuristics, 7*(1):77–97.

Cristianini, N. & Shawe-Taylor, J. (2000). *An Introduction to Support Vector Machines and Other Kernel-based Learning Methods.* Cambridge University Press. Cambridge, United Kingdom.

Culberson, J. C. (1992). Iterated greedy graph coloring and the difficulty landscape. Technical Report 92-07, Department of Computing Science, The University of Alberta, Edmonton, AB, Canada.

Cybenko, G. (1989). Approximation by superpositions of a sigmoidal function. *Mathematics of Control, Signals, and Systems, 2*(4):303–314.

Cybenko, G. (1996). Just-in-time learning and estimation. In Bittanti, S. & Picci, G. (Eds.), *Identification, Adaptation, Learning. The Science of Learning Models from data*, NATO ASI Series, pp. 423–434. Springer-Verlag. Berlin, Germany.

Darquennes, D. (2005). Programmation et applications des algorithmes de fourmilières. Mémoire de Licence, Facultés Universitaires Notre-Dames de la Paix, Namur, Belgium. Tentative title. In preparation.

Darwin, C. R. (1859). *On The Origin of Species by Means of Natural Selection. Or the preservation of favoured races in the struggle for life.* John Murray. London, United Kingdom.

de Boer, P.-T., Kroese, D. P., Mannor, S., & Rubinstein, R. Y. (2005). A tutorial on the cross-entropy method. *Annals of Operations Research, 134*(1):19–67.

De Bonet, J. S., Isbell, C. L., & Viola, P. (1997). MIMIC: Finding optima by estimating probability densities. In Mozer, M. C., Jordan, M. I., & Petsche, T. (Eds.), *Advances in Neural Information Processing Systems 9*, pp. 424–431, MIT Press.

de Werra, D. (1995). An introduction to timetabling. *European Journal of Operational Research, 19*:151–162.

de Werra, D. (1997). The combinatorics of timetabling. *European Journal of Operational Research, 96*:504–513.

Dean, A. & Voss, D. (1999). *Design and Analysis of Experiments.* Springer-Verlag. New York, NY, USA.

Demenage, M., Grisoni, P., & Paschos, V. T. (1998). Differential approximation algorithms for some combinatorial optimization problems. *Theoretical Computer Science, 209*:107–122.

den Besten, M. L. (2004). *Simple Metaheuristics for Scheduling. An empirical investigation into the application of iterated local search to deterministic scheduling problems with tardiness penalities.* PhD thesis, Technische Universität Darmstadt, Darmstadt, Germany.

Denis, M. (2005). Optimisation d'un algorithme génétique au moyen de race: Application au problème du voyageur de commerce. Mémoire de Licence, Université Libre de Bruxelles, Brussels, Belgium. Tentative title. In preparation.

Devroye, L., Gyorfi, L., & Lugosi, G. (1996). *A Probabilistic Theory of Pattern Recognition.* Springer-Verlag. New York, NY, USA.

Di Caro, G. (2004). *Ant Colony Optimization and its Application to Adaptive Routing in Telecommunication Networks.* PhD thesis, Université Libre de Bruxelles, Brussels, Belgium.

Di Gaspero, L. & Shaerf, A. (2001). Tabu search techniques for examination timetabling. In Burke, E. K. & Erben, W. (Eds.), *Practice and Theory of Automated Timetabling, 3rd International Conference, PATAT 2000*, number 2079 in LNCS, pp. 104–117, Springer-Verlag. Berlin, Germany.

Dorigo, M. (1992). *Ottimizzazione, apprendimento automatico, ed algoritmi basati su metafora naturale*. PhD thesis, Politecnico di Milano, Milano, Italy. In Italian.

Dorigo, M. (1998). Ants 1998—From Ant Colonies to Artificial Ants: 1st International Workshop on Ant Colony Optimization. `http://iridia.ulb.ac.be/~ants/ants98`.

Dorigo, M., Birattari, M., Blum, C., Gambardella, L. M., Mondada, F., & Stützle, T., editors. (2004). *Ant Colony Optimization and Swarm Intelligence, 4th International Workshop, ANTS 2004*, volume 3172 of *LNCS*. Springer-Verlag. Berlin, Germany.

Dorigo, M., Bonabeau, E., & Theraulaz, G. (2000). Ant algorithms and stigmergy. *Future Generation Computer Systems*, *16*(8):851–871.

Dorigo, M. & Di Caro, G. (1999). The ant colony optimization meta-heuristic. In Corne, D., Dorigo, M., & Glover, F. (Eds.), *New Ideas in Optimization*, pp. 11–32. McGraw-Hill. New York, NY, USA.

Dorigo, M., Di Caro, G., & Gambardella, L. M. (1999). Ant algorithms for distributed discrete optimization. *Artificial Life*, *5*(2):137–172.

Dorigo, M., Di Caro, G., & Sampels, M., editors. (2002). *Ant Algorithms, 3rd International Workshop, ANTS 2002*, volume 2463 of *LNCS*. Springer-Verlag. Berlin, Germany.

Dorigo, M., Di Caro, G., & Stützle, T. (2000). Ant algorithms. Guest editorial. *Future Generation Computer Systems*, *16*(8):v–vii.

Dorigo, M. & Gambardella, L. M. (1997). Ant Colony System: A cooperative learning approach to the traveling salesman problem. *IEEE Transactions on Evolutionary Computation*, *1*(1):53–66.

Dorigo, M., Maniezzo, V., & A.Colorni (1996). Ant System: Optimization by a colony of cooperating agents. *IEEE Transactions on Systems, Man, and Cybernetics—Part B*, *26*(1):29–41.

Dorigo, M., Maniezzo, V., & Colorni, A. (1991). The Ant System: An autocatalytic optimizing process. Technical Report 91-016 Revised, Dipartimento di Elettronica, Politecnico di Milano, Milano, Italy.

Dorigo, M., Middendorf, M., & Stützle, T., editors. (2000). *Proceedings of ANTS 2000—From Ant Colonies to Artificial Ants: 2nd International Workshop on Ant Algorithms*. IRIDIA, Université Libre de Bruxelles. Brussels, Belgium.

Dorigo, M. & Stützle, T. (2002). The ant colony optimization metaheuristic: Algorithms, applications and advances. In Glover, F. & Kochenberger, G. (Eds.), *Handbook of Metaheuristics*, pp. 251–285. Kluwer Academic Publisher. Norwell, MA, USA.

Dorigo, M. & Stützle, T. (2004). *Ant Colony Optimization*. MIT Press. Cambridge, MA, USA.

Dorigo, M., Zlochin, M., Meuleau, N., & M.Birattari (2002). Updating ACO pheromones using stochastic gradient ascent and cross-entropy methods. In Cagnoni, S., Gottlieb, J., Hart, E., Middendorf, M., & Raidl, R. (Eds.), *Applications of Evolutionary Computing, EvoWorkshop 2002: EvoCOP, EvoIASP, EvoSTIM/EvoPLAN*, volume 2279 of *LNCS*, pp. 21–30, Springer-Verlag. Berlin, Germany.

Draper, N. R. & Smith, H. (1981). *Applied Regression Analysis*. John Wiley & Sons. New York, NY, USA.

Dréo, J., Pétrowski, A., Siarry, P., & Taillard, E. (2003). *Métahauristiques pour l'optimisation difficile*. Éditions Eyrolles. Paris, France. In French.

Duda, R. O., Hart, P. E., & Stork, D. G. (2001). *Pattern Classification*. Second edition. John Wiley & Sons. New York, NY, USA.

Edmonds, J. (1965). Paths, trees, and flowers. *Canadian Journal of Mathematics*, *17*:449–467.

Efron, B. & Tibshirani, R. J. (1997). *An Introduction to the Bootstrap*. Chapman & Hall/CRC. Boca Raton, FL, USA.

Elman, J. L. (1990). Finding structure in time. *Cognitive Science*, *14*(2):179–211.

Etxeberria, R. & Larrañaga, P. (1999). Global optimization with bayesian networks. In *Proceedings of the Second Symposium on Artificial Intelligence*, pp. 332–339, La Habana, Cuba.

Fayyad, U., Piatetsky-Shapiro, G., & Smyth, P. (1996). The KDD process for extracting useful knowledge from volumes of data. *Communication of the ACM*, *39*(11):27–34.

Fogel, L. J. (1962). Toward inductive inference automata. In *Proceedings of the International Federation for Information Processing Congress*, pp. 395–399. Munich, Germany.

Fogel, L. J., Owens, A. J., & Walsh, M. J. (1966). *Artificial Intelligence through Simulated Evolution.* John Wiley & Sons. New York, NY, USA.

Forney, G. D. (1973). The Viterbi algorithm. *Proceedings of the IEEE, 61*(3):268–278.

Friedman, J. H. (1991). Multivariate adaptive regression splines. *The Annals of Statistics, 19*:1–141.

Friedman, J. H. (1994). Flexible metric nearest neighbor classification. Technical Report 113, Department of Statistics, Stanford University, Stanford, CA, USA. `http://www-stat.stanford.edu/~jhf/ftp/flexmet.ps.Z`.

Galilei, G. (1638). *Discorsi e Dimostrazioni Matematiche intorno a due nuove scienze attinenti alla Meccanica & i Movimenti Locali.* Elzevier. Leiden, The Netherlands.

Garey, M. R. & Johnson, D. S. (1979). *Computers and Intractability. A guide to the Theory of NP-Completeness.* W.H. Freeman and Company. New York, NY, USA.

Geman, S., Bienenstock, E., & Doursat, R. (1992). Neural networks and the bias/variance dilemma. *Neural Computation, 4*(1):1–58.

Gendreau, M. A., Hertz, A., & Laporte, G. (1994). A tabu search heuristic for the VRP. *Management Science, 40*:1276–1290.

Gent, I. P., Grant, S. A., MacIntyre, E., Prosser, P., Shaw, P., Smith, B. M., & Walsh, T. (1997). How not to do it. Technical Report 97.27, School of Computer Studies, University of Leeds, Leeds, United Kingdom.

Gent, I. P. & Walsh, T. (1994). How not to do it. Technical Report 714, Department of Artificial Intelligence, University of Edinburgh, Edinburgh, United Kingdom.

Glover, F. (1977). Heuristics for integer programming using surrogate constraints. *Decision Sciences, 8*:156–166.

Glover, F. (1986). Future paths for integer programming and links to artificial intelligence. *Computers & Operations Research, 13*(5):533–549.

Glover, F. & Kochenberger, G., editors. (2002). *Handbook of Metaheuristics.* Kluwer Academic Publisher. Norwell, MA, USA.

Goldberg, D. & Segrest, P. (1987). Finite markov chain analysis of genetic algorithms. In *Proceedings of the Second International Conference on Genetic Algorithms*, pp. 1–8, Lawrence Erlbaum. Hillsdale, NJ, USA.

Goldberg, D. E. (1989). *Genetic Algorithms in Search, Optimization and Machine Learning*. Addison-Wesley Publishing Company. Reading, MA, USA.

Golden, B. L., Assad, A. A., Wasil, E. A., & Backer, E. (1986). Experimentation in optimization. *European Journal of Operational Research*, *27*:1–16.

Golden, B. L. & Stewart, W. R. (1985). Empirical analysis of heuristics. In Lawler, E., Lenstra, J. K., Rinnooy Kan, A., & Shmoys, D. (Eds.), *The Traveling Salesman Problem: A guided Tour of Combinatorial Optimization*. John Wiley & Sons. New York, NY, USA.

Goldsman, D. & Nelson, B. L. (2001). Statistical selection of the best system. In Peters, B. A., Smith, J. S., Medeiros, D. J., & Rohrer, M. W. (Eds.), *Proceedings of the 2001 Winter Simulation Conference*, pp. 139–146, ACM. Arlington, VA, USA.

Good, P. I. (2001). *Resampling Methods*. Second edition. Birkhauser. Boston, MA, USA.

Goss, S., Aron, S., Deneubourg, J. L., & Pasteels, J. M. (1989). Self-organized shortcuts in the Argentine ant. *Naturwissenschaften*, *76*:579–581.

Grassé, P. P. (1959). La reconstruction du nid et les coordinations interindividuelles chez *Bellicositermes Natalensis et Cubitermes sp.* La théorie de la stigmergie: Essai d'interprétation du comportement des termites constructeurs. *Insectes Sociaux*, *6*:41–81.

Gratch, J., Chien, S., & DeJong, G. (1993). Learning search control knowledge for deep space network scheduling. In *Proceedings of the Tenth International Conference on Machine Learning*, pp. 135–142, Morgan Kaufmann. San Francisco, CA, USA.

Gutjahr, W. (2000). A graph-based ant system and its convergence. *Future Generation Computer Systems*, *16*(8):873–888.

Gutjahr, W. (2002). ACO algorithms with guarandeed convergence to the optimal solution. *Information Processing Letters*, *82*(3):145–153.

Hansen, P. & Mladenović, N. (1999). An introduction to variable neighborhood search. In Voss, S., Martello, S., Osman, I. H., & Roucairol, C. (Eds.), *Meta-Heuristics: Advances and Trends in Local Search Paradigms for Optimization*, pp. 433–458. Kluwer Academic Publisher. Boston, MA, USA.

Harik, G. R. (1999). Linkage learning via probabilistic modeling in the ecga. Technical Report IlliGAL-99010, Department of Computer Science, University of Illinois, Urbana, IL, USA.

Harik, G. R., Lobo, F. G., & Goldberg, D. E. (1999). The compact genetic algorithm. *IEEE Transactions on Evolutionary Computation*, *3*(4):287–297.

Hartl, R. F. (2005). MIC 2005: The 6th Metaheuristics International Conference. `http://www.mic2005.org`.

Hassin, R. & Khuller, S. (2001). Z-approximations. *Journal of Algorithms*, *41*(2):429–442.

Hecht-Nielsen, R. (1989). Theory of backpropagation neural networks. In *Proceedings of the International Joint Conference on Neural Networks*, volume 1, pp. 593–605, IEEE Publications. New York, NY, USA.

Heckerman, D. (1995). A tutorial on learning with bayesian networks. Technical Report MSR-TR-95-06, Microsoft Research, Redmond, WA, USA.

Hoeffding, W. (1963). Probability inequalities for sum of bounded random variables. *Journal of the American Statistical Association*, *58*:78–150.

Holland, J. (1975). *Adaptation in Natural and Artificial Systems*. University of Michigan Press. Ann Harbor, MI, USA.

Holm, S. (1979). A simple sequentially rejective multiple test procedure. *Scandinavian Journal of Statistics*, *6*:65–70.

Hooker, J. N. (1994). Needed: An empirical science of algorithms. *Operations Research*, *42*(2):201–212.

Hooker, J. N. (1995). Testing heuristics: We have it all wrong. *Journal of Heuristics*, *1*(1):33–42.

Hoos, H. H. & Stützle, T. (2004). *Stochastic Local Search. Foundations and Applications*. Morgan Kaufmann. San Francisco, CA, USA.

Hopfield, J. J. (1982). Neural networks and physical systems with emergent collective computational abilities. In *Proceedings of the National Academy of Science of the United States of America*, volume 79, pp. 2554–2558.

Hornik, K., Stinchcombe, M., & White, H. (1989). Multilayer feedforward networks are universal approximators. *Neural Networks*, *2*(5):359–366.

Hsu, J. (1996). *Multiple Comparisons*. Chapman & Hall. Boca Raton, FL, USA.

Hume, D. (1748). *An Enquiry Concerning Human Understanding*.

Ibaraki, T., Nonobe, K., & Yagiura, M., editors. (2005). *Metaheuristics: Progress as Real Problem Solvers*. Kluwer Academic Publisher. Boston, MA, USA. Post-conference proceedings of the 5th Metaheuristics International Conference, MIC 2003.

Idel, M. (1983). *Golem: Jewish Magical and Mystical Traditions on the Artificial Anthropoid*. State University of New York Press. Albany, NY, USA.

Igel, C. & Toussaint, M. (2003). On classes of functions for which the No Free Lunch results hold. *Information Processing Letters, 86*(6):317–321.

Jang, J.-S. R. (1993). Anfis: Adaptive-network-based fuzzy inference system. *IEEE Transactions on Systems, Man, and Cybernetics, 23*(3):665–685.

Johansen, T. A. & Foss, B. A. (1993). Constructing NARMAX models using ARMAX models. *International Journal of Control, 58*:1125–1153.

John, G. H. & Langley, P. (1996). Static versus dynamic sampling for data mining. In Simoudis, E., Han, J.-W., & Fayyad, U. (Eds.), *Proceedings of the 2nd International Conference on Knowledge Discovery and Data Mining*, pp. 367–370, AAAI Press. Menlo Park, CA, USA.

Johnson, D. S. (2002). A Theoretician's guide to the experimental analysis of algorithms. In Goldwasser, M. H., Johnson, D. S., & McGeoch, C. C. (Eds.), *Data Structures, Near Neighbor Searches, and Methodology: Fifth and Sixth DIMACS Implementation Challenges*, pp. 215–250, American Mathematical Society. Providence, RI, USA.

Johnson, D. S. & McGeoch, L. A. (1997). The travelling salesman problem: A case study in local optimization. In Aarts, E. H. L. & Lenstra, J. K. (Eds.), *Local Search in Combinatorial Optimization*, pp. 215–310. John Wiley & Sons. Chichester, United Kingdom.

Johnson, D. S., McGeoch, L. A., Rego, C., & Glover, F. (2001). 8th DIMACS implementation challenge. `http://www.research.att.com/~dsj/chtsp/`.

Jordan, M. I. & Jacobs, R. A. (1994). Hierarchical mixtures of experts and the EM algorithm. *Neural Computation, 6*:181–214.

Karp, R. M. (1972). Reducibility among combinatorial problems. In Miller, R. E. & Thatcher, J. W. (Eds.), *Complexity of Computer Computations*, pp. 85–103. Plenum Press. New York, NY, USA.

Kauffman, S. A. (1993). *The Origins of Order. Self-Organization and Selection in Evolution*. Oxford University Press. New York, NY, USA.

Kavli, T. (1993). ASMOD—an algorithm for adaptive spline modeling of observation data. *International Journal of Control, 58*:947–967.

Kearns, M. J. & Vazirani, U. V. (1997). *An Introduction to Computational Learning Theory.* MIT Press. Cambridge, MA, USA.

Khuri, A. I. (2003). *Advanced Calculus with Applications in Statistics.* Second edition. John Wiley & Sons. Hoboken, NJ, USA.

Kirkpatrick, S., Gelatt Jr., C. D., & Vecchi, M. P. (1983). Optimization by simulated annealing. *Science, 220*:671–680.

Kohavi, R. (1995). A study of cross-validation and bootstrap for accuracy estimation and model selection. In Mellish, C. S. (Ed.), *14th International Joint Conference on Artificial Intelligence*, volume 2, pp. 1137–1145, Morgan Kaufmann. San Mateo, CA, USA.

Kohavi, R. & John, G. H. (1997). Wrappers for feature subset selection. *Artificial Intelligence, 97*(1–2):273–324.

Kohonen, T. (1982). Self-organized formations of topologically correct feature maps. *Biological Cybernetics, 43*:59–69.

Kostuch, P. (2003a). Timetabling Competition. SA-based heuristic. `http://www.idsia.ch/ttcomp2002/docs/kostuch.pdf`.

Kostuch, P. (2003b). University course timetabling. Transfer Thesis, University of Oxford, Oxford, United Kingdom.

Kostuch, P. (2004). Personal communication.

Kubrick, S. (1968). 2001: A Space Odissey. Metro-Goldwyn-Mayer.

Kullback, S. (1959). *Information Theory and Statistics.* John Wiley & Sons.

Labella, T. H. & Birattari, M. (2004). Polyphemus: De abacorum racemo. Technical Report TR/IRIDIA/2004-15, IRIDIA, Université Libre de Bruxelles, Brussels, Belgium.

Lamarck, J.-B. (1809). *Philosophie zoologique, ou exposition des considérations relatives à l'histoire naturelle des animaux.*

Lanczos, C. (1985). *The Variational Principles of Mechanics.* Fourth edition. Dover Publications. New York, NY, USA.

Lang, F. (1927). Metropolis. Universum Film.

Larrañaga, P. & Lozano, J. A. (2001). *Estimation of Distribution Algorithms. A New Tool for Evolutionary Computation*. Kluwer Academic Publisher. Boston, MA, USA.

Larson, H. (1982). *Introduction to Probability Theory and Statistical Inference*. John Wiley & Sons. New York, NY, USA.

Lawler, E. L., Lenstra, J. K., Kan, A. H. G. R., & Shmoys, D. B. (1985). *The Travelling Salesman Problem*. John Wiley & Sons. Chichester, United Kingdom.

Leibniz, G. W. (1710). *Théodicée*.

Liang, K., Yao, X., & Newton, C. (2001). Adapting self-adaptive parameters in evolutionary algorithms. *Applied Intelligence*, *15*(3):171–180.

Lieber, D. (1999). *The Cross-Entropy Method for Estimating Probabilities of Rare Events*. PhD thesis, Technion, Israel nstitute of Technology, Haifa, Israel.

Ljung, L. (1987). *System Identification: Theory for the User*. Second edition. Prentice-Hall, Inc. Upper Saddle River, NJ, USA.

Lourenço, H. R. (1995). Job-shop scheduling: Computational study of local search and large-step optimization methods. *European Journal of Operational Research*, *83*:347–364.

Lourenço, H. R., Martin, O., & Stützle, T. (2002). Iterated local search. In Glover, F. & Kochenberger, G. (Eds.), *Handbook of Metaheuristics*, pp. 321–353. Kluwer Academic Publisher. Norwell, MA, USA.

Lunghi, M. (2004). Il ruolo della validazione dei modelli locali nell'uso del metodo della superficie di risposta per la configurazione di una metaeuristica. Tesi di Laurea, Università degli Studi di Ferrara, Ferrara, Italy. Tentative title. In preparation.

Mach, E. (1893). *The Science of Mechanics: A Critical and Historical Exposition of its Principles*. Open Court. Chicago, IL, USA.

Mandrioli, D. & Ghezzi, C. (1987). *Theoretical Foundations of Computer Science*. John Wiley & Sons. New York, NY, USA.

Manfrin, M. (2003). Metaeuristiche per la costruzione degli orari dei corsi universitari. Tesi di Laurea, Università degli Studi di Firenze, Firenze, Italy. In Italian.

Maniezzo, V. (1999). Exact and approximate nondeterministic tree-search procedures for the quadratic assignment problem. *INFORMS Journal on Computing*, *11*(4):358–369.

Marascuilo, L. & McSweeney, M. (1977). *Nonparametric and Distribution-Free Methods for the Social Sciences.* The Brooks/Cole Publishing Company. Monterey, CA, USA.

Maron, O. (1994). Hoeffding races: Model selection for MRI classification. Master's thesis, The Massachusetts Institute of Technology, Cambridge, MA, USA.

Maron, O. & Moore, A. W. (1994). Hoeffding races: Accelerating model selection search for classification and function approximation. In Cowan, J. D., Tesauro, G., & Alspector, J. (Eds.), *Advances in Neural Information Processing Systems*, volume 6, pp. 59–66, Morgan Kaufmann. San Francisco, CA, USA.

Maron, O. & Moore, A. W. (1997). The racing algorithm: Model selection for lazy learners. *Artificial Intelligence Review, 11*(1–5):193–225.

Martin, O. & Otto, S. W. (1996). Combining simulated annealing with local search heuristics. *Annals of Operations Research, 63*:57–75.

Martin, O., Otto, S. W., & Felten, E. W. (1991). Large-step Markov chains for the traveling salesman problem. *Complex Systems, 5*(3):299–326.

Masters, T. (1995). *Practical Neural Network Recipes in C++*. Academic Press. New York, NY, USA.

Maupertuis, P. L. M. (1750). *Essai de Cosmologie.*

McAllester, D., Selman, B., & Kautz, H. (1997). Evidence for invariants in local search. In *Proceedings of the 14th National Conference on Artificial Intelligence and 9th Innovative Applications of Artificial Intelligence Conference (AAAI-97/IAAI-97)*, pp. 321–326, AAAI Press. Menlo Park, CA, USA.

McGeoch, C. C. (1986). *Experimental Analysis of Algorithms.* PhD thesis, Carnegie Mellon, Pittsburgh, PA, USA.

McGeoch, C. C. (1992). Analyzing algorithms by simulation: Variance reduction techniques and simulation speedups. *ACM Computing Surveys, 24*(2):195–212.

McGeoch, C. C. (1996). Towards an experimental method for algorithm simulation. *INFORMS Journal on Computing, 2*(1):1–15.

McGeoch, C. C. (2002). A bibliography of algorithm experimentation. In Goldwasser, M. H., Johnson, D. S., & McGeoch, C. C. (Eds.), *Data Structures, Near Neighbor Searches, and Methodology: Fifth and Sixth DIMACS Implementation Challenges*, pp. 251–260, American Mathematical Society. Providence, RI, USA.

McGeoch, C. C. & Moret, B. M. E. (1999). How to present a paper on experimental work with algorithms. *SIGACT News*, *30*(4):85–90.

Mendenhall, W., Scheaffer, R., & Wackerly, D. (1986). *Mathematical statistics with applications*. Duxbury Press. Boston, MA, USA.

Metaheuristics Network (2000). Annex I to the contract: List of participants and description of work. Official Documentation of the Metaheuristics Network, a Training and Research Network funded by the Improving Human Potential Programme of the Commission of the European Community, contract number HPRN-CT-1999-00106.

Meuleau, N. & Dorigo, M. (2002). Ant colony optimization and stochastic gradient descent. *Artificial Life*, *8*(2):103–121.

Miagkikh, V. V. & Punch III, W. F. (1999). Global search in combinatorial optimization using reinforcement learning algorithms. In Angeline, P. J., Michalewicz, Z., Schoenauer, M., Yao, X., & Zalzala, A. (Eds.), *Proceedings of the Congress on Evolutionary Computation*, pp. 189–196, IEEE Publications. Piscataway, NJ, USA.

Minsky, M. L. & Papert, S. (1969). *Perceptrons: An introduction to computational geometry*. MIT Press. Cambridge, MA, USA.

Mitchell, T. M. (1997). *Machine Learning*. McGraw-Hill. New York, NY, USA.

Moll, R., Barto, A., Perkins, T., & Sutton, R. (1999). Learning instance-independent value functions to enhance local search. In Kearns, M. S., Solla, S. A., & Cohn, D. A. (Eds.), *Advances in Neural Information Processing Systems 11*, pp. 1017–1023, MIT Press. Cambridge, MA, USA.

Monasson, R., Zecchina, R., Kirkpatrick, S., Selman, B., & Troyansky, L. (1999). Determining computational complexity from characteristic 'phase transitions'. *Nature*, *400*:133–137.

Montgomery, D. C. (2000). *Design and Analysis of Experiments*. Fifth edition. John Wiley & Sons. New York, NY, USA.

Montgomery, D. C. & Peck, E. A. (1992). *Introduction to Linear Analysis*. Second edition. John Wiley & Sons. New York, NY, USA.

Moore, A. W. & Lee, M. S. (1994). Efficient algorithms for minimizing cross validation error. In *Proceedings of the Eleventh International Conference on Machine Learning*, pp. 190–198, Morgan Kaufmann. San Francisco, CA, USA.

Moore, A. W. & Schneider, J. (1996). Memory-based stochastic optimization. In Touretzky, D. S., Mozer, M. C., & Hasselmo, M. E. (Eds.), *Advances in Neural Information Processing Systems 8*, pp. 1066–1072, MIT Press. Cambridge, MA, USA.

Moscato, P. (1989). On evolution, search, optimization, genetic algorithms and martial arts: Towards memetic algorithms. Technical Report C3P Report 826, Caltech Concurrent Computation Program, Pasadena, CA, USA.

Moscato, P. & Norman, M. G. (1992). A memetic approach for the traveling salesman problem implementation of a computational ecology for combinatorial optimization on message-passing systems. In Valero, M., Onate, E., Jane, M., Larriba, J. L., & Suarez, B. (Eds.), *Parallel Computing and Transputer Applications*, pp. 177–186, IOS Press. Amsterdam, The Netherlands.

Mühlenbein, H., Bendisch, J., & Voigt, H.-M. (1996). From recombination of genes to the estimation of distributions. I. Binary parameters. In *Parallel Problem Solving from Nature, 4th International Conference, PPSN IV*, volume 1141 of *LNCS*, pp. 178–187, Springer-Verlag.

Myers, R. H. (1994). *Classical and Modern Regression with Applications.* Second edition. PWS-KENT Publishing Company. Boston, MA, USA.

Myers, R. H. & Montgomery, D. C. (2002). *Response Surface Methodology.* Second edition. John Wiley & Sons. New York, NY, USA.

Nelson, B. L., Swann, J., Goldsman, D., & Song, W. (2001). Simple procedure for selecting the best simulated system when the number of alternatives is large. *Operations Research, 49*(6):950–963.

Newall, J. P. (1999). *Hybrid Methods for Automated Timetabling.* PhD thesis, Department of Computer Science, University of Nottingham, Nottingham, United Kingdom.

Nilsson, N. J. (1965). *Learning Machines: Foundations of Trainable Pattern Classifying Systems.* McGraw-Hill. New York, NY, USA.

Nissen, V. (1994). Solving the quadratic assignment problem with clues from nature. *IEEE Transactions on Neural Networks, 5*(1):66–72.

Osman, I. H. & Kelly, J. P., editors. (1996). *Meta-Heuristics: The Theory and Applications.* Kluwer Academic Publisher. Boston, MA, USA. Post-conference proceedings of the 1st Metaheuristics International Conference, MIC'95.

Papadimitriou, C. H. & Steiglitz, K. (1998). *Combinatorial Optimization. Algorithms and Complexity.* Dover Publications. Mineola, NY, USA.

Papoulis, A. (1991). *Probability, Random Variables, and Stochastic Processes.* Third edition. McGraw-Hill. New York, NY, USA.

Parson, R. & Johnson, M. (1997). A case study in experimental design applied to genetic algorithms with applications to DNA sequence assembly. *American Journal of Mathematical and Management Sciences, 17*(3/4):369–396.

Pelikan, M., Goldberg, D. E., & Cantú-Paz, E. (1999). BOA: The Bayesian optimization algorithm. In Banzhaf, W., Daida, J., Eiben, A. E., Garzon, M. H., Honavar, V., Jakiela, M., & Smith, R. E. (Eds.), *Proceedings of the Genetic and Evolutionary Computation Conference*, pp. 525–532, Morgan Kaufmann. San Francisco, CA, USA.

Pelikan, M., Goldberg, D. E., & Lobo, F. (1999). A survey of optimization by building and using probabilistic models. Technical Report IlliGAL-99018, Department of Computer Science, University of Illinois, Urbana, IL, USA.

Pelikan, M. & Mühlenbein, H. (1999). The bivariate marginal distribution algorithm. In Roy, R., Furuhashi, T., & Chawdhry, P. K. (Eds.), *Advances in Soft Computing – Engineering Design and Manufacturing*, pp. 521–535, Springer-Verlag. London, United Kingdom.

Perrone, M. P. & Cooper, L. N. (1993). When networks disagree: Ensemble methods for hybrid neural networks. In Mammone, R. J. (Ed.), *Artificial Neural Networks for Speech and Vision*, pp. 126–142. Chapman & Hall. Boca Raton, FL, USA.

Pichitlamken, J. & Nelson, B. L. (2001). Selection-of-the-best procedures for optimization via simulation. In Peters, B. A., Smith, J. S., Medeiros, D. J., & Rohrer, M. W. (Eds.), *Proceedings of the 2001 Winter Simulation Conference*, pp. 401–407, ACM. Arlington, VA, USA.

Pierre, D. A. (1986). *Optimization Theory with Applications.* Dover Publications. New York, NY, USA.

Piscopo, C. & Birattari, M. (2002). Invention vs. discovery. A critical discussion. In Lange, S., Satoh, K., & Smith, C. H. (Eds.), *Discovery Science. 5th International Conference, DS2002*, volume 2534 of *LNCS*, pp. 457–462, Springer-Verlag. Berlin, Germany.

Powell, M. J. D. (1987). Radial basis function approximations to polynomials. In *12th Biennal Numerical Analysis Conference*, pp. 223–241.

Prais, M. & Ribeiro, C. C. (2000). Reactive grasp: An application to a matrix decomposition problem in tdma traffic assignment. *INFORMS Journal on Computing, 12*:164–176.

Priestley, M. B. (1988). *Non-linear and Non-stationary Time Series Analysis.* Academic Press. London, United Kingdom.

Quinlan, J. R. (1993a). Combining instance-based and model-based learning. In *Proceedings of the Tenth International Conference on Machine Learning*, pp. 236–243, Morgan Kaufmann. San Francisco, CA, USA.

Quinlan, R. (1993b). *C4.5. Programs for Machine Learning.* Morgan Kaufmann. San Mateo, CA, USA.

Rabiner, L. R. (1989). A tutorial on hidden markov models and selected applications in speech recognition. *Proceedings of the IEEE*, *77*(2):257–286.

Radcliffe, N. J. & Surry, P. D. (1995). Fundamental limitations on search algorithms: Evolutionary computing in perspective. In van Leeuwen, J. (Ed.), *Computer Science Today: Recent Trends and Developments*, volume 1000 of *LNCS*, pp. 275–291, Springer-Verlag. Berlin, Germany.

Rardin, R. R. & Uzsoy, R. (2001). Experimental evaluation of heuristic optimization algorithms: A tutorial. *Journal of Heuristics*, *7*(2):261–304.

Rechenberg, I. (1973). *Evolutionsstrategie: Optimierung technischer Systeme nach Prinzipien der biologischen Evolution.* Frommann-Holzboog. Stuttgart, Germany.

Reeves, C. R., editor. (1995). *Modern Heuristic Techniques for Combinatorial Problems.* McGraw-Hill. London, United Kingdom.

Reinelt, G. (1994). *The Traveling Salesman: Computational Solutions for TSP Applications*, volume 840 of *LNCS*. Springer-Verlag. Berlin, Germany.

Resende, M. G. C. & Pinho de Sousa, J., editors. (2003). *Metaheuristics : Computer Decision-Making.* Kluwer Academic Publisher. Boston, MA, USA. Post-conference proceedings of the 4th Metaheuristics International Conference, MIC 2001.

Ribeiro, C. C. & Hansen, P., editors. (2001). *Essays and Surveys in Metaheuristics.* Kluwer Academic Publisher. Boston, MA, USA. Post-conference proceedings of the 3rd Metaheuristics International Conference, MIC'99.

Robbins, H. & Monro, S. (1951). A stochastic approximation method. *Annals of Mathematical Statistics*, *22*:400–407.

Rose, H. J. (1928). *A Handbook of Greek Mythology including its extension to Rome.* Methuen. London, United Kingdom.

Rosenblatt, F. (1958). The perceptron: A probabilistic model for information storage and organization. *Psychological Rewiew, 65*:386–408.

Rossi-Doria, O. & Paechter, B. (2003). An hyperheuristic approach to course timetabling problem using evolutionary algorithm. Technical report, Napier University, Edinburgh, United Kingdom.

Rossi-Doria, O., Paechter, B., Blum, C., Socha, K., & Samples, M. (2002). A local search for the timetabling problem. In Burke, E. & De Causmaecker, P. (Eds.), *PATAT 2002, Proceedings of the 4th international conference on the Practice And Theory of Automated Timetabling*, pp. 115–119, KaHo St.-Lieven. Gent, Belgium.

Rossi-Doria, O., Sampels, M., Birattari, M., Chiarandini, M., Dorigo, M., Gambardella, L. M., Knowles, J., Manfrin, M., Mastrolilli, M., Paechter, B., Paquete, L., & Stützle., T. (2003). A comparison of the performance of different metaheuristics on the timetabling problem. In Burke, E. & De Causmaecker, P. (Eds.), *Practice and Theory of Automated Timetabling, 4th International Conference, PATAT 2002*, volume 2740 of *LNCS*, pp. 329–351, Springer-Verlag. Berlin, Germany.

Roy, R. K. (1990). *A Primer on the Taguchi Method.* Van Nostrand Reinhold. New York, NY, USA.

Rubinstein, R. Y. (1981). *Simulation and the Monte Carlo Method.* John Wiley & Sons. New York, NY, USA.

Rubinstein, R. Y. (1999a). The cross-entropy method for combinatorial and continuous optimization. *Methodology and Computing in Applied Probability, 1*(2):127–190.

Rubinstein, R. Y. (1999b). Rare event simulation via cross-entropy and importance sampling. In *Second International Workshop on Rare Event Simulation, RESIM'99*, pp. 1–17.

Rubinstein, R. Y. (2001). Combinatorial optimization, cross-entropy, ants and rare events. In Uryasev, S. & Pardalos, P. M. (Eds.), *Stochastic Optimization: Algorithms and Applications.* Kluwer Academic Publisher. Amsterdam, The Netherlands.

Rumelhart, D. E., Durbin, R., Golden, R., & Chauvin, Y. (1995). Backpropagation: The basic theory. In Chauvin, Y. & Rumelhart, D. E. (Eds.), *Backpropagation: Theory, Architectures and Applications*, pp. 1–35. Lawrence Erlbaum. Hillsdale, NJ, USA.

Rumelhart, D. E., Hinton, G. E., & Williams, R. J. (1986). Learning internal representations by back-propagating errors. *Nature*, *323*:533–536.

Sampels, M. (2002). Metaheuristics for the timetabling problem. Results of a comparison within the Metaheuristics Network. `http://iridia.ulb.ac.be/~msampels/ttmn.data/`.

Sampels, M., Blum, C., Mastrolilli, M., & Rossi-Doria, O. (2002). Metaheuristics for Group Shop Scheduling. In Guervós, J. J. M., Adamidis, P., & Beyer, H.-G. (Eds.), *Parallel Problem Solving from Nature, 7th International Conference, PPSN VII*, volume 2439 of *LNCS*, pp. 631–640, Springer-Verlag. Berlin, Germany.

Samuel, A. (1959). Some studies in machine learning using the game of checkers. *IBM Journal of Research and Development*, *3*:211–229.

Schaal, S. & Atkeson, C. G. (1994). Robot juggling: Implementation of memory-based learning. *IEEE Control Systems*, *14*(1):57–71.

Schaerf, A. (1995). A survey of automated timetabling. Technical Report CS-R9567, Centrum voor Wiskunde en Informatica, Amsterdam, The Netherlands.

Schiavinotto, T. (2004). Personal communication.

Schiavinotto, T. & Stützle, T. (2004). The linear ordering problem: Instances, search space analysis and algorithms. *Journal of Mathematical Modelling and Algorithms*, *3*(4):367–402.

Schumacher, C., Vose, M., & Whitley, D. (2001). The no free lunch and problem description length. In Spector, L., Goodman, E., Wu, A., Langdon, W., Voigt, H.-M., Gen, M., Sen, S., Dorigo, M., P.Pezeshk, Garzon, M., & Burke, E. (Eds.), *Proceedings of the Genetic and Evolutionary Computation Conference*, pp. 565–570, Morgan Kaufmann. San Francisco, CA, USA.

Schwefel, H.-P. (1981). *Numerical Optimization of Computer Models*. John Wiley & Sons. Chichester, United Kingdom.

Scott, R. (1982). Blade Runner. Warner Bros.

Shamma, J. S. & Athanas, M. (1990). Analysis of gain sheduled control for nonlinear plants. *IEEE Transactions on Automatic Control*, *35*:898–907.

Shavlik, J. W. & Dietterich, T. G., editors. (1990). *Readings in Machine Learning*. Morgan Kaufmann. San Mateo, CA, USA.

Shelley, M. W. (1818). *Frankenstein, or The Modern Prometheus*.

Sheskin, D. (2000). *Handbook of Parametric and Nonparametric Statistical Procedures.* Second edition. Chapman & Hall/CRC. Boca Raton, FL, USA.

Siegel, S. & Castellan, Jr., N. J. (1988). *Non Parametric Statistics for the Behavioral Sciences.* Second edition. McGraw-Hill. New York, NY, USA.

Skeppstedt, A., Ljung, L., & Millnert, M. (1992). Construction of composite models from observed data. *International Journal of Control, 55*(1):141–152.

Socha, K. (2003a). The influence of run-time limits on choosing ant system parameters. In Cantú-Paz, E., Foster, J., Deb, K., Lawrence, D., Roy, R., O'Reilly, U.-M., Beyer, H.-G., Standish, R., Kendall, G., Wilson, S., Harman, M., Wegener, J., Dasgupta, D., Potter, M., Schultz, A., Jonoska, N., Dowsland, K., & Miller, J. (Eds.), *Genetic and Evolutionary Computation - GECCO 2003*, volume 2723 of *LNCS*, pp. 49–60, Springer-Verlag. Berlin, Germany.

Socha, K. (2003b). Metaheuristics for the timetabling problem. Mémoire de DEA, Université Libre de Bruxelles, Brussels, Belgium.

Socha, K., Sampels, M., & Manfrin, M. (2003). Ant algorithms for the university course timetabling problem with regard to the state-of-the-art. In Raidl, G., Cagnoni, S., Cardalda, J. J. R., Corne, D. W., Gottlieb, J., Guillot, A., Hart, E., Johnson, C., Marchiori, E., Meyer, J.-A., & Middendorf, M. (Eds.), *Applications of Evolutionary Computing, EvoWorkshop 2003: EvoBIO, EvoCOP, EvoIASP, EvoMUSART, EvoROB, and EvoSTIM*, volume 2611 of *LNCS*, pp. 334–345, Springer-Verlag. Berlin, Germany.

Sommerville, I. (2001). *Software Engineering.* Sixth edition. Addison-Wesley Publishing Company. Harlow, United Kingdom.

Stenman, A., Gustafsson, F., & Ljung, L. (1996). Just in time models for dynamical systems. In *35th IEEE Conference on Decision and Control*, pp. 1115–1120, IEEE Publications. New York, NY, USA.

Stone, M. (1974). Cross-validation choices and assessment of statistical predictions. *Journal of the Royal Statistical Society, Series B, B36*:111–147.

Stützle, T. (2003). Iterated local search for the quadratic assignment problem (revised version). Technical Report AIDA-99-03, FG Intellektik, FB Informatik, Technische Universität Darmstadt, Darmstadt, Germany.

Stützle, T. & Dorigo, M. (2002). A short convergence proof for a class of ACO algorithms. *IEEE Transactions on Evolutionary Computation, 6*(4):358–365.

Stützle, T. & Hoos, H. H. (1996). Improving the Ant System: A detailed report on the $\mathcal{MAX}$–$\mathcal{MIN}$ Ant System. Technical Report AIDA-96-12, FG Intellektik, FB Informatik, Technische Universität Darmstadt, Darmstadt, Germany.

Stützle, T. & Hoos, H. H. (1997). The $\mathcal{MAX}$–$\mathcal{MIN}$ Ant System and local search for the traveling salesman problem. In Bäck, T., Michalewicz, Z., & Yao, X. (Eds.), *Proceedings of the 1997 IEEE International Conference on Evolutionary Computation (ICEC'97)*, pp. 309–314, IEEE Publications. Piscataway, NJ, USA.

Stützle, T. & Hoos, H. H. (1998). Improvements on the Ant System: Introducing the $\mathcal{MAX}$–$\mathcal{MIN}$ Ant System. In G. D. Smith, N. C. Steele, R. F. A. (Ed.), *Artificial Neural Networks and Genetic Algorithms*, pp. 245–249, Springer-Verlag. Vienna, Austria.

Stützle, T. & Hoos, H. H. (1999). $\mathcal{MAX}$–$\mathcal{MIN}$ Ant System and local search for combinatorial optimization problems. In Voss, S., Martello, S., Osman, I. H., & Roucairol, C. (Eds.), *Meta-Heuristics: Advances and Trends in Local Search Paradigms for Optimization*, pp. 137–154. Kluwer Academic Publisher. Dordrecht, The Netherlands.

Stützle, T. & Hoos, H. H. (2000). $\mathcal{MAX}$–$\mathcal{MIN}$ ant system. *Future Generation Computer Systems, 16*(8):889–914.

Su, L., Buntine, W. L., Newton, R., & Peters, B. S. (2001). Learning as applied to stochastic optimization for standard-cell placement. *IEEE Transactions on Computer-Aided Design of Integrated Circuits and Systems, 20*(4).

Sutton, R. S. & Barto, A. G. (1998). *Reinforcement Learning. An Introduction.* MIT Press. Cambridge, MA, USA.

Suykens, J. A. K. & Vandewalle, J., editors. (1998). *International Workshop on Advanced Black-Box Techniques for Nonlinear Modeling.* Katholieke Universiteit Leuven. Leuven, Belgium.

Syswerda, G. (1993). Simulated crossover in genetic algorithms. In Whitley, L. D. (Ed.), *Foundations of Genetic Algorithms 2*, pp. 239–255, Morgan Kaufmann. San Mateo, CA, USA.

Taguchi, G. (1987). *System of Experimental Design: Engineering Methods to Optimize Quality and Minimize Costs.* UNIPUB/Kraus International Publications. White Plains, NY, USA.

Taillard, E. D. (1991). Robust taboo search for the quadratic assignment problem. *Parallel Computing, 17*:443–455.

Taillard, E. D. (1995). Comparison of iterative searches for the quadratic assignment problem. *Location Science, 3*:87–105.

Takagi, T. & Sugeno, M. (1985). Fuzzy identification of system and its applications to modeling and control. *IEEE Transactions on Systems, Man, and Cybernetics*, *15*(1):116–132.

Tesauro, G. (1992). Practical issues in temporal difference learning. *Machine Learning*, *3*(4):257–277.

Tong, H. (1990). *Non-linear Time Series*. Oxford University Press. New York, NY, USA.

Toussaint, M. (2001). Self-adaptive exploration in evolutionary search. Technical Report IRINI-2001-05, Institut für Neuroinformatik, Ruhr-Universität Bochum, Bochum, Germany.

Vaessens, R. J. M., Aarts, E. H. L., & Lenstra, J. K. (1996). Job shop scheduling by local search. *INFORMS Journal on Computing*, *8*:302–317.

Van Breedam, A. (1995). Improvement heuristics for the vehicle routing problem based on simulated annealing. *European Journal of Operational Research*, *86*:480–490.

Van Breedam, A. (1996). An analysis of the effect of local improvement operators in genetic algorithms and simulated annealing for the vehicle routing problem. Technical Report 96/14, Faculty of Applied Economics, University of Antwerp, Antwerp, Belgium.

Vapnik, V. N. (1995). *The Nature of Statistical Learning Theory*. Springer-Verlag. New York, NY, USA.

Vapnik, V. N. (1998). *Statistical Learning Theory*. John Wiley & Sons. New York, NY, USA.

Vapnik, V. N. & Chervonenkis, A. J. (1971). On the uniform convergence of relative frequencies of events to their probabilities. *Theory of Probability and its Applications*, *16*:264–280. Previously published in Russian in 1968.

Vapnik, V. N. & Chervonenkis, A. J. (1991). The necessary and sufficient conditions for consistency of the method of empirical risk minimization. *Pattern Recognition and Image Analysis*, *1*(3):284–305.

Villacci, D., Bontempi, G., Vaccaro, A., & Birattari, M. (2004). The role of learning methods in the dynamic assessment of power components loading capability. *IEEE Transactions on Industrial Electronics*, *52*(1):280–290.

Viterbi, A. J. (1967). Error bounds for convolutional codes and an asymptotically optimal decoding algorithm. *IEEE Transactions on Information Theory*, *13*:260–269.

Voss, S., Martello, S., Osman, I. H., & Roucairol, C., editors. (1999). *Meta-Heuristics: Advances and Trends in Local Search Paradigms for Optimization.* Kluwer Academic Publisher. Boston, MA, USA. Post-conference proceedings of the 2nd Metaheuristics International Conference, MIC'97.

Wachowski, A. & Wachowski, L. (1999). The Matrix. Warner Bros.

Watkins, C. J. C. H. (1989). *Learning from Delayed Rewards.* PhD thesis, King's College, Cambridge, United Kingdom.

Weierstraß, K. (1885a). über die analytische darstellbarkeit sogenannter willkürlicher functionen einer reellen veränderlichen. *Sitzungsberichte der Königlich Preußsischen Akademie der Wissenschaften zu Berlin,* pp. 633–639. Part I.

Weierstraß, K. (1885b). über die analytische darstellbarkeit sogenannter willkürlicher functionen einer reellen veränderlichen. *Sitzungsberichte der Königlich Preußsischen Akademie der Wissenschaften zu Berlin,* pp. 789–805. Part II.

Weiss, S. & Indurkhya, N. (1995). Rule-based machine learning methods for functional prediction. *Journal of Artificial Intelligence Research, 3*:383–403.

Whitehead, S. D. & Ballard, D. H. (1991). Learning to perceive and act. *Machine Learning, 7*(7):45–83.

Whitmore, G. A. & Findlay, M. C., editors. (1978). *Stochastic Dominance: An Approach to Decision Making Under Risk.* D. C. Heath and Company. Lexington, MA, USA.

Widder, D. V. (1989). *Advanced Calculus.* Second edition. Dover Publications. New York, NY, USA.

Wolpert, D. (1992). Stacked generalization. *Neural Networks, 5*(2):241–259.

Wolpert, D. H. & Macready, W. G. (1996). No free lunch theorems for search. Technical Report SFI-TR-95-02-010, Santa Fe Institute, Santa Fe, NM, USA.

Wolpert, D. H. & Macready, W. G. (1997). No free lunch theorems for optimization. *IEEE Transactions on Evolutionary Computation, 1*(1):67–82.

Xu, J., Chiu, S. Y., & Glover, F. (1998). Fine-tuning a tabu search algorithm with statistical tests. *International Transactions in Operational Research, 5*(3):233–244.

Xu, J. & Kelly, J. (1996). A network flow-based tabu search heuristic for the veichle routing problem. *Transportation Science, 30*:379–393.

Yuan, B. & Gallagher, M. (2004). Statistical racing techniques for improved empirical evaluation of evolutionary algorithms. In Yao, X., Burke, E., Lozano, J. A., Smith, J., Merelo-Guervós, J. J., Bullinaria, J. A., Rowe, J., Tino, P., Kabán, A., & Schwefel, H.-P. (Eds.), *Parallel Problem Solving from Nature, 8th International Conference, PPSN VIII*, volume 3242 of *LNCS*, pp. 172–181, Springer-Verlag. Berlin, Germany.

Zadeh, L. A. & Desoer, C. A. (1963). *Linear System Theory*. McGraw-Hill. New York, NY, USA.

Zemel, E. (1981). Measuring the quality of approximate solutions to zero-one programming problems. *Mathematics of Operations Research*, *6*:319–332.

Zhang, W. & Dietterich, T. G. (1996). High-performance job-shop scheduling with a time-delay TD(λ) network. In Touretzky, D. S., Mozer, M. C., & Hasselmo, M. E. (Eds.), *Advances in Neural Information Processing Systems 8*, pp. 1024–1030, MIT Press. Cambridge, MA, USA.

Zhang, W. & Dietterich, T. G. (1998). Solving combinatorial optimization tasks by reinforcement learning: A general methodology applied to rescource-constrained scheduling. Technical report, Department of Computer Science, Oregon State University, Corvallis, OR, USA.

Zlochin, M., Birattari, M., & Dorigo, M. (2004). Towards a theory of practice in metaheuristics design. A machine learning perspective. Technical Report MCS04-01, Computer Science and Applied Mathematics, The Weizmann Institute of Science, Rehovot, Israel. Submitted for journal publication.

Zlochin, M., Birattari, M., Meuleau, N., & Dorigo, M. (2004). Model-based search for combinatorial optimization: A critical survey. *Annals of Operations Research*, *131* (1–4):373–395.

Zlochin, M. & Dorigo, M. (2002). Model based search for combinatorial optimization: A comparative study. In Guervós, J. J. M., Adamidis, P., & Beyer, H.-G. (Eds.), *Parallel Problem Solving from Nature, 7th International Conference, PPSN VII*, volume 2439 of *LNCS*, pp. 651–661, Springer-Verlag. Berlin, Germany.

Lo duca e io per quel cammino ascoso
intrammo a ritornar nel chiaro mondo;
e sanza cura aver d'alcun riposo,

salimmo sù, el primo e io secondo,
tanto ch'i' vidi de le cose belle
che porta 'l ciel, per un pertugio tondo.

E quindi uscimmo a riveder le stelle.
Dante, Inferno XXXIV, 133–139

My guide and I came on that hidden road
to make our way back into the bright world;
and with no care for any rest,

we climbed—he first, I following—until I saw,
through a round opening, some of those things
of beauty Heaven bears. It was from there

that we emerged, to see—once more—the stars.
Dante, Inferno XXXIV, 133–139